Exam Ref 70-742 Identity with Windows Server 2016

Andrew Warren

Exam Ref 70-742 Identity with Windows Server 2016

Published with the authorization of Microsoft Corporation by:
Pearson Education, Inc.

Copyright © 2017 by Pearson Education Inc.

All rights reserved. Printed in the United States of America. This publication is protected by copyright, and permission must be obtained from the publisher prior to any prohibited reproduction, storage in a retrieval system, or transmission in any form or by any means, electronic, mechanical, photocopying, recording, or likewise. For information regarding permissions, request forms, and the appropriate contacts within the Pearson Education Global Rights & Permissions Department, please visit www.pearsoned.com/permissions/. No patent liability is assumed with respect to the use of the information contained herein. Although every precaution has been taken in the preparation of this book, the publisher and author assume no responsibility for errors or omissions. Nor is any liability assumed for damages resulting from the use of the information contained herein.

ISBN-13: 978-0-7356-9881-9

ISBN-10: 0-7356-9881-3

Library of Congress Control Number: 2016962648

4 18

Trademarks

Microsoft and the trademarks listed at http://www.microsoft.com on the "Trademarks" webpage are trademarks of the Microsoft group of companies. All other marks are property of their respective owners.

Warning and Disclaimer

Every effort has been made to make this book as complete and as accurate as possible, but no warranty or fitness is implied. The information provided is on an "as is" basis. The authors, the publisher, and Microsoft Corporation shall have neither liability nor responsibility to any person or entity with respect to any loss or damages arising from the information contained in this book or programs accompanying it.

Special Sales

For information about buying this title in bulk quantities, or for special sales opportunities (which may include electronic versions; custom cover designs; and content particular to your business, training goals, marketing focus, or branding interests), please contact our corporate sales department at corpsales@pearsoned.com or (800) 382-3419.

For government sales inquiries, please contact governmentsales@pearsoned.com.

For questions about sales outside the U.S., please contact intlcs@pearson.com.

Editor-in-Chief	Greg Wiegand
Acquisitions Editor	Trina MacDonald
Development Editor	Rick Kughen
Managing Editor	Sandra Schroeder
Senior Project Editor	Tracey Croom
Editorial Production	Ellie Vee Design
Copy Editor	Christina Rudloff
Indexer	Julie Grady
Proofreader	Christina Rudloff
Technical Editor	Tim Warner
Cover Designer	Twist Creative, Seattle

Contents at a glance

	Introduction	*xi*
	Preparing for the exam	*xv*
CHAPTER 1	**Install and configure Active Directory Domain Services**	1
CHAPTER 2	**Manage and maintain AD DS**	77
CHAPTER 3	**Create and manage Group Policy**	149
CHAPTER 4	**Implement Active Directory Certificate Services**	241
CHAPTER 5	**Implement identity federation and access solutions**	295
	Index	*347*

Contents

Introduction   xi

Organization of this book xi

Microsoft certifications xii

Acknowledgments xii

Free ebooks from Microsoft Press xii

Microsoft Virtual Academy xii

Quick access to online references xiii

Errata, updates, & book support xiii

We want to hear from you xiii

Stay in touch xiv

Preparing for the exam   xv

Chapter 1 Install and configure Active Directory Domain Services   **1**

Skill 1.1: Install and configure domain controllers 1

    AD DS fundamentals   2

    Install a new forest   4

    Add or remove a domain controller   9

    Install AD DS on a Server Core installation   17

    Install a domain controller using Install from Media   18

    Install and configure a read-only domain controller   20

    Configure a global catalog server   24

    Configure domain controller cloning   28

    Upgrade domain controllers   33

    Transfer and seize operations master roles   36

    Resolve DNS SRV record registration issues   41

What do you think of this book? We want to hear from you!

Microsoft is interested in hearing your feedback so we can continually improve our books and learning resources for you. To participate in a brief online survey, please visit:

https://aka.ms/tellpress

Skill 1.2: Create and manage Active Directory users and computers 44
    Create, copy, configure, and delete users and computers   44
    Implement offline domain join   57
    Configure user rights   58
    Perform bulk Active Directory operations   60

Skill 1.3: Create and manage Active Directory groups and
    organizational units. 62
    Create and manage groups   63
    Create and manage OUs   69
    Delegate management of Active Directory with
    groups and OUs   71

Chapter summary 75

Thought experiment. 76

Thought experiment answer. 76

Chapter 2   Manage and maintain AD DS   77

Skill 2.1: Configure service authentication and account policies 77
    Create and configure MSAs and gMSAs   78
    Manage SPNs   80
    Configure Kerberos Constrained Delegation   82
    Configure virtual accounts   82
    Configure account policies   83
    Configure and apply Password Settings Objects   89
    Delegate password settings management   95

Skill 2.2: Maintain Active Directory 96
    Manage Active Directory offline   96
    Active Directory backup and recovery   102
    Manage Read Only Domain Controllers   110
    Managing AD DS replication   113

Skill 2.3: Configure Active Directory in a complex enterprise
    environment. 120
    Configure a multi-domain and multi-forest AD DS
    infrastructure   120
    Deploy Windows Server 2016 domain controllers
    within a preexisting AD DS environment   121

Upgrade existing domains and forests	122
Configure domain and forest functional levels	122
Configure multiple user principal name suffixes	123
Configure trusts	126
Configure AD DS sites and subnets	136

Chapter summary 145

Thought experiment.. 146

Thought experiment answers 147

Chapter 3 Create and manage Group Policy 149

Skill 3.1: Create and manage Group Policy Objects 149

Configure multiple local Group Policies	150
Overview of domain-based GPOs	156
Manage starter GPOs	162
Configure GPO links	164
Back up, restore, import, and copy GPOs	166
Create and configure a migration table	170
Reset default GPOs	174
Delegate Group Policy management	174
Detect health issues using the Group Policy Infrastructure Status dashboard	178

Skill 3.2: Configure Group Policy processing 179

Configure processing order and precedence	181
Configuring inheritance	182
Configure security filtering and WMI filtering	187
Configure loopback processing	195
Configure and manage slow-link processing and Group Policy caching	197
Configure client-side extension behavior	199
Force a Group Policy update	201

Skill 3.3: Configure Group Policy settings......................... 202

Configure software installation	202
Configure scripts	209
Import security templates	211

	Configure folder redirection	214
	Configure administrative templates	221

Skill 3.4: Configure Group Policy preferences 225

	Configuring Group Policy preferences	226
	Configure item-level targeting	236

Chapter summary 238

Thought experiment 239

Thought experiment answers 240

Chapter 4   Implement Active Directory Certificate Services   241

Skill 4.1: Install and configure AD CS 241

	Choosing between a standalone and an enterprise CA	243
	Install standalone CAs	246
	Install an AD DS integrated enterprise CA	252
	Install offline root and subordinate CAs	253
	Install and configure an Online Responder	266
	Implement administrative role separation	269
	Configure CA backup and recovery	272

Skill 4.2: Manage certificates 275

	Manage certificate templates	275
	Implement and manage certificate deployment, validation, and revocation	283
	Configure and manage key archival and recovery	288

Chapter summary 293

Thought experiment 293

Thought experiment answers 294

Chapter 5   Implement identity federation and access solutions   295

Skill 5.1: Install and configure AD FS 295

	Examine AD FS requirements	296
	Install the AD FS server role	300
	Configure the AD FS server role	300

Implement claims-based authentication, including relying party trusts	303
Configure authentication policies	310
Implement and configure device registration	313
Configure for use with Microsoft Azure and Microsoft Office 365	316
Configure AD FS to enable authentication of users stored in LDAP directories	317
Upgrade and migrate previous AD FS workloads to Windows Server 2016	318

Skill 5.2: Implement Web Application Proxy 319

Install and configure Web Application Proxy	319
Integrate Web Application Proxy with AD FS	322
Implement Web Application Proxy in pass-through mode	326
Publish Remote Desktop Gateway applications	327

Skill 5.3: Install and configure AD RMS 330

An AD RMS overview	330
Deploying an AD RMS server	331
Manage rights policy templates	339
Configure exclusion policies	343
Backup and restore AD RMS	344

Chapter summary 344

Thought experiment...345

Thought experiment answers....................................345

Index   347

What do you think of this book? We want to hear from you!

Microsoft is interested in hearing your feedback so we can continually improve our books and learning resources for you. To participate in a brief online survey, please visit:

https://aka.ms/tellpress

Introduction

The 70-742 exam focuses on the identity features and functionality available in Windows Server 2016. It covers the installation and configuration of Active Directory Domain Services (AD DS), and the managing and maintaining of AD DS, including configuring AD DS in a complex enterprise environment. Creating and managing Group Policy is a significant part of the exam. Also covered is how to implement Active Directory Certificate Services (AD CS), the identity federation and access solutions, along with Active Directory Federation Services (AD FS), Web Application Proxy, and Active Directory Rights Management Services (AD RMS).

This book is geared toward AD DS administrators who are looking to train in identity and access technologies with Windows Server 2016. It explains how to deploy and configure AD DS in a distributed environment, and how to implement Group Policy. In addition, the book covers how to deploy AD FS, AD RMS, and AD CS.

This book covers every major topic area found on the exam, but it does not cover every exam question. Only the Microsoft exam team has access to the exam questions, and Microsoft regularly adds new questions to the exam, making it impossible to cover specific questions. You should consider this book a supplement to your relevant real-world experience and other study materials. If you encounter a topic in this book that you do not feel completely comfortable with, use the "Need more review?" links you'll find in the text to find more information and take the time to research and study the topic. Great information is available on MSDN, TechNet, and in blogs and forums.

Organization of this book

This book is organized by the "Skills measured" list published for the exam. The "Skills measured" list is available for each exam on the Microsoft Learning website: *https://aka.ms/exam-list*. Each chapter in this book corresponds to a major topic area in the list, and the technical tasks in each topic area determine a chapter's organization. If an exam covers six major topic areas, for example, the book will contain six chapters.

Microsoft certifications

Microsoft certifications distinguish you by proving your command of a broad set of skills and experience with current Microsoft products and technologies. The exams and corresponding certifications are developed to validate your mastery of critical competencies as you design and develop, or implement and support, solutions with Microsoft products and technologies both on-premises and in the cloud. Certification brings a variety of benefits to the individual and to employers and organizations.

> **MORE INFO** **ALL MICROSOFT CERTIFICATIONS**
>
> For information about Microsoft certifications, including a full list of available certifications, go to *https://www.microsoft.com/learning*.

Acknowledgments

Andrew Warren When you start writing a book, you sit a while watching the cursor blink on your computer screen. Eventually, it dawns on you that it won't write itself, and so you begin. But the author is only the first stage in the process. Without my editor, Trina MacDonald, and the team at Pearson, my cursor might still be blinking. I'd also like to thank my wife and daughter for keeping the espresso machine full of beans and ready to go.

Free ebooks from Microsoft Press

From technical overviews to in-depth information on special topics, the free ebooks from Microsoft Press cover a wide range of topics. These ebooks are available in PDF, EPUB, and Mobi for Kindle formats, ready for you to download at:

https://aka.ms/mspressfree

Check back often to see what is new!

Microsoft Virtual Academy

Build your knowledge of Microsoft technologies with free expert-led online training from Microsoft Virtual Academy (MVA). MVA offers a comprehensive library of videos, live events, and more to help you learn the latest technologies and prepare for certification exams. You'll find what you need here:

https://www.microsoftvirtualacademy.com

Quick access to online references

Throughout this book are addresses to webpages that the author has recommended you visit for more information. Some of these addresses (also known as URLs) can be painstaking to type into a web browser, so we've compiled all of them into a single list that readers of the print edition can refer to while they read.

Download the list at *https://aka.ms/examref742/downloads*.

The URLs are organized by chapter and heading. Every time you come across a URL in the book, find the hyperlink in the list to go directly to the webpage.

Errata, updates, & book support

We've made every effort to ensure the accuracy of this book and its companion content. You can access updates to this book—in the form of a list of submitted errata and their related corrections—at:

https://aka.ms/examref742/errata

If you discover an error that is not already listed, please submit it to us at the same page.

If you need additional support, email Microsoft Press Book Support at *mspinput@microsoft.com*.

Please note that product support for Microsoft software and hardware is not offered through the previous addresses. For help with Microsoft software or hardware, go to *https://support.microsoft.com*.

We want to hear from you

At Microsoft Press, your satisfaction is our top priority, and your feedback our most valuable asset. Please tell us what you think of this book at:

https://aka.ms/tellpress

We know you're busy, so we've kept it short with just a few questions. Your answers go directly to the editors at Microsoft Press. (No personal information will be requested.) Thanks in advance for your input!

Stay in touch

Let's keep the conversation going! We're on Twitter: *http://twitter.com/MicrosoftPress*.

Important: How to use this book to study for the exam

Certification exams validate your on-the-job experience and product knowledge. To gauge your readiness to take an exam, use this Exam Ref to help you check your understanding of the skills tested by the exam. Determine the topics you know well and the areas in which you need more experience. To help you refresh your skills in specific areas, we have also provided "Need more review?" pointers, which direct you to more in-depth information outside the book.

The Exam Ref is not a substitute for hands-on experience. This book is not designed to teach you new skills.

We recommend that you round out your exam preparation by using a combination of available study materials and courses. Learn more about available classroom training at *https://www.microsoft.com/learning*. Microsoft Official Practice Tests are available for many exams at *https://aka.ms/practicetests*. You can also find free online courses and live events from Microsoft Virtual Academy at *https://www.microsoftvirtualacademy.com*.

This book is organized by the "Skills measured" list published for the exam. The "Skills measured" list for each exam is available on the Microsoft Learning website: *https://aka.ms/examlist*.

Note that this Exam Ref is based on this publicly available information and the author's experience. To safeguard the integrity of the exam, authors do not have access to the exam questions.

CHAPTER 1

Install and configure Active Directory Domain Services

Active Directory Domain Services (AD DS) provide the cornerstone of identity and access solutions in Windows Server 2016. It is therefore important that you understand how to implement an AD DS infrastructure to support the identity needs of your organization.

In this chapter, we cover how to install and configure domain controllers, and how to create and configure users, groups, computers, and organizational units (OUs). These skills are fundamental to implementing AD DS.

> **IMPORTANT**
> **Have you read page xv?**
> It contains valuable information regarding the skills you need to pass the exam.

Skills covered in this chapter:

- Install and configure domain controllers
- Create and manage Active Directory users and computers
- Create and manage Active Directory groups and OUs

Skill 1.1: Install and configure domain controllers

Domain controllers host the Windows Server 2016 AD DS server role and provide authentication and related services to your organization's computers and other networked devices. Before you can properly understand deployment scenarios for AD DS domain controllers, you must first understand the fundamentals of AD DS, including forests, trees, domains, sites, and OUs.

This section covers how to:
- AD DS fundamentals
- Install a new forest
- Add or remove a domain controller
- Install AD DS on a Server Core installation
- Install a domain controller using Install from Media
- Install and configure a read-only domain controller
- Configure a global catalog server
- Configure domain controller cloning
- Upgrade domain controllers
- Transfer and seize operations master roles
- Resolve DNS SRV record registration issues

AD DS fundamentals

AD DS consists of both logical and physical components. A physical component is something tangible, like a domain controller, while an AD DS forest is an intangible, logical component. AD DS consists of the following logical components:

- **Forest** A forest is a collection of AD DS domains that share a common schema and are bound by automatically created two-way trust relationships. Most organizations choose to implement AD DS with a single forest. Reasons to use multiple forests include the requirement to:
    - Provide for complete administrative separation between disparate parts of your organization.
    - Support different object types and attributes in the AD DS schema in different parts of your organization.
- **Domain** A domain is a logical administrative unit that contains users, groups, computers, and other objects. Multiple domains can be part of one or several forests, depending on your organizational needs. Parent-child and trust relationships define your domain structure.

EXAM TIP

A domain does not provide for administrative separation because all domains in a forest have the same forest administrator—the Enterprise Admins universal security group. For complete administrative separation, you must implement multiple AD DS forests.

- **Tree** A tree is a collection of AD DS domains that share a common root domain and have a contiguous namespace. For example, sales.adatum.com and marketing.adatum.com share the common root adatum.com; they also share a contiguous namespace, adatum.com. You can build your AD DS forest using a single tree, or you can use multiple trees. Reasons for using multiple trees include the requirement to support multiple logical namespaces within your organization, perhaps because of mergers or acquisitions.

- **Schema**   The AD DS schema is the collection of objects types and their properties, also known as attributes, that defines what sorts of objects you can create, store, and manage within your AD DS forest. For example, a user is a logical object type, and it has several properties, including a full name, a department, and a password. The relationship between objects and their attributes is held in the schema, and all domain controllers in a forest hold a copy of the schema.

- **OU**   An OU is a container within a domain that contains users, groups, computers, and other OUs. They are used to provide for administrative simplification. With OUs you can easily delegate administrative rights to a collection of objects by grouping them in an OU and assigning the right on that OU. You can also use Group Policy Objects (GPOs) to configure user and computer settings and link those GPO settings to an OU, streamlining the configuration process. One OU is created by default when you install AD DS and create a domain: Domain Controllers.

- **Container**   In addition to OUs, you can also use containers to group collections of objects together. There are a number of built-in containers, including: Computers, Builtin, and Managed Service Accounts. You cannot link GPOs to containers.

- **Site**   A site is a logical representation of a physical location within your organization. It can represent a large physical area, such as a city, or it can represent a smaller physical area, such as a collection of subnets defined by your datacenter boundaries. AD DS sites help to enable networked devices to determine where they are in relation to services with which they want to connect. For example, when a Windows 10 computer starts up, it uses its determined site location to try to find an adjacent domain controller to support the user's sign in. Sites also enable you to control AD DS replication by configuring an intersite replication schedule and interval.

EXAM TIP

A default site, Default-First-Site-Name, is created when you install AD DS and create your forest. All domain controllers belong to this site until you create additional sites and assign domain controllers to them. If you intend to create additional site objects, you should rename the default site.

- **Subnet**   A subnet is a logical representation of a physical subnet on your network. By defining subnets, you make it possible for a computer in your AD DS forest to determine its physical location in relation to services offered in the forest. No subnets exist by default. After you create subnets, you associate them with sites. A site can contain more than one subnet.

- **Partition**   Your AD DS is physically stored in a database on all of your domain controllers. Because some parts of your AD DS change infrequently, while others change often, a number of separate partitions are stored in the AD DS database.

> **NOTE   AD DS REPLICATION**
>
> When changes are made to AD DS, other instances of the changed partition must be updated. This process is referred to as AD DS replication. By splitting the database into several elements, the burden of the replication process is reduced.

These separate partitions are:

- **Schema**   A forest-level partition, which changes rarely. Contains the AD DS forest schema.
- **Configuration**   A forest-level partition that changes rarely, this partition contains the configuration data for the forest.
- **Domain**   Domain-level partition. This partition changes frequently, and a writeable copy of the partition is stored on all domain controllers. It contains the actual objects, such as users and computers, which exist within your forest.

> **NOTE   READ ONLY DOMAIN CONTROLLERS**
>
> Read Only Domain Controllers (RODCs) contain a read-only copy of the domain partition.

> **NOTE   APPLICATION DIRECTORY PARTITIONS**
>
> You can also create specific partitions to support directory-enabled applications that you deploy within your forest. For example, you can configure DNS to use a specific application directory partition for AD-integrated zone replication purposes.

- **Trust relationships**   A trust relationship, also sometimes referred to as a trust, is a security agreement between two domains in an AD DS forest, between two forests, or between a forest and an external security realm. This security agreement enables a user on one side of the trust to be assigned access to resources on the other side of the trust. In a trust relationship, one party is deemed to be trusting, while the other is said to be trusted. The resource-holding entity is trusting, while the user-holding entity is trusted. To help understand this, consider who is trusted and trusting when you lend someone your car keys.

Install a new forest

To install a new AD DS forest, you must deploy the first domain controller in that forest. This means deploying the AD DS server role on a Windows Server 2016 server computer and then promoting the server to a domain controller, and choosing the option to Add A New Forest.

To create a new forest, start by installing the AD DS role by using the following procedure:

1. Sign in to the Windows Server 2016 computer as a local administrator.
2. Launch Server Manager and then, on the Dashboard, click Add Roles And Features.
3. Click through the Add Roles And Features Wizard, and then, as shown in Figure 1-1, on the Server Roles page, select the Active Directory Domain Services check box, click Add Features, and then click Next.

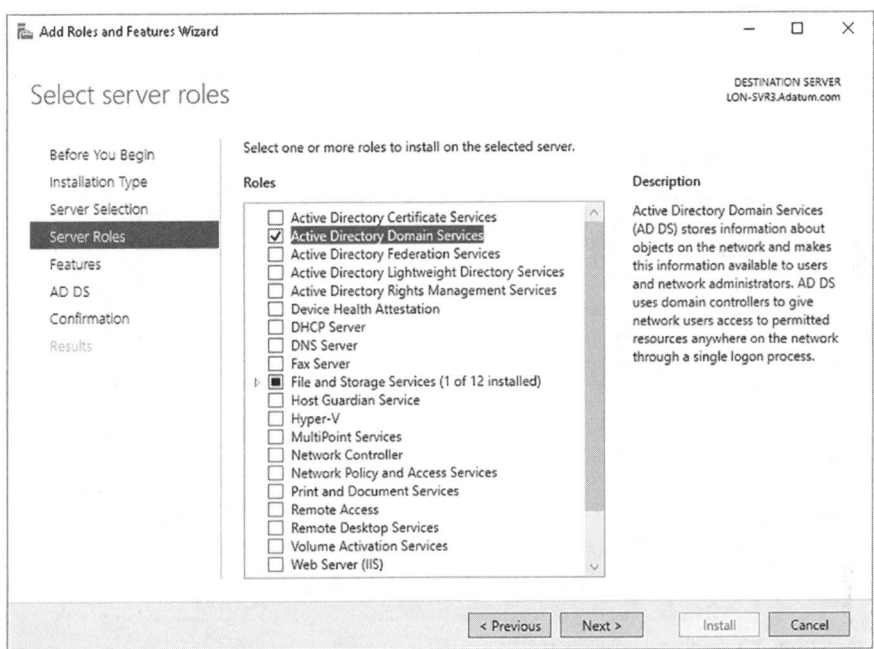

FIGURE 1-1 Installing the Active Directory Domain Services server role

4. Click through the rest of the wizard, and when prompted, click Install.
5. When installation is complete, click Close.

EXAM TIP

You can also use Windows PowerShell to install the necessary files. Run the following command at an elevated Windows PowerShell command prompt: Install-WindowsFeature AD-Domain-Services.

After you have installed the binaries for AD DS, you must create a new forest by promoting the first domain controller in the forest. To do this, use the following procedure:

1. In Server Manager, click the yellow warning triangle in Notifications, and then click Promote This Server To A Domain Controller.

EXAM TIP

You can also use Windows PowerShell to perform the promotion. Run the Install-ADDS-DomainController cmdlet. For example, run the Install-ADDSDomainController -InstallDns -DomainName adatum.com command to add the local server as an additional domain controller in the Adatum.com domain, and install the DNS server role.

2. In the Active Directory Domain Services Configuration Wizard, on the Deployment Configuration page, under Select The Deployment Operation, click Add A New Forest, and then type the name of the forest root domain, as shown in Figure 1-2. Click Next.

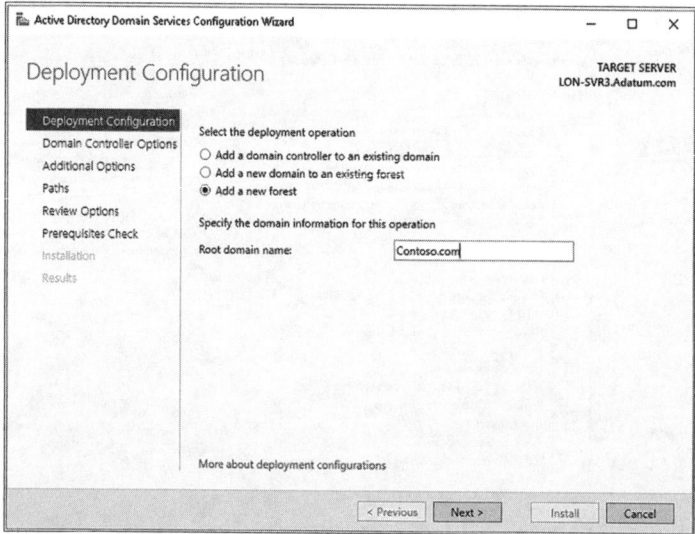

FIGURE 1-2 Adding a new forest

3. On the Domain Controller Options page, as shown in Figure 1-3, configure the following options, and then click Next:

   - **Forest Functional Level**   The forest functional level determines which forest-level features are available in your forest. The forest functional level also defines the minimum domain functional level for domains in your forest. Thus, choosing Windows Server 2012 at this level means that the minimum domain functional level is also Windows Server 2012. Choose between:
     - Windows Server 2008
     - Windows Server 2008 R2
     - Windows Server 2012
     - Windows Server 2012 R2
     - Windows Server 2016
   - **Domain Functional Level**   Determines the domain-level features that are available in this domain. Choose between:

- Windows Server 2008
- Windows Server 2008 R2
- Windows Server 2012
- Windows Server 2012 R2
- Windows Server 2016

> **NEED MORE REVIEW?** **WINDOWS SERVER 2016 FUNCTIONAL LEVELS**
>
> To review further details about domain and forest functional levels in Windows Server 2016, refer to the Microsoft TechNet website at *https://technet.microsoft.com/windows-server-docs/identity/ad-ds/windows-server-2016-functional-levels*.

- **Domain Name System (DNS) Server** DNS provides name resolution and is a critical service for AD DS. This option is selected by default, and unless you already have a configured DNS infrastructure, do not deselect this option.
- **Global Catalog (GC)** Global catalog servers provide forest-wide services. They are selected by default, and cannot be unselected. The first (and only) domain controller must be a global catalog server. When you have added additional domain controllers, you can revisit this setting.
- **Read Only Domain Controller (RODC)** Determines whether this domain controller is a read only domain controller. This option is not selected by default, and unavailable for the first (and currently only) domain controller in your forest.
- **Directory Services Restore Mode (DSRM) Password** Used when you start the domain controller in a recovery mode.

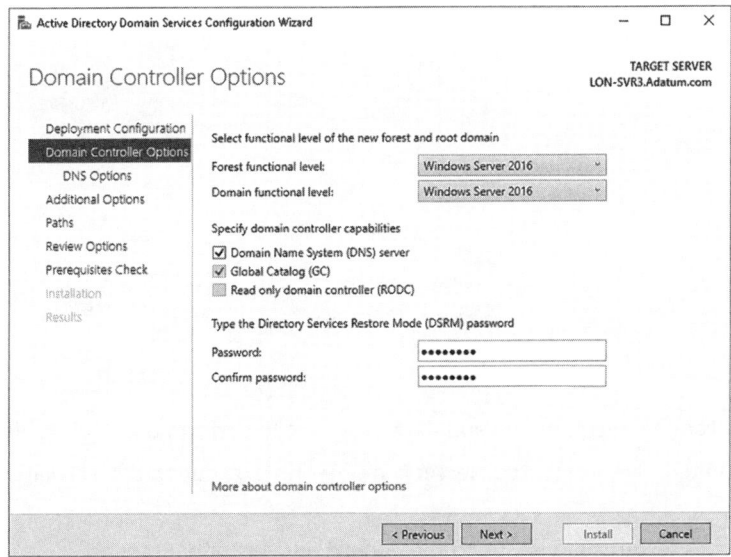

FIGURE 1-3 Configuring domain controller options

Skill 1.1: Install and configure domain controllers

4. On the Additional Options page, define the NetBIOS domain name. The NetBIOS protocol is not widely used anymore, and is based on a non-hierarchical naming structure. The default NetBIOS name is the first part of the AD DS forest name. For example, if your forest is called Contoso.com, the NetBIOS name defaults to CONTOSO; generally, you do not need to change this. Click Next.

5. As shown in Figure 1-4, define the location to store the AD DS database, log files, and SYSVOL content, and click Next. The defaults are:
   - Database folder: C:\Windows\NTDS
   - Log files folder: C:\Windows\NTDS
   - SYSVOL folder: C:\Windows\SYSVOL

EXAM TIP

There is usually little point in using different paths. However, you might achieve a small performance benefit by separating the SYSVOL, database, and log files if your server is installed with multiple physical hard disks, thereby distributing the load.

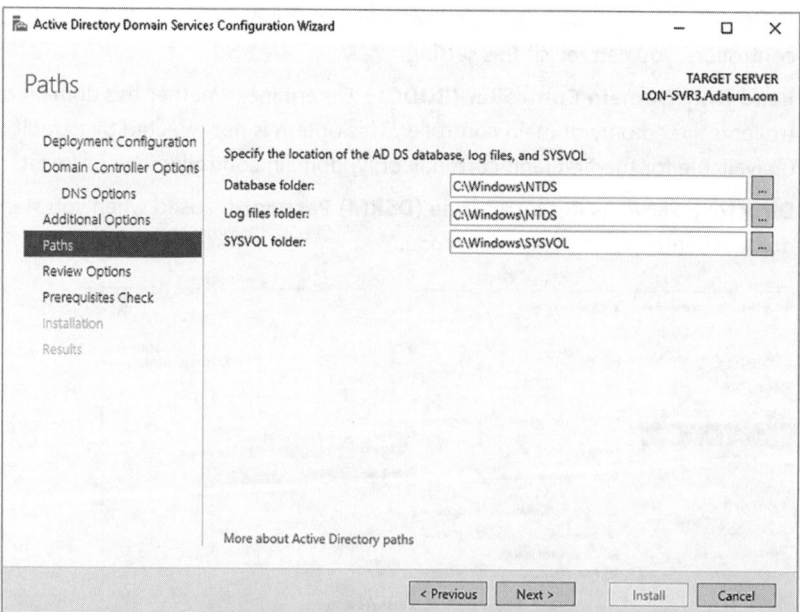

FIGURE 1-4 Configuring AD DS paths

6. Review the configuration options, and then click Next to perform prerequisite checks.
7. When prompted, click Install. Your server computer restarts during the installation process.
8. Sign in to your server computer using the domain administrator account.

> **NEED MORE REVIEW?** **INSTALL ACTIVE DIRECTORY DOMAIN SERVICES**
>
> To review further details about deploying AD DS, refer to the Microsoft TechNet website at *https://technet.microsoft.com/en-us/windows-server-docs/identity/ad-ds/deploy/install-active-directory-domain-services--level-100-*.

Add or remove a domain controller

After you have deployed the first domain controller in your AD DS forest, you can add additional domain controllers to provide for resilience and improved performance. The process for deploying additional domain controllers is broadly the same as that for the first domain controller: install the AD DS server role (either using Server Manager or Windows PowerShell), and then promote the domain controller (again, using either Server Manager or Windows PowerShell).

However, the specific options you select during the promotion process vary depending upon the details of the deployment. For example, adding a new domain controller in an existing domain is slightly different than adding a new domain controller in a new domain.

There are two basic scenarios for adding a new domain controller:

- **Add A New Domain Controller In An Existing Domain**   To complete this process, you must sign in as a member of the target domain's Domain Admins global security group.
- **Add A New Domain Controller In A New Domain**   To complete this process, you must sign in as a member of the forest root Enterprise Admins universal security group. This gives you sufficient privilege to modify the configuration partition of AD DS and create the new domain, either as part of the existing domain tree, or as part of a new domain tree.

A common reason to add a new domain is to create a replication boundary. Because most changes to the AD DS database occur in the domain partition, it is this partition that generates most AD DS replication traffic. By splitting your AD DS forest into multiple domains, you can split the volume of changes, and thereby reduce the replication between locations. For example, if A. Datum had a large deployment of computers in both Europe and in Canada, they could create two separate domains in the Adatum.com forest root domain: Europe.Adatum.com and Canada.Adatum.com. Changes in the Europe.Adatum.com domain are not replicated to domain controllers in Canada.Adatum.com, and vice versa.

Add a new domain controller in an existing domain

To add a new domain controller in an existing domain, sign in as a domain administrator and then complete the following procedure.

EXAM TIP

Signing in as a member of the Domain Admins global security group presupposes that the server computer you are intending to promote is a member of the target domain. If it is not, it is easier to add the server computer to the target domain first, and then complete the procedure. If you decide not to add the computer to the target domain, you must sign in as a local administrator and provide Domain Admin credentials during the promotion process. It is also a requirement that the server computer you are promoting can resolve names using the DNS service in your AD DS forest.

1. Add the Active Directory Domain Services server role.
2. In Server Manager, click Notifications, and then click Promote This Server To A Domain Controller.
3. In the Active Directory Domain Services Configuration Wizard, on the Deployment Configuration page, as shown in Figure 1-5, click Add A Domain Controller To An Existing Domain.

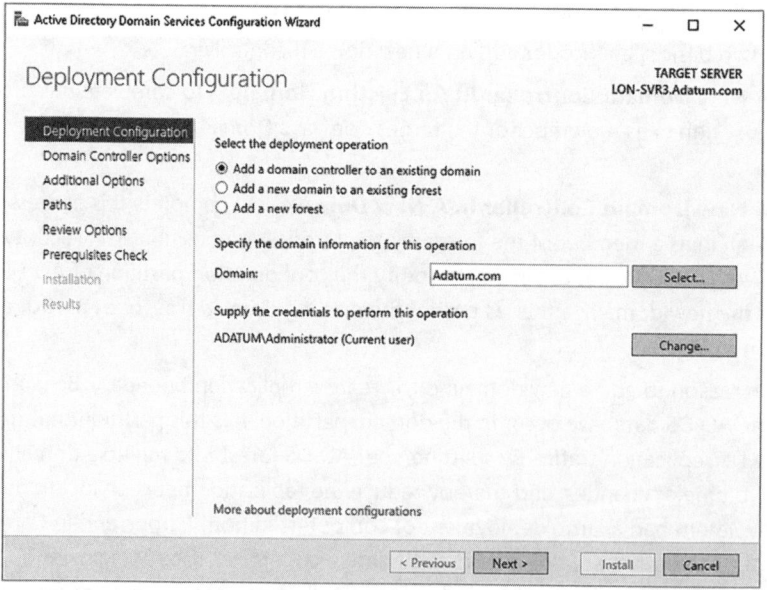

FIGURE 1-5 Deploying an additional domain controller in an existing domain

4. Specify the domain name. The default name is the same as the domain to which the server computer belongs. However, you can select from other available domains in the forest.
5. Specify the credentials of a user account with appropriate privilege to perform the promotion process. The default is the current user account. Click Next.
6. On the Domain Controller Options page, configure the Domain Name System (DNS) server (enabled by default), Global Catalog (GC) (enabled by default), and Read Only

Domain Controller (RODC) (not enabled by default) options. Unlike when promoting the first domain controller in a forest, you can enable the Read Only Domain Controller (RODC) to make this domain controller a read only domain controller.

7. In the Site name drop-down list, shown in Figure 1-6, select the site in which this domain controller is physically placed. The default is Default-First-Site-Name. Until you create additional AD DS sites, this is the only available site. You can move the domain controller after deployment.

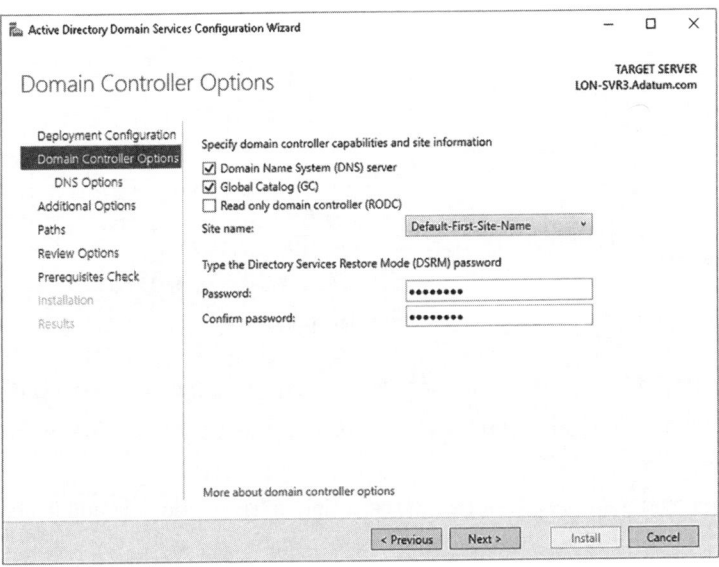

FIGURE 1-6 Configuring domain controller options for an additional domain controller

8. Enter the Directory Services Restore Mode (DSRM) password, and click Next.

9. On the Additional Options page, you must configure how this domain controller populates the AD DS database. You can configure the initial population from an online domain controller, selecting either Any Domain Controller, as shown in Figure 1-7, or specifying a particular domain controller. Alternatively, you can use the Install From Media (IFM) option. Click Next.

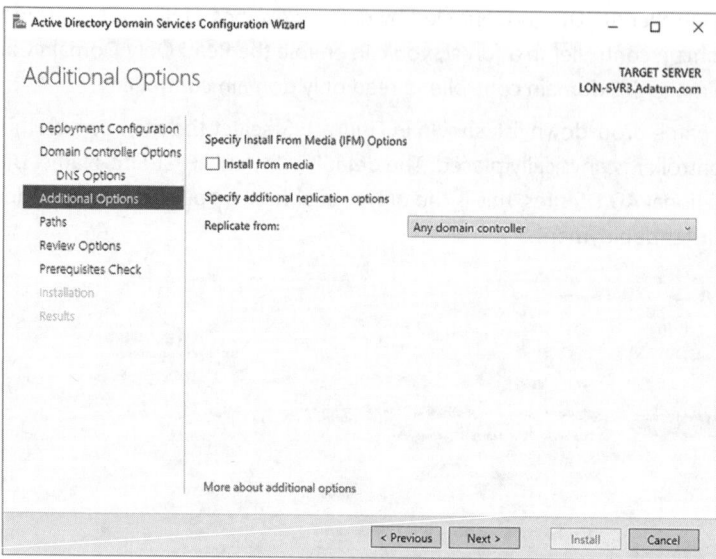

FIGURE 1-7 Configuring domain controller additional options

10. Configure the Paths, as before, and then click through the configuration wizard.
11. Click Install when prompted. Your server computer restarts during the promotion process.

After you have completed the promotion process, sign in using a domain admin account.

Add a new domain controller in a new domain

To add a new domain controller to a new domain in an existing forest, sign in as a member of the forest Enterprise Admin universal security group, and then complete the following procedure.

EXAM TIP

To sign in as a member of the Enterprise Admins universal security group presupposes that the server computer you are intending to promote is a member of one of the domains in your AD DS forest. If it is not, it is easier to add the server computer to the forest root domain first, and then complete the procedure. If you decide not to add the computer to the forest root domain, you must sign in as a local administrator and provide Enterprise Admin credentials during the promotion process. It is also a requirement that the server computer you are promoting can resolve names using the DNS service in your AD DS forest.

1. Add the Active Directory Domain Services server role.
2. In Server Manager, click Notifications, and then click Promote This Server To A Domain Controller.

3. In the Active Directory Domain Services Configuration Wizard, on the Deployment Configuration page, as shown in Figure 1-8, click Add A New Domain To An Existing Forest.

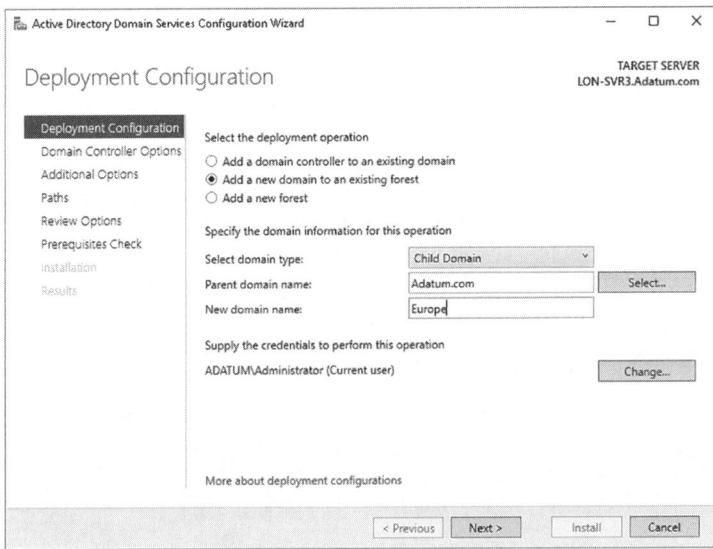

FIGURE 1-8 Adding a new child domain to an existing forest

4. You can then choose how the new domain is added. You can select:
   - **Child Domain**   Selecting this option creates a subdomain of the specified parent domain. In other words, the new domain is created in the existing domain tree.
   - **Tree Domain**   Select this option if you want to create a new tree in the same forest. The new tree shares the same forest schema, and has the same forest root domain, but you can define a non-contiguous namespace. This is useful when you want to create multiple DNS domain names in your AD DS forest infrastructure to support your organizational needs, but do not need, or want, to separate administrative function as is possible with a separate forest. If you choose Tree Domain, you must define the forest domain to which the tree is added. The default is the forest you are signed in to.
5. Enter the new domain name. In the case of a child domain, the name includes the parent domain as a suffix. For example, adding the Europe domain as a child of the Adatum.com domain creates the Europe.Adatum.com domain. If you create a new tree, you can enter any valid DNS domain name and it does not contain the forest root domain. Click Next.
6. On the Domain Controller Options page, select the domain functional level, and configure the DNS, GC, and RODC settings. Select the appropriate site name, and then finally, enter the DSRM password, and click Next.

7. On the DNS Options page, as shown in Figure 1-9, select the Create DNS Delegation check box. This creates a DNS delegation for the subdomain in your DNS namespace. Click Next.

> **NEED MORE REVIEW?** **UNDERSTANDING ZONE DELEGATION**
>
> To review further details about DNS delegation in Windows Server, refer to the Microsoft TechNet website at *https://technet.microsoft.com/library/cc771640(v=ws.11).aspx*.

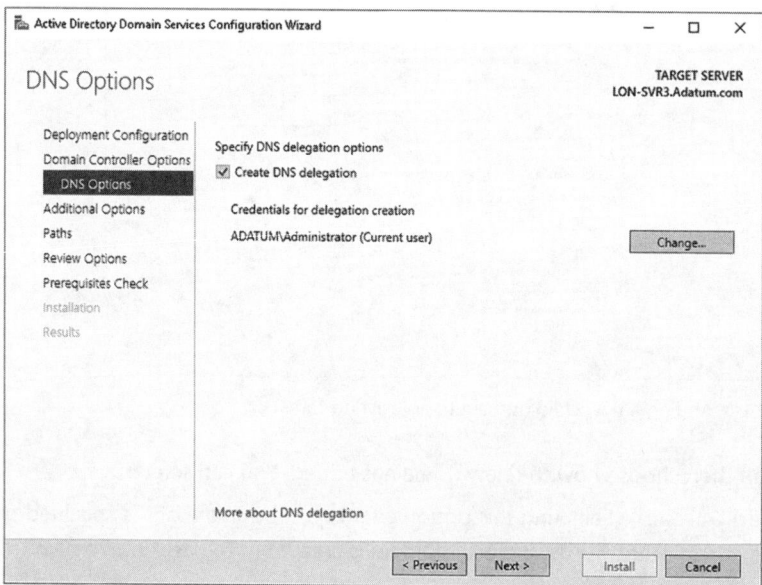

FIGURE 1-9 Adding a new child domain to an existing forest

8. Specify the NetBIOS domain name, and then click through the wizard. When prompted, click Install.
9. Your domain controller restarts during the promotion process. Sign in as a domain admin after the process is complete.

Removing domain controllers

From time to time, it might be necessary to decommission and remove a domain controller. This is a fairly straightforward process, and you can use Server Manager to complete the task.

1. Sign in using an account that has sufficient privilege. To remove a domain controller from a domain, sign in as a domain administrator. To remove an entire domain, sign in as a member of the Enterprise Admins universal security group.
2. Open Server Manager, and from the Manage menu, click Remove Roles And Features.
3. In the Remove Roles And Features Wizard, on the Before You Begin page, click Next.

4. Select the appropriate server on the Select Destination Server page, and then click Next.
5. On the Remove Server Roles page, clear the Active Directory Domain Services check box, click Remove Features, and then click Next.
6. In the Validation Results pop-up dialog box, shown in Figure 1-10, click Demote This Domain Controller.

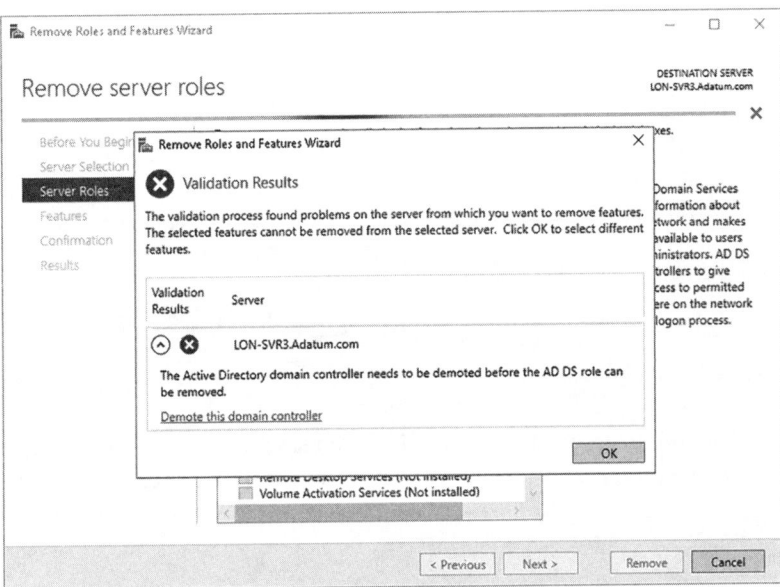

FIGURE 1-10 Removing AD DS

7. The Active Directory Domain Services Configuration Wizard loads, as shown in Figure 1-11. On the Credentials page, if necessary, specify user credentials that have sufficient privilege to perform the removal. Do not select the Force The Removal Of This Domain Controller check box unless the domain controller has failed and is not contactable. Click Next.

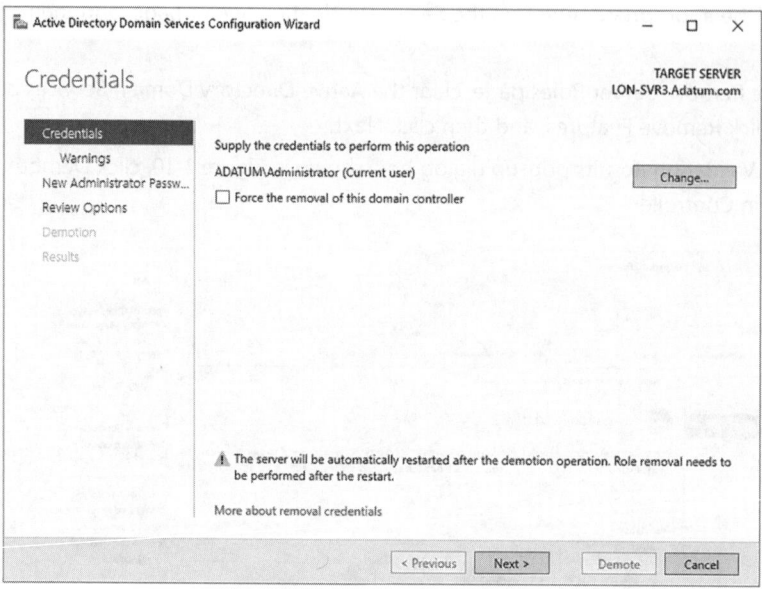

FIGURE 1-11 Demoting a domain controller

8. On the Warnings page, shown in Figure 1-12, you are prompted to confirm removal of the DNS and GC roles. Select the Proceed With Removal check box, and click Next.

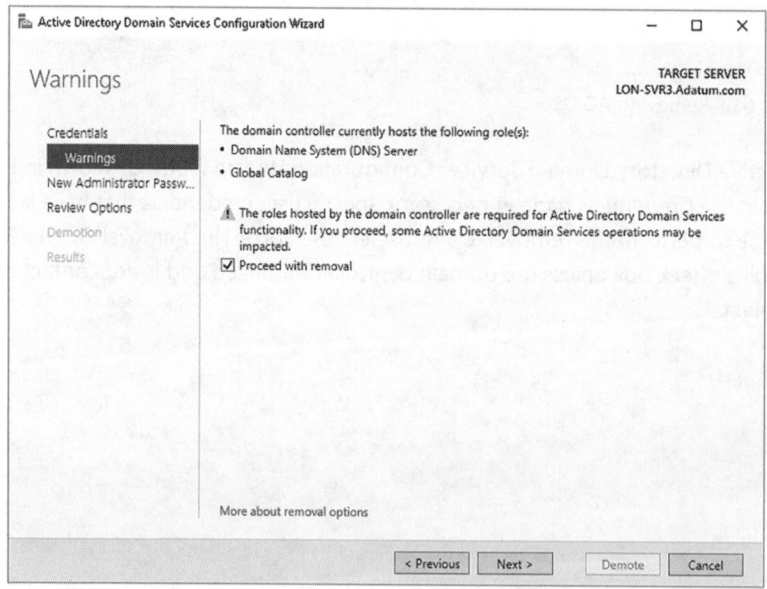

FIGURE 1-12 Removing optional components

9. On the New Administrator Password, enter and confirm the password that is set as the local administrator password, and click Next.

10. Review your choices, and then click Demote.
11. Your server is demoted and then restarts. Sign in using the local administrator account.

You can now verify the proper demotion and role removal. On a domain controller:

1. On a domain controller, open Active Directory Users And Computers. Verify that the demoted domain controller no longer is listed in the Domain Controllers OU.
2. Click the Computers container. You should see your demoted server computer.
3. Open Active Directory Sites And Services. Expand Sites, expand the Default-First-Site-Name site, and in Servers, delete the object that represents the server you demoted.

EXAM TIP
If the server to be decommissioned is the last domain controller in a domain, you must first remove all other computers from the domain, perhaps moving them to other domains within your forest. The procedure is then as described above.

You can also complete the demotion process by using Windows PowerShell. Use the following two cmdlets to complete the process from the Windows PowerShell command prompt:

```
Uninstall-addsdomaincontroller

Uninstall-windowsfeature AD-Domain_Services
```

NEED MORE REVIEW? DEMOTING DOMAIN CONTROLLERS AND DOMAINS
To review further details about demoting domain controllers, refer to the Microsoft TechNet website at *https://technet.microsoft.com/en-us/windows-server-docs/identity/ad-ds/deploy/demoting-domain-controllers-and-domains--level-200-*.

Install AD DS on a Server Core installation

You can deploy the AD DS server role on a Server Core installation. You can use Server Manager to remotely install the role, or you can use the Windows PowerShell Install-WindowsFeature AD-Domain-Services cmdlet.

After you have installed the required files, you can launch the Active Directory Domain Services Configuration Wizard from Server Manager to remotely configure the Server Core installation, or you can use the Windows PowerShell Install-ADDSDomainController cmdlet to complete the promotion process. In other words, the process for installing AD DS on a Server Core installation of Windows Server 2016 is the same as for a server with Desktop Experience.

EXAM TIP
You cannot deploy the AD DS server role on Nano Server. Consequently, you cannot use a Nano Server as a domain controller.

Install a domain controller using Install from Media

During the domain controller deployment process, the content of the AD DS database is replicated to the new domain controller. This replication includes the schema, configuration forest-wide partitions, as well as the appropriate domain partition. After this initial synchronization, replication occurs normally between the domain controllers.

This initial synchronization can present a challenge in some circumstances. For example, this can be challenging when you are deploying a domain controller in a location that is connected to your organization's network infrastructure using a low bandwidth connection. In this situation, the initial synchronization might take a long time, or use an excessive proportion of the available bandwidth.

To mitigate this, you can choose to deploy a domain controller and perform the initial AD DS synchronization using a local copy, or snapshot, of the AD DS database; this is known as performing an Install from Media (IFM) deployment. There are many steps involved in this process.

1. On an existing domain controller, using File Explorer, make a folder, for example C:\IFM, to store the AD DS snapshot.
2. Open an elevated command prompt and run the ntdsutil.exe command.
3. At the ntdsutil: prompt, type **Activate instance ntds**, and then press Enter.
4. At the ntdsutil: prompt, type **ifm**, and then press Enter.
5. At the ifm: prompt, as shown in Figure 1-13, type **create SYSVOL full C:\IFM**, and then press Enter.

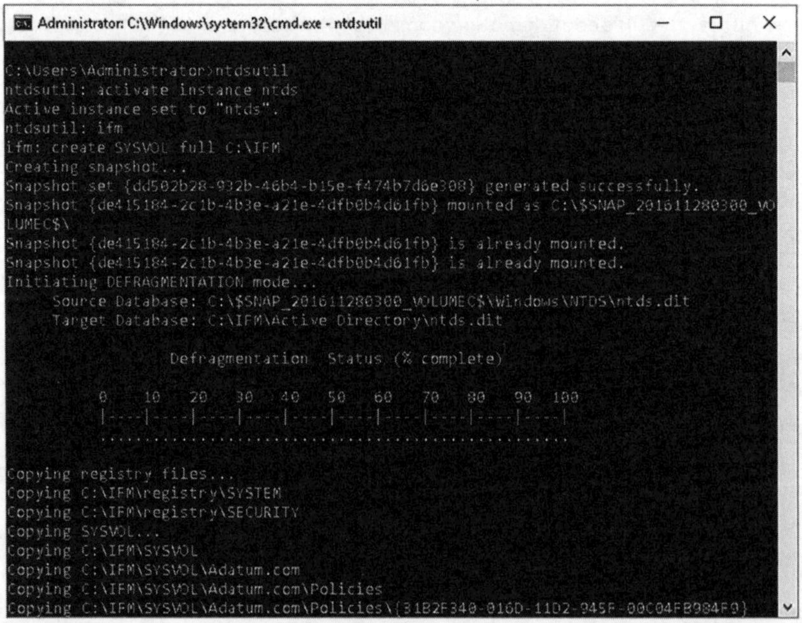

FIGURE 1-13 Creating an NTDS snapshot for IFM

6. At the ifm: prompt, type **quit** and then press Enter.
7. At the ntdsutil: prompt, type **quit** and then press Enter.
8. Close the command prompt.
9. Using File Explorer, copy the contents of the C:\IFM folder, shown in Figure 1-14, to removable storage, such as a USB memory stick.

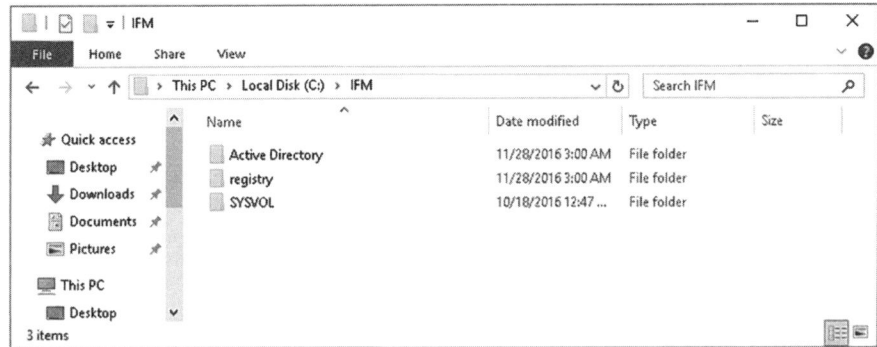

FIGURE 1-14 The folders created for an AD DS snapshot

10. At the server computer that you want to promote to a domain controller, install the Active Directory Domain Services server role in the usual way, either by using Server Manager, or by using Windows PowerShell.
11. Insert the memory stick containing the AD DS snapshot, or copy the snapshot files so that they are accessible on the target server computer, and then launch the Active Directory Domain Services Configuration Wizard from Server Manager, and click through the wizard.
12. On the Additional Options page, shown in Figure 1-15, select the Install From Media check box. In the Path box, enter the path to the local copy of the AD DS snapshot, click Verify, and then click Next.

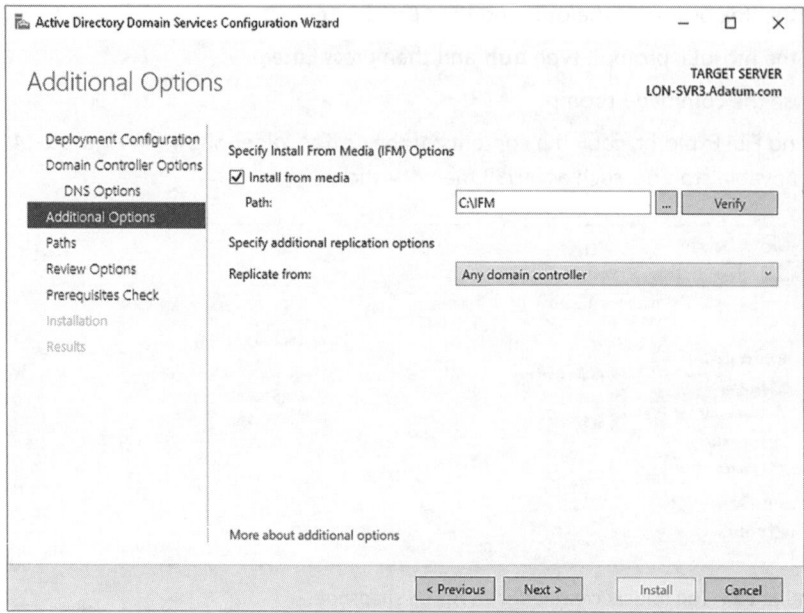

FIGURE 1-15 Choosing the Install From Media option

13. Click through the wizard, review your selections, and when prompted, click Install. Your server restarts during the promotion process.
14. Sign in as a domain administrator.

The domain controller now replicates in the normal way with other domain controllers in the forest. You might want to define the AD DS site to which the domain controller belongs, and then to configure a replication schedule to that site. These procedures are discussed in Chapter 2: Manage and maintain AD DS, Skill 2.3: Configure Active Directory in a complex enterprise environment.

EXAM TIP

You can also complete the deployment by using the Windows PowerShell Install-ADDSDomaincontroller -InstallationMediaPath x:\ifm command to promote the server computer.

Install and configure a read-only domain controller

An RODC is a domain controller that contains a read-only copy of AD DS. You can use RODCs to enable you to deploy domain controllers in offices where physical security cannot be guaranteed. For example, in a branch office, you might require a local domain controller, but do not have a physically secure computer room in which to install it.

Although RODCs offer several administrative benefits, before deploying them, you should consider the following factors:

- You should deploy only one RODC per site, per domain. If you deploy multiple RODCs per site, caching is inconsistent resulting in potential user and computer sign in problems.
- You can install the DNS server role along with the RODC role. Local clients can use the installed DNS role as with any other instance of DNS within your organization with one exception: dynamic updates. Because the DNS zone information is read only, clients cannot perform dynamic updates on the RODC instance of a DNS zone. In this situation, the RODC provides the clients with the name of a writable domain controller that the client can use to update its records.
- RODCs cannot perform the following AD DS functions:
  - **Operations master roles** Operations master roles need to be able to write to the AD DS database. Consequently, RODCs cannot hold any of the five operations master roles. Operations master roles are discussed later in this skill.
  - **AD DS replication bridgeheads** Because bridgeheads are responsible for AD DS replication, they must support both inbound and outbound AD DS replication. RODCs support only inbound replication, and therefore, cannot function as AD DS replication bridgeheads.
- RODCs cannot:
  - **Authenticate across trusts when a WAN connection is unavailable** If a branch office hosts users from several domains in your AD DS forest, users and computers from the domain of which the RODC is not a member cannot authenticate when a WAN link is unavailable. This is because the RODC caches credentials only for the domain accounts of which it is a member.
  - **Support applications that require constant AD DS interaction** Some applications, such as Microsoft Exchange Server, require AD DS interaction. RODC cannot support the required interactivity, and therefore, you must deploy writeable domain controllers in those locations that also host Exchange Servers.

Deploying an RODC

Before you deploy an RODC, you must ensure that there is at least one writable domain controller in your organization. You deploy RODCs in much the same way as you do all other domain controllers:

1. Install the Active Directory Domain Services server role on the server computer that you want to deploy as an RODC.
2. Launch the Active Directory Domain Services Configuration Wizard, and click through the wizard.
3. On the Domain Controller Options page, shown in Figure 1-16, select the Read Only Domain Controller (RODC) check box, and any other required options, and then click Next.

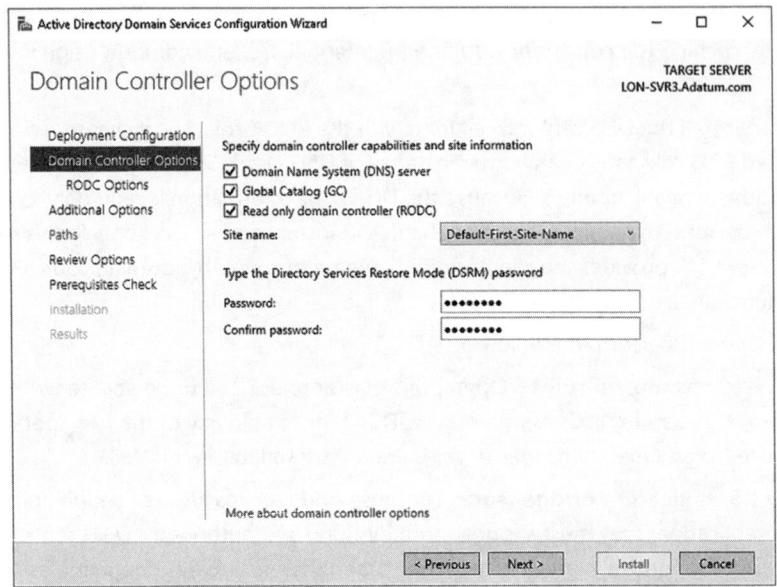

FIGURE 1-16 Installing an RODC

4. On the RODC Options page, shown in Figure 1-17, configure the following options, and then click Next.

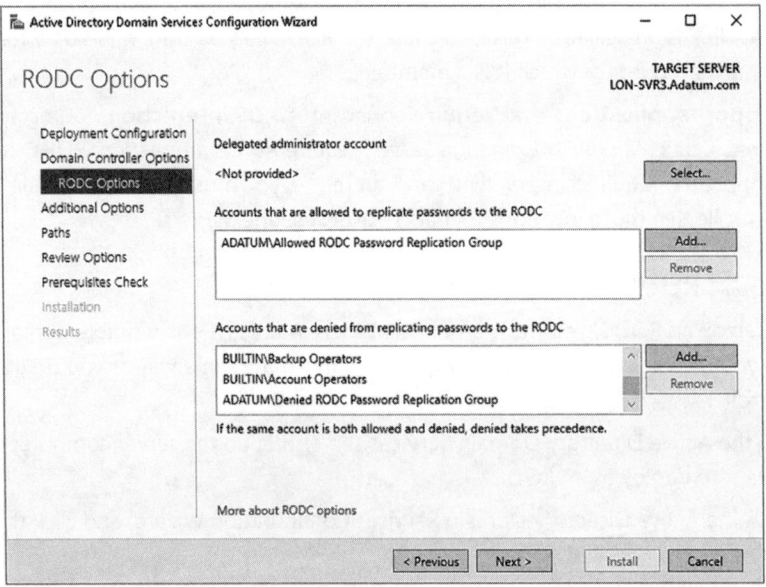

FIGURE 1-17 Configuring RODC options

- **Delegated Administrator Account** The delegated administrator(s) can perform local administration of the RODC without having equivalent domain administrator rights and privileges. Typically, an RODC delegated administrator can perform the following tasks:
    - Install and manage devices and drivers, hard disks, and updates
    - Manage the AD DS service
    - Manage server roles and features
    - View the event logs
    - Manage shared folders, apps, and services
- **Accounts That Are Allowed To Replicate Passwords To The RODC** By default, RODCs do not store sensitive password-related information. When a user signs in, the RODC forwards the sign in request to an online writeable domain controller elsewhere in the organization.

    However, to improve usability, you can define that certain user and computer accounts can be cached on the RODC, enabling local authentication to occur. You do this by defining an RODC password replication policy. Generally, you would only add the users and computers that are in the same local site as the RODC to the replication policy.

EXAM TIP

RODCs only store a subset of user and computer credentials. Consequently, if an RODC is stolen, security exposure is limited only to those cached accounts. This reduces the overall exposure, and helps reduce the administrative burden because only the cached accounts' passwords must be reset.

By default, as shown in Figure 1-17, the Allowed RODC Password Replication Group is enabled. After deploying the RODC, you can add users and computers to this group.

EXAM TIP

Also, there is a Denied RODC Password Replication Group. Members of this group can never have their credentials cached on the RODC. By default, this group contains Domain Admins, Enterprise Admins, and Group Policy Creator Owners.

- **Accounts That Are Denied From Replicating Passwords To The RODC** By default, the Denied RODC Password Replication Group is selected. After deploying the RODC, you can add users and computers to this group. Also, the following local groups are also denied from replicating passwords: Administrators, Server Operators, Backup Operators, and Account Operators.

EXAM TIP

The Allowed RODC Password Replication Group and Denied RODC Password Replication Group groups enable you to configure the password replication policy on all RODCs. However, if you have multiple branch offices—and therefore multiple RODCs—it is more secure to configure a separate group for each RODC for allowed password replication. In this instance, remove the Allowed RODC Password Replication Group, and add a group that you manually created, and then add the required members for that branch.

5. Click through the wizard, review your selections, and when prompted, click Install. Your server restarts during the promotion process.

EXAM TIP

You can use the Install-ADDSDomainController –ReadOnlyReplica Windows PowerShell command to install an RODC.

After you have deployed the RODC, you can configure the Allowed RODC Password Replication Group and Denied RODC Password Replication Group memberships to manage your RODC password replication policy.

Configure a global catalog server

In a single domain AD DS forest, any domain controller holds a copy of all objects within the forest. However, in multiple domain forests, this is no longer true. Although all domain controllers hold a copy of the schema and configuration partitions, they store only the local domain partition. Thus, if an application queries a domain controller in its local domain about the attributes of an object in another domain, there is no way for the local domain controller to satisfy that query.

This is where the global catalog is useful. The global catalog is a partial, read only copy of all objects in the forest and hosts a subset of all AD DS account schema attributes All domain controllers that are enabled as global catalog servers store a copy of this information locally. This enables them to satisfy queries for the attributes of objects that reside in other domains in the forest—without the requirement to petition a domain controller in that other domain.

EXAM TIP

In a single domain forest, configure all domain controllers as global catalog servers. In a multi-domain forest, unless all the domain controllers are global catalog servers, you must not configure the infrastructure master as a global catalog server.

You can configure a domain controller as a global catalog server during deployment of the domain controller. You select the Global Catalog (GC) check box on the Domain Controller Options page, shown in Figure 1-16, when you run the Active Directory Domain Services Configuration Wizard.

Alternatively, after installation, you can use the Active Directory Sites And Services tool:

1. On a domain controller, open Server Manager, click Tools, and then click Active Directory Sites And Services.
2. Expand the Sites node, expand the relevant site, expand the Server folder, and then expand the node for the domain controller that you want to modify.
3. Click the NTDS Settings object, as shown in Figure 1-18.

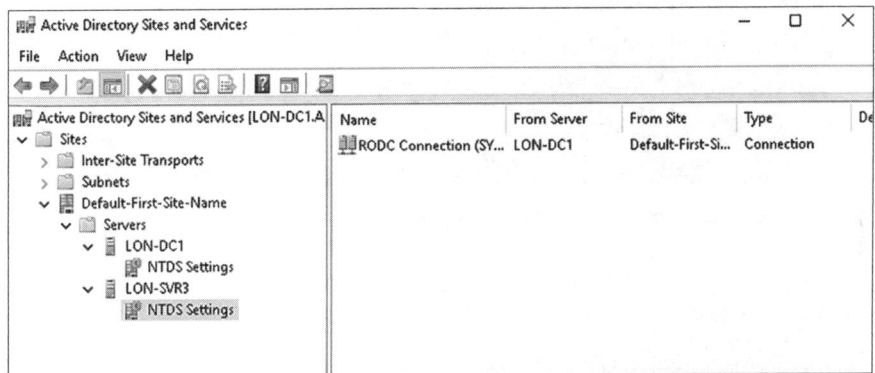

FIGURE 1-18 Configuring a global catalog server

4. Right-click the NTDS Settings node, and on the General tab, select the Global Catalog check box, as shown in Figure 1-19, and then click OK.

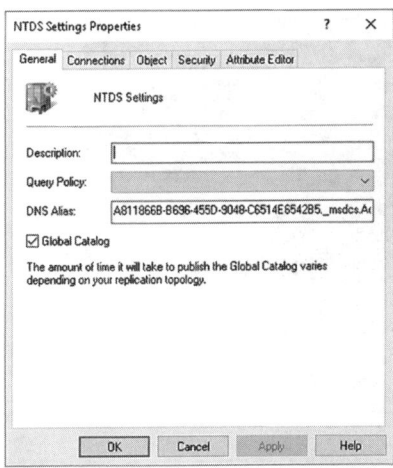

FIGURE 1-19 Enabling the global catalog server property

You can also use Windows PowerShell to make a domain controller a global catalog server.

1. Open Windows PowerShell (Admin).

2. Run the get-ADDomainController | select-object -property Name,IsGlobalCatalog command to query for a list of domain controllers and to verify their current global catalog status, as shown in Figure 1-20.

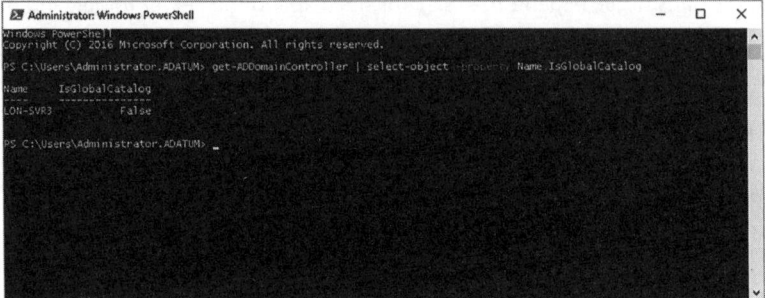

FIGURE 1-20 Getting a list of domain controllers

3. For the appropriate domain controller, run the following command, replacing LON-SVR3 with the name of your domain controller:

   Set-ADObject -Identity (Get-ADDomainController -Identity LON-SVR3).NTDSSettingsObjectDN -Replace @{options='1'}

4. Run the get-ADDomainController | select-object -property Name,IsGlobalCatalog command again to verify the change as shown in Figure 1-21.

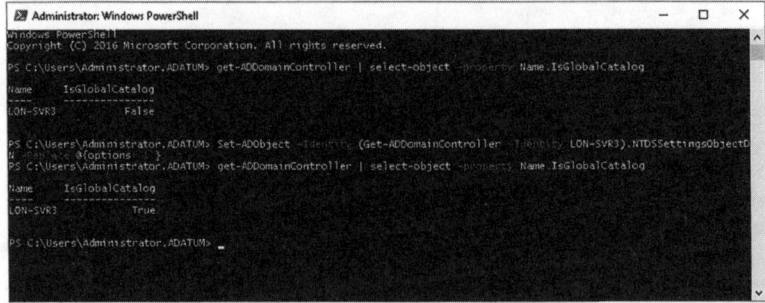

FIGURE 1-21 Configuring a domain controller as a global catalog server using Windows PowerShell

EXAM TIP

Many organizations now opt to make all domain controllers global catalog servers.

Adding attributes to the global catalog

It is important to note that the global catalog does not contain all attributes for all objects; rather, it contains a subset of the most useful attributes, known in Windows Server 2016 as the Partial Attribute Set. However, it is possible for you to modify which object attributes are stored in the global catalog; this is sometimes referred to as extending the partial attribute set. You can do this by using the following procedure:

> **NOTE CAUTION WHEN EDITING THE AD DS SCHEMA**
>
> Exercise great caution when editing the AD DS schema directly in this manner.

1. On the domain controller that has online access to the schema operations master role, run the regsvr32 schmmgmt.dll command at an elevated command prompt. This command enables the Active Directory Schema to be accessible through the management console.
2. Open the management console by running mmc.exe at an elevated command prompt.
3. In the Console1 – [Console Root] window, click File, and then click Add/Remove Snap-in.
4. In the Add Or Remove Snap-ins dialog box, in the Snap-in list, click Active Directory Schema, click Add, and then click OK.
5. Under Console Root in the navigation pane, expand Active Directory Schema, and then click Attributes. A long list of attributes is displayed.
6. You must know the specific attribute name to be able to modify its properties. Locate the attribute, right-click it, and then click Properties.
7. In the attribute Properties dialog box, the accountExpires Properties dialog box is shown in Figure 1-22, select the Replicate This Attribute To The Global Catalog check box, and then click OK.

FIGURE 1-22 Adding an attribute to the Global Catalog

8. Close the management console.

Configure domain controller cloning

It is relatively quick and straightforward to deploy domain controllers using the procedures outlined earlier in this chapter. But if you have many, broadly identical servers that you want to configure as domain controllers, a faster approach is to clone those domain controllers. This is especially relevant when your domain controllers are virtualized.

In versions of Windows Server prior to Windows Server 2012, cloning virtual domain controllers is prohibited. However, both Windows Server 2012 and Windows Server 2016 support virtual domain controller cloning. If you decide to deploy domain controllers by using cloning, there are the following potential advantages:

- **Fast deployment of domain controllers**   Not only does this make the initial deployment less time-consuming, it also offers the opportunity of responding quickly to domain controller outages by deploying a new clone.
- **Respond to increased demand**   Whether that's an increase in demand at a branch office, or elsewhere, you can deploy clones quickly when demand dictates.

Creating a clone

Before you can clone a virtual domain controller, you must ensure that your infrastructure meets the following requirements:

- **Windows Server 2012 or later**   Your domain controller guest virtual machines must run Windows Server 2012 or later.
- **PDC emulator operations master**   Your primary domain controller (PDC) emulator operations master must be running on a domain controller installed with Windows Server 2012 or later. Also, the PDC emulator role must be online when you start your cloned domain controllers for the first time.
- **Virtual machine generation identifiers**   You must use a hypervisor, such as Hyper-V on Windows Server 2012 or later, that supports virtual machine generation identifiers.

After you have verified these prerequisites, you can use the following procedure to clone a virtual domain controller. This consists of two stages: preparing the source domain controller, and preparing one or more target domain controller clones.

PREPARE THE SOURCE COMPUTER

1. Sign in to your domain controller as a member of the Domain Admins global security group.
2. Open the Active Directory Users And Computers console, navigate to the Users folder, and add the source computer to the Cloneable Domain Controllers global security group, as shown in Figure 1-23.

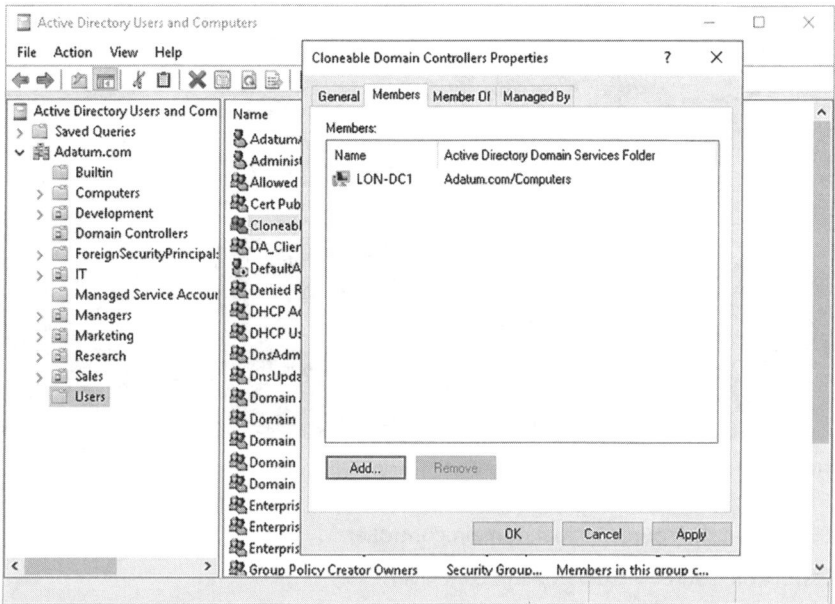

FIGURE 1-23 Adding a server to the Cloneable Domain Controllers security group

3. Run the Windows PowerShell Get-ADDCCloneingExcludedApplicationList cmdlet to check that all the apps and services on your source domain controller support cloning. Remove any unsupported apps.

EXAM TIP

If, after you clone a domain controller, you discover that the apps work, you can add the apps to the CustomDCCloneAllowList.xml file.

4. Run the Windows PowerShell Get-ADDCCloneingExcludedApplicationList -GenerateXML cmdlet.
5. Run the Windows PowerShell New-ADDCCloneConfigFile cmdlet, as shown in Figure 1-24, to generate a DCCloneConfig.xml file. This file is used to configure the clones. You specify a computer name, IP configuration, and site name for your intended clone. This information is written to DCCloneConfig.xml. If you intend to create multiple clones, typically, each must have a different DCCloneConfig.xml file.

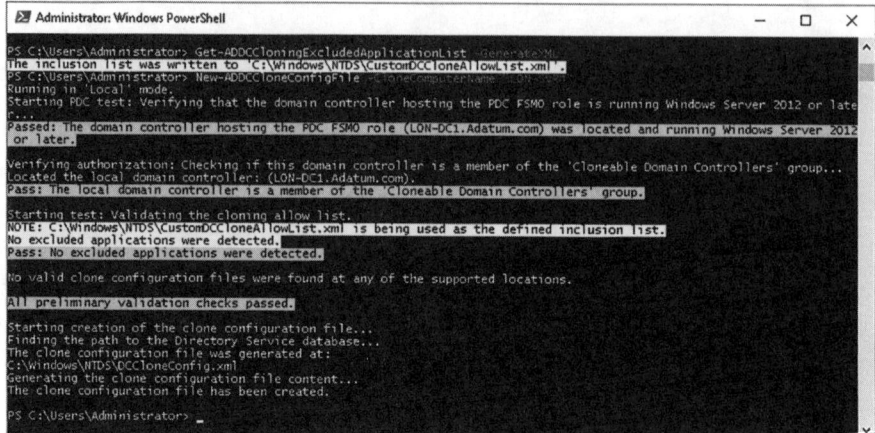

FIGURE 1-24 Creating the DCCloneConfig.xml using Windows PowerShell

6. Shut down the source virtual domain controller.
7. Export the source virtual domain controller:
   - Right-click the source domain controller virtual machine in the navigation pane, and then click Export.
   - In the Export Virtual Machine dialog box, in the Location text box, specify the folder where you want to store the virtual machine export, and then click Export.

EXAM TIP
Ensure that there are no checkpoints for your domain controller virtual machine before exporting.

8. If you are deploying multiple clones, you must now modify the DCCloneConfig.xml file for each one. Do this by mounting the VHD for the target domain controller clone and running the New-ADDCCloneConfigFile cmdlet and defining the unique information required for that clone. If you are deploying only a single clone, skip this step.

CREATE THE CLONE(S)

1. Ensure that the PDC emulator and a global catalog server are online and visible to your target clones.
2. In Hyper-V Manager, import the virtual machine:
   - **A.** In the Actions pane, click Import Virtual Machine.
   - **B.** In the Import Virtual Machine Wizard, on the Locate Folder page, in the Folder text box, type the path to the exported files for your virtual machine, and then click Next.
   - **C.** On the Select Virtual Machine page, as shown in Figure 1-25, if necessary, select the virtual machine in the list, and then click Next.

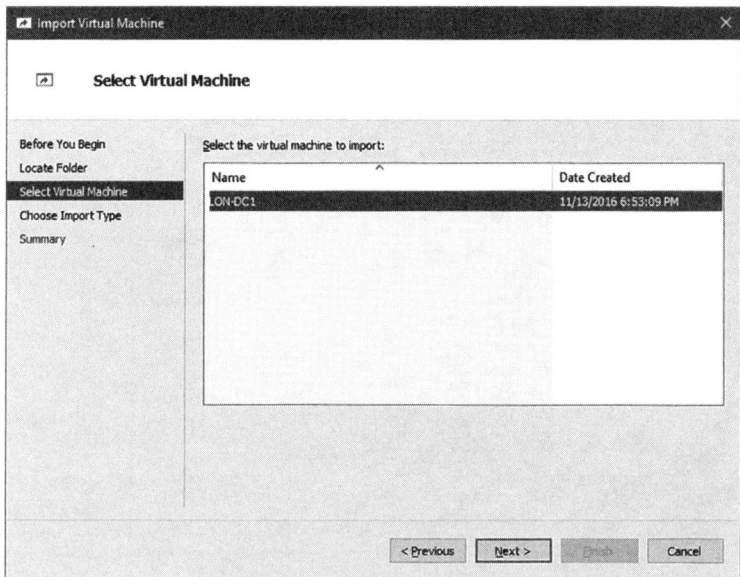

FIGURE 1-25 Importing a virtual machine

3. On the Choose Import Type page, shown in Figure 1-26, click Copy The Virtual Machine (Create A New Unique ID), and then click Next.

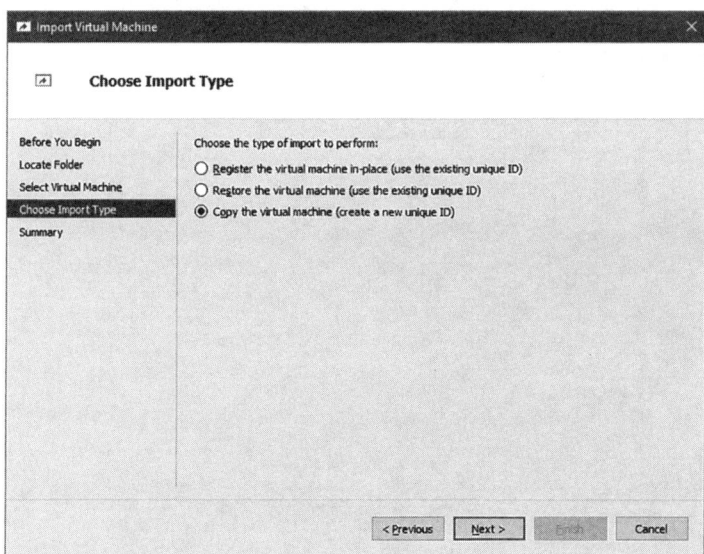

FIGURE 1-26 Specifying an import type

4. On the Choose Folders For Virtual Machine Files page, shown in Figure 1-27, select the Store The Virtual Machine In A Different Location check box, and for each folder location, specify a suitable folder path, and then click Next.

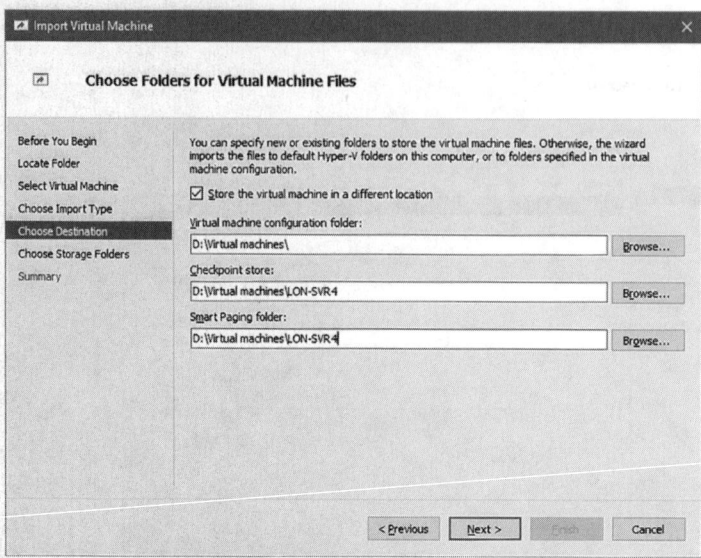

FIGURE 1-27 Specifying the location for imported virtual machine files

5. On the Choose Folders To Store Virtual Hard Disks page, shown in Figure 1-28, specify a suitable folder path, and then click Next.

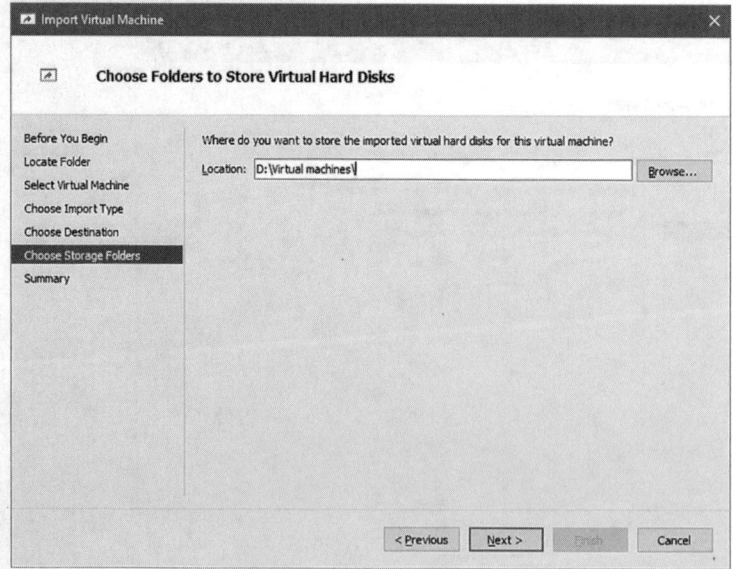

FIGURE 1-28 Specifying the location for imported virtual machine files

6. On the Completing Import Wizard page, click Finish. The virtual machine is imported, which can take up to 20 minutes or so.

7. After importing, in Hyper-V Manager, in the navigation pane, rename the imported virtual machine.
8. In Hyper-V Manager, in the Actions pane, click the newly imported virtual machine, click Start, and then click Connect to see the virtual machine starting. A "Domain Controller cloning is at x% completion" message is displayed during the completion of the cloning process.

> **NOTE REMINDER**
> Ensure that the PDC emulator and a global catalog server are online and accessible to your clone.

When your cloned domain controller starts, the following process occurs:

1. The clone verifies the presence of a virtual machine generation identifier. This is required, and if it does not exist, the computer starts normally (as if no DCCloneConfig.xml file exists) or renames DCCloneConfig.xml and restarts in DSRM. The administrator must then attempt to determine why no virtual machine generation identifier exists.
2. Assuming the presence of the virtual machine generation identifier, the clone determines if this identifier changed:
   - If it did not change, it is the original source domain controller. Any DCCloneConfig.xml file is renamed, and a normal startup occurs.
   - If it did change, the cloning process continues. If the DCCloneConfig.xml file exists, the computer gets the new computer name and IP address settings from the file, and the initialization continues, creating a new domain controller.

Upgrade domain controllers

If you are using an earlier version of Windows Server and want to upgrade your domain controllers to Windows Server 2016, you can perform an in-place upgrade. However, this process does pose some risks. It is generally safer to add a new Windows Server 2016 domain controller(s) to your existing infrastructure and then migrate roles to the newly deployed domain controller(s).

> **NOTE IN-PLACE UPGRADES**
> An in-place upgrade is one where the Windows Server 2016 is installed on the same server computer as is currently running an earlier version, for example, Windows Server 2008 R2.

Before you can deploy the first Windows Server 2016 domain controller into your existing infrastructure, you must determine that the current forest functional level and domain functional level are at least Windows Server 2008. You can do this by using the following procedure:

1. In the Active Directory Domains And Trusts console, in the navigation pane, right-click the Active Directory Domains And Trusts node, and then click Raise Forest Functional Level.
2. In the Raise Forest Functional Level dialog box, the current forest functional level is displayed, as shown in Figure 1-29.
3. If necessary, in the Select An Available Forest Functional Level list, click a level greater than Windows Server 2008, and then click Raise.

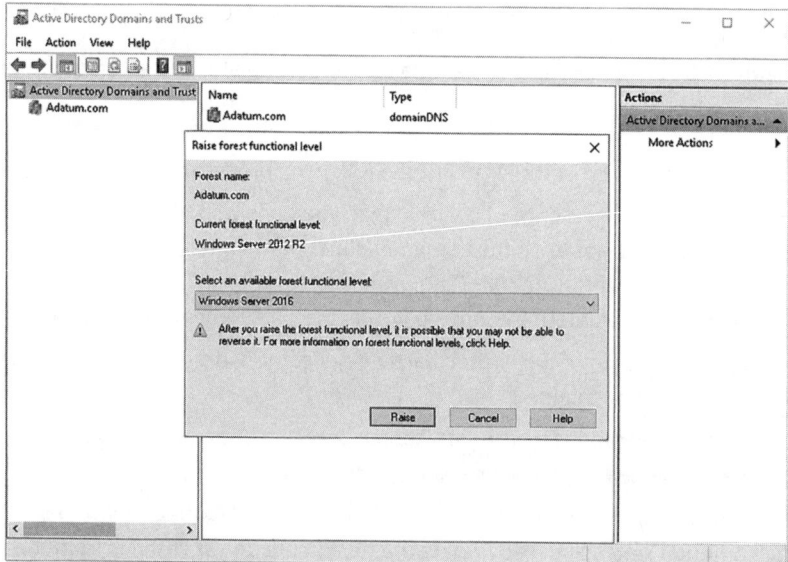

FIGURE 1-29 Verifying the forest functional level

4. In the navigation pane, locate and right-click the appropriate AD DS domain, and then click Raise Domain Functional Level.
5. In the Raise Domain Functional Level dialog box, the Current Domain Functional Level is displayed, as shown in Figure 1-30.
6. If necessary, in the Select An Available Domain Functional Level list, click a level greater than Windows Server 2008, and then click Raise.

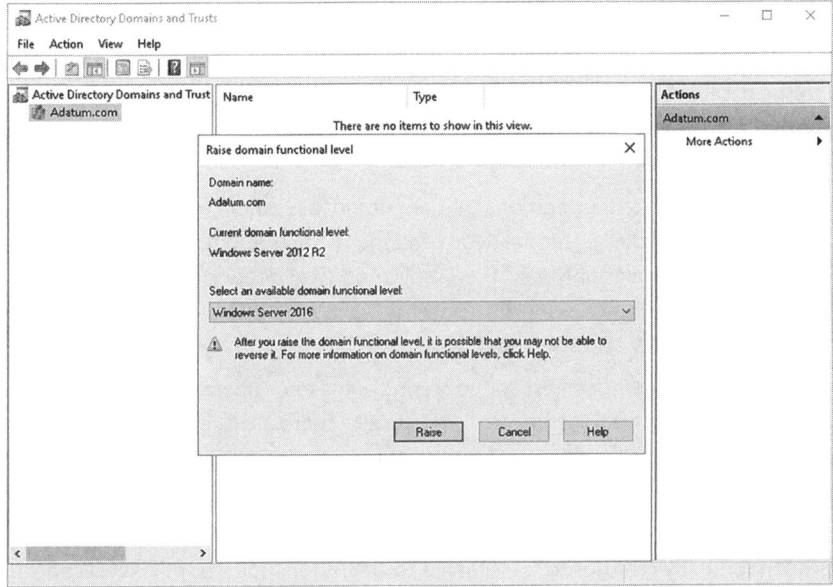

FIGURE 1-30 Verifying the domain functional level

After you have verified and, if necessary, raised the forest and domain functional levels, if your existing infrastructure is based on Windows Server 2008 or Windows Server 2008 R2, you must perform the following tasks:

- **Prepare your AD DS forest** On a domain controller in your existing forest, run adprep /forestprep.
- **Prepare your AD DS domain** On a domain controller in your existing forest, run adprep /domainprep.

If your current infrastructure is based on Windows Server 2012 or later, the Active Directory Domain Services Configuration Wizard performs these steps automatically. However, you can still choose to perform them as independent steps.

EXAM TIP

Adprep.exe is in the \Support\Adprep folder on your Windows Server 2016 DVD.

After you have raised the forest and domain functional levels (if necessary) and prepared your AD DS forest and domain, you can deploy the first Windows Server 2016 domain controller. Use the procedures discussed earlier in this chapter to complete this task. Then, you can transfer the operations master roles to your new Windows Server 2016 domain controller(s), as described in the next section. Finally, you can demote and remove your older domain controllers.

Transfer and seize operations master roles

The AD DS database supports multimaster updates. Broadly speaking, this means that a change to the database can be made on any instance, or replica, of the database. That change is then replicated to all other instances of the database on all other domain controllers throughout your forest.

However, there are certain operations that are not ideally suited to a multimaster approach. For example, handling user password changes is safer and more secure when handled by a single domain controller only, and then replicated to all other domain controllers.

What are operations master roles?

To handle the sort of operations best suited to single-master updates, Windows Server AD DS supports the notion of operations masters. Specifically, there are five operations master role holders (also sometimes called flexible single master operations (FSMO) roles). Two of these are forest-wide operations masters:

- **Schema master**   The schema master maintains the schema and is responsible for propagating any changes to the schema to the other copies of this AD DS partition on all other domain controllers in the forest. Because the schema rarely changes, the temporary absence of this operations master might easily go unnoticed. However, it must be online when you make changes to the schema, for example, when you install an application, such as Exchange Server, that requires additional object types and attributes for existing object types.

- **Domain naming master**   The domain naming master handles the addition or removal of domains in your AD DS forest. Because these sort of changes are infrequent, if the domain naming master is temporarily unavailable, you might not realize it straight away.

EXAM TIP

By default, both these roles are assigned to the first domain controller in your AD DS forest.

You can use the Windows PowerShell get-ADForest cmdlet to retrieve information about the current Schema and Domain naming master role holders, as shown in Figure 1-31.

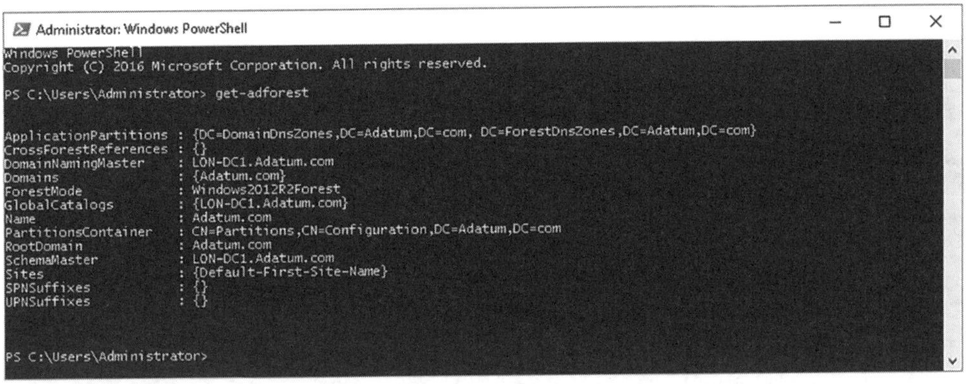

FIGURE 1-31 Determining the current forest operations master roles

The remainder of the operations masters are domain-wide. This means each domain holds these three operations master roles, and they are specific to that domain. They are:

- **PDC emulator** Performs several critical domain-wide operations:
  - Acts as a time source in the domain
  - Propagates password changes
  - Provides a primary source for GPOs for editing purposes
- **Infrastructure master** Maintains inter-domain references, and consequently, this role is only relevant in multidomain forests. For example, the infrastructure master maintains the integrity of an object's security access control list when that list contains security principals from another domain.

EXAM TIP

You should not assign the infrastructure master role to a global catalog server unless your forest consists of only a single domain. The only exception to this is if all domain controllers are also global catalog servers, in which case, the infrastructure master role is redundant.

- **RID master** Provides blocks of IDs to each of the domain controllers in its domain. Each object in a domain requires a unique ID.

EXAM TIP

By default, all these roles are assigned to the first domain controller you promote in a given domain.

You can use the Windows PowerShell Get-AdDomain cmdlet to retrieve information about the current Schema and Domain naming master role holders, as shown in Figure 1-32.

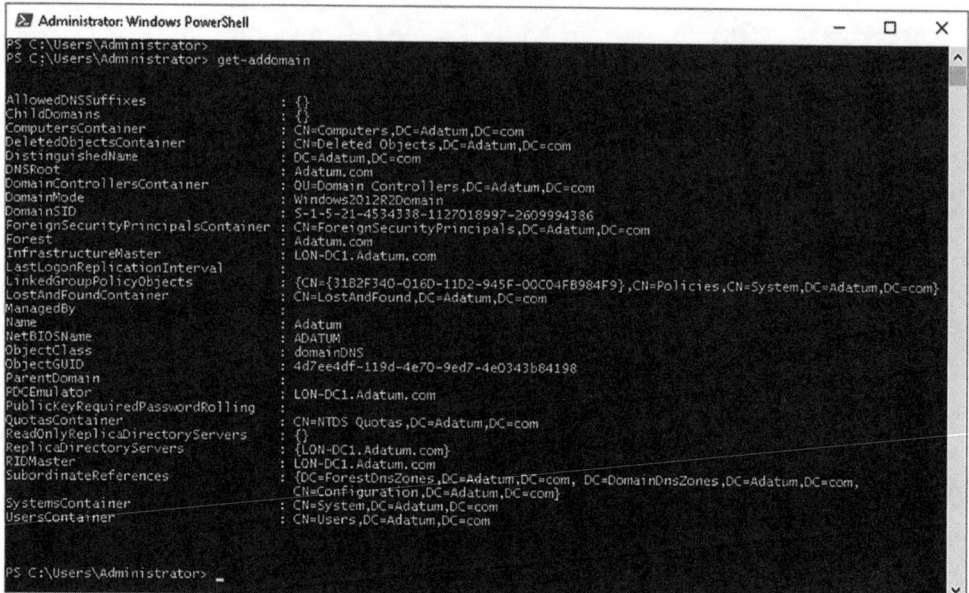

FIGURE 1-32 Determining the current domain operations master roles

Generally, if one of these forest-wide or domain-wide operations masters is unavailable for a short period, it probably does not affect day-to-day operations in your AD DS infrastructure. However, extended periods of unavailability can pose significant challenges and might result in problems.

EXAM TIP

Absence of the PDC Emulator will often have an immediate and noticeable effect. Users might experience problems signing in if it is unavailable.

Transferring roles

If you anticipate the need to shut down the domain controller that hosts an operations master role for an extended period, consider transferring that role. To transfer a role, use the appropriate following procedure.

For the schema master:

1. On the domain controller to which you want to transfer the role, open the Active Directory Schema console.

2. Right-click the Active Directory Schema node in the navigation pane, and then click Change Active Directory Domain Controller. Select the domain controller that you want to transfer the role to, and click OK.

3. Right-click the Active Directory Schema node in the navigation pane, and then click Operations Master.

4. In the Change Schema Master dialog box, shown in Figure 1-33, verify that the target domain controller appears in the Change text box, and then click Change, click Yes, click OK, and then click Close.

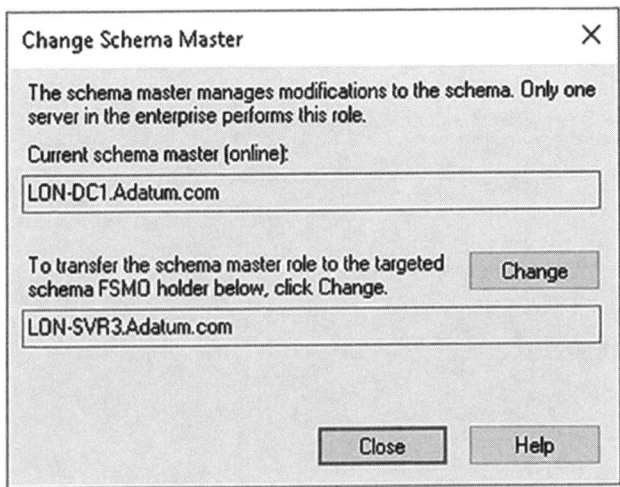

FIGURE 1-33 Transferring the schema master role

For the domain naming master:

1. On the target domain controller, open the Active Directory Domains And Trusts console.
2. Right-click the Active Directory Domains And Trusts node in the navigation pane, and then click Change Active Directory Domain Controller. Select the domain controller that you want to transfer the role to, and click OK.
3. Right-click the Active Directory Domains And Trusts node in the navigation pane, and then click Operations Master.
4. In the Operations Master dialog box, verify that the target domain controller appears in the Change text box, and then click Change, click Yes, click OK, and then click Close.

For any of the three domain-wide operations masters:

1. On the target domain controller, open the Active Directory Users And Computers console.
2. Right-click the appropriate domain in the navigation pane, and then click Operations Masters.

3. In the Operations Masters dialog box, shown in Figure 1-34, on either the RID, PDC, or Infrastructure tab, verify that the target domain controller appears in the Change text box, and then click Change, click Yes, click OK, and then click Close.

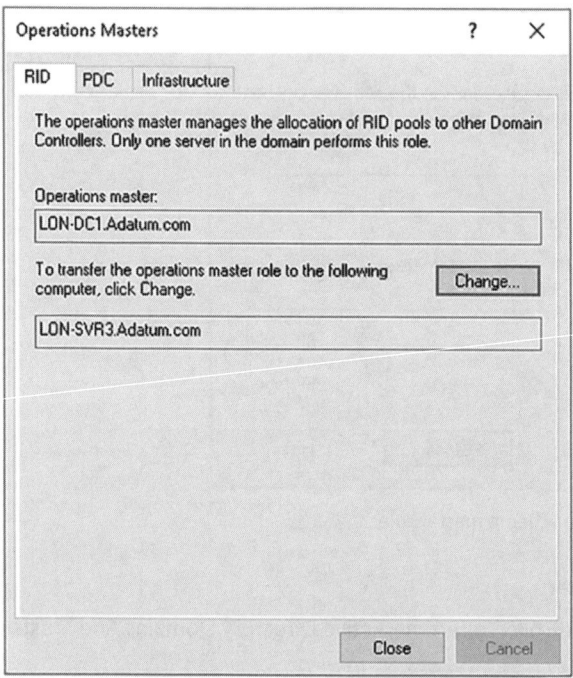

FIGURE 1-34 Transferring the domain-wide operations master roles

You can also move these roles with the Windows PowerShell Move-ADDirectoryServer-OperationMasterRole cmdlet. For example, to transfer the PDC emulator master to LON-SVR3, use the following command:

```
Move-ADDirectoryServerOperationMasterRole -Identity "LON-SVR3"
 -OperationMasterRole PDCEmulator
```

Seizing roles

It is not always possible to anticipate the removal of an operations master role holder. Consequently, if a domain controller hosting one of the operations master roles becomes unavailable, and you cannot quickly and easily get it operational again, you might consider seizing the operations master roles held by the failed domain controller.

If you must seize a role, you cannot use the management console to perform the task. Instead, you must use the Move-ADDirectoryServerOperationMasterRole -force cmdlet. Each role is assigned a number identifier, as described in Table 1-1.

TABLE 1-1 Operations master roles

Identifier	Role
0	PDC Emulator
1	RID master
2	Infrastructure master
3	Schema master
4	Domain naming master

For example, to seize the PDC Emulator, RID master, and Infrastructure master roles, assigning them to LON-SVR3, use the following command:

```
Move-ADDirectoryServerOperationMasterRole -Identity "LON-SVR3" -OperationMasterRole 0,1,2 -Force
```

> **NEED MORE REVIEW? MOVE (TRANSFERRING OR SEIZING) FSMO ROLES**
>
> To review further details about seizing FSMO roles, refer to the Microsoft TechNet website at *http://social.technet.microsoft.com/wiki/contents/articles/6736.move-transfering-or-seizing-fsmo-roles-with-ad-powershell-command-to-another-domain-controller.aspx*.

You can also use the Ntdsutil.exe command line tool to transfer or seize operations master roles.

> **NEED MORE REVIEW? USING NTDSUTIL.EXE TO TRANSFER OR SEIZE FSMO ROLES**
>
> To review further details about using Ntdsutil.exe to seize roles, refer to the Microsoft TechNet website at *https://support.microsoft.com/en-us/kb/255504*.

Resolve DNS SRV record registration issues

To locate services provided by AD DS, domain controllers register service location (SRV) records in DNS. These SRV records, shown in Figure 1-35, enable DNS clients to locate the appropriate services. For example, when a user signs in from a Windows 10 computer, Windows 10 uses DNS to obtain a list of adjacent domain controllers that can provide authentication services.

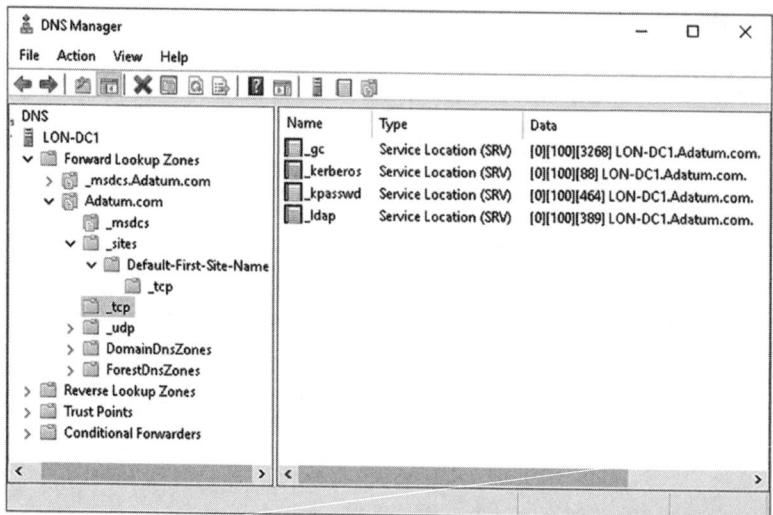

FIGURE 1-35 The DNS Manager console displays AD DS SRV records

A SVR record consists of several elements that identify the AD DS service. These are the service, the protocol, the priority and weight, the protocol port number, and the host FQDN offering the service, as shown in Figure 1-36.

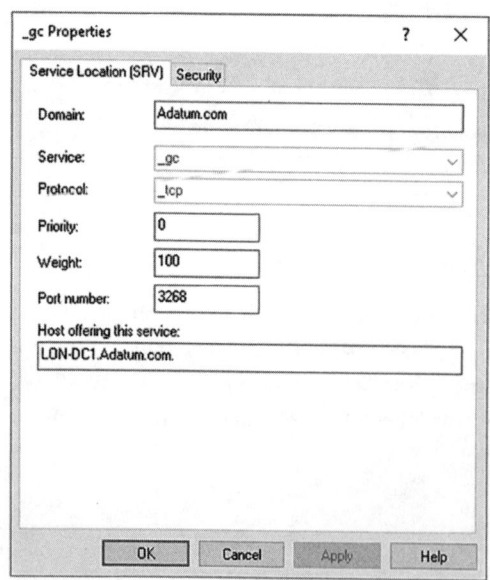

FIGURE 1-36 The global catalog SRV record for the Adatum.com domain

For example, if a Microsoft Exchange Server computer is attempting to locate a domain controller running the Global Catalog service in the Adatum.com domain, it queries DNS for _gc._tcp.Adatum.com.

To help clients obtain access to geographically adjacent instances of AD DS services, information about sites is provided in the SRV records on DNS. For example, when a Windows 10 computer starts up, it looks for site-specific SRV records in DNS. A typical DNS response to the client's query includes:

- A list of the domain controllers in the same site as the client
- A list of the domain controllers in the next closest site

EXAM TIP

This assumes that no domain controllers were available in the same site and that the Try Next Closest Site GPO setting is enabled.

- A random list of available domain controllers in the domain, if there is no domain controller in the next closest site

Troubleshooting registration

Each domain controller runs the NETLOGON service. This service is responsible for, among other things, registering the domain controller's SRV records in DNS. If you determine that a domain controller's SRV records are not appearing in DNS correctly, restart the NETLOGON service. This should force the records to register correctly.

You can also use the nslookup.exe DNS testing command line tool to verify the correct registration of SRV records. For example, to ensure that the correct records are registered for the Adatum.com domain, from a command prompt, perform the following procedure:

1. Type **nslookup** and then press Enter.
2. Type **set type=all** and then press Enter.
3. Type **_ldap._tcp.dc._msdcs.Adatum.com** and then press Enter.

The output returned should look something like Figure 1-37.

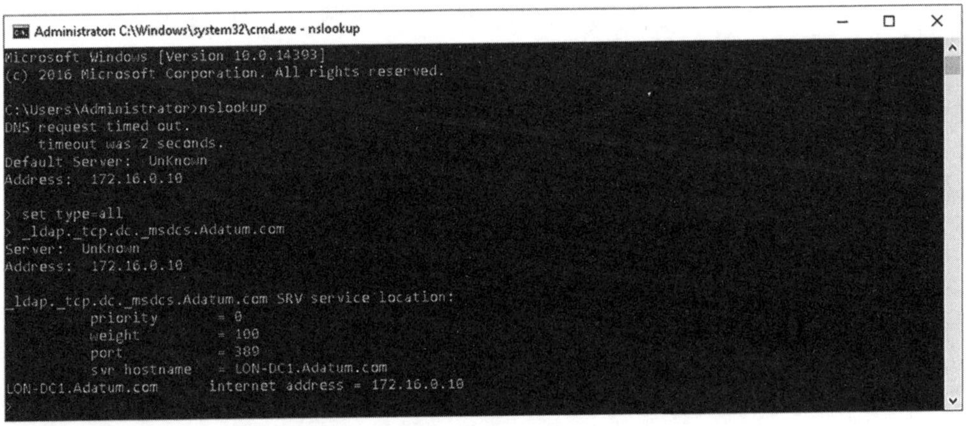

FIGURE 1-37 Using NSLOOKUP to troubleshoot SRV registration in DNS

Skill 1.2: Create and manage Active Directory users and computers

After you have installed and deployed your domain controllers, you can start to populate AD DS with objects, including users and computers. You can use several graphical tools accessible from Server Manager to perform these administrative tasks, or you can use Windows PowerShell to help automate these tasks.

> **This section covers how to:**
> - Create, copy, configure, and delete users and computers
> - Implement offline domain join
> - Configure user rights
> - Perform bulk Active Directory operations

Create, copy, configure, and delete users and computers

For every user in your organization, you must create a user account in AD DS. This identifies them as an individual when they attempt to perform tasks (rights) or access resources (permissions).

You can populate this user account with properties (attributes) that describe the user. These could include their full name, contact details, their role in your organization, their department, and many settings that define the scope of their abilities within your network.

It's important that before you start this process, you spend a little time thinking about a naming standard for your user accounts. The user account name must identify the user clearly, and must be unique within your organization. Typically, organizations use a combination of a user's last name and initials to yield a unique name. If your organization is large, this might require careful consideration because many users might share a last name, and some might share both first name and last name.

In AD DS, it's not only users that must have an account. Computers that connect to your organization's networked resources must also be identified. In some respects, this is simpler because you make the decision about the computer account name when you deploy the computer and name it during the installation process. Therefore, it's critical that when you deploy your users' computers, you consider the device name carefully.

Adding user accounts

There are several tools that you can use to create and manage user accounts, including Windows PowerShell, the dsadd.exe command-line tool, Active Directory Users and Computers, shown in Figure 1-38, and the Active Directory Administrative Center, shown in Figure 1-39. For the purposes of procedures in this chapter, we will use Active Directory Users and Computers and Windows PowerShell.

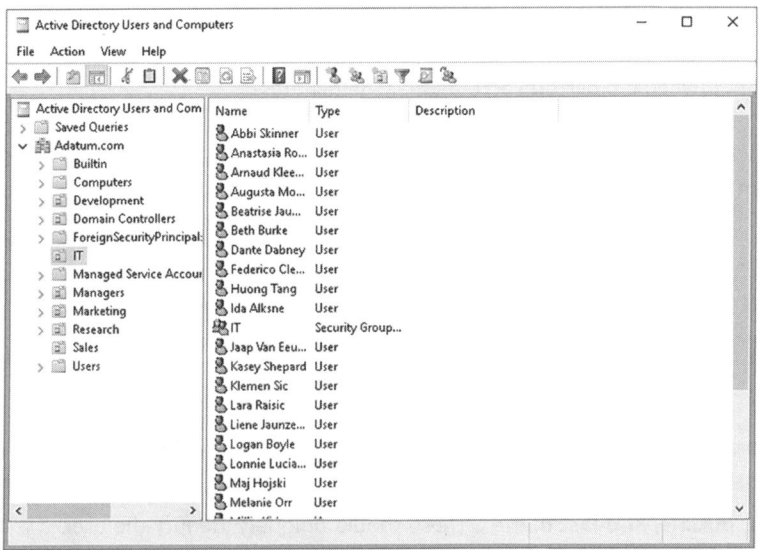

FIGURE 1-38 Active Directory Users and Computers

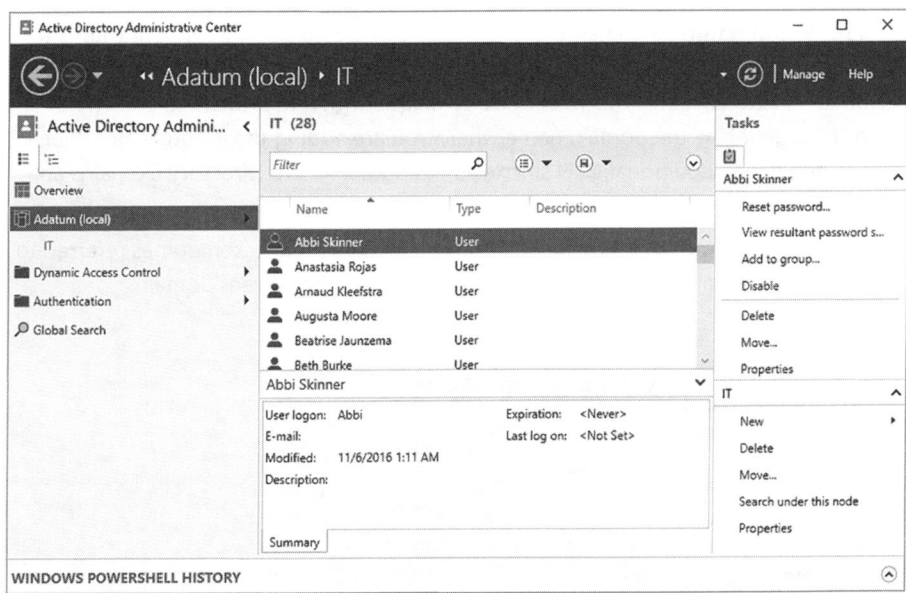

FIGURE 1-39 The Active Directory Administrative Center

After defining your user account naming standard, use the following procedure to add a user account:

1. Sign in as a member of the Domain Admins global security group.

EXAM TIP

In fact, you can sign in as a member of the Account Operators group. Members of this group have sufficient privilege to perform account management tasks.

2. Open the Active Directory Users And Computers console, and then select the OU in which you want to create your user account.

EXAM TIP

You can create user accounts in the Builtin, Computers, and Users containers, too, but it is best practice to consolidate your users in OUs for management purposes.

3. Right-click the OU, point to New, and then click User.
4. In the New Object – User dialog box, shown in Figure 1-40, enter the following information, and then click Next:
   - **First name, initials, and last name** These should uniquely identify the user. These elements combined to create the user's full name, which must be unique within the AD DS container where you create it. However, it is advisable to try to ensure that the name is unique within the forest.
   - **User logon name** This name is combined with the adjacently displayed suffix (@Adatum.com in Figure 1-40) to create a user principal name (UPN); for example, BurkeB@Adatum.com. This UPN must be unique within the AD DS forest. The UPN suffix is generally the domain name where you are adding the account. However, you can define additional UPN suffixes by using the Active Directory Domains and Trusts console.
   - **User logon name (pre-Windows 2000)** This name is also sometimes referred to as the SAM account name. It must be unique within the current domain.

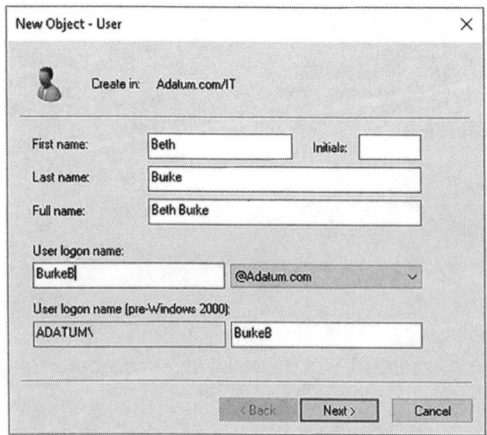

FIGURE 1-40 Adding a user account

5. Next, enter a password and confirm the password, as shown in Figure 1-41. Whatever you enter must meet the current password complexity rules in your domain. Configure the remaining settings, and click Next:

   - **User Must Change Password At Next Logon** It is good practice to force a user to choose a new password when they first sign in.
   - **User Cannot Change Password** Select this option if the user account is a specialist account, such as one used by an app or service rather than a person. This option is mutually exclusive with User Must Change Password At Next Logon.
   - **Password Never Expires** Likewise, choose this option if the user account is a specialist account, such as one used by an app or service. This option is also mutually exclusive with User Must Change Password At Next Logon.
   - **Account Is Disabled** It is good practice to disable all user accounts until the user is ready to sign in for the first time. Many organizations add user accounts and create email accounts for new start employees before the new employee's first day. However, leaving a user account enabled and unused, with its initial password, is not secure.

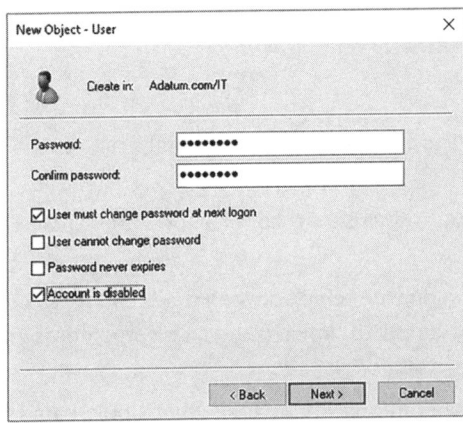

FIGURE 1-41 Configuring password and account options

6. When prompted, click Finish.

After you have created the account, you must modify its properties so that you can configure group memberships, organizational details, and more advanced account properties. To do this, use the following procedure:

1. In Active Directory Users And Computers, locate the OU that contains your new user account.
2. Right-click the account, and then click Properties. There are a huge number of configurable user account properties, but the following are the most critical.
3. In the User Properties dialog box, click the Account tab, shown in Figure 1-42, and then configure the following settings:

FIGURE 1-42 Modifying user account properties

- **Logon Hours**   Specify the days and times of the week when the account can be used. The default is Always.
- **Log On To**   Define which computers the user account can be signed in at. The default is All Computers.
- **Unlock Account**   This option can only be selected when the account has been locked. This occurs when a user attempts to sign in using an incorrect password and exceeds the threshold of incorrect passwords.
- **Account Options**   Aside from the options you defined when you created the account (user must change password at next logon, and so on), you can enable some more advanced options for accounts that are used in sensitive situations requiring more security. Settings include: Smart Card Is Required For Interactive Logon, Account Is Sensitive And Cannot Be Delegated, and This Account Supports Kerberos AES 256 Bit Encryption.
- **Account Expires**   You can configure an expiration date for an account. This is often useful for accounts used by interns or temporary staff. After the account is expired, you can reassign the account to the next intern and reconfigure the expiration setting.

4. On the Profile tab, shown in Figure 1-43, the following settings.

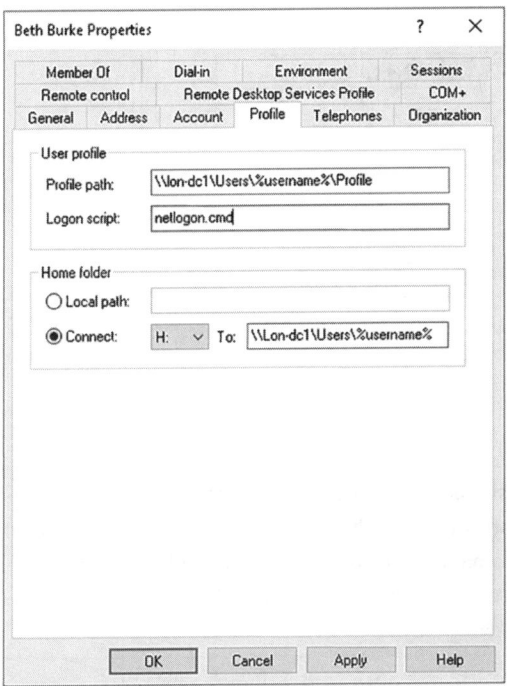

FIGURE 1-43 Modifying user profile properties

- **Profile Path** If you define a profile path on a shared folder, the user's desktop and app settings roam with the user account. When a user signs out, her desktop and app settings are saved to this location. Define a UNC name and use the variable %username% to define a subfolder off the shared folder. For example, as shown in Figure 1-43, the UNC name points to the shared folder Users on the server LON-DC1. A subfolder for this user, named after the user account, will be created automatically when you click Apply, as shown in Figure 1-44. Beneath that, a subfolder for the user's profile is automatically created.

- **Logon Script** Specify the name of a batch file to use as a logon script for this user. You must not specify the path to this file; all scripts must be stored in the NETLOGON shared folder (part of SYSVOL) so that they can be replicated to all domain controllers. Generally, this field is seldom used. Most administrators prefer to apply logon scripts by using GPOs.

- **Home Folder** It's good practice to create a personal storage area on your network for each user. This is referred to as a home folder. If you use the variable %username% to define a subfolder off a valid shared folder, the username is applied when the user's home folder is automatically created. Specify a drive letter to use to map to the user's home folder.

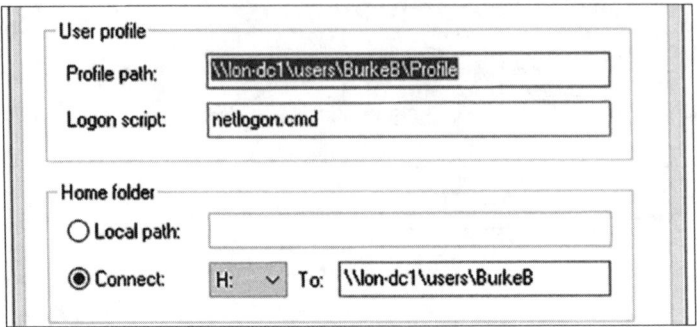

FIGURE 1-44 Applying user profile options

EXAM TIP

Ensure that you create the required shared folders before you create your first user accounts. That way, Windows Server can automatically create the required user subfolders and correctly assign permissions automatically. Also, use of the variable %username% means that if you copy this account, the variable is substituted with the details for the account you are creating as a copy.

5. On the Member Of tab, shown in Figure 1-45, add the user to the required groups, and then click OK. Groups are discussed in the next skill.

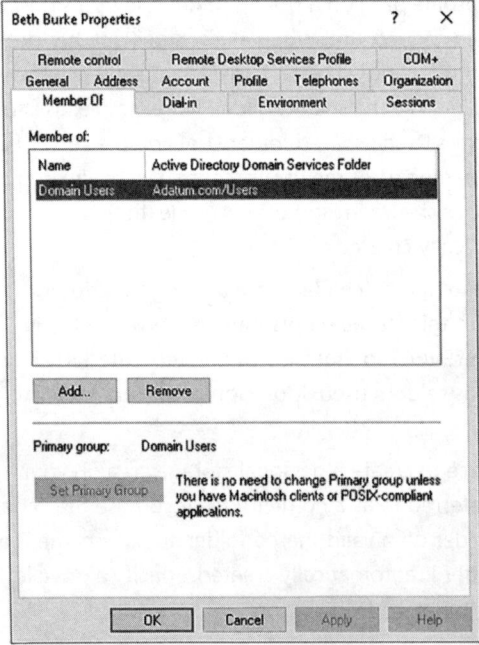

FIGURE 1-45 Modifying group memberships

Configure templates

If you have many, broadly similar user accounts to add, you can consider using templates to help speed up the process. A template user account is an ordinary user account populated with common properties and settings. You copy the account in Active Directory Users And Computers, and then configure only the unique individual settings:

- First Name and Last Name
- Full Name
- User Logon Name
- Password

EXAM TIP

It's a very good idea to disable a template account and to configure the User Cannot Change Password setting; this helps prevent use of the account.

The following user account properties are copied when you create and copy a template account:

- Group Memberships
- Home Directories
- Profile Settings
- Logon Scripts
- Logon Hours
- Password Settings
- Department Name
- Manager

EXAM TIP

Although the notion of a template account might seem attractive, there are easier and quicker ways to manage user accounts in bulk. Most administrators use Windows PowerShell scripts to create multiple accounts.

Managing user accounts

When your user accounts have been created, you must be prepared to manage these accounts. You can use Active Directory Users and Computers or Windows PowerShell to perform the following typical management tasks:

- **Resetting passwords** Right-click the relevant user account, and then click Reset Password. In Windows PowerShell, use the Set-ADAccountPassword cmdlet. For example, to reset Beth Burke's password, use the following command:

```
Set-ADAccountPassword 'CN=Beth Burke,OU=IT,DC=Adatum,DC=com' -Reset -NewPassword
(ConvertTo-SecureString -AsPlainText "Pa55w.rd" -Force)
```

- **Unlocking accounts** Right-click the relevant user account, and then click Unlock. In Windows PowerShell, use the Unlock-ADAccount cmdlet.
- **Renaming accounts** Right-click the relevant user account, and then click Rename. Type the new full name and press Enter. In the Rename User dialog box, shown in Figure 1-46, type the relevant information and click OK. In Windows PowerShell, use the Rename-ADObject cmdlet.

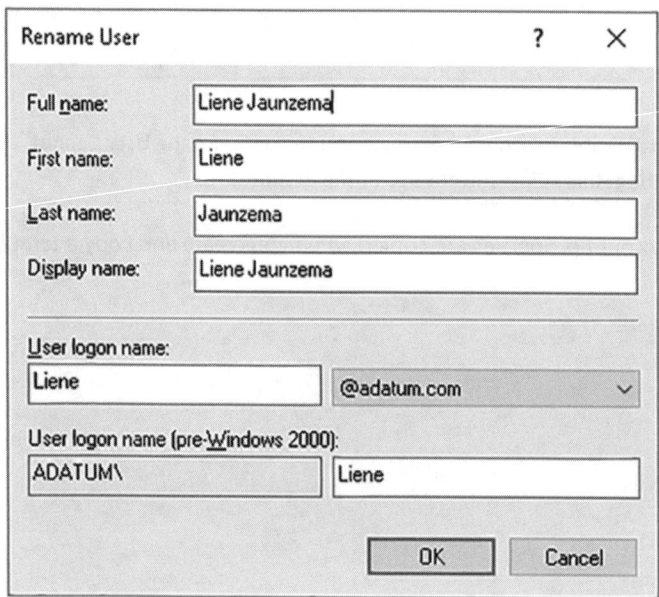

FIGURE 1-46 Renaming a user account

- **Moving users** Right-click the relevant user account, and then click Move. In the Move dialog box, click the new location, and then click OK. In Windows PowerShell, use the Move-ADObject cmdlet. For example, to move Beth Burke from IT to Marketing in the Adatum.com domain, use the following command:

```
Move-ADObject -Identity 'CN=Beth Burke,OU=IT,DC=Adatum,DC=com' -TargetPath
'OU=Marketing,DC=Adatum,DC=com'
```

EXAM TIP

You can also use the Dsmod.exe command-line tool to accomplish many of these tasks.

You can use Windows PowerShell cmdlets to perform all common user management tasks. Table 1-2 lists the important cmdlets and explains their use.

TABLE 1-2 Common Windows PowerShell cmdlets for user management

Cmdlet	Use
New-ADUser	Creates user accounts.
Set-ADUser	Modifies the properties of user accounts.
Remove-ADUser	Deletes user accounts.
Set-ADAccountPassword	Resets the password of a user account.
Set-ADAccountExpiration	Modifies the expiration date of a user account.
Unlock-ADAccount	Unlocks a user account.
Enable-ADAccount	Enables a user account.
Disable-ADAccount	Disables a user account.

Manage inactive and disabled accounts

There are many reasons why accounts might become inactive, including:

- An employee leaves your organization
- An intern or temporary member of staff leaves
- A member of staff is away on a sabbatical, or is ill for an extended period
- An employee is on parental leave

Whatever the reason, it is good practice to disable accounts that are inactive to help ensure the security of your network. To Disable an unused account, in Active Directory Users And Computers, right-click the user account, and then click Disable Account. To enable a disabled account, locate the user account, right-click it, and then click Enable Account.

Add and manage computer accounts

For computer devices that your organization owns, you should create an AD DS account for the computer. This helps to secure your organization's network infrastructure because the computer can identify itself to the AD DS domain of which it is a member.

By default, computer accounts are created and stored in the default Computers container. This is not an OU and, therefore, you cannot delegate administration on it, nor apply GPOs to it. In larger organizations, consider placing your computers in OUs rather than the Computers container.

To add a computer to the domain, you must sign in with an account that has sufficient privilege. In fact, you require permissions to add a computer object within the domain. Also, you require local administrator privilege on the computer itself. By default, the following groups have the permissions to create computer objects in any OU:

- Enterprise Admins
- Domain Admins
- Administrators
- Account Operators

EXAM TIP

Standard users can add a maximum of 10 computers to a domain. Use the Active Directory Services Interfaces Editor (ADSI Edit) console to increase the machine account quota if 10 is insufficient.

You can then add the computer account using one of two strategies:

- **Add the computer account in one step** When you join a computer to a domain, you can supply credentials to create the required computer account at the same time as you change the client computer's settings. This is a simple, one-step process.

- **Pre-create the computer account** You can create the computer account in AD DS first, and then, from the client computer, add the computer to your domain. This two-step approach enables you to separate the administrative tasks of adding computers to the domain, and managing computer accounts. Also, any GPOs configured on the computer's AD DS container apply more quickly.

To add a Windows 10 computer to a domain in a single step, use the following procedure:

1. Sign in to the Windows 10 computer as a local administrator.
2. Right-click Start, and then click System.
3. In System, click Advanced System Settings.
4. In the System Properties dialog box, on the Computer name tab, click Change.
5. In the Computer Name/Domain Changes dialog box, shown in Figure 1-47, select Domain, and then type the domain name.

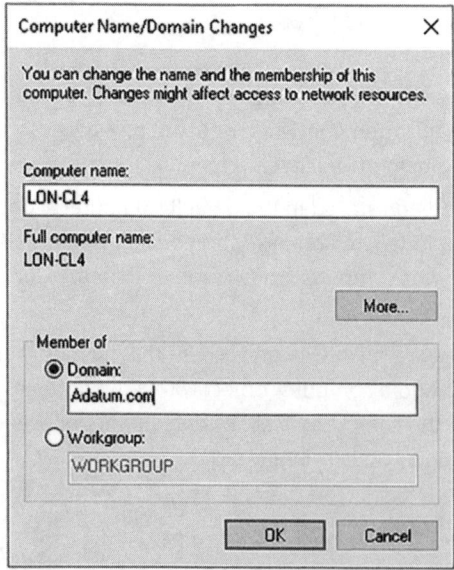

FIGURE 1-47 Adding a computer to a domain

6. Click OK, and in the Windows Security dialog box, enter the User Name and Password of a user account in the domain that has sufficient privilege to add a computer account, then click OK.
7. In the Computer Name/Domain Changes pop-up dialog box, shown in Figure 1-48, click OK.

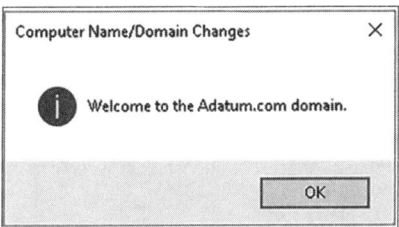

FIGURE 1-48 Completing the add to domain process

8. Click OK to the warning that you must restart your computer.
9. In the System Properties dialog box, click Close, and then when prompted, click Restart Now.
10. Sign in using a domain account to your computer.
11. On your domain controller, open Active Directory Users And Computers.
12. Navigate to the Computers container, and locate the new computer account.
13. If necessary, right-click the new account, and then click Move, as shown in Figure 1-49.

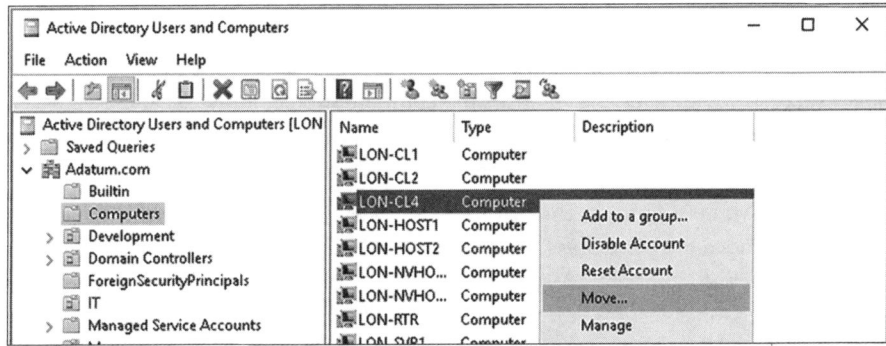

FIGURE 1-49 Moving a computer account

14. Select the new OU location for the computer, and then click OK.

Generally, computer accounts do not require much management. You might need to add a computer to a security group, which is an almost identical process to adding a user to a group. You can use Active Directory Users and Computers or the Active Directory Administrative Center to perform computer management.

You can also use Windows PowerShell. Table 1-3 lists the common Windows PowerShell computer management cmdlets.

TABLE 1-3 Common Windows PowerShell cmdlets for computer management

Cmdlet	Use
New-ADComputer	Creates a new computer account.
Get-ADComputer	Displays the properties of a computer account.
Set-ADComputer	Modifies the properties of a computer account.
Remove-ADComputer	Deletes a computer account.
Test-ComputerSecureChannel	Verifies or repairs the trust relationship between a computer and the domain.
Reset-ComputerMachinePassword	Resets the password for a computer account.

RESET THE SECURE CHANNEL

Occasionally, you might need to reset the computer's secure channel. When a computer signs in to the AD DS domain, it establishes a secure channel with the domain controller; the secure channel is sometimes referred to as a trust. Under some circumstances, this trust becomes unavailable, and the computer cannot establish the secure channel. This can result in users being unable to sign in at the computer, and in the failure of the application of GPOs on the computer.

Often, when a secure channel failure has occurred, users receive the following message when they attempt to sign in:

"The trust relationship between the workstation and the primary domain failed."

Some administrators remove the computer from the domain, adding it temporarily to a workgroup, and then after restarting the computer, they add it to the domain again. This is usually successful. However, this removes the computer object in AD DS and creates a new one, albeit with the same name. Because the object is new, and has a new security identity (SID), any group memberships for the computer are lost; this might not be a concern.

However, if you use group memberships extensively, it is better to reset the secure channel rather than remove the computer from the domain. You can reset the channel by using Active Directory Users and Computers, Windows PowerShell, or the Dsmod.exe command-line tool. Resetting the channel ensures that the computer's SID remains the same, and this means that group memberships are retained.

EXAM TIP

You can also use the Netdom.exe or Nltest.exe command-line tools.

In Active Directory Users and Computers, to reset the secure channel.

1. Right-click the computer, click Reset Account, and then click Yes, as shown in Figure 1-50.
2. Rejoin the computer to the domain, and then restart the computer.

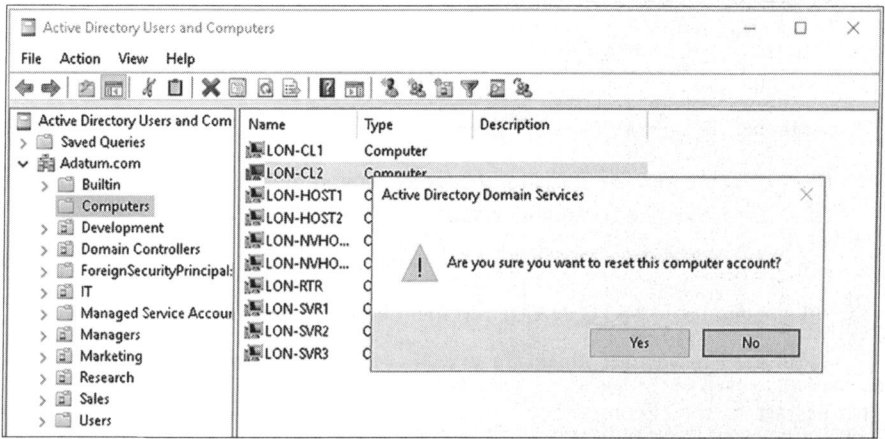

FIGURE 1-50 Resetting the computer account

To use Windows PowerShell, on the computer, run the following command in an elevated Windows PowerShell command prompt:

```
Test-ComputerSecureChannel -Repair
```

To use the Dsmod.exe command-line tool, use the following command on the computer, and then rejoin the computer to the domain:

```
dsmod computer "ComputerDN" -reset
```

Implement offline domain join

Usually, when you add a computer to an AD DS domain, the domain controllers of the domain are online and accessible from the computer that you want to add. However, sometimes, it is not possible to perform an online domain join, for example, when the computer to be added is connected to a domain controller by an intermittent remote connection.

In Windows Server 2016, for client computers running Windows 7 or newer, you can use a feature known as offline domain join to bypass this problem. To perform an offline domain join, you use the Djoin.exe command-line tool. Djoin.exe generates a metadata blob, similar to a configuration file, which is used on the client computer to complete the join process. When you run Djoin.exe, you must specify the domain name you want to join, the name of the computer to be added to the domain, and the name and location of the file that will store this information.

To perform an offline domain join, use the following procedure:

1. On a domain controller, open an elevated command prompt and run djoin.exe /provision. The format for this command is:

   ```
   djoin.exe /Provision /Domain <DomainName> /Machine <MachineName> /SaveFile <filepath>
   ```

   For example, to add LON-CL4 to the Adatum.com domain, use the following command:

   ```
   djoin.exe /provision /domain adatum.com /machine LON-CL4 /savefile c:\cl4.txt
   ```

2. Next, copy the join file to the target computer and then use the djoin.exe /requestODJ command. The command format is:

   ```
   djoin.exe /requestODJ /LoadFile <filepath> /WindowsPath %systemroot% /Localos
   ```

   For example, to add LON-CL4, run the following command:

   ```
   djoin.exe /requestODJ /loadfile c:\LON-CL4.txt /windowspath C:\Windows /Localos
   ```

3. Restart the target computer.

Configure user rights

User rights are different from permissions. Permissions give the ability to access something, such as a folder or printer, while rights are the ability to do something, such as manage a printer.

Rights are sometimes described as being the assignment of management abilities; this is often true, because many rights enable users to perform management tasks. However, not all rights are administrative. Some are for simple, user-oriented tasks, such as the right to allow logon locally, or change the system time.

It is typical to assign rights by adding users to groups that already are assigned that right. For example, members of the local Administrators group can perform many management tasks through the assignment of rights to that group. By adding a user to the Administrators group, that user enjoys those rights.

However, if you want to grant a user a right directly, or, indeed, to assign a right to a group, it is important that you know how to do it. The tool most frequently used to assign rights in a non-domain environment is the Local Security Policy. In an AD DS forest, administrators use GPOs to assign these rights.

To modify user rights, use the following procedure:

1. Open the Group Policy Management console.
2. Navigate to the Group Policy Objects container.
3. In the details pane, right-click the Default Domain Policy, and then click Edit.

4. In the Group Policy Management Editor, in the navigation pane, expand Computer Configuration, expand Policies, expand Windows Settings, expand Security Settings, expand Local Policies, and then, as shown in Figure 1-51, click User Rights Assignment.

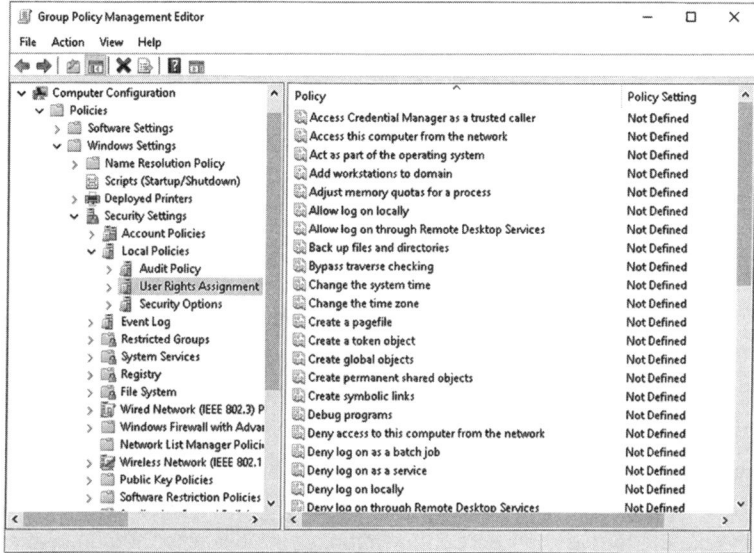

FIGURE 1-51 Locating the User Rights Assignment node

5. In the details pane, select the right that you want to assign by double-clicking it.
6. In the Right Properties dialog box, shown in Figure 1-52, select the Define These Policy Settings, click Add User Or Group, select the appropriate user or group, and click OK.

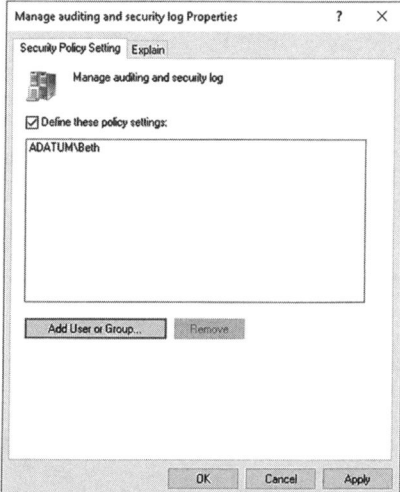

FIGURE 1-52 Assigning a right

7. In the Right Properties dialog box, click OK.

> **NEED MORE REVIEW?** **USER RIGHTS ASSIGNMENT**
>
> For a list of common user rights, refer to the Microsoft TechNet website at *https://technet.microsoft.com/library/dn221963(v=ws.11).aspx*.

Perform bulk Active Directory operations

Bulk operations are when an administrator performs a single task to complete multiple activities, and can include the following common administrative tasks:

- Automate the creation of Active Directory accounts
- Automate unlocking of disabled accounts using Windows PowerShell
- Automate password resets using Windows PowerShell
- Change the properties of many users in a single step, such as department name or street address

In a small organization, the requirement to perform bulk operations is less likely. However, in large organizations, the need likely exists to add and configure blocks of users on a regular basis. This might take the form of bulk account creation, or of bulk account management, such as changing the accounts' properties.

There are several methods you can employ to perform bulk account management, including using comma separated value (CSV) files, and Windows PowerShell scripts. Using CSV files can make working with multiple AD DS objects quicker and easier.

An example CSV file might look like this:

```
FullName, Department

Abbie Parsons, Sales

Allan Yoo, Sales

Erin Bull, Sales
```

After you have created a properly formatted CSV file, you can use it with a Windows PowerShell script to perform your bulk operation.

> **EXAM TIP**
>
> You use the Windows PowerShell Import-csv cmdlet to read a CSV file's contents into a variable in memory for use by a script.

For example, to create new accounts with Windows PowerShell and a CSV file, you could use the following basic script.

```
$users=Import-CSV -LiteralPath "C:\new-users.csv"

    foreach ($user in $users)

    {

        New-ADUser $user.FullName -AccountPassword (Read-Host -AsSecureString "Enter password") -Department $user.Department

    }
```

> **NEED MORE REVIEW?** **CREATING BULK USERS IN ACTIVE DIRECTORY USING POWERSHELL**
>
> To review further details about using Windows PowerShell to create AD DS user objects in Windows Server 2016, refer to the Microsoft MSDN website at *https://blogs.msdn.microsoft.com/amitgupta/2012/02/06/creating-bulk-users-in-active-directory-using-powershell/*.

Using Windows PowerShell to modify AD DS objects

To perform bulk operations on user or computer objects, or indeed, group objects, you must pass a list of the desired objects to a Windows PowerShell cmdlet that then performs the required modification. Often, the cmdlet that performs this modification is one of the following:

- Set-ADUser
- Set-ADComputer
- Set-ADGroup
- Set-ADOrganizationalUnit

For example, if you wanted to modify the company name of all users following a merger, you could use the following command:

```
Get-ADUser -Filter {company -like "A Datum"} | Set-ADUser -Company "Contoso"
```

To disable all user accounts in the Sales department, you could use the following command:

```
Get-ADUser -Filter {Department -like "Sales"} | Disable-ADAccount
```

To reset the password for all users in the Marketing department, you could use the following command:

```
Get-ADUser -Filter {Department -like "Marketing"} | Set-ADAccountPassword -Reset -NewPassword (ConvertTo-SecureString -AsPlainText "Pa55w.rd" -Force)
```

> **NEED MORE REVIEW?** **ACTIVE DIRECTORY BULK USER MODIFICATION**
>
> To review further details about using Windows PowerShell to manage AD DS objects in bulk, refer to the Microsoft TechNet website at *https://blogs.technet.microsoft.com/poshchap/2014/05/14/active-directory-bulk-user-modification/*.

Skill 1.3: Create and manage Active Directory groups and organizational units

In addition to users and computers, all AD DS forests contain groups and OUs. You can use graphical tools to create and manage groups and OUs, or alternatively, you can use Windows PowerShell cmdlets.

In some senses, groups and OUs are similar; they both contain objects, such as users, computers, or even other groups or OUs. Strictly speaking, however, groups *have* members and OUs *contain* objects.

OUs and groups are also used in different ways. Typically, you implement groups in AD DS to assign rights or permissions, whereas you use OUs to streamline management through the application of GPOs or through management delegation.

By default, a Windows Server 2016 domain controller contains several built-in group accounts, including those listed in Table 1-4.

TABLE 1-4 Default AD DS Windows Server 2016 groups

Name	Description
Server Operators	A domain local group created with the default abilities to install and share software on the server, manage disks and backup the server.
Account Operators	A domain local group with the ability to create and manage user and group accounts. Members can also delete accounts that they have created.
Print Operators	A domain local group that can install, share, and manage printers and print queues.
Administrators	This domain local group has rights to perform any function on a Windows Server 2016 server computer. Members can create new accounts, delete accounts, manage disks and printers, set security and auditing policies and so on.
Users	A domain local group that inherits the permissions to use resources. Typically read permissions to disks and the permissions to submit print jobs. These accounts can have a Profile and a home directory.
Guests	A domain local group with limited access to the server. These accounts cannot have either Profiles or home directories.
Backup Operators	A domain local group that has the rights to back up the server. Members also have the rights to restore the same data.
Network Configuration Operators	Members have certain network management privileges.
Remote Desktop users	Members can sign in remotely to this server (used for remote desktop services).
Domain Computers	A global group that contains all workstations and servers in the domain.
Domain Controllers	A global group that contains all domain controllers in the domain.
Domain Guests	A Global group automatically added to all Local Guests groups.
Domain Admins	A Global group automatically added to all Local Administrators groups.
Domain Users	A Global group automatically added to all Local Users groups.
Enterprise Admins	A universal group (only in the forest root domain) that has full administrative control of all objects in the forest.

In addition to these groups, Windows Server also supports the notion of *special identities*. These are treated as groups within the operating system in as much as you can grant them permissions and rights, like any other group. However, the membership list is not editable; that is, you cannot assign a user (or another group) to a special identity. Rather, the membership is implied based on the characteristics of a user in a given situation. These *special identities* are:

- **Everyone** This identity represents everybody and includes both users with an account, and guests without an account—assuming the guest account is enabled.
- **Authenticated Users** This identity is more specific and includes everybody except guests.
- **Anonymous Logon** This identity is used by resources that do not require a username or password to permit access. It does not include guests.
- **Interactive** A user that is attempting to access a resource on the local computer belongs to the Interactive identity.
- **Network** A user that is attempting to access a resource on a remote computer belongs to the Network identity.
- **Creator Owner** Any individual that creates an object, such as a file, belongs to the Creator Owner identity for that object. A user that belongs to this identity has full control of the object.

> **This section covers how to:**
> - Create and manage groups
> - Create and manage OUs
> - Delegate management of Active Directory with groups and OUs

Create and manage groups

When considering groups, it is important to determine when it is appropriate to use the built-in default groups or the special identities, and when it is necessary to create and configure additional groups to suit your specific organizational needs.

Configure group nesting

In Windows Server 2016, it is possible to configure group nesting. This is the process of adding a group as a member of another group. The purpose behind group nesting is one of scaling. If it is sometimes logical to group users together and assign the group permissions (or rights) rather than the individuals that make up the group, on occasion, it is logical to group groups. This is particularly relevant in large, multidomain AD DS forests.

To facilitate group nesting, AD DS in Windows Server 2016 supports three group scopes and two group types. These are:

- **Scopes** Define the scope (or range) of abilities:
    - **Domain Local** Can only be granted rights and permissions within the local security authority. That is, a domain local account can only be granted rights and permissions on resources in the local domain. A domain local group can contain:
        - Users from any domain in the forest
        - Global groups from any domain in the forest
        - Universal groups from any domain in the forest
    - **Global** Can be granted rights and permissions to any resource in any domain in the forest. A global group can contain:
        - Users from anywhere in the forest
        - Global groups from the same domain
    - **Universal** Used for forest-wide operations, and allow for the assignment of permissions and rights in any domain in the forest. Universal groups can contain:
        - User accounts, global groups, and other universal groups from any domain in the entire forest
- **Types** Define the purpose of the group:
    - **Security** Used to assign permissions or rights. Can also be used for the purposes of email distribution lists.
    - **Distribution** Used only for the purposes of email distribution lists.

EXAM TIP

Universal group membership lists are maintained in the Global Catalog, whereas other groups memberships are not.

In Windows Server 2016, there is a recommended strategy for nesting groups referred to as IGDLA, which is an abbreviation for the following:

- **Identities** User and computer accounts that represent business functions within your organization.
- **Global groups** Contain identities and belong to domain local groups. Generally, these are named after the objects that are members. For example, Sales, Marketing, European users.
- **Domain local groups** Granted permissions and rights on objects. Generally named after the functions members perform. For example, Administrators, Print Operators.
- **Access** The access that you grant on a resource to the domain local group.

In a large multidomain forest, you can also use Universal groups to help manage nesting. This is referred to as IGUDLA:

- **Identities** User and computer accounts.
- **Global groups** Contain identities and belong to Universal groups.

- **Universal**   Consolidates multiple global groups from other domains into a single entity.
- **Domain local groups**   Contains Universal groups and granted permissions and rights on objects.
- **Access**   The access that you grant on a resource.

You do not have to implement either of these strategies. In fact, in a single domain forest, there is little difference between the groups as the scope for all groups is then the same, as is the potential membership of any group. However, it is recommended that you at least consider using IGDLA in a single domain forest in case later, you add additional domains.

Convert groups, including security, distribution, universal, domain local, and domain global

If you create a group and define its scope and type, and later, you want to change the scope and/or type, this is permissible in certain circumstances, as summarized in the following list:

- **Global to universal**   Permitted only if the group that you want to rescope is not a member of another global group. This is because a universal group cannot belong to a global group.
- **Domain local to universal**   Permitted only if the group that you want to rescope does not contain another domain local group. This is because a universal group cannot contain a domain local group.
- **Universal to global**   Permitted only if the group that you want to rescope does not have another universal group as a member. This is because a universal group cannot belong to a global group.
- **Universal to domain local**   Always permitted.

If you want to change the type of the group, this is always permissible but with the following caveats:

- **Distribution to security**   Always permitted.
- **Security to distribution**   Always permitted, but any rights and permissions assigned to the group are lost because distribution groups cannot be assigned permissions or rights.

> **NEED MORE REVIEW?   GROUP SCOPE**
>
> To review further details about group scope, refer to the Microsoft TechNet website at *https://technet.microsoft.com/en-us/library/cc755692(v=ws.10).aspx*.

Create, configure, and delete groups

The process of creating and managing groups is straightforward. As with users and computers, you can use Active Directory Users and Computers, the Active Directory Administrative Center, or Windows PowerShell to perform all group management tasks.

To create a group in Active Directory Users and Computers, use the following procedure:

1. Locate the appropriate OU. Right-click the OU, point to New, and then click Group.
2. In the New Object – Group dialog box, shown in Figure 1-53, type the Group name. The Group name (pre-Windows 2000) autocompletes.

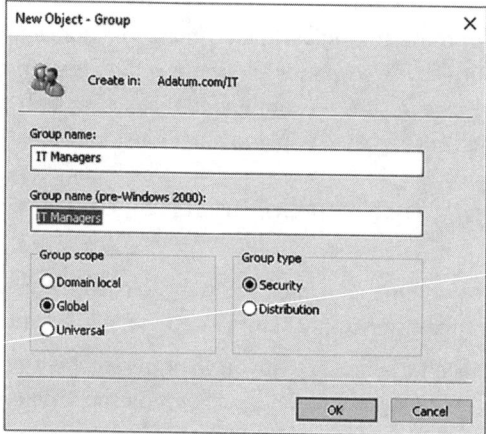

FIGURE 1-53 Adding a group

3. Specify the group scope and type. The default is global security. Click OK.

After you add the group, in the details pane in Active Directory Users and Computers, double-click the group to configure its properties, including members. To add a member, click the Members tab, as shown in Figure 1-54, click Add, browse and select your user or group, and then click OK.

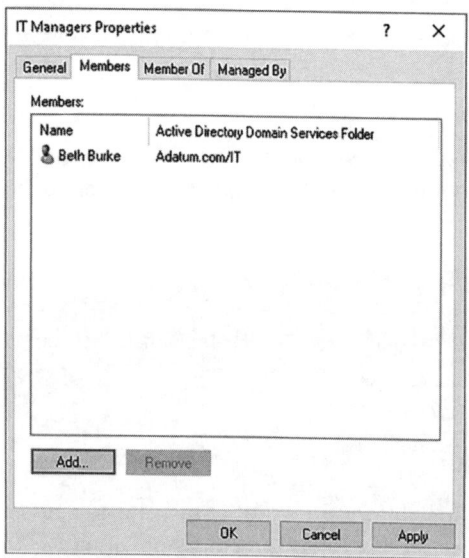

FIGURE 1-54 Configuring a group

You can configure group managers. This enables you to delegate responsibility for management of the group, as shown in Figure 1-55.

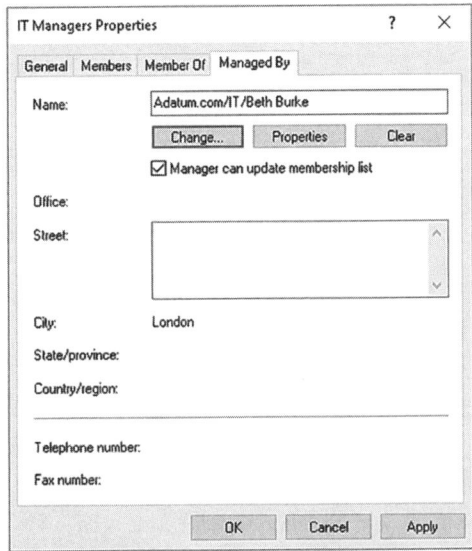

FIGURE 1-55 Assigning a group manager

You can easily delete a group from Active Directory Users and Computers. Right-click the group and then click Delete. At the confirmation prompt, click Yes.

You can perform all group management tasks by using Windows PowerShell. Table 1-5 shows the group management cmdlets.

TABLE 1-5 Common Windows PowerShell cmdlets for group management

Cmdlet	Use
New-ADGroup	Creates new groups
Set-ADGroup	Modifies properties of groups
Get-ADGroup	Displays properties of groups
Remove-ADGroup	Deletes groups
Add-ADGroupMember	Adds members to groups
Get-ADGroupMember	Displays members of groups
Remove-ADGroupMember	Removes members from a group
Add-ADPrincipalGroupMembership	Adds group membership to objects
Get-ADPrincipalGroupMembership	Displays group membership of objects
Remove-ADPrincipalGroupMembership	Removes group membership from an object

For example, to create a new group called IT Managers in the IT OU in the Adatum.com domain, you can use the following command:

```
New-ADGroup -Name "IT Managers" -SamAccountName ITManagers -GroupCategory Security
-GroupScope Global -DisplayName " IT Managers" -Path "OU=IT,DC=Adatum,DC=Com"
-Description "Members of this group are RODC Administrators"
```

To add members, you can use the following command:

```
Add-ADGroupMember "IT Managers" "Beth", "Ida"
```

To enumerate the current group members, use the following command:

```
Get-ADGroupMember "IT Managers"
```

Manage group membership using Group Policy

Although you can manually maintain group memberships by using either Windows PowerShell or the graphical tools, such as Active Directory Users and Computers, it can be time-consuming, especially in a large organization.

In Windows Server 2016 AD DS, you can use GPOs to maintain group membership. This means you can manage group membership automatically from a single point. This is called *Restricted Groups*.

Using Restricted Groups, you can configure the membership of a specific group, and you can also configure that a specific group must be a member of another group. Or you can configure both to create group nesting. To implement Restricted Groups, on your domain controller, open the Group Policy Management console.

1. Navigate to the Group Policy Objects container.
2. In the details pane, right-click the Default Domain Policy, and then click Edit. You can, of course, create your own GPO and link it to the appropriate OU
3. In the Group Policy Management Editor, in the navigation pane, expand Computer Configuration, expand Policies, expand Windows Settings, expand Security Settings, and then click the Restricted Groups node.
4. Right-click Restricted Groups, and then click Add Group.
5. In the Add Group dialog box, browse and locate the group you want to restrict, and click OK.
6. Then, in the Group Properties dialog box, shown in Figure 1-56, to restrict membership of the group, under the Configure Membership For Group heading, click Add, and then add any users or groups that must belong to the group.
7. Optionally, under the This Group Is A Member Of heading, browse and locate any groups of which this group must be a member. Click OK.

FIGURE 1-56 Restricting group membership

EXAM TIP
You can only implement the Restricted Groups feature in domain-level GPOs. You cannot use local group policies on Windows client or Windows Server operating systems.

Create and manage OUs

OUs enable you to manage your AD DS domain more easily by grouping users, groups, and computers together in a container, and then apply configuration settings to that container by using GPOs. In addition, you can configure security settings on your OUs so that a subset of management permissions are assigned to a user or group on that OU, and therefore objects within that OU; this is known as *delegation*.

Before you start creating OUs and populating them with users, groups, and computers, it's worth spending some time thinking about what you want to achieve with them. Most organizations consolidate their AD DS objects into OUs based on one of the following strategies:

- **Business units** This might represent the department, such as Sales or Research. It might represent a product line, such as Aviation or Paints.
- **Geographical location** Depending on the size of your organization, this might be office location, city location, or even country or continent. Remember that you can use AD DS site objects to control physical network behavior, so using geographical OUs must mean something in terms of delegation or configuration.
- **Hybrid** A combination of both these strategies. It is likely this will suit only the largest organizations. It is also probable that your OUs will be nested, perhaps first by region

and then by department, or the other way around, depending on the management structure of your organization.

After you have considered how best to implement OUs, you can start to create them, and then move objects, such as users and computers, into them. Generally, most OU management is performed using graphical tools, such as Active Directory Users and Computers. However, you can use Windows PowerShell. Table 1-6 lists the common Windows PowerShell OU management cmdlets.

TABLE 1-6 Common Windows PowerShell cmdlets for OU management

Cmdlet	Use
New-ADOrganizationalUnit	Creates OUs
Set-ADOrganizationalUnit	Modifies properties of OUs
Get-ADOrganizationalUnit	Displays properties of OUs
Remove-ADOrganizationalUnit	Deletes OUs

To create an OU in AD DS, open the Active Directory Users and Computers console. Navigate to the domain object, and then use the following procedure:

1. Right-click the domain (or OU, if you are creating nested OUs), point to New, and then click Organizational Unit.

2. In the New Object – Organizational Unit dialog box, shown in Figure 1-57, in the Name box, type the name for your OU, and then click OK.

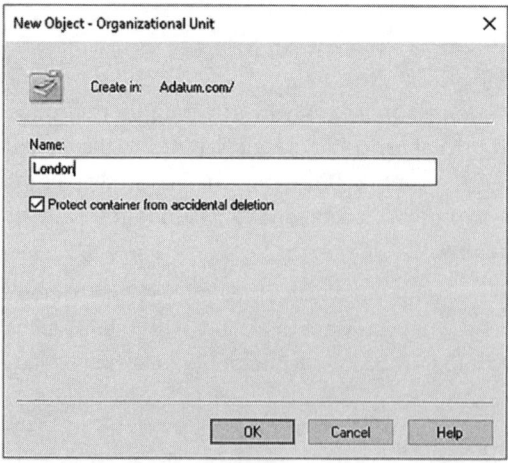

FIGURE 1-57 Adding an OU

After you have created your OU, you can begin to create, or move, objects into the OU. Once this task is completed, you can create and link GPOs to the OUs to configure user and computer settings for objects within the OU. GPOs are discussed in more detail later in Chapter 3: Create and manage Group Policy.

Delegate management of Active Directory with groups and OUs

Having created your OUs and populated them with the required objects, you can optionally delegate administration of them to groups within AD DS.

> **NOTE DELEGATION NOT SEPARATION**
> Remember that although you can delegate administrative responsibility for certain tasks to specific users or groups on a designated OU, you cannot separate administration. Members of the Domain Admins group can perform all management tasks on even delegated OUs in the current domain. Members of the Enterprise Admins group can manage all OUs in all domains in the forest. The only way to achieve administrative separation is by implementing multiple AD DS forests, each with a separate Enterprise Admins group.

You can delegate tasks by using the Delegation Of Control Wizard in Active Directory Users and Computers. Alternatively, you can manually assign specific object-level AD DS permissions using the Security tab on AD DS objects; this, however, can be a time-consuming and fiddly process.

To delegate control using the Delegation Of Control Wizard, use the following procedure:

1. In Active Directory Users and Computers, locate and right-click your OU, and then click Delegate Control.
2. In the Delegation Of Control Wizard, on the Welcome page, click Next.
3. On the Users or Groups page, click Add, and locate the user or group to which you want to delegate the specific task you are configuring. Click OK, and then click Next.

> **EXAM TIP**
> Even if you intend to delegate to a single user, it is still best practice to delegate to a group of which the single user is the only member. This makes things easier if later, you must delegate to a different user. Instead of having to start over, you can simply remove the old user and add the new user to the group.

4. On the Tasks To Delegate page, shown in Figure 1-58, in the Delegate The Following Common Tasks list, select the check box for the task(s) you want to delegate, and click Next.

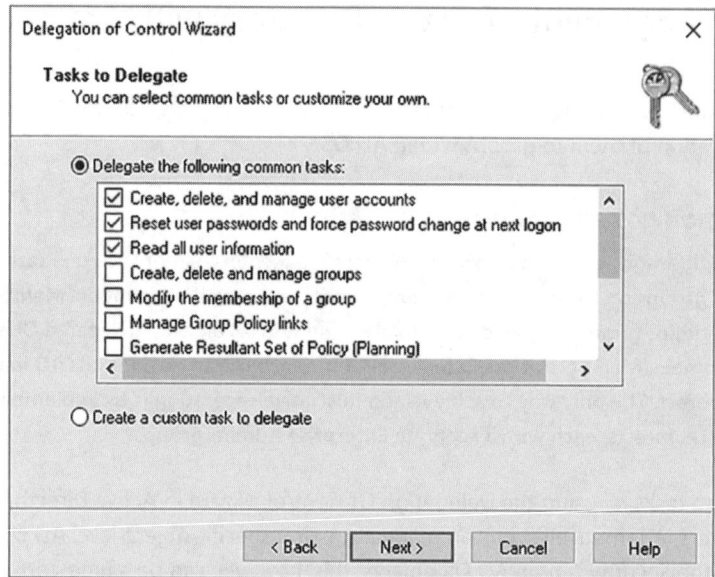

FIGURE 1-58 Delegating a common task

EXAM TIP

Common tasks are: User management, group management, limited GPO management, and inetOrgPerson management.

5. AD DS permissions are configured. Click Finish.

You can run the Delegation Of Control Wizard as many times as you require to assign the necessary permissions. However, for more advanced tasks, or specialist permissions, you must use custom tasks. For example, to delegate the ability to create and delete computer objects, you must use the custom task option.

1. Launch the Delegation Of Control Wizard, specify the user or group to which you want to delegate your custom task, and then, on the Tasks To Delegate page, click Create A Custom Task To Delegate, and click Next.

2. On the Active Directory Object Type page, shown in Figure 1-59, select This Folder, Existing Objects In This Folder, And Creation Of New Objects In This Folder. This option enables the delegated administrator to manage all aspects of the selected object types. Click Next.

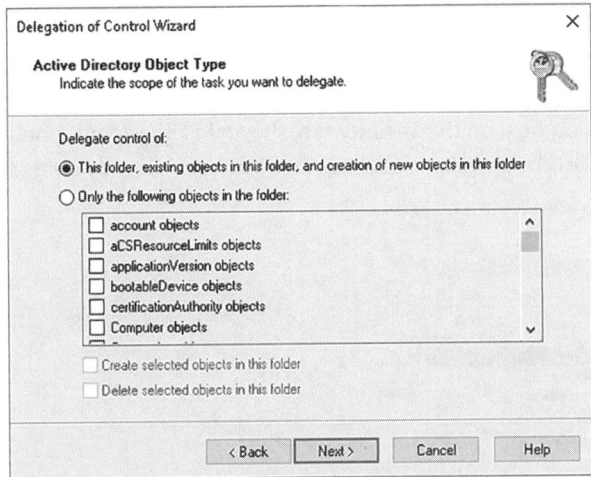

FIGURE 1-59 Delegating a custom task

3. On the Permissions page, select the Creation/Deletion Of Specific Child Objects, as shown in Figure 1-60, and then select the Create Computer objects and Delete Computer objects check boxes. Click Next.

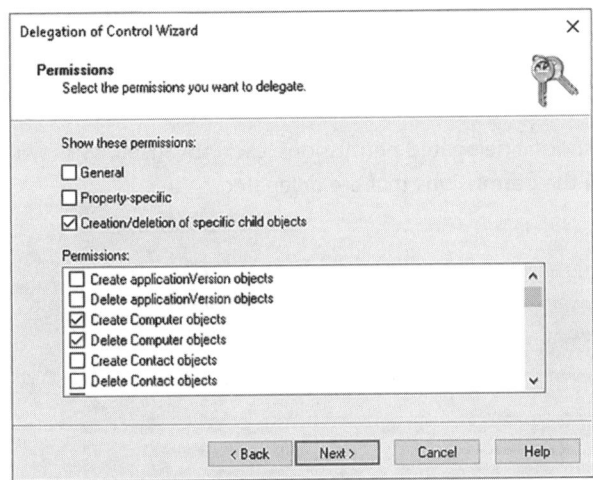

FIGURE 1-60 Selecting the object type

4. Click Finish. AD DS permissions are configured.

There comes a point when using the Delegation Of Control Wizard is itself too time-consuming. Although relatively simple, to have to repeatedly step through the wizard to assign another custom task, and then another, would take longer than just configuring the AD DS permissions directly. To view and edit the AD DS permissions on an object, use the following procedure.

1. In Active Directory Users and Computers, click the View menu, and then click Advanced Features. This enables the Security tab on all objects.
2. Right-click your OU, and then click Properties.
3. In the OU Properties dialog box, on the Security tab, shown in Figure 1-61, you can see the permissions for the OU. These will include any that you have recently delegated.

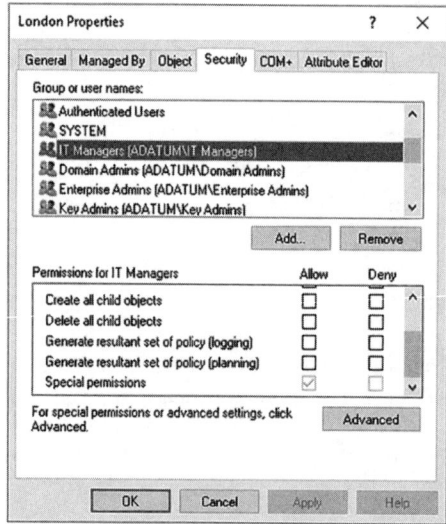

FIGURE 1-61 Viewing AD DS object permissions

4. If you want to view the specific delegated permissions, click Advanced, as shown in Figure 1-62. You can see the permissions that are delegated.

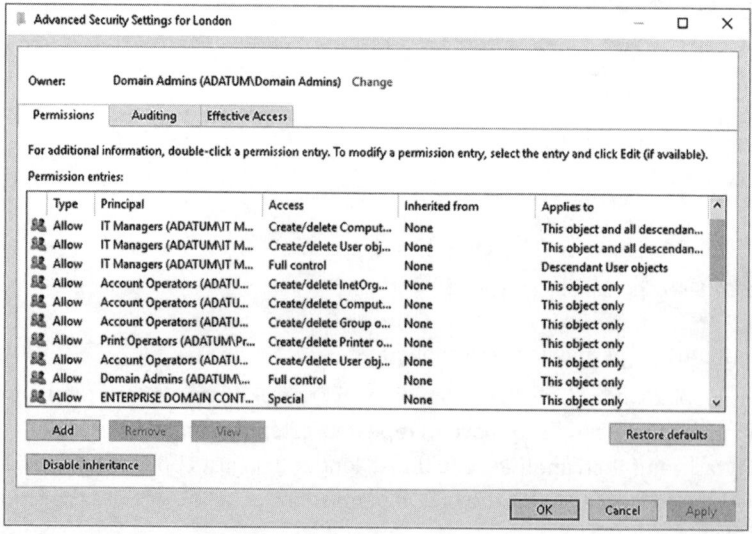

FIGURE 1-62 Viewing Advanced AD DS object permissions

5. You can now use the Add button to configure specific permissions without needing to use the Delegation Of Control Wizard, as shown in Figure 1-63.

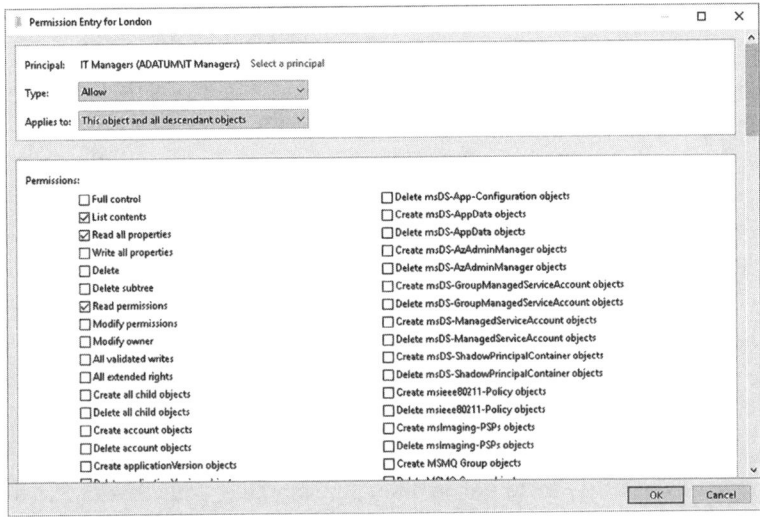

FIGURE 1-63 Manually adding AD DS object permissions

6. Click OK three times to complete the process.

Chapter summary

- AD DS consists of both logical and physical components.
- You create your AD DS forest by deploying the first domain controller in it.
- You create your AD DS forest structure based on trees of domains.
- RODCs can be deployed in locations that are physically less secure than offices with dedicated computer rooms.
- You can use Windows PowerShell to easily manage users, groups, computers, and OUs.
- OUs are used to help delegate administration within an AD DS forest, and also to enable easier configuration of AD DS objects through the use of linked GPOs.
- Groups in AD DS can be nested to support larger organizations.

Thought experiment

In this thought experiment, demonstrate your skills and knowledge of the topics covered in this chapter. You can find answers to this thought experiment in the next section.

You work in support at A. Datum. As a consultant for A. Datum, answer the following questions about implementing AD DS within the A. Datum organization:

1. A. Datum is acquiring a pharmaceuticals company, Contoso. It is important that users can access resources in the Contoso organization from their computers in A. Datum. However, Contoso wants to maintain complete administrative separation. What type of AD DS structure can you recommend based on this scenario?

2. A. Datum has several departments in their London, UK, offices. These are IT, Research, Sales, and Marketing. Computers within each of these departments have very different configuration requirements. How can you easily accommodate these differences, while streamlining administration as much as possible?

3. One of your sales offices supports a hundred or so users. Currently, users experience problems when they try to sign in during the morning. You discover that their link to the head office is unreliable and sometimes unavailable. You decide to deploy a domain controller at this office. What considerations are there with your decision?

Thought experiment answer

This section contains the solution to the thought experiment. Each answer explains why the answer choice is correct.

1. Complete AD DS administrative separation can only be achieved by implementing two AD DS forests.

2. Create OUs based on department and move the appropriate computer accounts into the relevant OUs. Create and link GPOs to the OUs and configure the GPOs to configure the required computer settings.

3. It is possible that the branch office is less secure than the head office. Using an RODC would help to protect the security of user accounts. Enabling caching of the user accounts used only at the branch would enable sign in even if the head office link is down.

CHAPTER 2

Manage and maintain AD DS

After you have deployed and configured your domain controllers, you must configure service accounts, account policies, and other security settings. You also must be prepared to maintain the Active Directory Domain Services (AD DS) server role to ensure availability of this critical identity service. This maintenance might involve performing backup and recovery procedures, and maintaining the AD DS database.

If you are deploying AD DS in a large enterprise organization, you must also configure more advanced aspects of AD DS, including how to establish and configure a multi-forest AD DS infrastructure. For organizations with multiple locations, you also need to know how to create subnets and sites, and to configure and manage both intrasite and intersite AD DS replication.

Skills covered in this chapter:

- Configure service authentication and account policies
- Maintain Active Directory
- Configure Active Directory in a complex enterprise environment

Skill 2.1: Configure service authentication and account policies

Many apps and services that you install on Windows Server run in the security context of a user account, known as a service account. Like all user accounts, it is important that these service accounts are not compromised. Windows Server 2016 provides Managed Service Accounts (MSAs) and Group Managed Service Accounts (gMSAs) to help you more easily manage service accounts.

Account policies enable you to control fundamental security features, such as password complexity, length, expiration, and lockout. You can use these features to help secure your network, and the apps and services that run within it.

> **This section covers how to:**
> - Create and configure MSAs and gMSAs
> - Manage SPNs
> - Configure Kerberos Constrained Delegation
> - Configure virtual accounts
> - Configure account policies
> - Configure and apply Password Settings Objects
> - Delegate password settings management

Create and configure MSAs and gMSAs

In earlier versions of Windows Server, it was common to create standard user accounts for the purposes of running apps or services. For example, you might create a user account called Email and configure the email program you installed to run in the context of the Email user account.

Using standard user accounts in this way does raise some considerations, including:

- **Account password management**   The password for these standard user accounts must be periodically changed to help maintain security of your apps and services. Failure to change the account password results in failure of your apps or service.
- **Service Principal Names**   Service Principal Names (SPNs) are unique identifiers for a specific service instance and are used to associate a service instance with a service account. If you use a standard user account with SPNs, it could result in additional administrative effort and cause possible authentication issues that might result in app failure.

One possible workaround is to use the local system (NT AUTHORITY\SYSTEM), the local service (NT AUTHORITY\LOCAL SERVICE), or the network service (NT AUTHORITY\NETWORK SERVICE) accounts to configure your app. However, these three accounts might not provide sufficient security, nor have sufficient privilege for many situations.

Windows Server 2016 provides both MSAs and gMSAs to help you mitigate these issues:

- **MSAs**   Unlike standard user accounts, MSAs inherit some of their structure from computer objects, including the way that password changes are handled. This provides the following benefits:
    - Automatic password management
    - Simplified SPN management

> **EXAM TIP**
>
> MSAs are stored in the Managed Service Accounts container in your AD DS domain. To view these accounts, in Active Directory Users and Computers, enable the Advanced Features view.

- **gMSAs** Enable you to extend the function of MSAs to multiple servers in your AD DS domain. This is useful where you are using load balancing. To use gMSAs, your AD DS environment must meet the following requirements:
    - Client computers must run at least Windows 8
    - You must create a key distribution services (KDS) root key for your domain
    - At least one domain controller must be running Windows Server 2012 or later

When you create a gMSA, you must define the collection of computers that can retrieve password information from AD DS. This can be a list of computer objects, or an AD DS group that contains the desired computer objects.

In Windows Server 2016, you use the same Windows PowerShell cmdlets to create and manage gMSAs as you do MSAs. This means that in Windows Server 2016, all MSAs are managed as gMSAs. To create gMSAs, start by creating the KDS root key. On a domain controller, use the following Windows PowerShell cmdlet to complete this task:

`Add-KdsRootKey –EffectiveImmediately`

EXAM TIP

Although the EffectiveImmediately parameter instructs AD DS to make the required change immediately, in fact, the key does not become effective for a further 10 hours. This is to allow AD DS to replicate the change throughout your forest.

After creating the KDS root key, use the Active Directory Module for Windows PowerShell new-ADServiceAccount cmdlet from any domain controller to create your gMSAs. For example:

`New-ADServiceAccount –Name LON-IIS-GMSA –DNSHostname LON-DC1.Adatum.com – PrincipalsAllowedToRetrieveManagedPassword LON-DC1$, LON-DC2$, LON-IIS$`

Use the PrincipalsAllowedToRetrieveManagedPassword parameter to define which computers, or groups, can access the gMSA password properties.

When you have created your new gMSA, you must associate it with the server computers on which it is to be used. To do this, use the Active Directory Module for Windows PowerShell Add-ADComputerServiceAccount cmdlet to complete this task. For example:

`Add-ADComputerServiceAccount –identity LON-DC1 –ServiceAccount LON-IIS-GMSA`

Next, you must install the gMSA on the servers where it is to be used. Use the Install-ADServiceAccount cmdlet. For example:

`Install-ADServiceAccount –Identity LON-IIS-GMSA`

Finally, configure the required service or app to use the configured gMSA. Use the following procedure to complete the task:

1. On the target server(s), in Server Manager, click Tools, and then click Services.

2. Locate the appropriate service, double-click it, and then on the Log On tab, shown in Figure 2-1, click This Account, and then type the name of your account. For example, type ADATUM\LON-IIS-GMSA.

FIGURE 2-1 Configuring a service account

3. Clear the Password, and Confirm Password check boxes, and click OK.

Manage SPNs

SPNs are similar in concept to Domain Name System (DNS) alias records (CNAMEs), but rather than being a pointer for a computer record in a DNS zone, SPNs point to domain accounts. SPNs are used by Kerberos, the authentication protocol in Windows Server 2016 AD DS domain controllers. They associate a service with a service logon account, enabling a client computer app to request that the service authenticate an account, even if the client app does not know the account name. Before Kerberos can use SPNs, services must register their SPNs in AD DS.

SPNs consist of several elements, and must be unique within your AD DS forest. These elements are:

- **Service class** Identifies the class of a service. For example, www for a web server. There are several well-known service classes.
- **Host** The computer name on which the service runs. Usually this is a fully qualified domain name (FQDN), such as LON-SVR2.Adatum.com.
- **Port** Optionally used to identify the port number used by a service. Enables you to differentiate between multiple instances of the same services installed on a specific computer. For example, a secure website uses TCP port 443.

- **Service name** An optional element that is based on the DNS name of the domain, or of a service locator (SRV) or Mail Exchanger (MX) record within the domain. This element identifies services that are domain-wide.

This creates an SPN comprising these elements:

```
<service class>/<host>:<port>/<service name>
```

For example:

```
WebService/LON-SVR2.Adatum.com:443
```

Generally, there is little management of SPNs required. But occasionally, you might be required to force registration. You can use the Setspn.exe command-line tool to register SPNs.

EXAM TIP

Using gMSAs significantly reduces the likelihood of you having to manually reconfigure SPNs.

For example, to register an SPN for IIS on LON-SVR2 in the Adatum.com domain using the LON-IIS-GMSA group MSA, use the following command, as shown in Figure 2-2.

```
setspn -A WebService/lon-svr2.adatum.com:433 lon-iis-gmsa
```

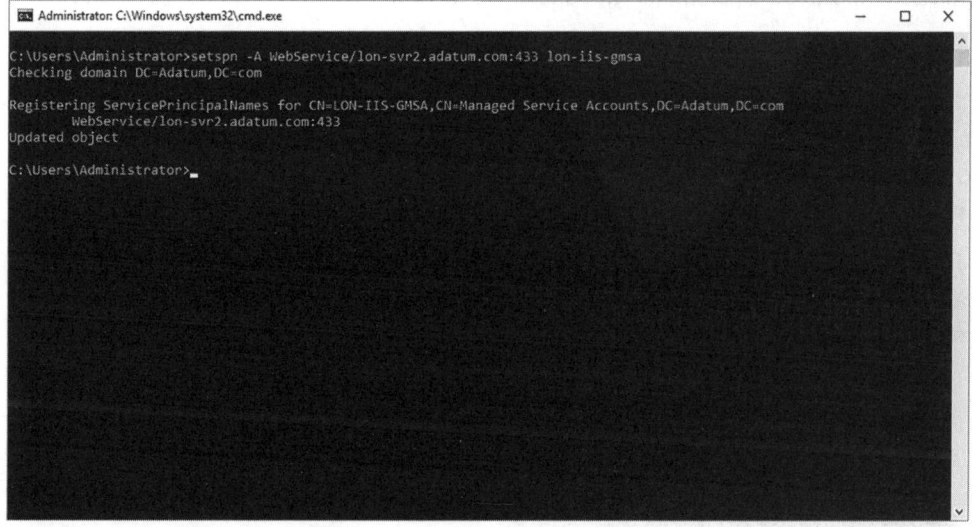

FIGURE 2-2 Adding an SPN

NEED MORE REVIEW? MANUAL SPN REGISTRATION

To review further details about manually registering SPNs, refer to the Microsoft MSDN website at *https://msdn.microsoft.com/library/ms191153.aspx*.

Configure Kerberos Constrained Delegation

In some situations, app or services might make connections to remote apps or services installed on other server computers. In essence, these connections are being made on behalf of client computers connecting to the originating app or service.

Typically, this scenario occurs when a front-end service communicates with a back-end service on behalf of users on client computers using the back-end app. To support this scenario, it is necessary to use authentication delegation; this is the process where the authenticating authority (in Windows Server 2016, this is a domain controller) allows a service to act on behalf of another service. The problem is that in earlier versions of Windows Server, there is no way to prevent the delegation from extending to a third, or even fourth service. Kerberos constrained delegation in Windows Server 2016 prevents this.

To configure constrained delegation to allow a front-end app access to a back-end service on the behalf of users, you must use one of the following cmdlets for the security principal that runs your front-end service:

- Get-ADUser
- Get-ADComputer
- Get-ADServiceAccount

Next, pass that security principal object as the argument using the PrincipalsAllowedToDelegateToAccount parameter with one of the following Windows PowerShell cmdlets:

- Set-ADUser
- Set-ADComputer
- Set-ADServiceAccount

For example:

```
$computer = Get-ADComputer -Identity WEBSVR1

Set-ADComputer LON-SVR2 -PrincipalsAllowedToDelegateToAccount $computer
```

> **NEED MORE REVIEW? HOW KERBEROS CONSTRAINED DELEGATION WORKS**
>
> To review further details about Kerberos Constrained Delegation (KCD), refer to the Microsoft TechNet website at *https://technet.microsoft.com/library/cc995228.aspx#Anchor_0*.

Configure virtual accounts

You cannot create, delete, or manage the passwords for virtual accounts. They exist automatically and are a representation of the local computer account when used to access apps or resources.

To configure a service to use a virtual account, use the following procedure:

1. In Server Manager, click Tools, and then click Services.
2. Locate the appropriate service, double-click it, and then on the Log On tab, shown in Figure 2-3, click This Account, and then type the name of your account. For example, type NT SERVICE\LON-SVR2$.

FIGURE 2-3 Configuring a virtual account for a service

3. Clear the Password and Confirm Password check boxes, and click OK.

Configure account policies

Account policies enable you to configure password-related settings, including the password policy, account lockout settings, and Kerberos policy settings. These settings are accessible through the Default Domain Policy in the Group Policy Management Editor.

To view and configure these settings, use the following procedure:

1. In Server Manager, click Tools, and then click Group Policy Management.
2. In Group Policy Management, expand your forest, expand the Domains folder, and expand the domain you want to configure.
3. Click the Group Policy Objects folder, and then, in the Details pane, as shown in Figure 2-4, right-click the Default Domain Policy, and then click Edit.

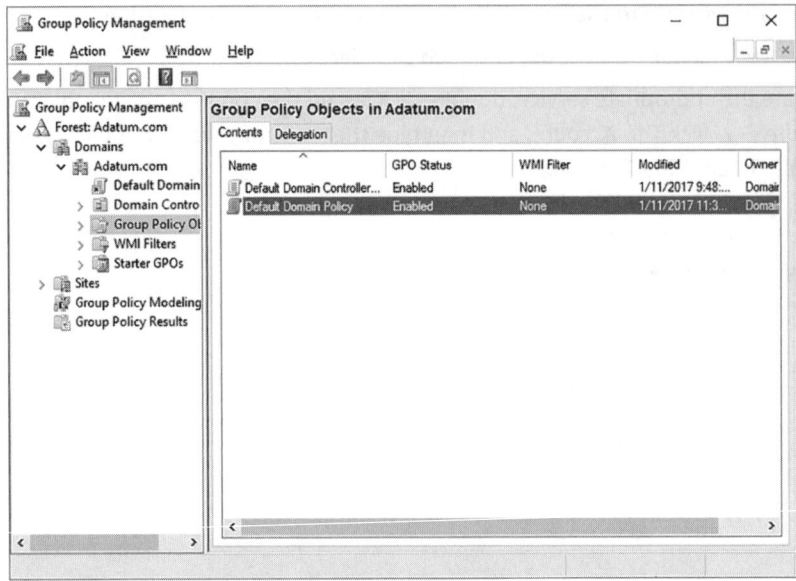

FIGURE 2-4 Viewing available default Group Policy Objects

4. In the Group Policy Management Editor, under the Default Domain Policy node, expand Computer Configuration, expand Policies, expand Windows Settings, expand Security Settings, and then click Account Policies, as shown in Figure 2-5.

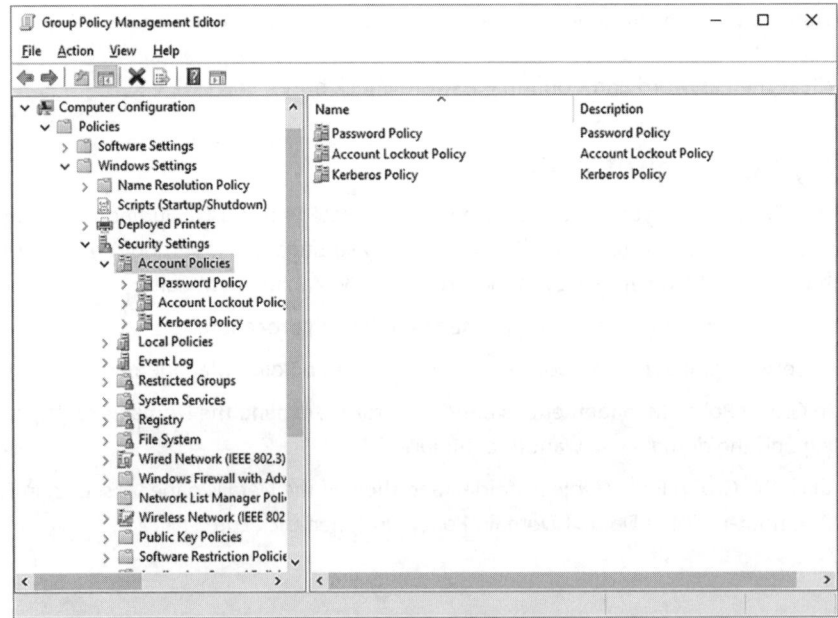

FIGURE 2-5 Editing Account Policies in the Default Domain Policy

Configure domain and local user password policy settings

Password policies enable you to define settings that control how your domain users' passwords are managed. To configure domain password policy settings, in the Group Policy Management Editor, under the Account Policies folder, in the Password Policy folder, shown in Figure 2-6, you can configure the following password settings:

- **Enforce Password History**   Prevents users from reusing passwords. The default value is 24.
- **Maximum Password Age**   Ensures that users change their passwords within the defined period. Default is 42 days.
- **Minimum Password Age**   Prevents users from changing their passwords until this period has expired. Helps prevent users from cycling through a range of passwords back to their favorite password by changing their password 24 times very rapidly. The default is one day.
- **Minimum Password Length**   Ensures passwords are not too short. Longer passwords are more difficult to guess, especially if complex passwords are also enforced. Default is seven characters.
- **Password Must Meet Complexity Requirements**   Helps to ensure that passwords are more difficult to guess. Enabled by default. When enabled, passwords must meet several complexity requirements:
    - Cannot contain user's name or their account user name
    - Must contain at least six characters
    - Must contain characters from at least three of the following four groups:
    - Uppercase letters [A–Z]
    - Lowercase letters [a–z]
    - Numerals [0–9]
    - Special, non-alphanumeric characters, such as !@#)(*&^%
- **Store Passwords Using Reversible Encryption**   Provides support for older apps that require knowledge of a user's password. In many cases, storing passwords using reversible encryption is the same as storing clear text passwords and should be avoided unless absolutely necessary. This is disabled by default.

EXAM TIP

You can enable individual user accounts to store passwords using reversible encryption if necessary.

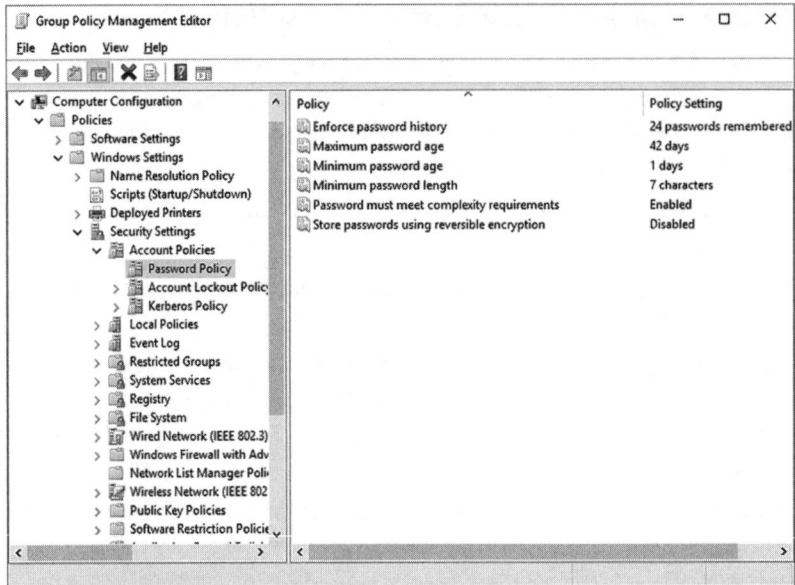

FIGURE 2-6 Editing the domain password policy

For computers in a workgroup, you can configure a local account policy. To configure local password policies, on the target computer, in Server Manager, click Tools, and then click Local Security Policy. Expand Account Policies, and, as shown in Figure 2-7, click Password Policy. You can also configure a local account lockout policy.

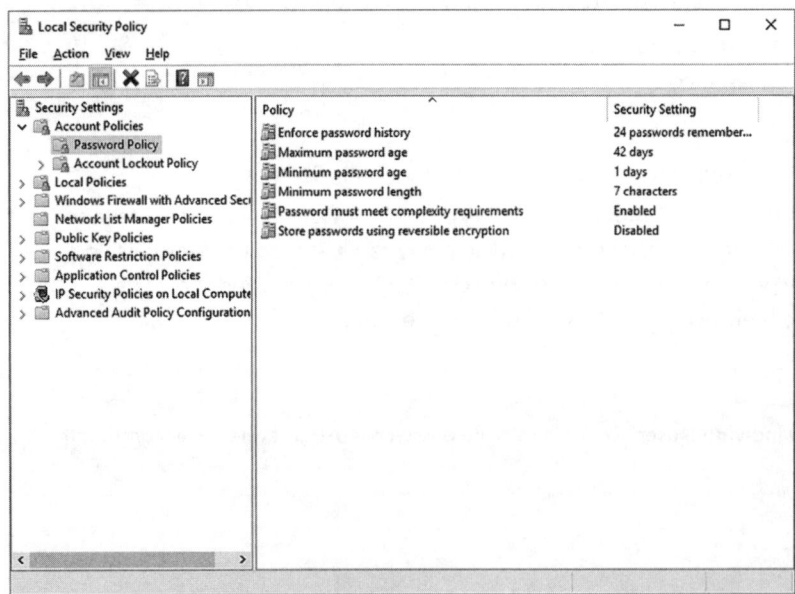

FIGURE 2-7 Editing the local password policy

86   CHAPTER 2   Manage and maintain AD DS

> **EXAM TIP**
>
> Settings that you configure in the Local Security Policy are overridden by settings configured in the Domain Security Policy for server computers that are part of an AD DS domain.

Configure account lockout policy settings

Account lockout settings define what happens when a user enters an incorrect password. If a user's account is locked, they cannot sign in until their account is unlocked. In the Account Lockout Policy folder, shown in Figure 2-8, you can configure the following lockout settings:

- **Account Lockout Duration** Defines the lockout duration in minutes. After an account is locked, when this period has expired, the account is automatically unlocked. An administrator can unlock the account manually at any time. To always use manual unlocking, configure the lockout duration to 0. By default, this setting is not enabled.

- **Account Lockout Threshold** Determines how many incorrect sign in attempts a user can make before their account is locked. By default, a value of 0 is assigned; this effectively disables account lockout.

- **Reset Account Lockout Counter After** Determines how many minutes must pass before the account lockout threshold is reset. Used in conjunction with the account lockout threshold value, you can effectively configure a system sensitivity to incorrect passwords. For example, configuring a value of 5 in conjunction with an account lockout threshold of 2 means that any two incorrect passwords in a five-minute period locks the account. Changing this value to 30 makes the system more sensitive because the account is locked out after two incorrect sign in attempts in a 30-minute period. By default, this setting is not enabled.

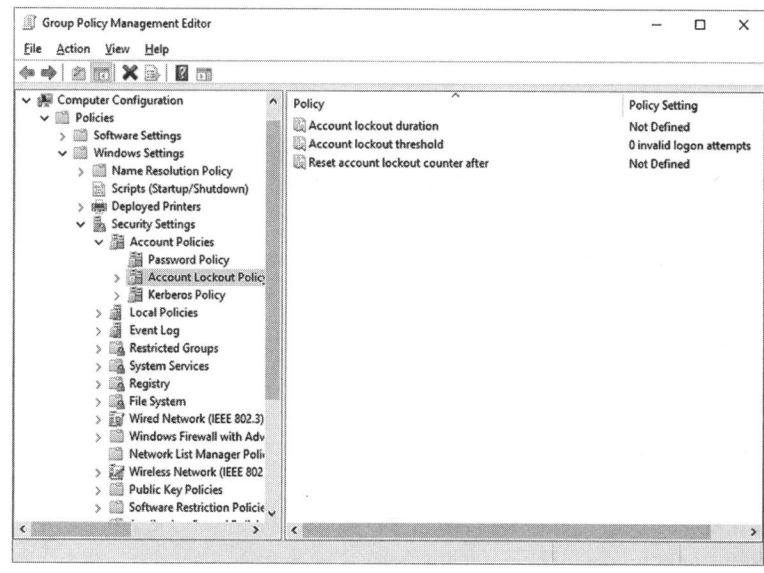

FIGURE 2-8 Editing the account lockout policy

To manually unlock an account, open the user account properties in Active Directory Users and Computers. On the Account tab, shown in Figure 2-9, select the Unlock Account check box, and then click OK.

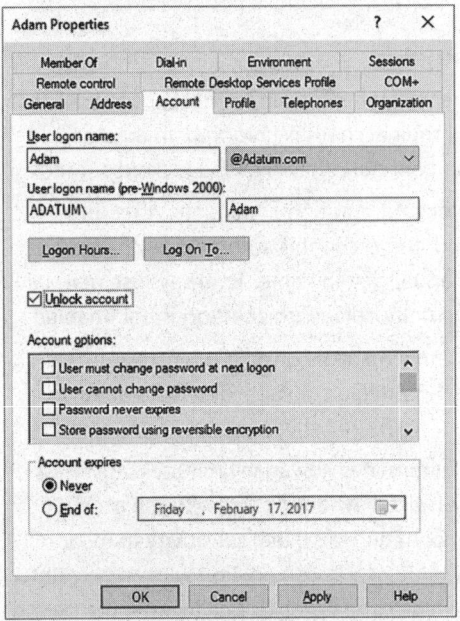

FIGURE 2-9 Unlocking an account

Configure Kerberos policy settings

Kerberos provides the authentication architecture for Windows Server 2016. When users sign in, they receive a Kerberos ticket granting ticket from a domain controller. When a user attempts to connect to a server, they receive a service ticket. The Kerberos policy settings enable you to control aspects of ticket handling and renewal.

In the Kerberos Policy folder, shown in Figure 2-10, you can configure the following Kerberos settings:

- **Enforce User Logon Restrictions** Forces domain controllers to perform additional validation on a user's rights policy, helping to add security. The default is Enabled.
- **Maximum Lifetime For Service Ticket** Defines the maximum age of a user's service ticket. Must be at least 10 minutes and not greater than the maximum lifetime of a user ticket. The default is 600 minutes.
- **Maximum Lifetime For User Ticket** Determines the maximum age of a user's ticket granting ticket. The default is 10 hours.
- **Maximum Lifetime For User Ticket Renewal** Determines for how long a user can renew their ticket granting ticket. The default is 7 days.

- **Maximum Tolerance For Computer Clock Synchronization** Determines the sensitivity to a disparity between the client computer's time and that of the domain controller. The default is five minutes.

EXAM TIP

The domain controller that holds the primary domain controller (PDC) emulator operation master role is the time source for the domain.

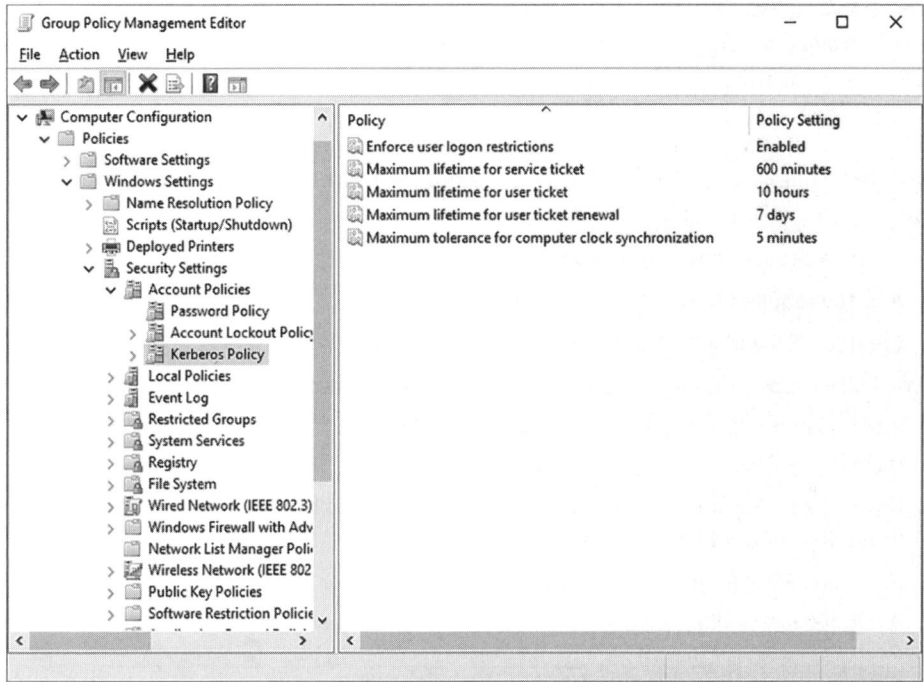

FIGURE 2-10 Editing the Kerberos policy

Configure and apply Password Settings Objects

You can only configure Account Policies for your domain; you cannot configure a separate policy for organizational units (OUs) within your domain. In early versions of Windows Server, the need to configure a different account policy for business groups or geographical locations often meant having to configure multiple domains within the AD DS forest.

However, in Windows Server 2016 you can implement multiple account policies by using Password Settings Objects (PSOs). Using PSOs you can implement and configure account policies that impact users and groups rather than just containers, which means you have more targeted administrative control.

EXAM TIP

PSOs were introduced in Windows Server 2008.

In addition to PSOs, Windows Server 2016 creates a container called Password Settings Container; this stores the PSOs that you create and apply in your domain.

EXAM TIP

You can only apply PSOs to users, InetOrgPerson objects, and global security groups. If you want to apply a PSO to an OU, create a shadow group and apply the PSO to that group. A shadow group is a global security group that you manually create and add all users in an OU to the membership list of the shadow group.

To implement PSOs, you must create the PSO and then link it to the appropriate user or group object. For example, to configure a more stringent password policy for administrator accounts, use the following high-level procedure:

1. Create a Secure Admins global security group.
2. Add the required user accounts to the group.
3. Create a PSO and link it to the Secure Admins group.

If you link multiple PSOs to a single object, the following precedence rules apply:

- If there are no PSOs linked to a user, Windows Server AD DS applies the Default Domain Policy Account Policy settings.
- If you link a PSO directly to a user object, that PSO takes precedence over any PSOs linked to groups of which the user is a member.
- If you link PSOs to groups, AD DS compares the PSOs for all global security groups of which the user object is a member.

EXAM TIP

If you link multiple PSOs directly to a user object or group object, the PSO that has the lowest precedence value is applied. The msDS-PasswordSettingsPrecedence PSO attribute holds the precedence value.

Although the settings in a PSO are identical to the password policies that you apply in the Default Domain Policy, you do not use the Group Policy Management Editor to configure or apply them. Instead, you use Windows PowerShell or the Active Directory Administrative Center console.

EXAM TIP

Your AD DS domain functional level must be at least Windows Server 2008 to support PSOs.

Creating PSOs with Windows PowerShell

To create and apply PSOs using Windows PowerShell, use the following two cmdlets:

- **New-ADFineGrainedPasswordPolicy** Creates the PSO and assigns the properties that you define by using cmdlet parameters, shown in Table 2-1.
- **Add-FineGrainedPasswordPolicySubject** Links the PSO to the user or group that you define by using the cmdlet parameters.

For example, as shown in Figure 2-11, the following commands create and link a new PSO named Admins to the Secure Admins global security group:

```
New-ADFineGrainedPasswordPolicy Admins -ComplexityEnabled:$true
-LockoutDuration:"00:45:00" -LockoutObservationWindow:"00:45:00" -LockoutThreshold:"0"
-MaxPasswordAge:"24.00:00:00" -MinPasswordAge:"2.00:00:00" -MinPasswordLength:"8"
-PasswordHistoryCount:"30" -Precedence:"1" -ReversibleEncryptionEnabled:$false -Protecte
dFromAccidentalDeletion:$true

Add-ADFineGrainedPasswordPolicySubject Admins -Subjects "Secure Admins"
```

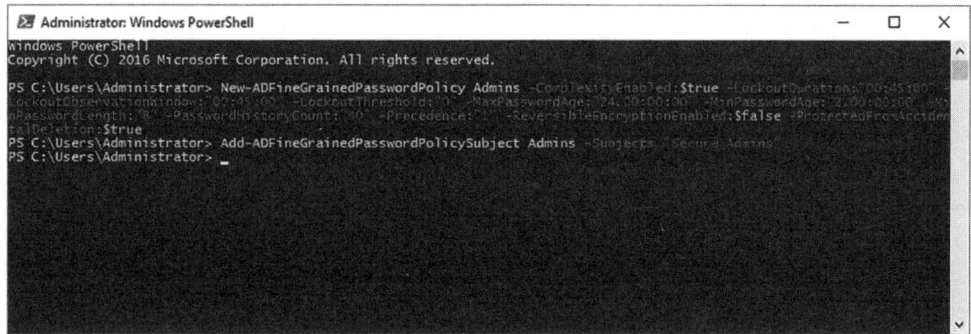

FIGURE 2-11 Creating and applying a PSO with Windows PowerShell

TABLE 2-1 PSO settings

Setting	Format of Setting	Explanation
Password Policy Settings		
Name	String	Defines the name of your PSO.
ComplexityEnabled	True or False	Determines whether complex passwords are enforced.
MinPasswordLength	Integer	Defines the minimum length of passwords.
MaxPasswordAge	Time: dd.hh:mm:ss	Determines the maximum number of days before users must change their passwords.
MinPasswordAge	Time: dd.hh:mm:ss	Determines the minimum amount of time that must elapse before users can change their passwords.
PasswordHistoryCount	Integer	Specifies the number of password changes that must occur before passwords can be reused.
ReversibleEncryptionEnabled	True or False	Defines whether reversible encryption is allowed.
Account Lockout Settings		
LockoutThreshold	Integer	Specifies the number of incorrect password sign in attempts before an account is locked.
LockoutObservationWindow	Time: hh:mm:ss	Determines how many minutes must pass before the account lockout threshold is reset.
LockoutDuration	Time: hh:mm:ss	Specifies for how long the account is locked before being unlocked automatically.
PSO Specific Settings		
Precedence	Integer	Determines how multiple PSOs linked to the same object apply.
PSOApplied	List of distinguished names	Determines to which users or global security groups the PSO should apply.
ProtectedFromAccidentalDeletion	True or False	Specifies whether the PSO must be protected against inadvertent deletion.

Creating PSOs with the Active Directory Administrative Center

To create and link PSOs using the Active Directory Administrative Center console, use the following procedure:

1. In Active Directory Administrative Center, click Manage, click Add Navigation Nodes, in the Add Navigation Node dialog box, select the appropriate target domain, click the >> button, and then click OK, as shown in Figure 2-12.

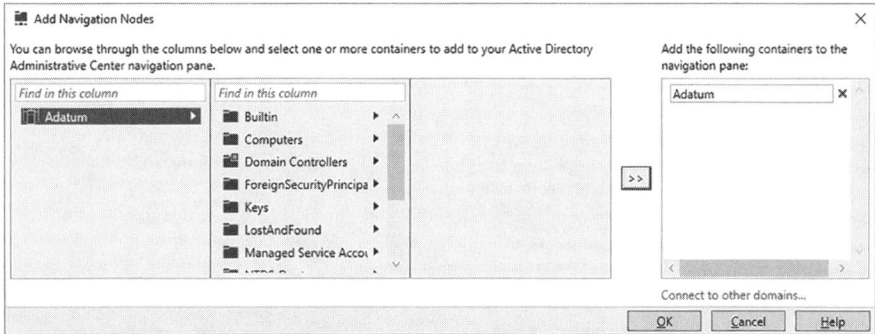

FIGURE 2-12 Adding a navigation node

2. In the navigation pane, expand your domain, click the System container, and then click Password Settings Container, as shown in Figure 2-13. Press Enter.

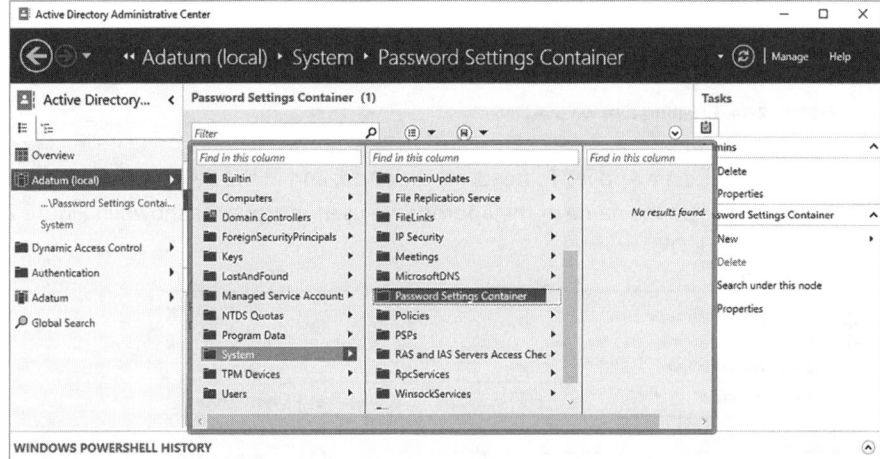

FIGURE 2-13 Selecting the Password Settings Container

3. In the Tasks pane, click New, and then click Password Settings.
4. In the Create Password Settings: dialog box, configure the required settings for the new PSO, as shown in Figure 2-14.

FIGURE 2-14 Creating a new PSO

5. Under the Directly Applies To heading, click Add, and in the Select Users Or Groups dialog box, type the name of the appropriate user or group, as shown in Figure 2-15, and then click OK.

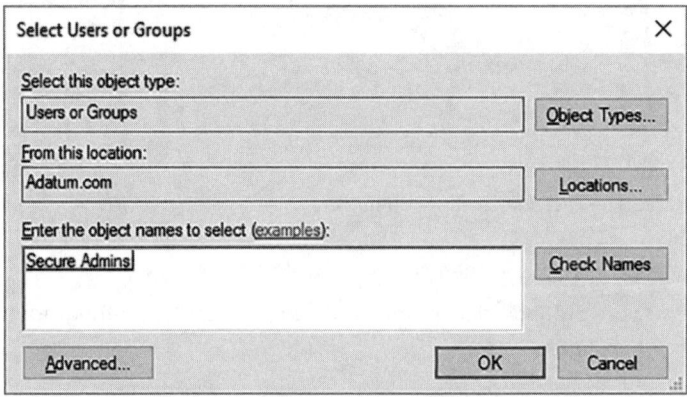

FIGURE 2-15 Selecting the group to which the PSO is linked

6. Click OK.

Delegate password settings management

To delegate the management of password settings, you can use the following Delegate Control Wizard in Active Directory Users and Computers, as described in the following procedure:

1. In Active Directory Users and Computers, locate and right-click the appropriate OU, and then click Delegate Control.
2. In the Delegation Of Control Wizard, on the Welcome page, click Next.
3. On the Users Or Groups page, click Add, and locate the user or group to which you want to delegate password settings management. Click OK, and then click Next.
4. On the Tasks To Delegate page, shown in Figure 2-16, in the Delegate The Following Common Tasks list, select the Reset User Passwords And Force Password Change At Next Logon check box, and then click Next. Click Finish when prompted.

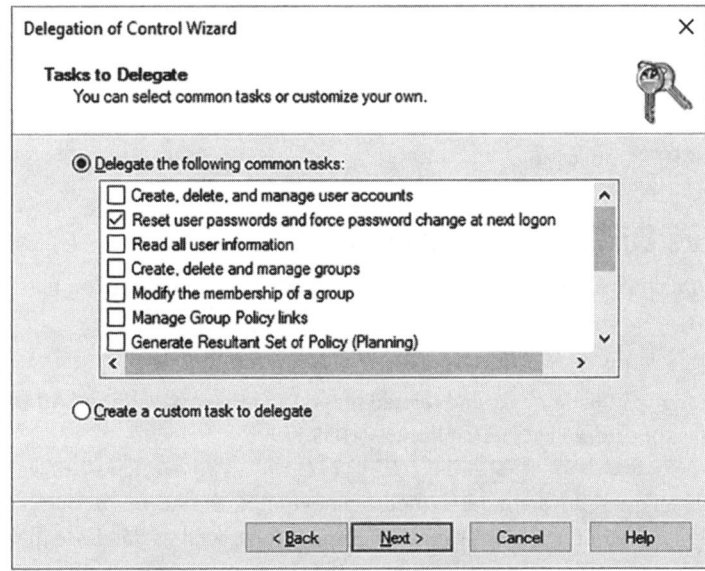

FIGURE 2-16 Delegating password settings management

Delegation of administrative functions is covered in detail in Chapter 1: Install and configure Active Directory Domain Services, Skill 1.3: Create and manage Active Directory groups and OUs, in the Delegate management of Active Directory with groups and OUs section.

Skill 2.2: Maintain Active Directory

For the most part, AD DS is a very robust and reliable directory service and requires little maintenance. However, from time to time, it might be necessary to perform database defragmentation to optimize AD DS. To help protect against data loss or database corruption, you should also know how to backup and restore AD DS.

You can deploy read only domain controllers (RODCs) to branch offices or other locations where physical server security cannot be guaranteed. Because the RODC maintains a read-only copy of AD DS, it is important that you know how to configure and manage replication to the RODC, and how to manage a password replication policy to RODCs in your branch offices.

This section covers how to:
- Manage Active Directory offline
- Active Directory backup and recovery
- Manage Read Only Domain Controllers
- Managing AD DS replication

Manage Active Directory offline

AD DS is stored in domain controllers in a database and a collection of related log files.

EXAM TIP

You define the location of the database and related files during the installation of AD DS. By default, these files are stored in %SystemRoot%\NTDS.

Most AD DS database operations are performed online; that is, the AD DS service is running and is accessible on the network. However, some operations, such as database maintenance, must be performed offline. Often, this means that you must restart the domain controller in directory services restore mode (DSRM). While the server is in DSRM, it cannot service client sign in requests, nor perform any other AD DS tasks. In order to enable your network to continue operating correctly, you must have additional domain controllers that can continue to provide directory-related services.

In Windows Server 2016, for some database-related tasks, you can also stop the AD DS service rather than restarting the domain controller in DSRM.

EXAM TIP

The ability to stop AD DS in this manner is known as restartable AD DS, and is only available in Windows Server 2012 and later.

Using restartable AD DS to perform maintenance tasks can help you complete maintenance tasks more quickly, thereby reducing the downtime of your domain controller.

Perform offline defragmentation of an AD DS database

When you perform offline defragmentation of the AD DS database, you enable unused space in the database to be made available to the file system. At the completion of the defragmentation, you have a compacted AD DS database. You use the NtdsUtil.exe command-line tool to perform offline AD DS database maintenance.

To compact your AD DS, use the following procedure:

1. On your domain controller, in Server Manager, click Tools, and then click Services to open the Services console.
2. Stop the Active Directory Domain Services service, as shown in Figure 2-17.

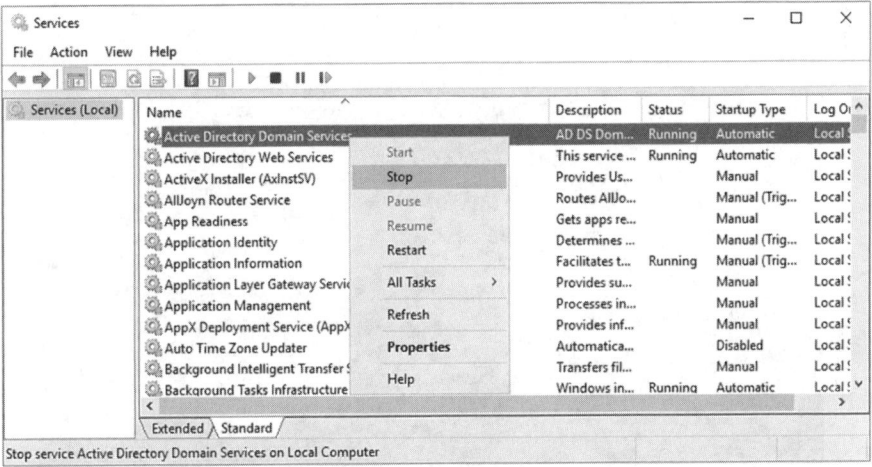

FIGURE 2-17 Stopping the Active Directory Domain Services service

3. You are prompted to stop related services, such as DNS Server, Kerberos Key Distribution Center, Intersite Messaging, and DFS Replication. Click Yes to stop these services.
4. Open an elevated command prompt.
5. Run the NtdsUtil.exe command.
6. Run the following commands, shown in Figure 2-18:
   - Activate instance NTDS
   - Files
   - Compact to C:\
   - Integrity

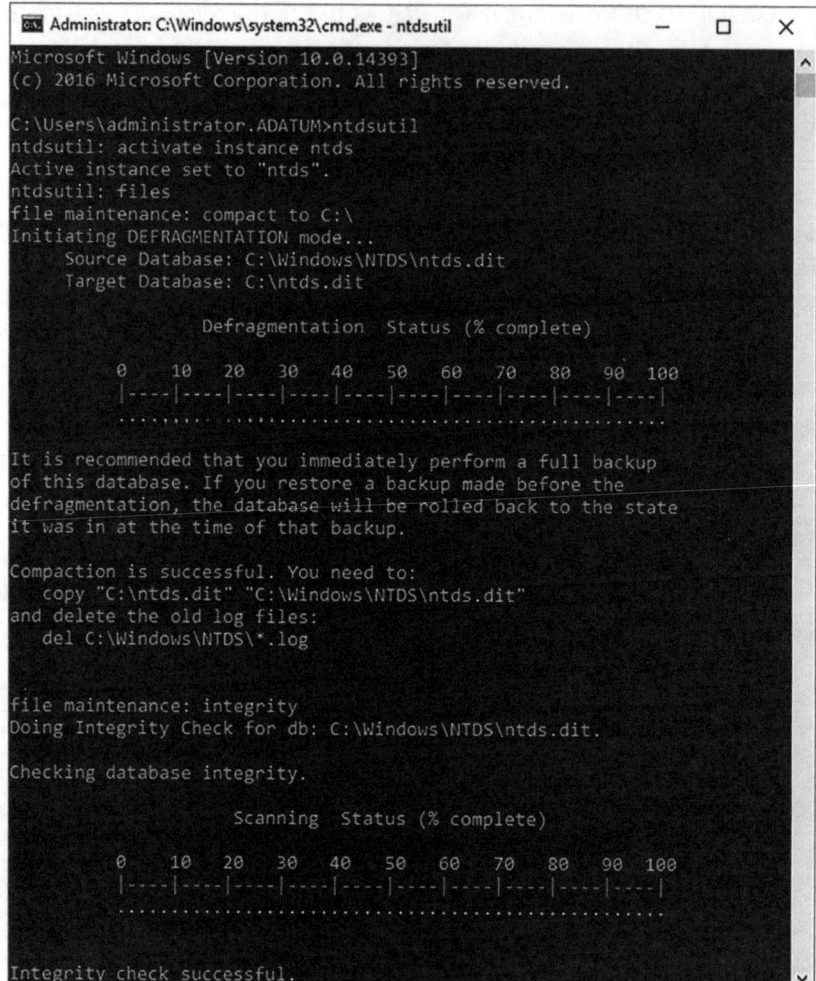

FIGURE 2-18 Defragmenting the AD DS database

7. Complete the database maintenance by running the following commands at the elevated command prompt:
   - Quit
   - Quit
   - Copy C:\ntds.dit C:\Windows\NTDS\ntds.dit
   - Del C:\Windows\NTDS*.log
   - Exit

8. In the Services console, start the Active Directory Domain Services. Related services are also started.

> **NEED MORE REVIEW? COMPACT THE DIRECTORY DATABASE FILE**
>
> To review further details about AD DS database compaction, refer to the Microsoft TechNet website at *https://technet.microsoft.com/library/cc794920(v=ws.10).aspx*.

Perform metadata cleanup

Metadata cleanup is a task that you must perform after you have forcibly removed a domain controller from your AD DS forest, perhaps following server failure. The metadata identifies the domain controller in AD DS. If this is not cleaned up, it can impact AD DS replication, as well as the Distributed File System (DFS) replication.

You can perform metadata cleanup by using Active Directory Users and Computers and Active Directory Sites and Services. You can also use the NtdsUtil.exe command line tool.

USING GRAPHICAL TOOLS

Use the following procedure to perform AD DS metadata cleanup by using graphical tools:

1. On a domain controller, in Server Manager, click Tools, and then click Active Directory Users And Computers.
2. Navigate to the Domain Controllers folder, right-click the domain controller that you previously removed from the domain, and then click Delete. Click Yes to confirm the operation.
3. In the Deleting Domain Controller dialog box, shown in Figure 2-19, select the Delete This Domain Controller anyway check box, and then click Delete.

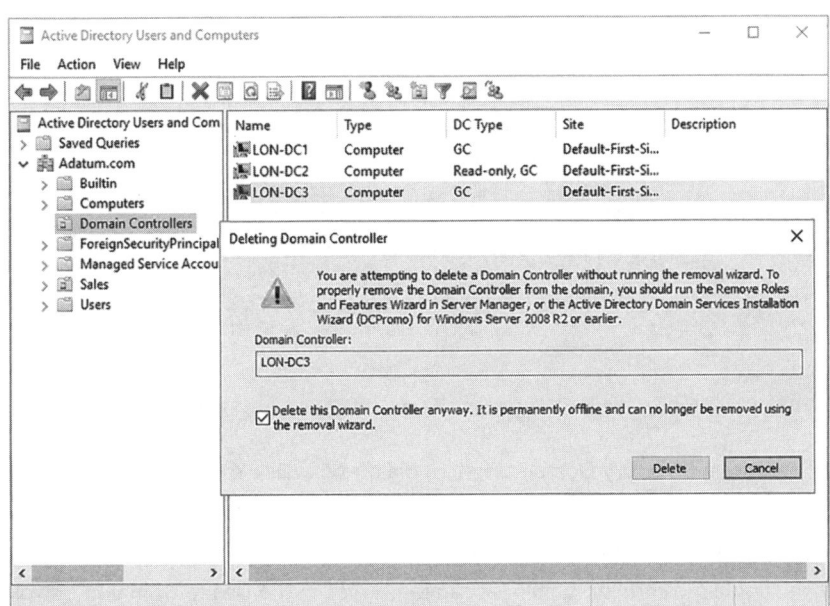

FIGURE 2-19 Forcibly removing a domain controller

4. If the domain controller is a global catalog server, click Yes to confirm deletion.

5. If the domain controller that you removed holds one or more operations master roles, you must move the roles to an online domain controller. Click OK to move the roles to the suggested domain controller. You cannot use a different domain controller from the one suggested by the deletion process. If you want to use a different domain controller to host the operations master roles, move them after you complete the metadata cleanup process. You can read more about transferring operations master roles in Skill 1.1: Install and configure domain controllers, in the Transfer and seize operations master roles section.

6. In Server Manager, click Tools, and then click Active Directory Sites And Services.

7. Navigate to the site object that contains your removed domain controller. Expand the Servers folder, and locate the server that you removed.

8. Select the NTDS Settings. Right-click the NTDS Settings node, and then click Delete, as shown in Figure 2-20.

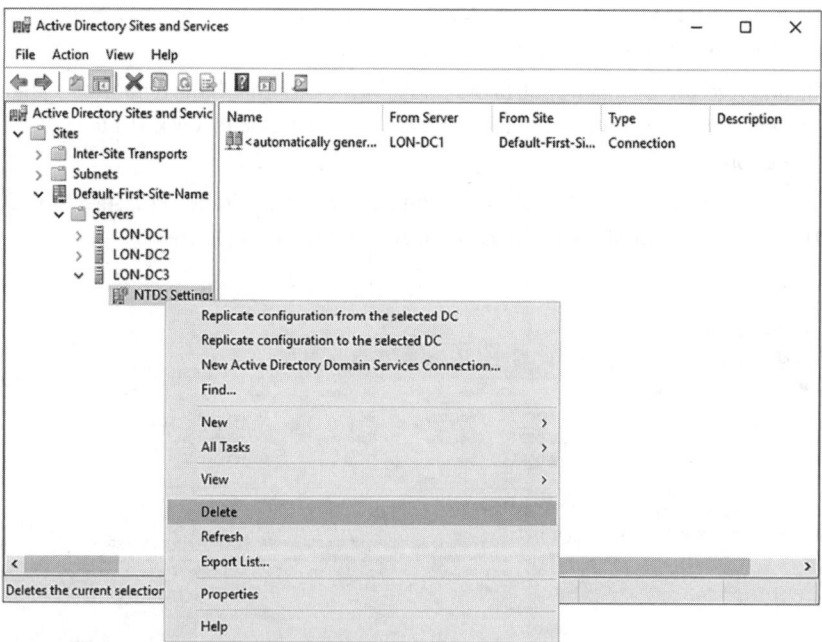

FIGURE 2-20 Deleting the NTDS Settings object

9. In the Active Directory Domain Services dialog box, click Yes to confirm deletion.

10. In the Deleting Domain Controller dialog box, select the Delete This Domain Controller Anyway check box, and then click Delete.

11. If the domain controller is a global catalog server, in the Delete Domain Controller dialog box, click Yes.

12. If the domain controller that you removed holds one or more operations master roles, you must move the roles to an online domain controller. Click OK to move the roles to the suggested domain controller. You cannot use a different domain controller from the one suggested by the deletion process. If you want to use a different domain controller to host the operations master roles, move them after you complete the metadata cleanup process.

13. Finally, in the navigation console, right-click the domain controller that was forcibly removed, and then click Delete. Click Yes to confirm the operation.

USING NTDSUTIL.EXE

You can also use the NtdsUtil.exe command line tool at an elevated command prompt to complete the preceding task. During this process, you must select the target domain controller by first selecting its domain and site. Use the following procedure to complete the task:

1. Run the NtdsUtil.exe command.
2. Run the following commands in order, as shown in Figure 2-21:
   - Metadata cleanup
   - Connections
   - Connect to server <server-name>
     (where <server-name> is an online domain controller)
   - Quit
   - Select Operation Target
   - List domains
   - Select Domain X
     (where X is the domain that contains the domain controller you forcibly removed)
   - List sites
   - Select Site Y
     (where Y is the site that contains the domain controller you forcibly removed)
   - List servers in site
   - Select Server Z
     (where Z is the offline domain controller you want to remove)
   - Quit
   - Remove selected server
   - In the Server Remove Confirmation Dialog window, click Yes to complete the process.
   - Quit

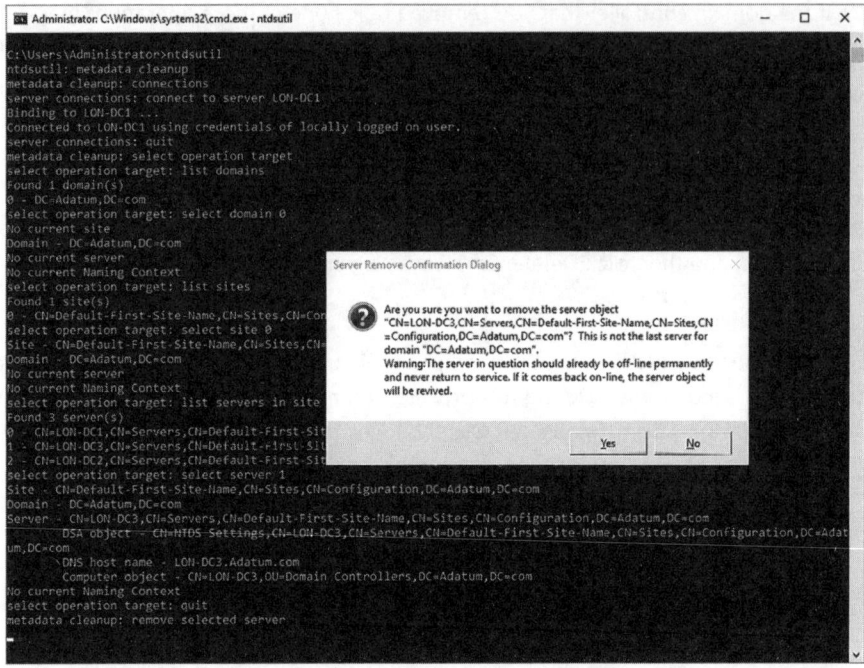

FIGURE 2-21 Using NtdsUtil.exe to forcibly remove a domain controller

> **NEED MORE REVIEW?** **CLEAN UP SERVER METADATA**
>
> To review further details about AD DS metadata cleanup, refer to the Microsoft TechNet website at *https://technet.microsoft.com/library/cc816907(v=ws.10).aspx*.

Active Directory backup and recovery

AD DS is a critical service, and as such, it is important that you know how to protect it from data loss and corruption. You can help to protect AD DS by implementing the Active Directory recycle bin, and by implementing a suitable backup and recovery procedure.

Configure and restore objects by using the Active Directory Recycle Bin

The first line of protection against data loss in AD DS is the Active Directory Recycle Bin. To enable the Active Directory Recycle Bin, in the Active Directory Administrative Centre, shown in Figure 2-22, in the Tasks list, click Enable Recycle Bin. You can also use the Windows PowerShell `Enable-ADOptionalFeature` cmdlet.

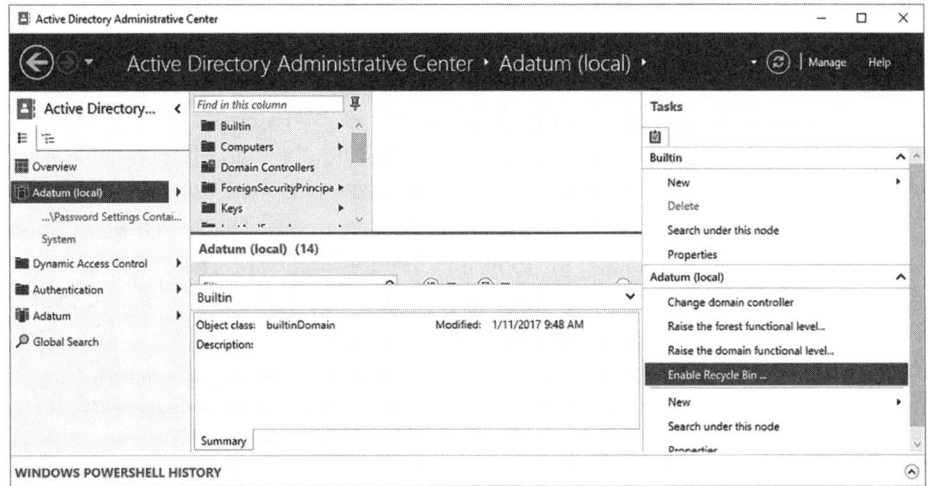

FIGURE 2-22 Enabling the Active Directory Recycle Bin

> **EXAM TIP**
>
> Once you enable the Active Directory Recycle Bin, you cannot disable it.

After you have enabled the Active Directory Recycle Bin, you see a Deleted Objects container in the Active Directory Administrative Center. When you delete AD DS objects, they are stored in the Deleted Objects folder, shown in Figure 2-23.

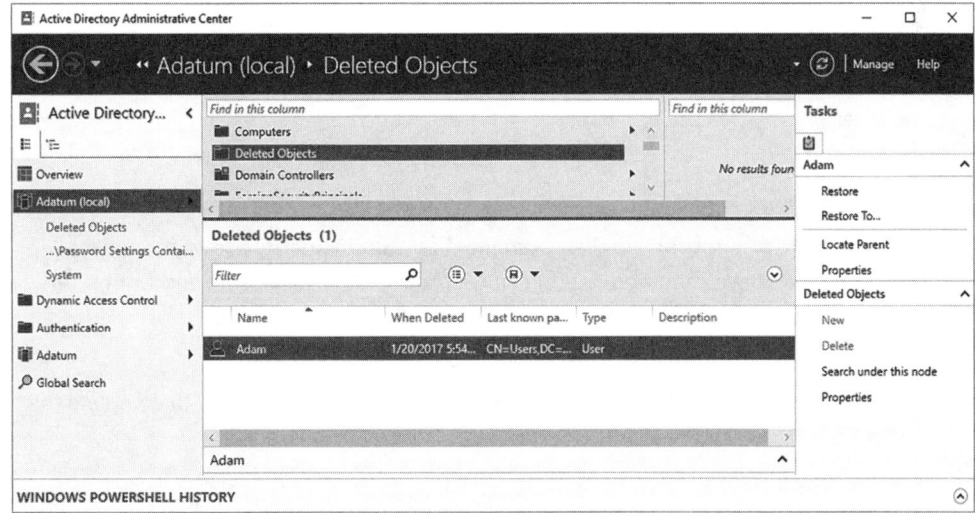

FIGURE 2-23 Viewing deleted objects in the Active Directory Recycle Bin

PERFORM OBJECT AND CONTAINER RECOVERY

To recover a deleted object, in the Deleted Objects folder, right-click a deleted object and then click Restore or Restore To. Choosing Restore enables you to recover the object to its original location in AD DS. Using the Restore To option allows you to specify an alternative location for the object. When you recover a deleted object from the Active Directory Recycle Bin, all the object's attributes are restored, including group memberships and access rights.

By default, deleted objects are recoverable for 180 days after their deletion. However, you can reconfigure this value by changing the tombstoneLifetime and msDS-DeletedObjectLifetime values using Windows PowerShell. For example, to change the recoverable period to 30 days in the Adatum.com domain, run the following two commands:

```
Set-ADObject -Identity "CN=Directory Service,CN=Windows NT,CN=Services,CN=Configur
ation,DC=Adatum,DC=com" -Partition "CN=Configuration,DC=Adatum,DC=com" -Replace:@
{"tombstoneLifetime" = 30}

Set-ADObject -Identity "CN=Directory Service,CN=Windows NT,CN=Services,CN=Configurati
on,DC=Adatum,DC=com" -Partition "CN=Configuration,DC=Adatum,DC=com" -Replace:@{"msDS-
DeletedObjectLifetime" = 30}
```

Configure Active Directory snapshots

An Active Directory snapshot is a copy of the state of AD DS at a given point. You can create snapshots by using the NtdsUtil.exe command line tool using the following procedure:

1. Open an elevated command prompt on a domain controller.
2. Run NtdsUtil.exe and then run the following commands, in this order, to complete the process:
   - Activate instance NTDS
   - Snapshot
   - Create
   - List all
   - Quit

After you create a snapshot, you can examine it by using NtdsUtil.exe to mount the snapshot. Once you have mounted it, you can use Active Directory Users and Computers to view the snapshot. To mount a snapshot, use the following procedure:

1. Open an elevated command prompt on a domain controller.
2. Run NtdsUtil.exe and then run the following commands, in this order, to complete the process:
   - Activate instance NTDS
   - Snapshot
   - List all

- Mount <GUID>

  (where <GUID> is the unique identity of the snapshot you want to mount)
- Quit
- Quit

3. At the elevated command prompt, run the following command:
   - dsamain -dbpath c:\$snap_datetime_volumec$\windows\ntds\ntds.dit -ldapport 50000

Leave the dsamain.exe command running and complete the next procedure to view a snapshot:

1. From Server Manager, open Active Directory Users And Computers.
2. Right-click the root node, and then click Change Domain Controller.
3. In the Change Directory Server dialog box, click <Type A Directory Server Name[:port] here>.
4. Type the name of the domain controller followed by the port number you specified earlier. For example, type LON-DC1:50000, and then press Enter, and then click OK.

You can now view the mounted snapshot. When you have finished examining the snapshot, use the NtdsUtil.exe command to unmount the snapshot:

1. In NtdsUtil.exe, run the following commands:
   - Activate instance NTDS
   - Snapshot
   - Unmount <GUID>
   - Quit
   - Quit

Back up Active Directory and SYSVOL

Although useful, you cannot rely on the Active Directory Recycle Bin or AD DS snapshots as a means of providing for AD DS recovery. Also, neither of these methods can help protect the data stored in SYSVOL.

> **EXAM TIP**
>
> SYSVOL is a folder maintained by all domain controllers in your forest and contains scripts and Group Policy related files.

To provide protection against data loss or corruption of AD DS, you should consider implementing a backup and recovery solution. You can use the Windows Server Backup feature to provide this solution.

Windows Server Backup consists of a command line tool, Wbadmin.exe, and a graphical console, which you can use to backup, and if necessary, restore AD DS.

To install the Windows Server Backup feature, you can use Server Manager, as shown in Figure 2-24.

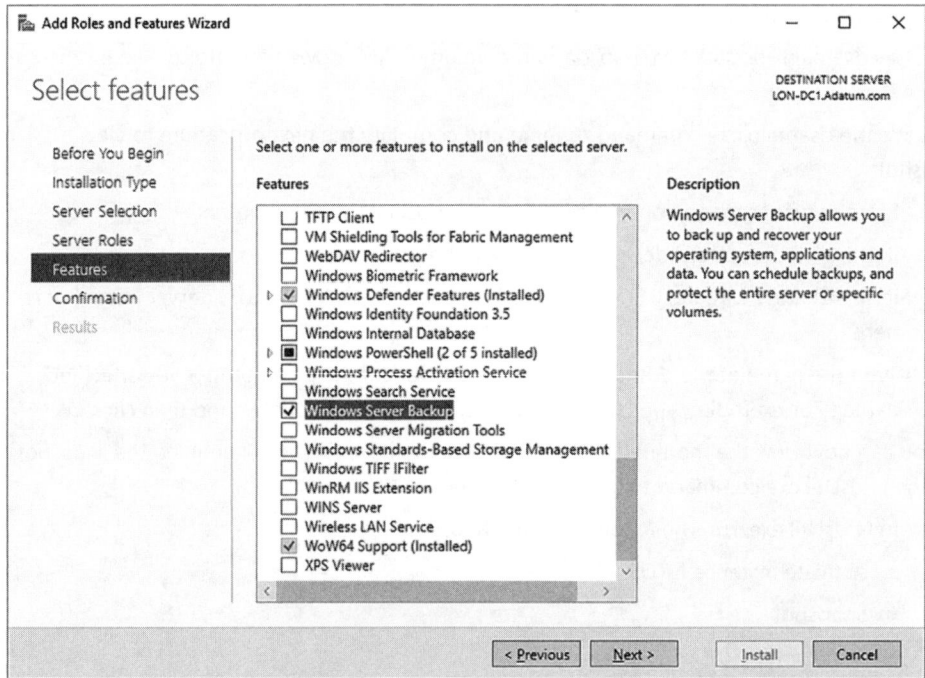

FIGURE 2-24 Installing Windows Server Backup

Windows Server Backup enables you to perform the following types of backup:

- **Bare Metal Recovery** In the event of total server failure, perhaps following the loss of a physical hard disk, you can use a bare metal recovery backup to completely recover a server to the point when the backup was performed.
- **System State** The system state consists of the server's configuration, including the roles and features installed. This includes the AD DS database and SYSVOL content.
- **Selected Volumes** Allows you to perform a backup of specific folders, or even files.

After installing the Windows Server Backup feature, you can use Windows Server Backup to back up AD DS using the following procedure.

1. On your domain controller, click Start, point to Windows Accessories, and then click Windows Server Backup.
2. In Windows Server Backup, in the navigation pane, right-click Local Backup, and then click Backup Once.
3. In the Backup Once Wizard, on the Backup Options page, click Different Options, and click Next.
4. On the Select Backup Configuration page, click Custom, and then click Next.
5. On the Select Items For Backup page, click Add Items.
6. In the Select Items dialog box, select the System State check box, as shown in Figure 2-25, and then click OK.

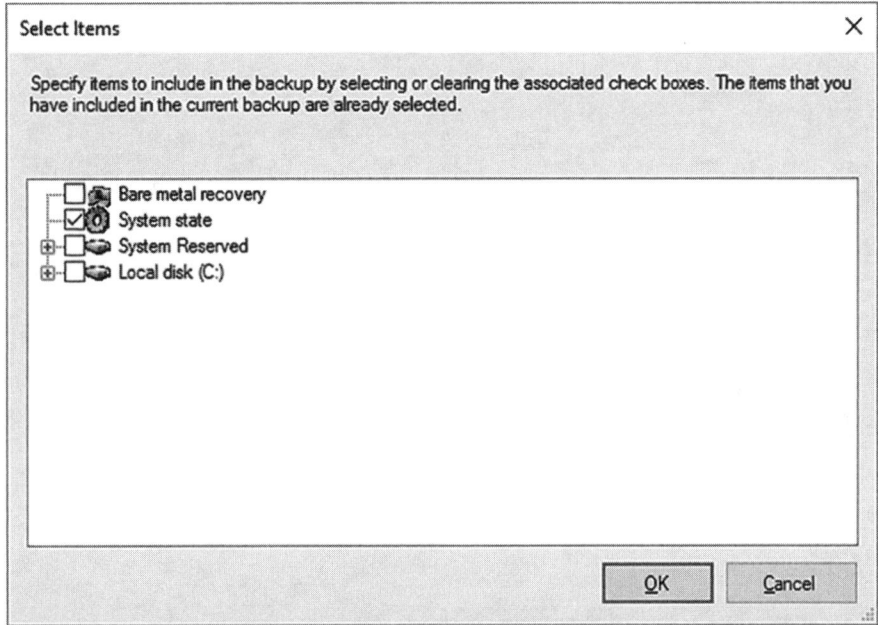

FIGURE 2-25 Selecting the items to backup

7. On the Select Items For Backup page, shown in Figure 2-26, click Next.

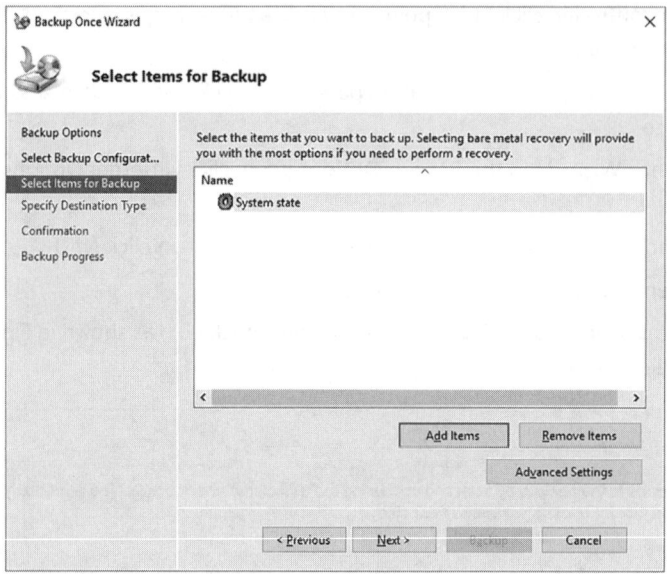

FIGURE 2-26 Selecting System State for backup

8. On the Specify Destination Type page, select the destination. Choose between Local drives and Remote Shared folder. Click Next.

9. If you selected a remote folder, on the Specify Remote Folder page, in the Location box, type the UNC name to the shared folder that you want to use as a backup target, as shown in Figure 2-27.

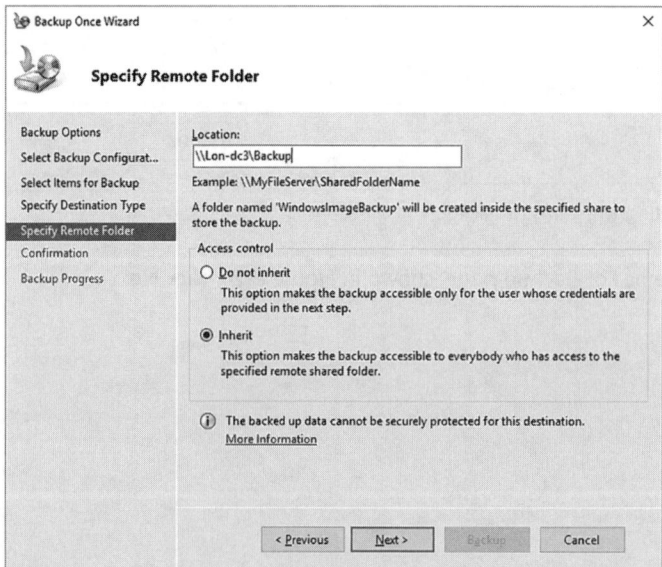

FIGURE 2-27 Specifying the backup target

10. In the Access Control section, click either Do Not Inherit or Inherit. This setting controls who has access to the target backup files. If you want to limit access to the user that performs the backup, click Do Not Inherit, and then click Next. Otherwise, to enable the backup to be accessible by everyone with permissions on the remote folder, click Inherit, and then click Next.
11. On the Confirmation page, click Backup.

> **NEED MORE REVIEW?** **WBADMIN**
>
> To find out about using Wbadmin.exe command line backup and restore options, refer to the Microsoft TechNet website at *https://technet.microsoft.com/library/cc754015(v=ws.11).aspx*.

Perform Active Directory restore

Depending upon the situation, the way that you recover your AD DS varies. For example, if a domain controller becomes unavailable, but you have one or more other domain controllers for the same domain, you can simply remove the domain controller, cleanup the metadata, and deploy a new domain controller to replace the failed one.

However, you might decide that you would prefer to restore the AD DS on a domain controller rather than replace the server unit; perhaps because it contains other apps, services, or data that you cannot easily replace. Or perhaps because you just need to recover a few deleted objects. In this situation, you can perform an AD DS restore operation.

When you restore AD DS, it is important to consider the nature of the database; it is a multimaster database, which means that even while one domain controller is offline, changes can still take place on other instances of the database on other domain controllers. If you simply restore the AD DS database to a point in time when you last performed a backup, then that point in time is overwritten by AD DS replication from other domain controllers when the restore operation is completed. This might be desirable; after all, if there have been changes since the last backup, typically, you would want to include them.

However, if you are attempting to restore only a part of your AD DS, you don't want to overwrite it with replicated changes. For example, rather than dealing with a failed domain controller, you attempt to recover objects that were accidentally deleted. If you performed a backup operation, and later inadvertently deleted an AD DS object, that deletion would be replicated after your restore operation.

To help mitigate this issue, you can perform either nonauthoritative restore or authoritative restore operations. Using an authoritative restore means that the restored data is not overwritten by replicated changes.

> **EXAM TIP**
>
> If you enabled the Active Directory Recycle Bin, you can recover objects from the Deleted Objects folder as an alternative to using an authoritative restore.

To perform a nonauthoritative AD DS restore operation, start your domain controller in DSRM. Then, open the Windows Server Backup console and use the Restore Wizard to restore the System State data from a previous backup. This is a straightforward procedure. Then start your domain controller normally. Changes made since the last backup are now replicated to the domain controller.

To perform an authoritative AD DS restore operation, start the domain controller in DSRM, restore the System State, and then open an elevated command prompt. At the command prompt, run the NtdsUtil.exe command. Then run the following commands:

- Authoritative restore
- Restore object <object DN>

The object's DN will look something like this: CN=Adam ,OU=Sales,DC=adatum,DC=com. Restart your domain controller normally. If you want to mark an entire OU as authoritative, at the NtdsUtil.exe prompt, run the following commands:

- Authoritative restore
- Restore subtree <object DN>

The object(s) marked as authoritative are not overwritten, and are replicated from the restored domain controller throughout your forest.

Manage Read Only Domain Controllers

An RODC is a domain controller that contains a read only copy of AD DS. You can use RODCs to enable you to deploy domain controllers in offices were physical security cannot be guaranteed.

Deploying RODCs is covered in Chapter 1: Install and configure Active Directory Domain Services, Skill 1.1: Install and configure domain controllers, in the Install and configure an RODC section.

Configure Password Replication Policy for RODC

By default, RODCs do not store sensitive password-related information. Consequently, when a user signs in, the RODC forwards the sign in request to a writeable domain controller within your organization.

However, to improve usability, you can define that specific user and computer accounts can be cached on the RODC, enabling local authentication to occur. You do this by defining an RODC password replication policy. Generally, you would only add the users and computers that are in the same local site as the RODC to the replication policy.

To configure a replication policy for an RODC, you use two Domain Local security groups:

- **Allowed RODC Password Replication Group** Add user or computers to this group to enable their passwords to be cached on the RODC.
- **Denied RODC Password Replication Group** Add user or computers to this group to prevent their passwords to be cached on the RODC.

EXAM TIP

In addition, the following local groups are also denied from replicating passwords: Administrators, Server Operators, Backup Operators, and Account Operators.

These groups are automatically created when you deploy an RODC and enable you to configure the password replication policy on all RODCs. But if you have multiple branch offices, and therefore multiple RODCs, it is more secure to configure a separate group for each RODC for allowed password replication. In this instance, remove the Allowed RODC Password Replication Group, and add a group that you manually created, and then add the required members for that branch. Use the following procedure to complete this task:

1. In Active Directory Users and Computers, create a global security group that contains users and computers that have permissions.
2. Locate the Domain Controllers OU.
3. Right-click your RODC, and click Properties.
4. In the Properties dialog box, on the Password Replication Policy tab, shown in Figure 2-28, remove the Allowed RODC Password Replication Group.

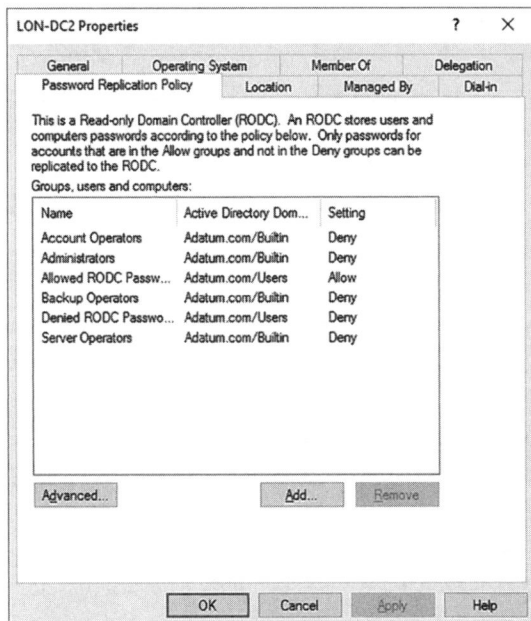

FIGURE 2-28 Configuring an RODC password replication policy

5. Click Add, and as shown in Figure 2-29, click Allow Passwords For The Account To Replicate To This RODC for the account you are adding to the password replication policy, and then click OK.

FIGURE 2-29 Specifying the Allow policy

6. In the Select Users, Computers, Service Accounts, or Groups dialog box, enter the group name whose members' passwords are to be replicated to this RODC, and then click OK twice.

7. Add the required users and computers to the group you just added.

You can complete a similar procedure to modify the server specific deny replication policy. Remove the Denied RODC Password Replication Group from the Password Replication Policy, and add your own group with members whose passwords won't be replicated to the target RODC.

You can use the Advanced view on the Password Replication Policy tab to view which user or computer passwords are replicated to the RODC. You can also determine the effective policy for a selected user or computer. Use the following procedure:

1. In Active Directory Users and Computers, in the Domain Controllers OU, right-click your RODC, and click Properties.

2. On the Password Replication Policy tab, click Advanced.

3. In the Advanced Password Replication Policy dialog box, on the Policy Usage tab, shown in Figure 2-30, in the Display Users And Computers That Meet The Following Criteria list, click:

- **Accounts Whose Passwords Are Stored On This Read-Only Domain Controller**   Enables you to see which users and computers have had their passwords cached on the RODC.

- **Accounts That Have Been Authenticated To This Read-Only Domain Controller**   Enables you to see which users and computers have signed in using the RODC.

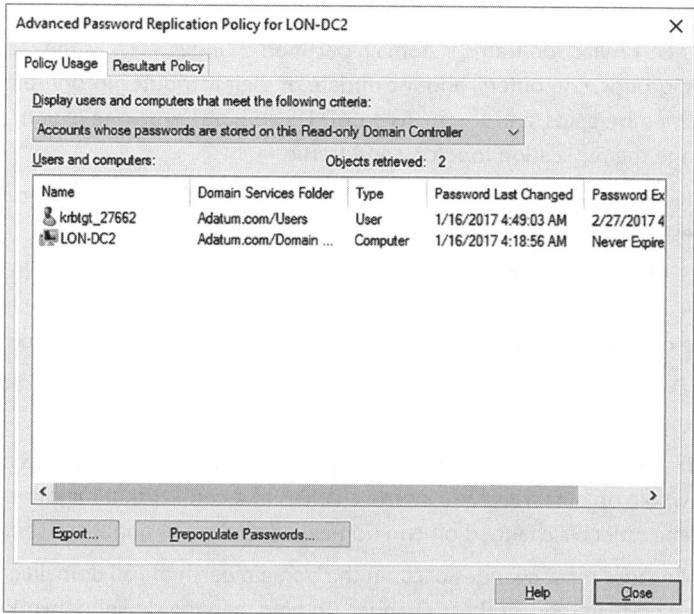

FIGURE 2-30 Viewing the advanced password replication policy settings

4. Use the Prepopulate Passwords button to retrieve passwords for listed users. This can help reduce sign in time for configured users.
5. On the Resultant Policy tab, add users or computers to determine what the resultant password policy is for the selected objects. This is useful when you have multiple Allow or Deny groups configured on the Password Replication Policy tab.

Managing AD DS replication

AD DS is a database that resides on Windows Server domain controllers and consists of several partitions. These are:

- **Schema** A forest-level partition that rarely changes and holds the forest schema.
- **Configuration** A forest-level partition that also changes rarely and contains the configuration data for the forest.
- **Domain** A domain-wide partition that changes frequently, and a writeable copy of the partition is stored on all domain controllers.

EXAM TIP
You can also create and configure application partitions. These store non-domain data, such as DNS zone information, and can be configured to replicate to specified domain controllers.

Changes in the schema and configuration partitions are infrequent. Consequently, the significant bulk of AD DS replication traffic is domain partition changes, such as the creation of new objects (users, groups, computers) and the update of their attributes (properties such as passwords, group memberships, and so on). As an AD DS administrator, one of your roles is to monitor and manage the replication topology and traffic.

AD DS replication is the process of synchronizing the various copies of the AD DS database throughout your forest. This replication has the following characteristics:

- **Multimaster** With the exception of certain specific elements, AD DS is a multimaster database. In essence, this means all copies are writable and can be updated. This offers the advantage of removing single points of failure, and can also improve performance.
- **Pull-based** Domain controllers pull changes from their replication partners rather than push changes.
- **Fine-grained** To avoid replication conflicts, replication is based on attributes of objects and not whole objects. This reduces the chances of a conflict that might otherwise occur if the same object is changed on two domain controllers at about the same time.
- **Site-aware** Because most changes occur in the domain partition, all domain controllers within a domain request these changes. To help manage slower network links between locations, you can configure AD DS sites, and then configure how AD DS replication is handled between sites. This is known as intersite replication.
- **Automatically generated topology** Windows Server generates the AD DS replication topology automatically, creating a resilient and efficient infrastructure. In many circumstances, you might not need to manually reconfigure the topology.

When discussing AD DS replication, it is helpful to keep in mind that there are two types of replication:

- **Intrasite** This occurs between domain controllers in the same AD DS site. Windows Server manages AD DS replication on the assumption that high-speed persistent networks connect domain controllers within a site. Intrasite replication usually requires little manual intervention because Windows Server efficiently manages it automatically. However, you must devise and implement a suitable AD DS site infrastructure and place domain controllers in the appropriate site.
- **Intersite** This occurs between domain controllers in different AD DS sites. Windows Server manages replication on the assumption that domain controllers might not be connected by persistent high-speed networks. You have more manual control over the replication process, including the interval and schedule.

> ***NEED MORE REVIEW?* ACTIVE DIRECTORY REPLICATION**
>
> To review further details about how AD DS replication works, refer to the Microsoft TechNet website at *https://technet.microsoft.com/library/cc961788.aspx*.

Monitor and manage replication

Intrasite replication consists of a network of connection objects between domain controllers, which are replication partners. Connection objects are one-way, pull-based replication pathways between one domain controller and its replication partner.

A component called the knowledge consistency checker (KCC) generates an optimized topology for replication by creating these connection objects automatically. This topology contains sufficient connection objects to create a maximum of three hops between any two domain controllers, thereby reducing delays in the propagation of replication data.

If you deploy an additional domain controller in a site, or conversely, remove one, the knowledge consistency checker regenerates the replication topology to account for the change.

> **EXAM TIP**
>
> The knowledge consistency checker runs periodically—every 15 minutes by default.

Figure 2-31 shows the connection objects in the Default-First-Site-Name site in the Adatum.com domain.

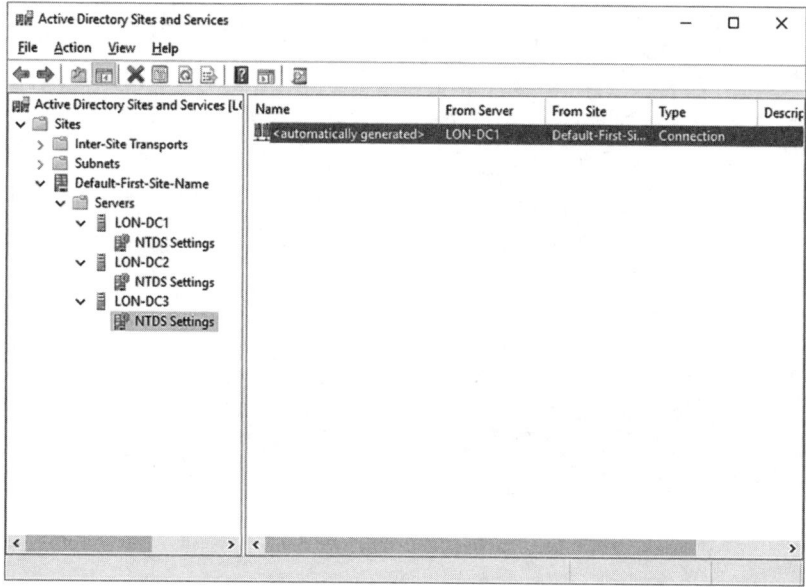

FIGURE 2-31 Viewing a connection object

Although you can manually create persistent connection objects within a site if you want, this is not usually necessary and not recommended; this is because the knowledge consistency checker does not evaluate manually created connection objects. It is more likely that you might need to create and configure connection objects to manage intersite replication. This is discussed in Skill 2.3: Configure Active Directory in a complex enterprise environment, in the Configure AD DS sites and subnets section.

You can view and manage AD DS replication by using the Active Directory Sites and Services tool, as shown in Figure 2-31. For example, you can force replication over a connection object between two domain controllers by using the following procedure:

1. In Active Directory Sites and Services, navigate to the server object that you want to update.
2. Under the server object, click the NTDS Settings node, and in the details pane, right-click the <automatically generated> object.
3. Click Replicate Now on the context menu. This pulls changes from the designated replication partner.

You can also use Repadmin.exe and the DcDiag.exe command-line tools:

- **Repadmin**   Use this tool to check the status of replication on your domain controllers or to reconfigure the replication topology:
    - Display the replication partners for a domain controller by using `repadmin /showrepl DC_LIST`, as shown in Figure 2-32. Replace DC_LIST with the names of your domain controller(s). You can use an asterisk as a wildcard.

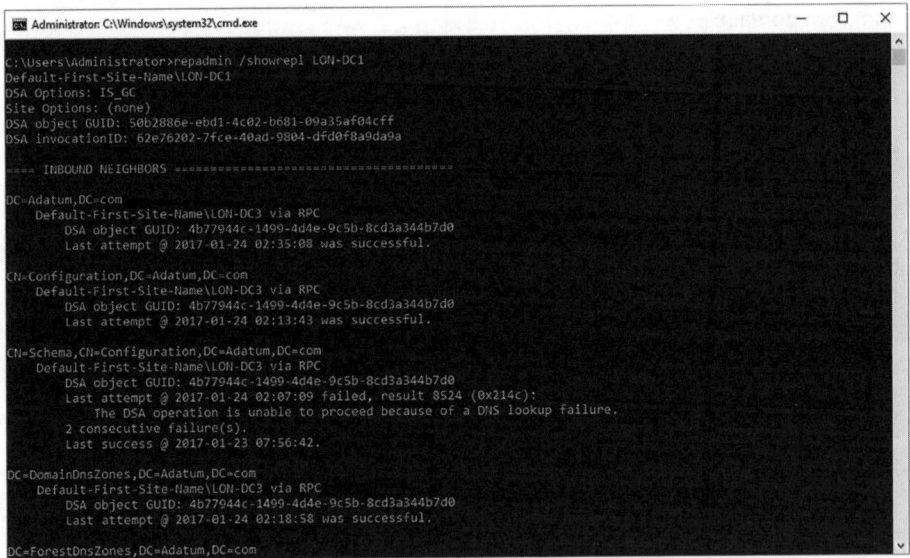

FIGURE 2-32 Running Repadmin

- Display connection objects for a domain controller by using `repadmin /showconn DC_LIST`.
- Display metadata about an object by using `repadmin /showobjmeta DC_LIST Object`. Replace object with the AD DS distinguished name or GUID of your object.
- Launch the knowledge consistency checker by using `repadmin /kcc`.

- Force replication between partners by using `repadmin /replicate Destination_DC_LIST Source_DC_Name Naming_Context`.
- Synchronize a domain controller with all replication partners by using `repadmin /syncall DC/A /e`.

> **NEED MORE REVIEW? REPADMIN SYNTAX**
>
> To review further details about using Repadmin.exe, refer to the Microsoft TechNet website at *https://technet.microsoft.com/library/cc736571(v=ws.10).aspx*.

- **DcDiag** Use Dcdiag.exe to perform tests against your AD DS replication topology, as shown in Figure 2-33. You can also use several parameters to run specific tests, including: FrsEvent, DFSREvent, Intersite, KccEvent, Replications, Topology, and VerifyReplicas.
- Use with the following parameters to perform.

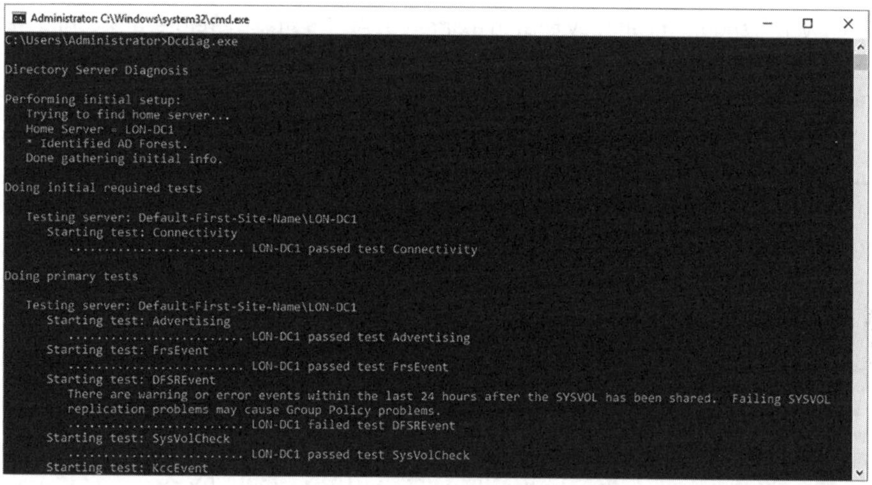

FIGURE 2-33 Running Dcdiag

> **NEED MORE REVIEW? DCDIAG.EXE**
>
> To review further details about using Dcdiag.exe, refer to the Microsoft TechNet website at *https://technet.microsoft.com/library/cc731968(v=ws.11).aspx*.

You can also use a number of Windows PowerShell cmdlets, as shown in 2, to monitor and manage replication in Windows Server 2016.

TABLE 2-2 Windows PowerShell cmdlets for AD DS replication

Cmdlet	Explanation
Get-ADReplicationConnection	Provides information about a specified AD DS replication connection(s) based on filters that you specify
Get-ADReplicationFailure	Provides a description of a replication failure
Get-ADReplicationPartnerMetadata	Provides replication metadata from one or more replication partners
Get-ADReplicationSite	Provides information about a specified site(s) based on applied filters
Get-ADReplicationSiteLink	Provides information about a specified site link(s) based on applied filters
Get-ADReplicationSiteLinkBridge	Provides information about a specified site link bridge(s) based on applied filters
Get-ADReplicationSubnet	Provides information about a specified subnet(s) based on applied filters

Configure replication to RODCs

RODCs, by their nature, exist in different physical locations from writable domain controllers. Typically, this should mean they exist in a different AD DS site. Therefore, any configuration of RODC replication is intersite rather than intrasite. This requires that you have correctly configured the site objects in AD DS and moved the domain controllers to the appropriate site(s).

The knowledge consistency checker automatically creates connection objects for RODCs. But if you are experiencing problems, use the Repadmin.exe command-line tool to force the knowledge consistency checker to regenerate the topology. Use the following high-level procedure:

1. Add the site with the RODC to a site link and ensure that the selected site link also contains a site with a writable domain controller.
2. Force replication of the configuration partition to the RODC by using `Repadmin.exe`.
3. Regenerate the replication topology by using `repadmin /kcc` on the RODC.

> **NEED MORE REVIEW? REESTABLISHING REPLICATION FOR AN RODC**
>
> To review further details about using configuring AD DS replication for an RODC, refer to the Microsoft TechNet website at *https://technet.microsoft.com/library/dd736126(v=ws.10).aspx*.

Upgrade SYSVOL replication to Distributed File System Replication

SYSVOL folders reside in the %SystemRoot%\SYSVOL folder on all domain controllers and contain logon scripts and Group Policy Templates. In earlier versions of Windows Server, AD DS uses the File Replication Service (FRS) to synchronize the contents of the SYSVOL folder among domain controllers.

In Windows Server 2008 and newer, you use DFS Replication (DFSR) to manage SYSVOL replication, replacing the FRS replication infrastructure. DFSR provides for a more efficient and reliable means to replicate SYSVOL.

If you upgraded your domain controllers from Windows Server 2003, it is possible that they might still be using FRS to replicate SYSVOL. You can check this by using the Dfsrmig.exe command-line tool as follows:

1. Open an elevated command prompt.
2. Run the `Dfsrmig.exe /GetGlobalState` command.

If the returned message is `Current DFSR global status: 'Eliminated'`, your SYSVOL replication is already using DFSR. If you receive the message `DFSR migration has not yet initialized`, then you should migrate to DFSR. During the migration, the configuration moves through four phases, or states:

- **State 0** This is the start state. FRS is being used to replicate SYSVOL.
- **State 1** The prepared state. FRS continues to replicate SYSVOL, however, the local DFSR service creates a replicated copy of SYSVOL.
- **State 2** The redirected state. DFSR begins to replicate SYSVOL, and FRS maintains only a local replica of SYSVOL.
- **State 3** The eliminated state. FRS is no longer used, and DFSR provides all SYSVOL replication.

Use the following procedure to migrate SYSVOL replication to DFSR:

1. At the command prompt, run `dfsrmig /setglobalstate 1`. Then run the `Dfsrmig.exe /GetMigrationState` command to verify all domain controllers have reached the prepared state.
2. At the command prompt, run `dfsrmig /setglobalstate 2`. Then run the `Dfsrmig.exe /GetMigrationState` command to verify all domain controllers have reached the redirected state.
3. At the command prompt, run `dfsrmig /setglobalstate 3`. Then run the `Dfsrmig.exe /GetMigrationState` command to verify all domain controllers have reached the eliminated state.
4. On each domain controller, open the Services console and verify that the File Replication Service is disabled.

> **NEED MORE REVIEW? DFSRMIG.EXE**
>
> To review further details about using the Dfsrmig.exe command-line tool, refer to the Microsoft TechNet website at *https://technet.microsoft.com/library/dd641227(v=ws.11).aspx*.

Skill 2.3: Configure Active Directory in a complex enterprise environment

In large networked environments, it is possible that using a single AD DS domain is undesirable. It is also possible that a single AD DS forest is not appropriate. As a result, it is important that you know how and when to configure multiple AD DS forests and domains, and where necessary, create the required trust relationships between them.

As your network grows and spans multiple locations, it is necessary to configure AD DS sites to help optimize network services, including AD DS replication. Before you create sites, it is also necessary to create subnet objects that map to the physical Internet Protocol (IP) subnets in your network.

> **This section covers how to:**
> - Configure a multi-domain and multi-forest AD DS infrastructure
> - Deploy Windows Server 2016 domain controllers within a preexisting AD DS environment
> - Upgrade existing domains and forests
> - Configure domain and forest functional levels
> - Configure multiple user principal name suffixes
> - Configure trusts
> - Configure AD DS sites and subnets

Configure a multi-domain and multi-forest AD DS infrastructure

Although we discuss forests and domains in Chapter 1, perhaps a quick reminder would be beneficial.

- **Forest** A collection of domains sharing a common schema and bound by automatically generated two-way trust relationships. Generally, using a single forest is desirable for most organizations because it simplifies administration. However, reasons to consider using multiple forests include the requirement to:
  - Provide for complete administrative separation between disparate parts of your organization.
  - Support different object types and attributes in the AD DS schema in different parts of your organization.
- **Domain** A logical administrative containing users, groups, computers, and other objects. Parent-child and trust relationships define your domain structure. A domain does not provide for administrative separation because all domains in a forest have the same forest administrator: the Enterprise Admins universal security group.

- **Tree** A collection of AD DS domains that share a common root domain and have a contiguous namespace. Reasons for using multiple trees include the requirement to support multiple logical namespaces within your organization, perhaps as a result of mergers or acquisitions.

Adding a forest

When you want to deploy a new forest in an existing AD DS environment, you start the process by deploying the first domain controller in that forest. The server computer on which you deploy the new forest is almost certainly a member of a workgroup. You must therefore sign in as a member of the Administrators local security group.

Essentially, the process for deploying an additional forest is identical to creating the first forest. This procedure is discussed in the "Install a new forest" section in Chapter 1, "Install and configure Active Directory Domain Services.".

After you have deployed the new forest, you can configure any required trust relationships between the forests to support your administrative and business needs.

Adding a new domain

Similarly, when you want to create a new domain within your AD DS forest, you start by deploying the first domain controller in that domain, and then choosing the Add A New Domain Controller In A New Domain option in the Deployment Wizard. You must sign in as a member of the forest root Enterprise Admins universal security group to complete this process.

You have two choices when adding a new domain:

- **Child Domain** Creates a subdomain of the specified parent domain. In other words, the new domain is created in the existing domain tree.
- **Tree Domain** Creates a new tree in the same forest. This option is useful when you want to create multiple DNS domain names in your AD DS forest infrastructure to support your organizational needs, but do not need, or want, to separate administrative function as is possible with a separate forest.

These procedures are covered in Chapter 1: Install and configure Active Directory Domain Services, Skill 1.1: Install and configure domain controllers, in the Add A New Domain Controller In A New Domain section. After you have deployed the new domain, you do not need to configure any additional trusts.

Deploy Windows Server 2016 domain controllers within a preexisting AD DS environment

These procedures are covered in Chapter 1: Install and configure Active Directory Domain Services, Skill 1.1: Install and configure domain controllers, in the Add Or Remove A Domain Controller section.

Upgrade existing domains and forests

Upgrading existing domains and forests is covered in Chapter 1: Install and configure Active Directory Domain Services, Skill 1.1: Install and configure domain controllers, in the Upgrade Domain Controllers section.

Configure domain and forest functional levels

Forest and domain functional levels provide new features within your AD DS infrastructure while providing compatibility with important features from earlier versions of Windows Server. When you deploy AD DS, you can select a suitable forest and domain functional level based on your requirements. You can also change the forest and domain functional levels following deployment. The following forest and domain functional levels exist:

- **Forest Functional Level** Determines which forest-level features are available. Also defines the minimum domain functional level for domains in your forest. Select from:
    - Windows Server 2008
    - Windows Server 2008 R2
    - Windows Server 2012
    - Windows Server 2012 R2
    - Windows Server 2016

> ***NEED MORE REVIEW?*** **FEATURES THAT ARE AVAILABLE AT FOREST FUNCTIONAL LEVELS**
>
> To review details about forest functional level features, refer to the Microsoft TechNet website at *https://technet.microsoft.com/library/understanding-active-directory-functional-levels(v=ws.10).aspx#Features that are available at forest functional levels*.

- **Domain Functional Level** Determines the domain-level features available in your domain. Select from:
    - Windows Server 2008
    - Windows Server 2008 R2
    - Windows Server 2012
    - Windows Server 2012 R2
    - Windows Server 2016

> ***NEED MORE REVIEW?*** **FEATURES THAT ARE AVAILABLE AT DOMAIN FUNCTIONAL LEVELS**
>
> To review details about domain functional level features, refer to the Microsoft TechNet website at *https://technet.microsoft.com/library/understanding-active-directory-functional-levels(v=ws.10).aspx#Features that are available at domain functional levels*.

You can raise the forest functional level by using the following procedure:

1. In the Active Directory Domains And Trusts console, in the navigation pane, right-click the Active Directory Domains And Trusts node, and then click Raise Forest Functional Level.
2. In the Raise Forest Functional Level dialog box, the current forest functional level is displayed, as shown in Figure 2-34.
3. In the Select An Available Forest Functional Level list, click the desired level, and then click Raise.

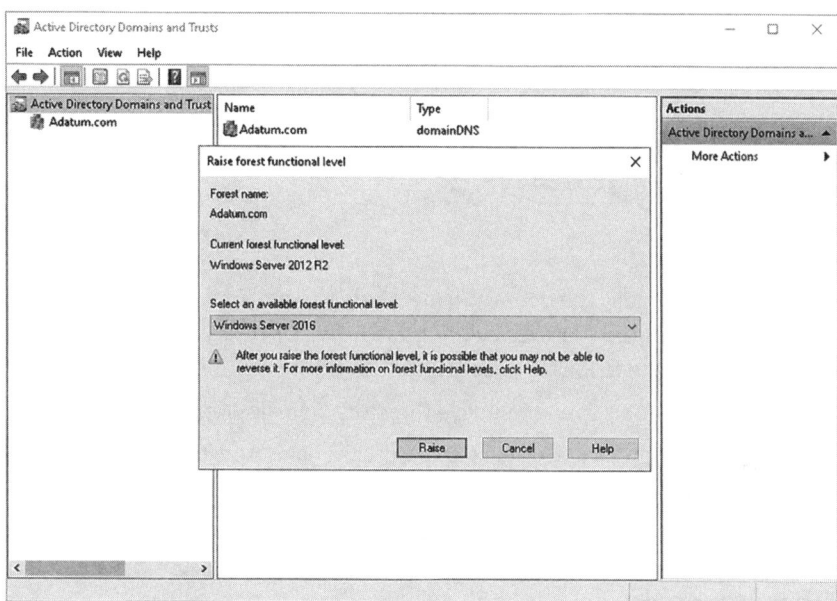

FIGURE 2-34 Viewing the forest functional level

To raise a domain's domain functional level, use the following procedure:

1. In the Active Directory Domains And Trusts console, in the navigation pane, locate and right-click the appropriate AD DS domain, and then click Raise Domain Functional level.
2. In the Raise Domain Functional Level dialog box, the current domain functional level is displayed.
3. In the Select An Available Domain Functional Level list, click the appropriate level, and then click Raise.

Configure multiple user principal name suffixes

User principal name (UPN) suffixes enable you to define the unique forest-wide name for an object, such as a user. For example, when you create a new user account, you define the user's user logon name. This name is combined with the adjacently displayed suffix (@Adatum.com in Figure 2-35) to create a user principal name (UPN); for example, BurkeB@Adatum.com. This UPN must be unique within the AD DS forest.

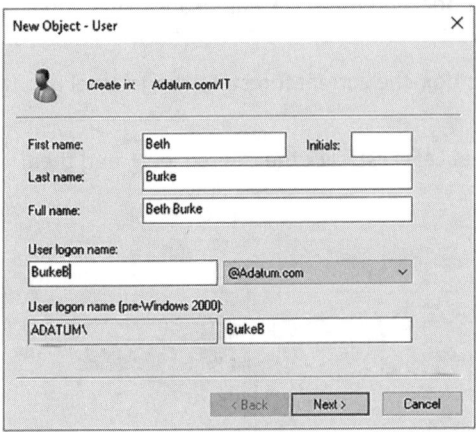

FIGURE 2-35 Adding a user account

The UPN suffix is generally the domain name where you are adding the account. However, you can define additional UPN suffixes by using the Active Directory Domains and Trusts console. To do this, use the following procedure:

1. From Server Manager, open the Active Directory Domains And Trusts console.
2. In the console, right-click the Active Directory Domains And Trusts node in the navigation pane, and then click Properties.
3. In the Active Directory Domains And Trusts [Server name] dialog box, on the UPN Suffixes tab, shown in Figure 2-36, in the Alternative UPN suffixes box, type a new suffix, and then click Add.

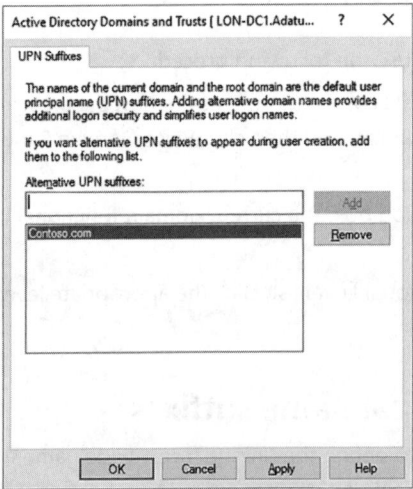

FIGURE 2-36 Adding a UPN suffix

4. After you have added all the suffixes you require, click OK.

Next, you must modify the user accounts that you want to use the new suffix. You can do this using the following procedure:

1. Open Active Directory Users And Computers and locate the accounts that you want to modify.
2. Right-click the accounts, and then click Properties.
3. In the Properties For Multiple Items dialog box, shown in Figure 2-37, on the Account tab, select the UPN suffix check box.

FIGURE 2-37 Assigning the UPN suffix

4. In the UPN suffix list, click the new suffix, and then click OK.

You can also use Windows PowerShell to reconfigure the UPN suffix for multiple accounts by using the get-ADUser and Set-ADUser cmdlets. For example, to change the UPN suffix for all users in the Sales OU in the Adatum.com domain to Sales.Contoso.com, use the following procedure:

1. Open Windows PowerShell on a domain controller.
2. Run the following script:

```
$new_suffix = "Sales.Contoso.com"

$users = Get-ADUser -Filter {UserPrincipalName -like '*'} -SearchBase "OU=Sales,DC=Adatum,DC=Com"

foreach ($user in $users) {

    $userName = $user.UserPrincipalName.Split('@')[0]

    $UPN = $userName + "@" + $new_suffix

        Write-Host $user.Name $user.UserPrincipalName $UPN

    $user | Set-ADUser -UserPrincipalName $UPN }
```

Configure trusts

A trust relationship is a security agreement between two domains in an AD DS forest, between two forests, or between a forest and an external security realm. Trust relationships enable a security principal in one domain, such as a user or computer, to potentially gain access to a resource in another domain; potentially, because in addition to a trust, the security principal must be granted permissions on the resource by the resource-holding domain administrator. In a one-way trust relationship, one party is deemed to be trusting, while the other is said to be trusted. The resource-holding entity is trusting, while the user-holding entity is trusted. In a two-way trust relationship, both parties are both trusting (resource-holding) and trusted (user-holding).

In Windows Server 2016, domains in the same forest are configured automatically with two-way transitive trusts so that, in principle, a user in any domain in the forest has the potential to access a resource anywhere else in the forest. By default, in a multi-domain forest, the following trust types exist:

- **Parent/child**   Two-way transitive trust between a parent domain and its child domain.
- **Tree-root**   Two-way transitive trust between a new AD DS domain tree and the existing AD DS forest root domain.

> **EXAM TIP**
>
> A transitive trust is one that applies through an intermediate security realm. For example, if A trusts B, and B trusts C, A also trusts C.

But you can also create trusts manually to satisfy certain technical or administrative requirements. These are:

- **Forest**   A transitive one-way or two-way trust, depending on configuration, between two AD DS forests. Enables users in one forest (or both forests) to enable resources in the other.
- **External**   A non-transitive one-way or two-way trust, depending on configuration, between your AD DS forest and another AD DS domain, such as an older Windows NT 4.0 domain. Enables users in your forest to access resources in the other domain, and users in the remote forest to access your resources.
- **Realm**   A transitive or non-transitive, one-way or two-way trust, depending on configuration, that enables authentication between your Windows Server AD DS forest and a Kerberos v5 realm based on a non-Windows directory service.
- **Shortcut**   A non-transitive one-way or two-way trust, depending on configuration, between domains in your AD DS forest that can help improve authentication performance. Use shortcut trusts for domains within the same forest but in different AD DS domain trees.

To create trust relationships, you use the Active Directory Domains and Trusts tool. It is important to note that to configure any of these trusts, it must be possible for the two parties in the trust to be able to resolve one another's names; this requires DNS configuration. For example, to configure a forest trust, each domain controller that you use to configure the trust must be able to resolve the SRV records for the remote forest.

Configure forest trusts

To configure a forest trust, use the following procedure:

1. Configure DNS so that domain controllers in each forest can resolve one another's names and SRV records. Create a DNS stub zone (or configure conditional forwarding) for the remote DNS zone.

> **NEED MORE REVIEW?** **ADD A STUB ZONE**
>
> To review further details about adding a DNS stub zone, refer to the Microsoft TechNet website at *https://technet.microsoft.com/library/cc754190(v=ws.11).aspx*.

2. Open the Active Directory Domains And Trusts console on a domain controller in the first AD DS forest.
3. Right-click the forest root domain in the navigation pane, and then click Properties.
4. In the Domain Properties dialog box, click the Trusts tab, shown in Figure 2-38, and then click New Trust.

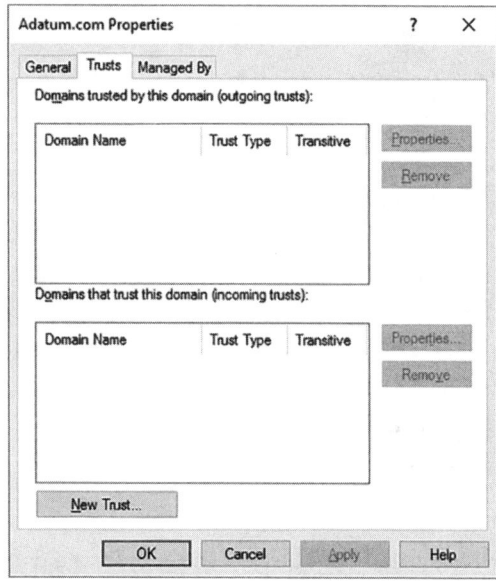

FIGURE 2-38 Viewing the available trusts

5. In the New Trust Wizard, click Next, and then, on the Trust Name page, in the Name box, type the FQDN of the remote forest, as shown in Figure 2-39, and then click Next.

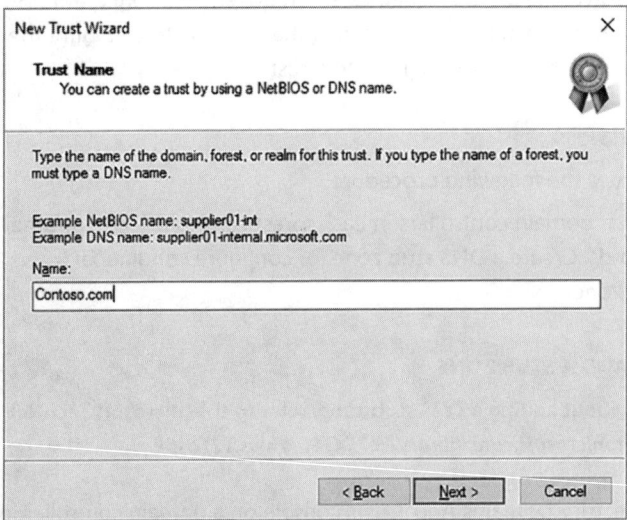

FIGURE 2-39 Defining the remote DNS name

6. On the Trust Type page, shown in Figure 2-40, click Forest trust, and then click Next.

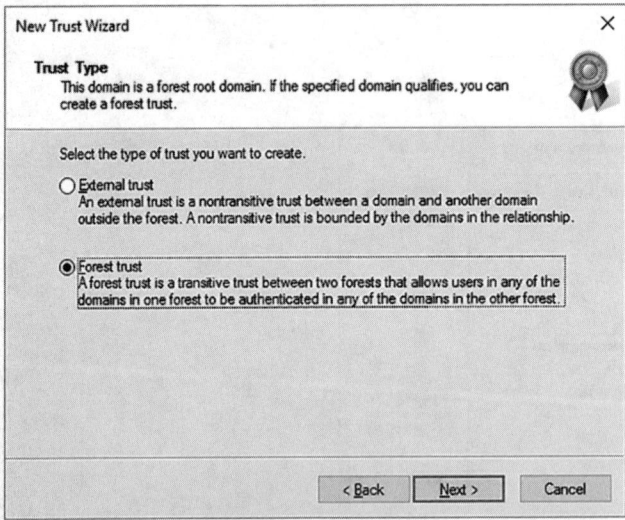

FIGURE 2-40 Specifying the trust type

7. On the Direction Of Trust page, shown in Figure 2-41, select the appropriate direction. Choose between Two-Way, One-Way Incoming, and One-Way Outgoing. For example, click Two-Way, and then click Next.

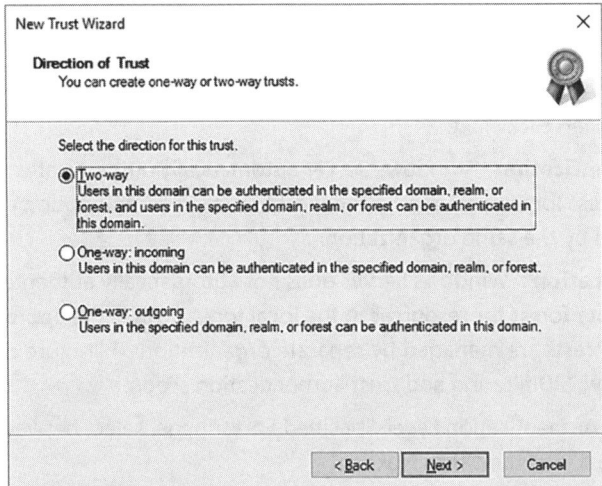

FIGURE 2-41 Defining the trust direction

8. On the Sides Of Trust page, shown in Figure 2-42, click Both This Domain And The Specified Domain, and then click Next.

EXAM TIP

To configure the trust using a single step, you must provide credentials with the necessary privilege in the remote forest. That is, a user that belongs to the remote Enterprise Admins universal security group. If you don't have these credentials, then you must ask the administrator in the remote forest to complete their end of the configuration of the forest trust by repeating this process.

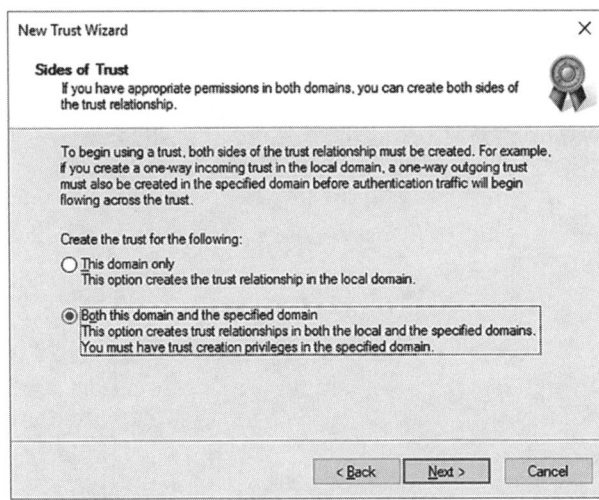

FIGURE 2-42 Defining whether to configure both sides of the trust

9. On the User Name And Password page, enter the credentials required to configure the trust in the remote forest, and then click Next.
10. On the Outgoing Trust Authentication Level-Local Forest page, select between the two available options, and then click Next.
    - **Forest-Wide Authentication**   Windows Server automatically authenticates users from the remote forest for all resources in the local forest. Select this option if both forests are managed by the same organization.
    - **Selective Authentication**   Windows Server does not automatically authenticate users from the remote forest for resources in the local forest. This is the appropriate option if your two forests are managed by separate organizations. For more details, see the section below: SID filtering and trust authentication scope.
11. On the Outgoing Trust Authentication Level-Specified Forest page, select between the two available options, and then click Next:
    - **Forest-Wide Authentication**   Windows Server automatically authenticates users from the local forest for all resources in the remote forest. Select if both forests are managed by the same organization.
    - **Selective Authentication**   Windows Server does not automatically authenticate users from the local forest for resources in the remote forest. Select if your two forests are managed by separate organizations. For more details, see the section below: SID filtering, and trust authentication scope.
12. Click Next twice, and then on the Confirm Outgoing Trust page, click Yes, confirm the outgoing trust. This enables you to verify that the trust is working. Click Next.
13. On the Confirm Incoming Trust page, click Yes, confirm the incoming trust. This enables you to verify that the trust is working. Click Next.
14. Click Finish, and then, in the Domain Properties dialog box, shown in Figure 2-43, click OK.

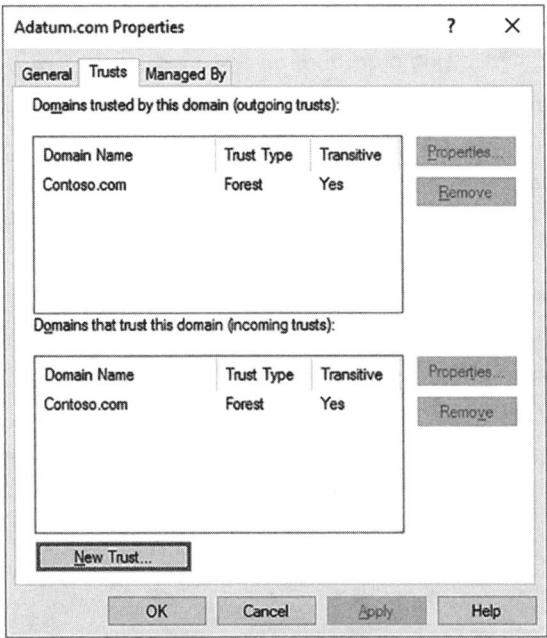

FIGURE 2-43 Viewing the configured trusts

After you configure the trust, you can then assign access to resources. A common way to achieve this is to select remote users and groups through the trust by using the Locations option when browsing users and groups, as shown in Figure 2-44.

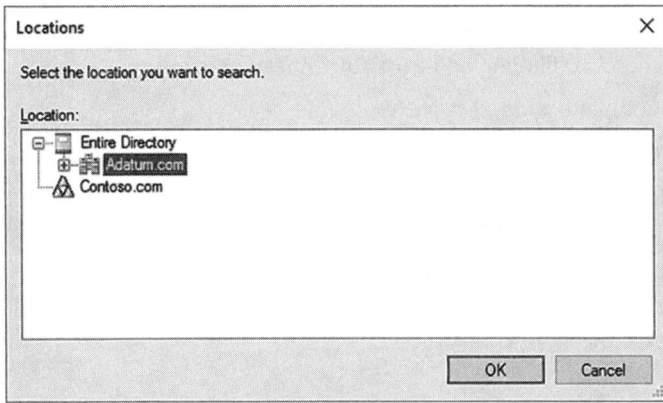

FIGURE 2-44 Selecting the location to search for security principals

Skill 2.3: Configure Active Directory in a complex enterprise environment   **CHAPTER 2**   **131**

Configure external trusts

To configure an external trust, use the following procedure:

1. Configure DNS so that domain controllers in each forest can resolve one another's names and SRV records.
2. In the Active Directory Domains And Trusts console on a domain controller in the first AD DS forest, right-click the forest root domain in the navigation pane, and then click Properties.
3. In the Domain Properties dialog box, click the Trusts tab, and then click New Trust.
4. In the New Trust Wizard, click Next, and then, on the Trust Name page, in the Name box, type the FQDN of the remote forest, and then click Next.
5. On the Trust Type page, click External Trust, and then click Next.
6. On the Direction Of Trust page, select the appropriate direction. Choose between Two-way, One-Way Incoming, and One-Way outgoing. For example, click Two-Way, and then click Next.
7. On the Side Of Trust page, click Both This Domain And The Specified Domain, and then click Next.
8. On the User Name And Password page, enter the credentials required to configure the trust in the remote forest, and then click Next.
9. On the Outgoing Trust Authentication Level-Local Domain page, choose between Domain-Wide Authentication and Selective Authentication, and then click Next. For more details, see the section below: SID filtering and trust authentication scope.
10. On the Outgoing Trust Authentication Level-Specified Domain page, choose between Domain-Wide Authentication and Selective Authentication and then click Next. For more details, see the section: SID filtering and trust authentication scope.
11. On the Trust Selections Complete page, click Next.
12. On the Trust Creation Complete page, click Next.
13. On the Confirm Outgoing Trust page, click Yes, and confirm the outgoing trust. This enables you to verify that the trust is working. Click Next.
14. In the Active Directory Domain Services dialog box, shown in Figure 2-45, acknowledge the message about SID filtering, and click OK. For more details, see the section: SID filtering and trust authentication scope.

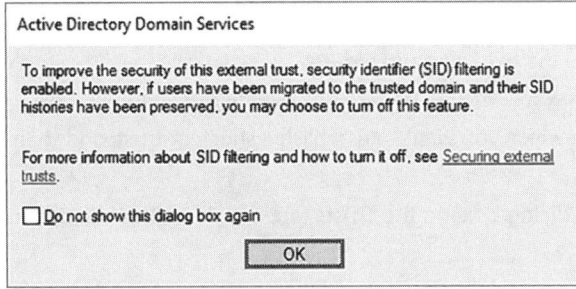

FIGURE 2-45 Acknowledging the SID filtering message

15. In the Domain Properties dialog box, click OK.

Configure realm trusts

To configure a realm trust, use the following procedure:

1. Configure DNS so that domain controllers in each security authority can resolve one another's names.
2. In Active Directory Domains And Trusts, in the navigation pane, right-click the domain node for the domain with which you want to establish a shortcut trust, and then click Properties.
3. In the Domain Properties dialog box, on the Trusts tab, click New Trust, and then click Next.
4. On the Trust Name page, type the FQDN of the domain, and then click Next.
5. On the Trust Type page, click Realm trust, as shown in Figure 2-46, and then click Next.

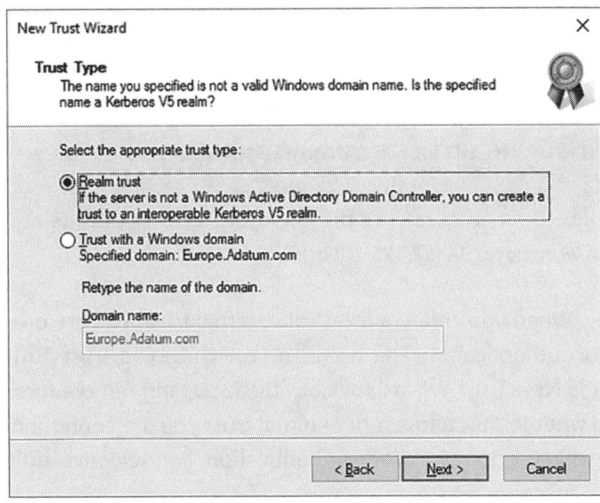

FIGURE 2-46 Configuring a realm trust

6. Complete the wizard using the guidance provided for forest or external trusts.

Skill 2.3: Configure Active Directory in a complex enterprise environment **CHAPTER 2** **133**

Configure shortcut trusts

To configure a shortcut trust, use the following procedure:

1. In Active Directory Domains And Trusts, in the navigation pane, right-click the domain node for the domain with which you want to establish a shortcut trust, and then click Properties.
2. In the Domain Properties dialog box, on the Trusts tab, click New Trust, and then click Next.
3. On the Trust Name page, type the FQDN of the domain, and then click Next.
4. On the Trust Type page, click Shortcut trust, and then click Next.
5. Complete the wizard using the guidance provided for forest or external trusts.

SID filtering and trust authentication scope

By their very nature, trusts give users from another domain the potential to access resources in your domain. This can pose security risks. There are a number of features in Windows Server 2016 that you can use to help mitigate these potential security risks. These are:

- **SID Filtering** After you set up a forest of external trust, you are warned that SID filtering has been enabled. SID filtering controls the way that SIDs are used during authentication to resources in a trusting domain. If a user belongs to groups, the SIDs of those groups are presented to resource-holding servers through the trust when the user attempts authentication.

    If a user that belongs to the Domain Admins group signs in at a trusted domain, that user's SID history contains an entry for a group, Domain Admins, which also exists in your resource-holding domain. This gives the remote user potentially more access than is desirable. SID filtering helps prevent this by instructing the resource-holding domain to filter out SIDs from the account-holding domain that is not the primary SIDs of security principals.

> **NEED MORE REVIEW? CONFIGURING SID FILTER QUARANTINING ON EXTERNAL TRUSTS**
>
> To review further details about SID filtering, refer to the Microsoft TechNet website at *https://technet.microsoft.com/library/cc794757(WS.10).aspx*.

- **Authentication Scope** When you create a forest or external trust, you are prompted to configure the scope of authentication. This occurs on the Outgoing Trust Authentication Level pages of the New Trust Wizard for both the local, and remote forests or domains, depending on whether it is a forest or external trust you are configuring. You choose between forest-wide (or domain-wide) authentication, and selective authentication.

Choosing forest-wide (or domain-wide) effectively means that all users from the remote forest (or domain) are considered to be Authenticated Users. This limits your administrative control – or simplifies it, depending upon your viewpoint.

However, if you choose Selective authentication, although all users in the remote forest (or domain) are considered to be trusted, you must explicitly grant them permissions to authenticate against server resources in your local forest (or domain). This provides for more control, but can be time-consuming to configure.

If the remote forest (or domain) is a part of your organization, it is usually acceptable to choose forest-wide (or domain-wide) authentication during the setup of the trust. If, however, the remote forest (or domain) is part of a different organization, choose selective authentication when prompted.

EXAM TIP
You can reconfigure the authentication scope setting for your forest or external trust after you have established the trust by using the Active Directory Domains and Trusts tool.

> **NEED MORE REVIEW?** **ENABLE SELECTIVE AUTHENTICATION OVER A FOREST TRUST**
>
> To review further details about selective authentication, refer to the Microsoft TechNet website at *https://technet.microsoft.com/library/cc794747(WS.10).aspx*.

Configure name suffix routing

A unique name suffix is a UPN suffix or DNS forest name, such as Adatum.com or Contoso.com, that is not subordinate to any other another name suffix. To help simplify authentication through forest trusts, by default, Windows Server routes all unique name suffixes to the trusting domain.

To further simplify administration, all child name suffixes are also routed. Thus, users with the suffix Sales.Contoso.com, which is a subordinate of Contoso.com, have a suffix that is a child of Contoso.com.

If, for any reason, you want to disable name suffix routing through a forest trust, you can do so by using the Active Directory Domains and Trusts console by selecting the appropriate domain in the navigation pane. Then, use the following procedure:

1. In the Active Directory Domains And Trusts console, in the navigation pane, right-click the appropriate domain, and then click Properties.
2. In the Domain Properties dialog box, on the Trusts tab, under either Domains Trusted By This Domain (Outgoing Trusts) or Domains That Trust This Domain (Incoming Trusts), click the appropriate forest trust, and then click Properties.

3. Click the Name Suffix Routing tab, and under Name Suffixes In The <domain name> Forest, perform one of the following:
   - Click the suffix that you want to enable, and then click Enable.
   - Click the suffix that you want to disable, and then click Disable.
4. Click OK twice.

> **NEED MORE REVIEW? ENABLE OR DISABLE AN EXISTING NAME SUFFIX FROM ROUTING**
> To review further details about name suffix routing, refer to the Microsoft TechNet website at *https://technet.microsoft.com/library/cc731648(v=ws.11).aspx*.

Configure AD DS sites and subnets

AD DS sites and subnets enable you to create logical objects in the AD DS configuration partition that map to physical entities in your organization's network; namely, your organization's physical IP subnets and geographical locations. By creating AD DS subnet objects, computers that are members of your AD DS infrastructure can determine in which physical subnet they are located. By associating subnets with AD DS sites, computers can determine in which geographic location they reside.

Information about where a computer is can be used by that computer to locate services that are adjacent rather than distant. For example, using a local domain controller to attempt to sign in rather than one that is physically remote can speed up sign in times.

> **EXAM TIP**
> Because AD DS sites and subnet objects are part of the AD DS configuration partition, you must be a member of the forest Enterprise Admin universal security group to create or configure them.

Create AD DS sites

There are a number of reasons to create sites. These are:

- **Replication Management** You can exert more control over intersite replication than is possible with intrasite replication.
- **Group Policy Application** You can create Group Policy Objects (GPOs) and link them to site objects. This applies the policy settings to users and computers that are at a specific location.
- **Service Location** You can use information stored in a computer's service location (SRV) resource record to determine which site it is in.

When you deploy AD DS, a default site called Default-First-Site-Name is created. All domain controllers are configured as part of this site until you create additional sites and move your domain controllers into those sites.

To create an AD DS site, use the following procedure:

1. In Server Manager, click Tools, and then click Active Directory Sites And Services.
2. In Active Directory Sites And Services, in the navigation pane, click Sites.
3. Right-click Sites, and then click New Subnet.
4. In the New Object – Site dialog box, shown in Figure 2-47, in the Name box, type the name for your site. For example, type London.

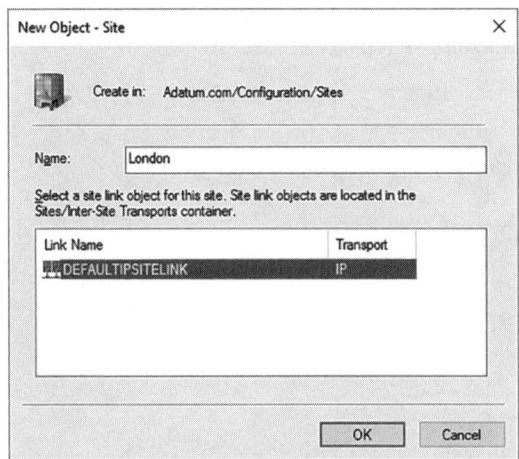

FIGURE 2-47 Creating a new site

5. In the Link Name list, click the appropriate site link object. It is likely that at this stage, only the DEFAULTIPSITELINK object exists. This is the default connection object created to support the AD DS intersite replication topology. You can create and configure your own site links later. For now, click DEFAULTIPSITELINK, and click OK.
6. In the Active Directory Domain Services pop-up dialog box, click OK to acknowledge the message about next steps.
7. Create your additional sites. Initially, use the DEFAULTIPSITELINK object for the selected link object for each site.

You can also use the Windows PowerShell New-ADReplicationSite cmdlet. For example, to create a new site called London, use the following command:

```
New-ADReplicationSite -Name "London"
```

Create AD DS subnets

Now create a logical map of your physical infrastructure by creating IP subnets. These should map exactly to the physical subnets within your network, otherwise this can lead to poor performance and potential problems with service availability.

To create an AD DS subnet, use the following procedure:

1. In Server Manager, click Tools, and then click Active Directory Sites And Services.
2. In Active Directory Sites And Services, in the navigation pane, expand Sites, and then click Subnets.
3. Right-click Subnets, and then click New Subnet.
4. In the New Object – Subnet dialog box, shown in Figure 2-48, in the Prefix box, type the prefix for your IP subnet. For example, type 172.16.0.0/16.

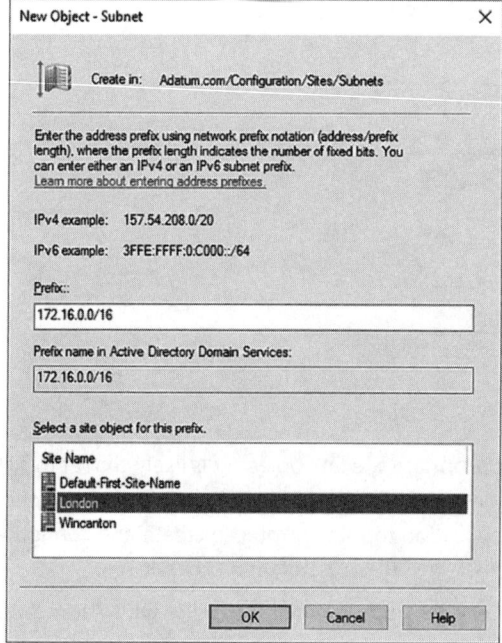

FIGURE 2-48 Adding a subnet

5. In the Select A Site Object For This Prefix, select the appropriate site. For example, click London, and then click OK.
6. Create any additional subnets for your organization, and map each to the appropriate site. Remember that a site can contain multiple subnets, but a subnet can only be associated with a single site.

You can also use the Windows PowerShell New-ADReplicationSubnet cmdlet. For example, to create a subnet called 172.16.0.0/16, use the following command:

    New-ADReplicationSubnet -Name "172.16.0.0/16"

To create the same subnet, but link it to a site called London, use the following command:

    New-ADReplicationSubnet -Name "172.16.0.0/16" -Site London

Create and configure site links

The next step in establishing your intersite replication configuration is to create and configure site links. Initially, all of your sites are connected by the automatically created DEFAULTIPSITE-LINK object, but you can create your own site links.

To create a site link, use the following procedure:

1. In Active Directory Sites And Services, in the navigation pane, expand Sites, expand Inter-Site Transports, and then click IP.

EXAM TIP
You can choose between two transports for your site links: IP and SMTP. The SMTP site link uses the Simple Mail Transfer Protocol to route site-to-site data. This is useful when you are connecting sites together, which are likely to be connected by non-persistent and slow links. The IP transport should be selected in almost all situations.

2. Right-click IP, and then click New Site Link.
3. In the New Object – Site Link dialog box, shown in Figure 2-49, in the Name box, type a meaningful descriptive name of what the site link connects. For example, type London <> Wincanton.

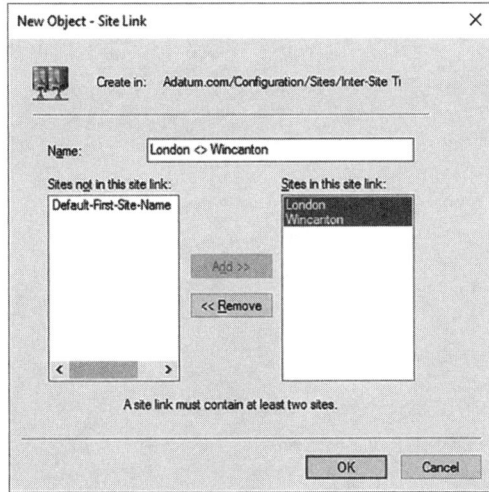

FIGURE 2-49 Adding a site link

4. In the Sites Not In This Site Link list, click the sites (at least two) that are interconnected by this site link, and then click Add>>.
5. Click OK.

You can also use the Windows PowerShell `New-ADReplicationSiteLink` cmdlet. For example, to create a new site link between the sites London and NewYork, use the following command:

```
New-ADReplicationSiteLink -Name "London-NewYork" -SitesIncluded London,NewYork
```

Next, you must configure the site link:

1. In the details pane, right-click the site link, and then click Properties.
2. In the Site Link Properties dialog box, shown in Figure 2-50, configure the following properties, and then click OK.
    - **Cost**   This is an arbitrary number that should represent a preference as to whether the link should be used if there are multiple paths available. For instance, if there are two possible paths between two sites in your infrastructure, but one has a higher end-to-end cost, the lower cost path is used, unless it's unavailable. The default value is 100.
    - **Replicate Every**   This is the replication interval and defaults to 180 minutes. Reduce this to help to ensure any changes are propagated more quickly throughout the domain controllers in your organization. 15 minutes is the lowest configurable value.
    - **Schedule**   The schedule is the replication availability window. During the configured time, replication can occur at the specified 'Replicate every' interval. If you want to prevent replication from occurring during working hours, for example, you can use the Schedule to configure that.

FIGURE 2-50 Configuring the site link properties

After you have created all the required site links, and moved all the domain controllers into the correct sites, if you no longer need the DEFAULTIPSITELINK, you can delete it.

When to use site link bridges

Generally, creating and configuring site links is sufficient to enable a fully-routable, fault tolerant intersite replication topology. This is because all site links are automatically bridged by default, meaning that all site links are transitive.

Site link bridges enable you to create transitive links between sites when site links cannot provide the required behavior. There are two situations in which site link bridges might be required:

- **Your IP network is not fully routed** You can enable site link bridges to enable transitive links where your IP network is not capable of doing this automatically.
- **You want more control over the replication flow** You can control how the replication of AD DS flows through your sites by disabling the Bridge All Site Links option, and then creating site link bridges. Replication traffic flows transitively through sites linked by site link bridges, but does not route beyond the site link bridge.

> **NEED MORE REVIEW? CREATING A SITE LINK BRIDGE DESIGN**
>
> To review further details about implementing site link bridges, refer to the Microsoft TechNet website at *https://technet.microsoft.com/library/cc753638(v=ws.10).aspx*.

Move domain controllers between sites

After you have configured the subnets and sites to mirror your network's physical topology, you must move the domain controllers into the appropriate sites. It is assumed that the domain controllers already are assigned the appropriate IP configuration so that they are physically in the correct subnet.

> **EXAM TIP**
>
> During deployment of a domain controller, you are prompted to which site you want to deploy the domain controller.

To move a domain controller between sites after deployment, use the following procedure:

1. In Active Directory Sites And Services, in the navigation pane, expand the Default-First-Site-Name object.
2. Expand the Servers folder, and then click the server that you want to move.
3. Right-click the server, and then click Move.
4. In the Move Server dialog box, shown in Figure 2-51, click the site to which you want to move the domain controller, and then click OK.

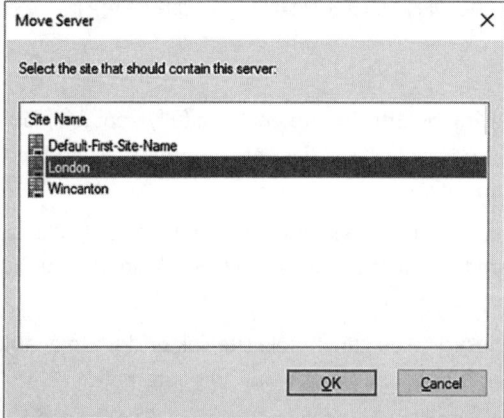

FIGURE 2-51 Moving a domain controller

You can also use the Windows PowerShell `Move-ADDirectoryServer` cmdlet to move domain controllers between sites.

You do not need to move servers or client computers. These devices determine their own site placement by using their IP configuration to determine their subnet. From AD DS, they then determine their site.

After you have completed the process of creating and configuring your subnets, sites, and site links, and after you have moved your domain controllers to the appropriate sites, as shown in Figure 2-52, it is then a good idea to run a knowledge consistency check to rebuild the replication topology. You can do this from Active Directory Sites and Services by locating the NTDS Settings object under the server object in a given site. Right-click the NTDS Settings object, point to All Tasks, and then click Check Replication Topology.

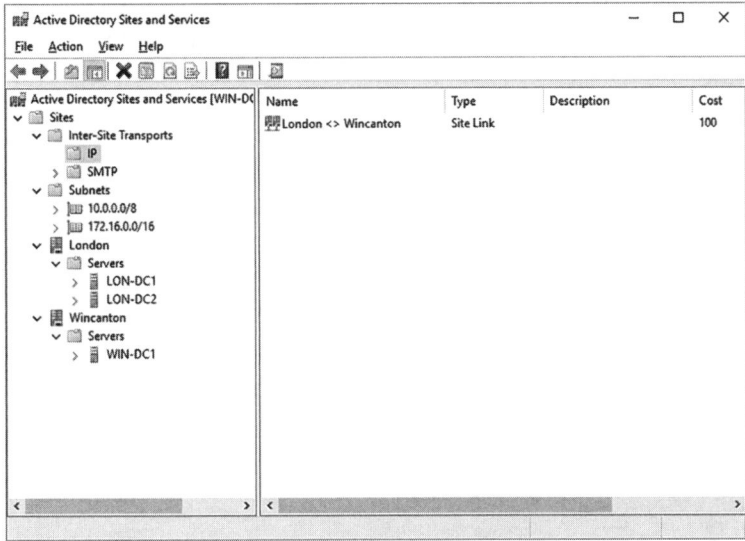

FIGURE 2-52 The completed intersite replication topology

Manage registration of SRV records

When you deploy domain controllers, they register important records in the appropriate DNS zone on your DNS server. These records, known as SRV resource records, enable computers and users to locate domain controller services. AD DS services, such as the Kerberos authentication service, use SRV records to advertise themselves to clients in an AD DS network.

A typical SRV record consists of a number of elements:

- **Service Name And Port** Identifies the service and the associated Transmission Control Protocol (TCP) or User Datagram Protocol (UDP) port. For example, common SRV records include Lightweight Directory Access Protocol (LDAP) over TCP port 389, Kerberos over port 88, the Kerberos V5 authentication protocol (KPASSWD) on port 464, and the global catalog service on port 3268.

- **Protocol** Indicates whether TCP or UDP is used. A service can use both, but is required to register separate SRV records that indicate this.
- **Hostname** Provides the name of the host offering the service. Client computers must then use host records in DNS to determine the IP address being used by the specified host.
- **Options** SRV records are also assigned preference, weight, and priority values. These are used when there are multiple records that point to the same service or server and you want to control which servers are used first. For example, an AD DS domain controller registers its Kerberos authentication service DNS resource records with a priority value of 0 and a weight of 100, as shown in Figure 2-53. You can change these initial values to determine which host offering the Kerberos authentication service is used by clients. DNS clients attempt to use the server with the lowest priority value. If multiple servers have the same priority value, clients use the server in proportion to their weight values.

FIGURE 2-53 Viewing the details of an SRV record

EXAM TIP

You can configure these values using the DNS Manager console or the Windows PowerShell **Add-DnsServerResourceRecord** or **Set-DnsServerResourceRecord** cmdlets using the **Priority, Weight,** and **Preference** parameters.

SRV records are stored in DNS in a hierarchy that includes not only the protocol information, but also the site information; this enables computers to locate services based on the AD DS site in which the service is offered. Figure 2-XY shows the DNS structure of the registered SRV records.

Generally, you do not need to manually register or maintain SRV records. Assuming that your DNS servers are configured with DNS zones that support dynamic updates, when you add domain controllers, or move them to different sites, they update their DNS records automatically.

Manage site coverage

It is important that all physical sites have access to a domain controller. If, after you have completed your intersite replication configuration, there are sites without domain controllers, you have a number of possible solutions:

- **Add the subnet to a site**   If there are only a few computers at a branch office that do not merit a domain controller, to ensure client computers can locate domain services, add the subnet at that location to an adjacent site.
- **Deploy an RODC**   If there are sufficient computers to merit a local domain controller, deploy an RODC.
- **Rely on automatic site coverage**   A domain controller from an adjacent site also registers its SRV records for the smaller site enabling client computers to locate that domain controller.

> ***NEED MORE REVIEW?*** **FINDING A DOMAIN CONTROLLER IN THE CLOSEST SITE**
>
> To review further details about automatic site coverage, refer to the Microsoft TechNet website at *https://technet.microsoft.com/library/Cc978016*.

Chapter summary

- You can use gMSAs to simplify account administration for services.
- SPNs enable client computers to locate services.
- You can use PSOs to create account policies for specific users or groups of users.
- The NtdsUtil.exe command-line tool enables you to perform many AD DS database administration tasks, including offline defragmentation.
- Metadata cleanup in the process of cleaning up the AD DS database following the forced removal of a domain controller.
- Enabling the Active Directory Recycle Bin can make recovering AD DS objects much simpler in many circumstances but is not a replacement for backup.
- RODCs are ideal for deployment to less physically secure locations, such as branch offices.
- You can configure multiple UPN suffixes in your AD DS forest to support specific naming conventions without needing to change the domain name(s) or reconfigure DNS settings.

- Trust relationships enable a security principal in one domain, such as a user or computer, to potentially gain access to a resource in another domain.
- Forest-wide authentication is recommended when you implement a forest trust between two AD DS forests, both of which are managed by your organization.
- In simple networked environments, you can use the default intersite configuration objects: Default-First-Site-Name and DEFAULTIPSITELINK.
- SRV resource records enable computers to locate domain-wide services, or services available in their local site.

Thought experiment

In this thought experiment, demonstrate your skills and knowledge of the topics covered in this chapter. You can find answers to this thought experiment in the next section.

You work in support at A. Datum. As a consultant for A. Datum, answer the following questions about managing advanced AD DS environments for the A. Datum organization:

1. You are planning a new AD DS deployment. The business consists of two separate divisions, each with their own IT departments and management structures. What high-level AD DS structure does this suggest and why?

2. A fellow administrator has deployed an app that runs on servers and connects to a SQL Server database at the backend. Clients connect to the app to retrieve customer data. After 42 days, you experience a problem with users being unable to access their data. What might be going on here? What could you do to resolve the issue?

3. Your AD DS forest consists of two trees, one for Adatum.com, and one for Contoso.com. Contoso.com consists of multiple child domains: Europe.Contoso.com, Americas.Contoso.com, and Pacific.Contoso.com. Each of these has child domains according to business group. For example, Sales.Europe.Contoso.com. Users in the Sales.Pacific.Contoso.com domain need to access resources in the Adatum.com, but they are finding access is slow. You have eliminated physical network performance issues, so what else might be going on, and what could you do to mitigate the problem?

Thought experiment answers

This section contains the solution to the thought experiment. Each answer explains why the answer choice is correct.

1. This scenario initially suggests using multiple forests. This is because a separate AD DS forest, each with its own separate management team, could represent each division. However, it is important to ask questions of the management team and look at how the IT departments work. It might not be necessary for the AD DS deployment to use multiple forests. Creating a single forest, perhaps with multiple trees to support naming might be appropriate. In other words, the fact that the organization has separate IT departments in two divisions doesn't necessarily mean you have to configure your AD DS infrastructure to perpetuate that.

2. The 42-day interval hints at the problem. Users, by default, are required to change their passwords every 42 days. Perhaps when your colleague installed the app, he or she used a standard user account to run the service that connects to the SQL Server? If this is the case, you must use a gMSA to configure the service that connects to the SQL Server. This makes managing passwords for service accounts much easier.

3. It is possible that poor access times are a result of the way trusts work. The access from the Sales.Europe.Contoso.com domain to resources in Adatum.com must transit up the Contoso.com tree. By configuring a shortcut trust between Adatum.com and Sales.Europe.Contoso.com, you might improve performance.

CHAPTER 3

Create and manage Group Policy

Group Policies enable you to centrally configure and manage objects within your Active Directory Domain Services (AD DS) network infrastructure. To implement Group Policy Objects (GPOs) within AD DS, you must know how to create and manage GPOs; how to configure Group Policy processing, including order, precedence, inheritance, and enforcement; how to configure specific settings within a GPO; and how to implement GPO preferences, including configuring printer preferences, network drive mappings, and power options.

Skills covered in this chapter:
- Create and manage Group Policy Objects
- Configure Group Policy processing
- Configure Group Policy settings
- Configure Group Policy preferences

Skill 3.1: Create and manage Group Policy Objects

With GPOs linked to your sites, domains, and organizational units (OUs), you can quickly and easily manage large numbers of both users and computers that require the same settings. Examples include: computers at the same physical location, users in the same department, or computers with a specific base configuration that require particular settings.

After you have devised and implemented your organization's OU infrastructure, and moved the user and computer objects into the relevant OUs, you can create GPOs, configure the desired settings, and then link them to the appropriate OU.

Using GPOs enables you to more easily manage many aspects of your AD DS infrastructure, including:

- **Windows and app settings** Use GPOs to provide a consistent interface for Windows and the installed apps. By standardizing settings, you can more easily support your users' needs.

- **Software deployment** You can use GPOs to deploy, update, and remove desktop apps from your organization's computers.
- **Folder redirection** Windows enables users to configure a Start menu, to customize their desktop appearance, and to store files in a personal storage area, sometimes referred to as a home folder. With folder redirection in GPOs you can redirect these local folders to a network location. This can help make back up of user data easier, and can enable user roaming between computer devices, while retaining the users' personalized settings.
- **Security settings** Many of the configurable settings in GPOs relate to operating system security. You can use GPOs to apply standard security settings to collections of users or computers.
- **Infrastructure settings** GPOs also contain configurable settings for things like wireless network profiles, and Windows Firewall rules and settings.

> This section covers how to:
> - Configure multiple local Group Policies
> - Overview of domain-based GPOs
> - Manage starter GPOs
> - Configure GPO links
> - Back up, restore, import, and copy GPOs
> - Create and configure a migration table
> - Reset default GPOs
> - Delegate Group Policy management
> - Detect health issues using the Group Policy Infrastructure Status dashboard

Configure multiple local Group Policies

Although this chapter focuses on domain-based GPOs, Windows Server 2016 and Windows 10 both support local Group Policies. Using local GPOs enables you to apply settings to a computer and its local user accounts; this can be useful if the computer is not part of your AD DS forest.

EXAM TIP

If you apply local GPOs to a computer that is part of your AD DS forest, site-based and domain-based GPOs also apply. Any settings you configure using local GPOs that are also configured as part of a site or domain GPO are overridden.

You can create multiple local GPOs. These are:

- **Local Group Policy** This GPO contains the settings that apply to the local computer, irrespective of which user signs in. This policy contains both a computer and user node.
- **Administrators and Non-Administrators Local Group Policy** These user-specific policies apply to users based on whether they belong to the local administrators group or not. This enables you to customize settings for administrators. These two policies contain only a user node.
- **User specific Local Group Policy** Windows 8 and Windows Server 2012 and newer enable support for user specific local Group Policies. This contains only a user node.

If you implement multiple local GPOs, they are processed in the following order:

1. Local Group Policy
2. Administrators and Non-Administrators Group Policy
3. User-specific Local Group Policy

EXAM TIP

If settings apply in several policies, the policy that is applied last takes precedence.

To create multiple local GPOs, use the following procedure:

1. Sign in as a local administrator.
2. Click Start, type mmc.exe and then press Enter.
3. In the management console, click File, and then click Add/Remove Snap-In.
4. In the Add Or Remove Snap-ins dialog box, shown in Figure 3-1, in the snap-in list, click Group Policy Object Editor, and then click Add.

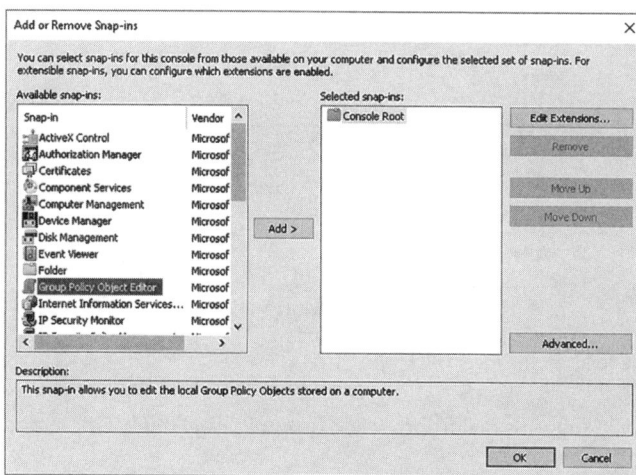

FIGURE 3-1 Adding the Group Policy Object Editor snap-in to a management console

5. In the Select Group Policy Object dialog box, on the Welcome To The Group Policy Wizard page, shown in Figure 3-2, click Browse.

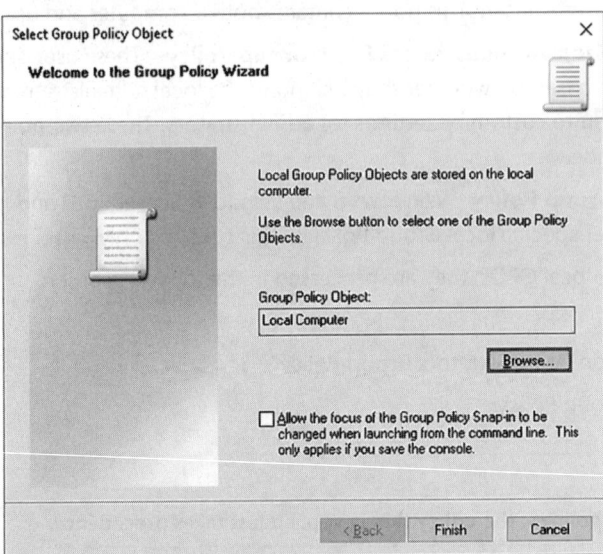

FIGURE 3-2 Setting the GPO focus to the local computer

6. In the Browse For A Group Policy Object dialog box, on the Computers tab, click This Computer, as shown in Figure 3-3, and then click Finish.

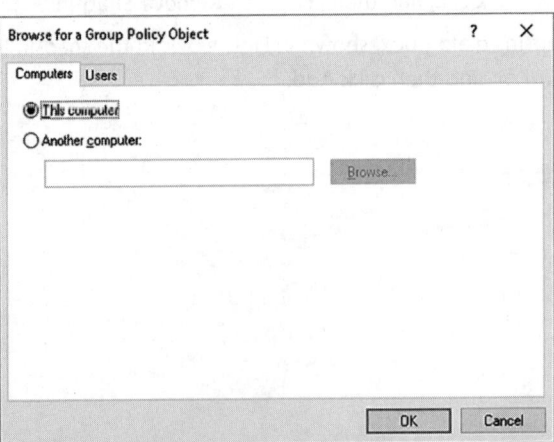

FIGURE 3-3 Setting the focus of the local GPO

7. In the Add Or Remove Snap-ins dialog box, click Group Policy Object Editor, and click Add.

8. In the Select Group Policy Object dialog box, on the Welcome To The Group Policy Wizard page, click Browse.

9. In the Browse For A Group Policy Object dialog box, on the Users tab, shown in Figure 3-4, click Administrators, click OK, and then click Finish.

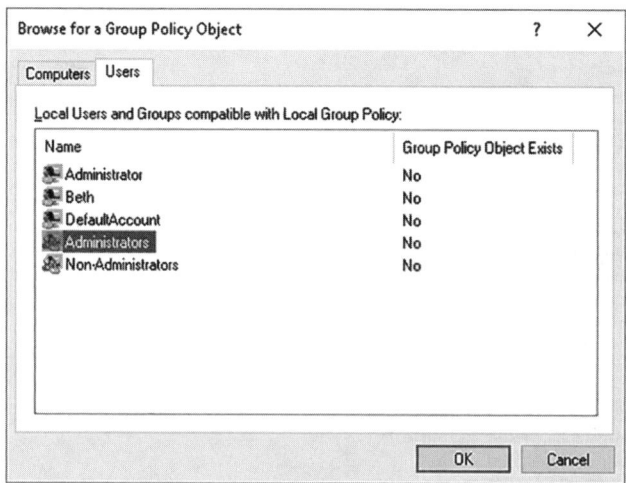

FIGURE 3-4 Setting the GPO focus to the Administrators group

10. In the Add Or Remove Snap-ins dialog box, click Group Policy Object Editor, and click Add.
11. In the Select Group Policy Object dialog box, on the Welcome To The Group Policy Wizard page, click Browse.
12. In the Browse For A Group Policy Object dialog box, on the Users tab, click Non-Administrators, click OK, and then click Finish.
13. If you want to configure local GPOs for specific users, in the Add Or Remove Snap-Ins dialog box, click Group Policy Object Editor, and click Add.
14. In the Select Group Policy Object dialog box, on the Welcome To The Group Policy Wizard page, click Browse.
15. In the Browse For A Group Policy Object dialog box, on the Users tab, click the specific user account for which you want to create a GPO, click OK, and then click Finish.

EXAM TIP

You cannot apply local GPOs to security groups.

16. In the Add Or Remove Snap-ins dialog box, shown in Figure 3-5, click OK.

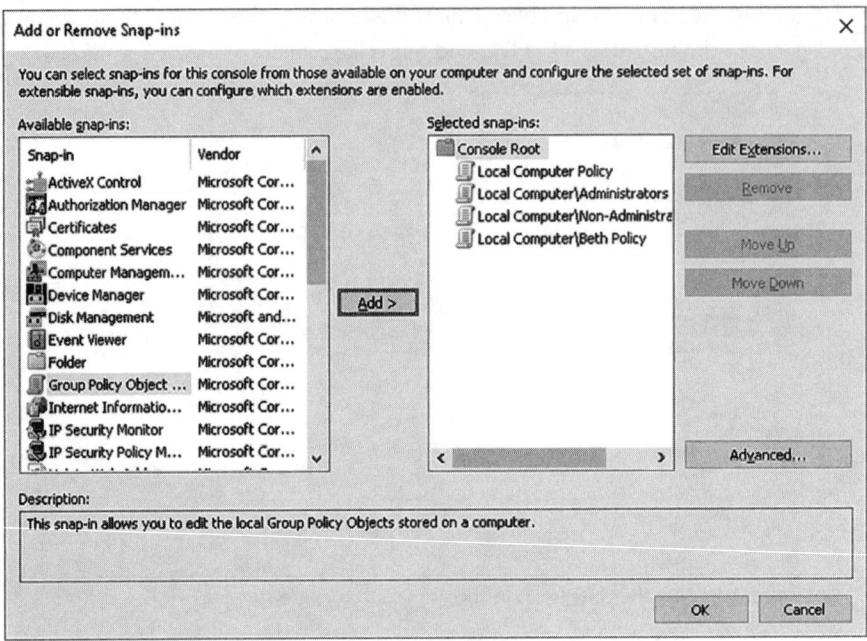

FIGURE 3-5 All local GPOs defined within the management console

17. In the Console 1 – [Console Root] dialog box, shown in Figure 3-6, expand the relevant policy, and configure the required settings.

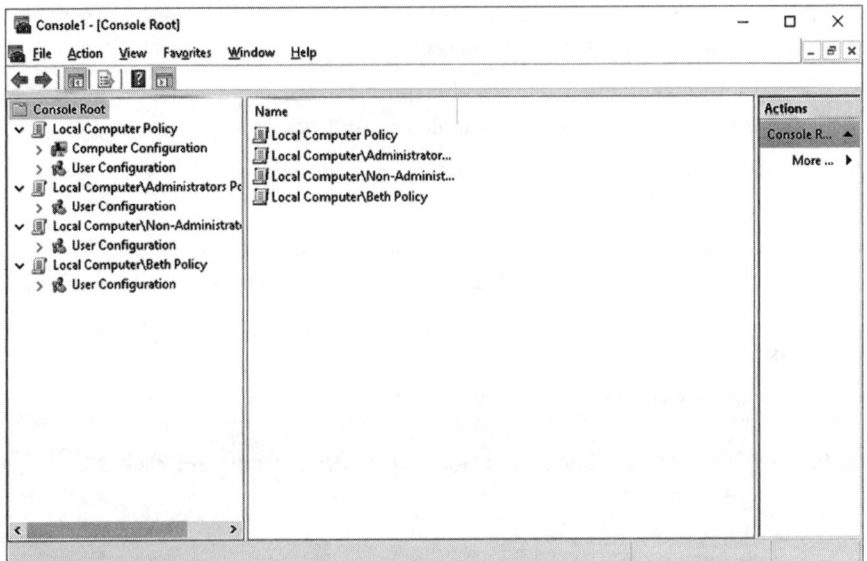

FIGURE 3-6 Completed console with four local GPOs displayed

154 CHAPTER 3 Create and manage Group Policy

To configure one of the local policies, such as the Local Computer Policy, use the following procedure:

1. In the Console 1 – [Console Root] dialog box, in the navigation pane, expand the Local Computer Policy, and then click Computer Configuration.
2. Under the Computer Configuration node, expand the required folder. For example, expand Windows Settings, and locate the appropriate setting, as shown in Figure 3-7.

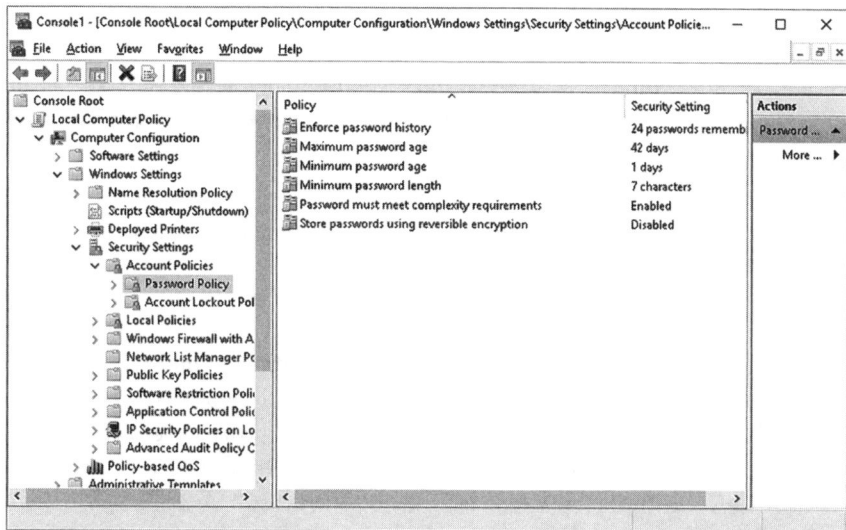

FIGURE 3-7 Configuring specific local GPO settings

3. In the details pane, double-click the required setting and configure the desired value, and then click OK.
4. Under the User Configuration node, expand the required folder(s), locate the appropriate setting(s), and configure the desired value.
5. When you have configured all the local GPOs, you can close the console. If you are likely to reconfigure the policies, consider saving the management console with the configured snap-ins.

Although the ability to configure multiple local GPOs is a significant improvement over only being able to configure a single local GPO, the process still lacks the flexibility and centralization offered by using domain-based GPOs. Also, remember that any settings configured using local GPOs can be overwritten by domain-based GPOs.

Overview of domain-based GPOs

Domain-based GPOs apply to computer and user objects that are part of an AD DS domain. Using domain-based GPOs enables you to more easily manage the user and computer objects in your AD DS infrastructure.

Structure of GPOs

GPOs consist of two components stored in two different locations. These components are:

- **Group Policy container** This is an object stored in the AD DS database. It is replicated to other domain controllers using the intrasite or intersite AD DS replication schedule, as appropriate. This object defines the fundamental attributes of the GPO. Each GPO is assigned a globally unique identity (GUID) by AD DS.

- **Group Policy template** This is a collection of files and folders stored in the SYSVOL shared folder on all domain controllers. These files contain the actual GPO settings. The settings for a specific GPO are stored in:

    %SystemRoot%\SYSVOL\Domain\Policies\{GUID}

    The {GUID} is the globally unique identity of the GPO. The contents of the SYSVOL folder, including the Group Policy template folders, are replicated between domain controllers using a different replication agent. In Windows Server 2008 and earlier, SYSVOL is replicated by the File Replication Service (FRS). In newer versions of Windows Server, SYSVOL replication is handled by the Distributed File System Replication agent (DFSR).

EXAM TIP

Because these two GPO components are replicated between domain controllers using different replication agents, you can occasionally get temporary synchronization issues between these two components. Generally, these issues automatically resolve.

Available GPO management tools

You can create and manage GPOs in your domain using several different tools. These are:

- **Group Policy Management** This management console, shown in Figure 3-8, enables you to perform all GPO-related management tasks, including creation, linking, filtering, modeling, and troubleshooting.

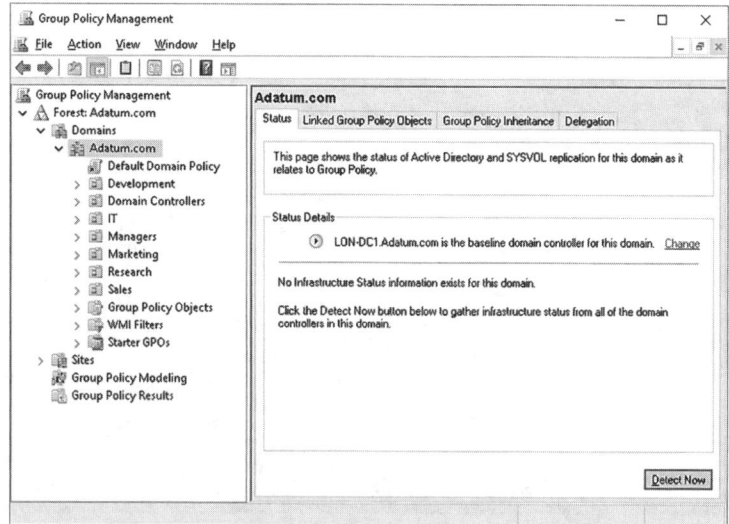

FIGURE 3-8 The Group Policy Management console

- **Group Policy Management Editor** You can launch this console from within Group Policy Management by selecting a GPO, and then selecting Edit. You can view and configure available settings in the GPO using this console, shown in Figure 3-9.

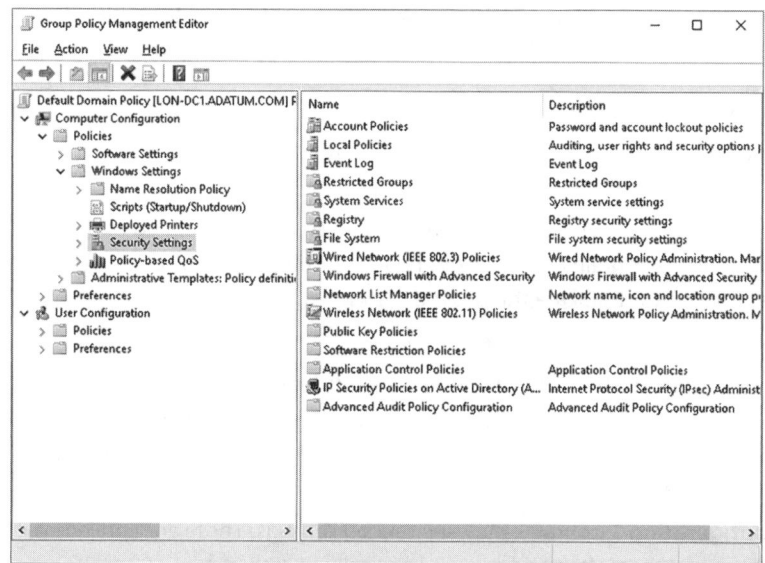

FIGURE 3-9 The Group Policy Management Editor console

- **Windows PowerShell** You can also use a number of Windows PowerShell cmdlets to create, link, and configure GPOs. For example, the new-gpo cmdlet is used to create a GPO, as shown in Figure 3-10.

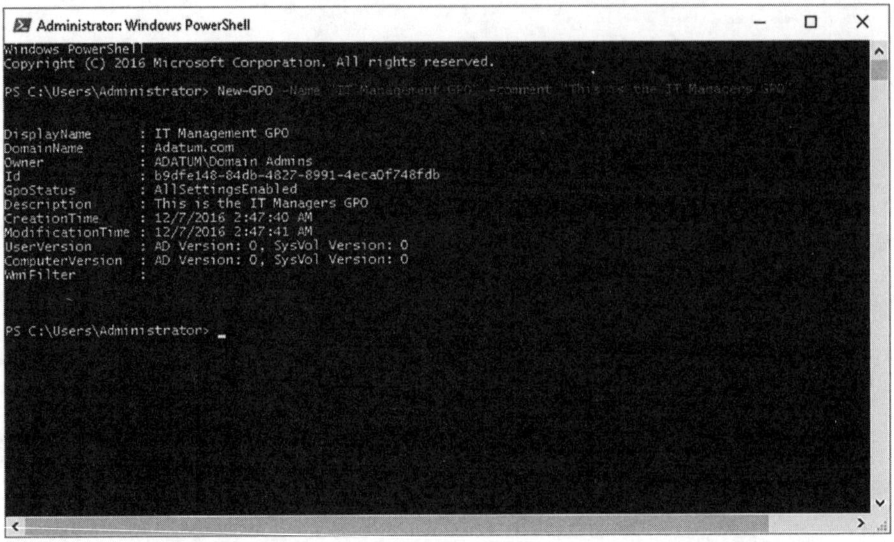

FIGURE 3-10 Creating a new GPO using Windows PowerShell

> **NEED MORE REVIEW? GROUP POLICY CMDLETS IN WINDOWS POWERSHELL**
>
> To review further details about using Windows PowerShell to manage GPOs, refer to the Microsoft TechNet website at *https://technet.microsoft.com/library/ee461027.aspx*.

Configuring specific settings

After you have created your GPOs, you must configure the available settings. You use the Group Policy Management Editor to perform this task.

As shown in Figure 3-9, a GPO consists of several nodes, each containing folders and subfolders. These folders contain collections of related settings. This structure helps make it easier for the administrator to locate the desired setting.

A policy consists of two top-level nodes:

- **Computer Configuration**   Contains the settings that are applied to the computer objects in a container to which this GPO is linked. These settings are applied on affected computers during startup and thereafter, and are automatically refreshed every 90 to 120 minutes.
- **User Configuration**   Contains the user-related settings. These are applied when a user signs in and thereafter, and are automatically refreshed every 90 to 120 minutes.

> **NOTE EFFECTIVENESS**
>
> Even if a policy setting is applied, it does not necessarily mean that it is immediately effective. Often, computer settings only apply after a restart, and user settings sometimes only apply following a sign out and sign in procedure.

Beneath each of these nodes, there are some folders and many subfolders that group settings, including:

- **Software Settings**   Enables you to deploy, update, and remove software from computers in your domain. Contains a single subfolder:
    - **Software Installation**   Enables you to add packages for deployment in your organization.
- **Windows Settings**   Enables you to configure the basic settings for your computers or users. Contains several subfolders, including:
    - **Scripts**   You can configure startup and shutdown or logon and logoff scripts that process when a computer starts or a user signs in.
    - **Security Settings**   Consolidates the various security settings that you can apply, including: account policies and user rights; event log settings; restricted groups; system services; registry and file system permissions; Windows Firewall rules and settings; software and application control settings, and many others.
    - **Folder Redirection**   You can redirect desktop, Start menu, and the user's personal folder, amongst others.
- **Administrative Templates**   Contains registry settings that control user, computer, and app behavior and settings. There are many thousands of settings, but these have been grouped logically into folders to help make their purpose more obvious. These include:
    - Control Panel
    - Desktop
    - Network
    - Shared Folders
    - Start Menu and Taskbar
    - System
    - Windows Components
    - All Settings

When you start to configure specific settings, you see that they fall into several different types. Some require that you configure one or more values, as shown in Figure 3-11.

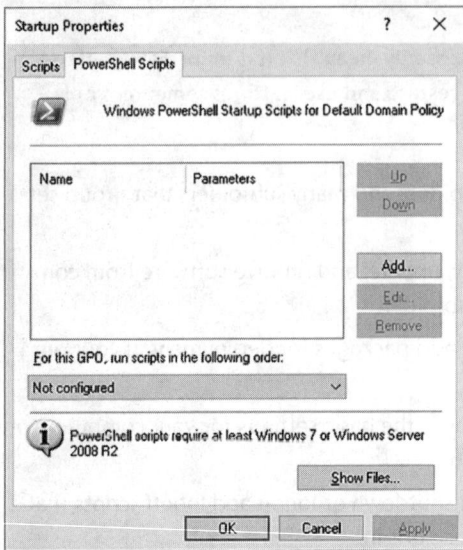

FIGURE 3-11 Configuring a GPO setting

Others require that you turn on or turn off a setting by enabling or disabling it, as shown in Figure 3-12. These settings have three possible values: Enabled, Disabled, and Not Configured (usually the default). The last of these three is rather interesting because the resultant value on a client computer (or signed in user) depends on whether the same setting is configured elsewhere; that is, in another GPO that also affects this computer or user. We learn about this behavior in more detail later.

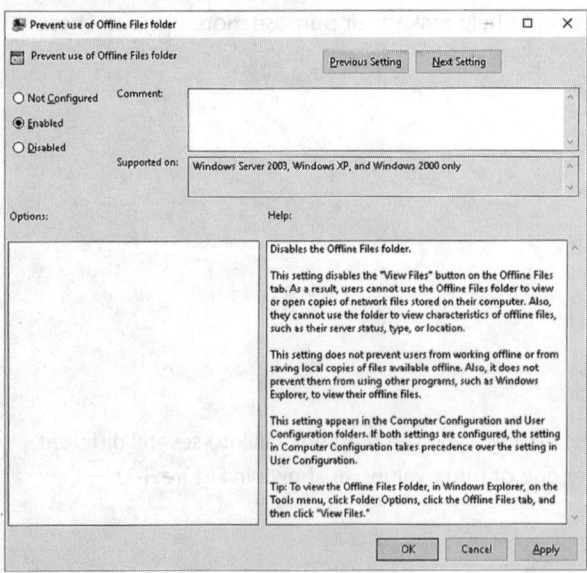

FIGURE 3-12 Configuring a GPO setting

160 CHAPTER 3 Create and manage Group Policy

Linking GPOs

When you have created a GPO and you have configured its settings, you must then link it to a container object in AD DS for it to apply to objects. You can link GPOs to:

- Sites
- Domains
- OUs

Linking a GPO to a container object is known as *scoping*. The scope determines which computers and users are impacted by the settings in a GPO. For example, if you link a GPO to the domain container, all computer and user objects within the domain are impacted by the configuration settings within that GPO. If you link the GPO to an OU, only objects within that OU (and any sub-OUs) are affected.

> *NOTE* **INHERITANCE**
>
> Settings configured at the domain level are inherited by objects in OUs within that domain. You can control this inheritance behavior; this is discussed in Skill 3.2: Configure Group Policy processing.

It is important that you understand that proper OU planning is required before you begin to create, configure, and link GPOs.

Client-side extensions

Although domain controllers store and make available the various GPOs that you create and configure, it is the responsibility of the client computer to connect to the domain controller and request and apply the necessary GPOs. A service called the Group Policy Client connects and downloads the required GPOs. Then, a series of components on the client, known as client-side extensions, process the GPO settings.

There are several client-side extensions on a Windows computer that process different GPO settings. These include:

- Registry policy
- Internet Explorer maintenance policy
- Software Installation policy
- Folder Redirection policy
- Scripts policy
- Security policy
- Internet Protocol security (IPsec) policy
- Wireless policy
- Encrypting File System recovery policy
- Disk quota policy

EXAM TIP

Open the registry and navigate to the HKLM\Software\Microsoft\Windows NT\CurrentVersion\Winlogon\GPExtensions key in the registry. You can see a list of the available client-side extensions here.

Manage starter GPOs

In larger organizations, you might find that you must create many GPOs, some of which share many settings. If this is the case, you can consider using *Starter GPOs*. A Starter GPO is a template GPO that you can use for creating a new GPO.

If you populate the Starter GPO with the most common settings, you can quickly create additional GPOs that contain those common settings. To create Starter GPOs, use the following procedure:

1. Open the Group Policy Management console and navigate to the Starter GPOs node beneath your domain node, as shown in Figure 3-13.

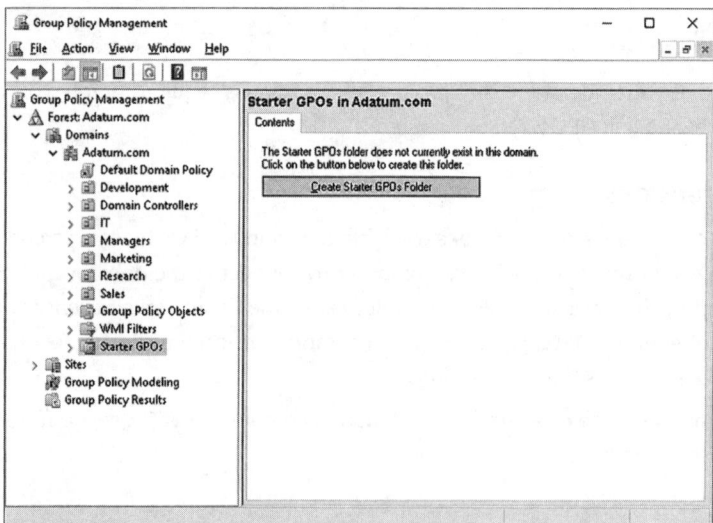

FIGURE 3-13 Configuring the Starter GPOs folder

2. In the details pane, click Create Starter GPOs Folder. The Starter GPOs folder is created and populated with two default Starter GPOs:
   - Group Policy Remote Update Firewall Ports
   - Group Policy Reporting Firewall Ports

You must now create and configure the required Starter GPOs:

1. Right-click the Starter GPOs node in the navigation pane, and then click New.
2. In the New Starter GPO dialog box, type the name for your Starter GPO, and then click OK.

3. In the Starter GPOs folder, shown in Figure 3-14, right-click the new Starter GPO, and then click Edit.

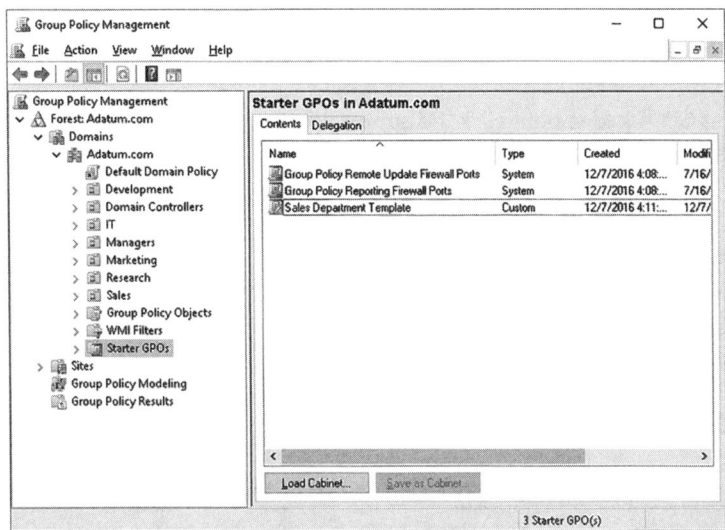

FIGURE 3-14 Creating Starter GPOs

4. In the Group Policy Starter GPO Editor, shown in Figure 3-15, configure the required settings.

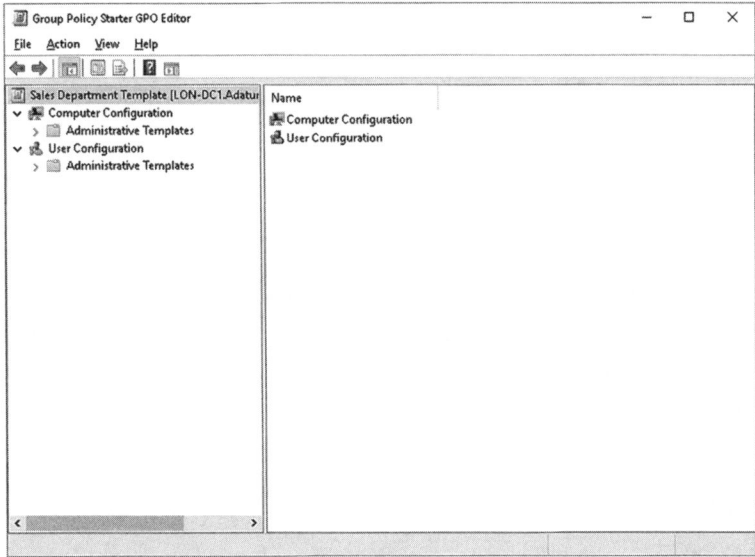

FIGURE 3-15 Configuring Starter GPO settings

EXAM TIP
Starter GPOs contain only the Administrative Template node.

5. Close the Group Policy Starter GPO Editor.

To create a new GPO based on a Starter GPO:

1. In the Starter GPOs folder, right-click the appropriate Starter GPO, and then click New GPO from Starter GPO.
2. In the New GPO dialog box, type the GPO name, and click OK.
3. Click the Group Policy Objects node in the navigation pane, shown in Figure 3-16, and your new policy is listed along with default GPOs and any others previously created.

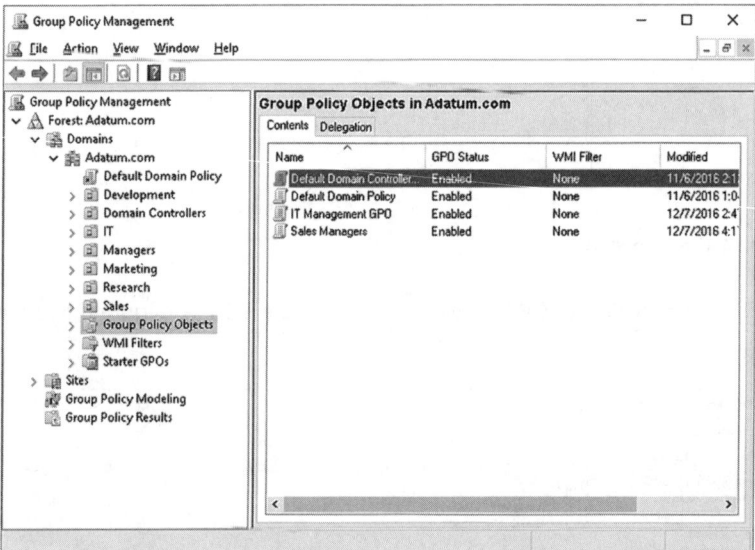

FIGURE 3-16 The newly created GPO

NOTE IMPORT AND EXPORT
It's possible to export Starter GPOs to a .CAB file. It is also possible to import Starter GPOs from a .CAB file. Use the Load Cabinet and Save As Cabinet buttons in the Starter GPOs folder, as shown in Figure 3-14.

Configure GPO links

To make a GPO effective, you must link it to a container. To link a GPO to a container, you can use the Group Policy Management console or the Windows PowerShell New-GPLink cmdlet.

As mentioned earlier, you can link GPOs to the following AD DS containers:

- **Sites** Use site-linked GPOs for settings that apply to computers or users based on their specific location. Obviously, you must have defined both subnet and site objects in AD DS and moved your domain controllers into the appropriate sites.

EXAM TIP
Be aware that site-linked GPOs can sometimes impose delays on the application of GPOs for clients in a specific site location but in a different domain from the domain controllers situated at the site.

- **Domains** Use domain-linked GPOs for settings that apply to most, or all, of the users and computers in your domain. If the same settings apply to multiple domains in your forest, you should copy the GPOs from one domain to the other and then link them at the other domain.
- **OUs** For settings that are more specific, consider linking your GPOs to an OU. Then place the appropriate users and computers into the OU. Note that all objects in the OU receive settings from the linked GPO by default, unless you choose to configure some form of GPO filtering.

The procedure for linking an existing GPO to a container is as follows:

1. In the Group Policy Management console, right-click the appropriate container, and then click Link An Existing GPO.
2. In the Select GPO dialog box, shown in Figure 3-17, in the Look In This Domain list, select the current domain, and then in the Group Policy objects list, click the appropriate GPO, and click OK.

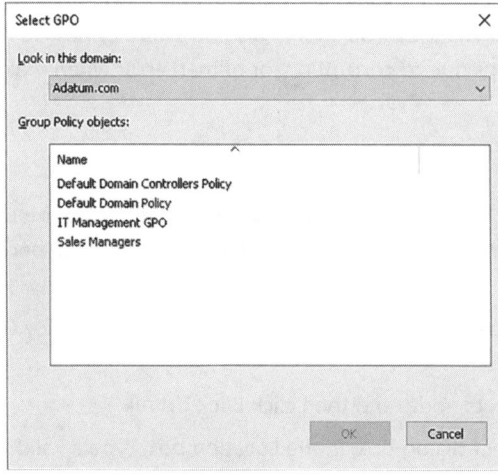

FIGURE 3-17 Linking a GPO

> **NOTE CREATING AND LINKING IN A SINGLE STEP**
>
> You can also create and link a GPO in one step. Right-click the container, and then click Create A GPO In This Domain, and Link It Here. Enter the GPO name, and click OK. You must then edit the GPO and configure the required settings.

You can use the Windows PowerShell New-GPLink cmdlet to link a GPO to a container. For example, to link the GPO called IT Managers to the IT OU in the Adatum.com domain, use the following command:

```
New-GPLink -Name "IT Managers" -target "ou=IT, dc=Adatum,dc=com"
```

To create the same GPO and link it in one step, use the following command:

```
New-GPO -Name "IT Managers" | New-GPLink -target "ou=IT,dc=Adatum,dc=com" -LinkEnabled Yes
```

If multiple GPOs are linked to the same container, you must configure the link order. The link order determines in which order the GPOs apply. This becomes important if the same setting is configured in several different GPOs as it determines which setting applies. Link order is discussed in Skill 3.2: Configure Group Policy processing.

EXAM TIP

You can link a single GPO to multiple AD DS containers simultaneously.

Back up, restore, import, and copy GPOs

It is important that you back up your GPOs when you have made significant changes to them, or, indeed, are about to make significant changes. You should also be aware of how to restore your GPOs should the need arise, perhaps due to corruption, or human error when making configuration changes.

Back up GPOs

You can perform all backup and restore operations using the Group Policy Management console, or with Windows PowerShell cmdlets. To back up all GPOs in your domain, perform the following procedure:

1. Open the Group Policy Management console and navigate to the Group Policy Objects node.
2. Right-click the Group Policy Objects node, and then click Back Up All.
3. In the Back Up Group Policy Object dialog box, in the Location box, type a valid path to a folder where you want to store your backups, as shown in Figure 3-18. Optionally, enter a description, and then click Back Up.

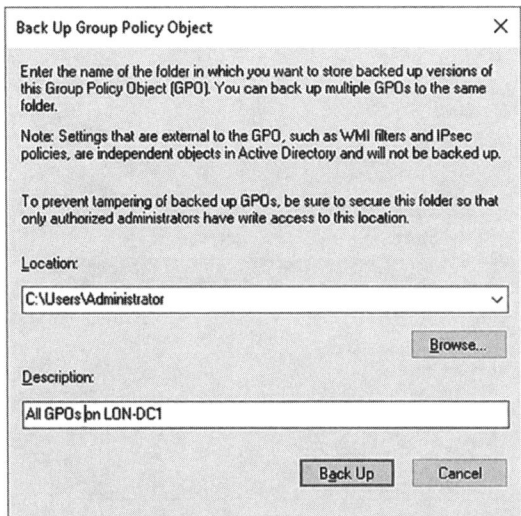

FIGURE 3-18 Specifying a backup location

4. On the Backup progress page, click OK.

To back up all GPOs to a shared folder called \\LON-DC1\Backup using Windows PowerShell, run the following command:

```
Backup-Gpo -All -Path \\LON-DC1\Backup
```

To back up a specific GPO, in the Group Policy Objects node, click and then right-click the specific GPO you want to back up, and then click Back Up. The process is like the process for backing up all GPOs. To use Windows PowerShell to back up a specific GPO, in this case, called Sales Managers, use the following command:

```
Backup-Gpo -Name "Sales Manager" -Path C:\Users\Administrator -Comment "Weekly Backup"
```

Restore GPOs

To restore a GPO, use the following procedure:

1. Right-click the appropriate GPO in the Group Policy Objects node, and then click Restore from Backup.
2. In the Restore Group Policy Object Wizard, on the Welcome page, click Next.
3. On the Backup Location page, enter the location where you saved your backup GPOs, and then click Next.
4. On the Source GPO page, shown in Figure 3-19, select the appropriate version of the backed up GPO. Click Next.

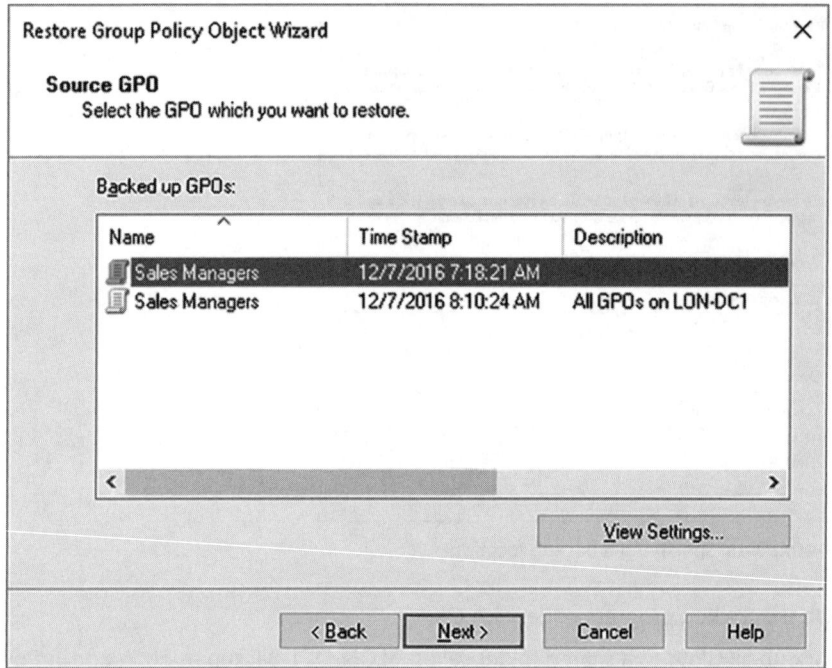

FIGURE 3-19 Selecting a backup to restore

5. On the Completing The Restore Group Policy Object Wizard page, click Finish, and when prompted, click OK.

You can also use the Windows PowerShell restore-gpo cmdlet. To restore the Sales Managers GPO from the \\LON-DC1\Backup folder, use the following command:

```
Restore-GPO -Name "Sales Managers" -Path \\LON-DC1\Backup
```

Manage backups

You can also manage your backups from the Group Policy Management console. You can use the Manage Backups option to view the settings in a backup, to delete a backup, and to restore a backup.

To access the Manage Backups tool, in the Group Policy Management console:

1. Right-click the Group Policy Objects node, and then click Manage Backups.
2. In the Manage Backups dialog box, shown in Figure 3-20, select the backup you want to manage, and then click Restore, Delete, or View Settings, as required.

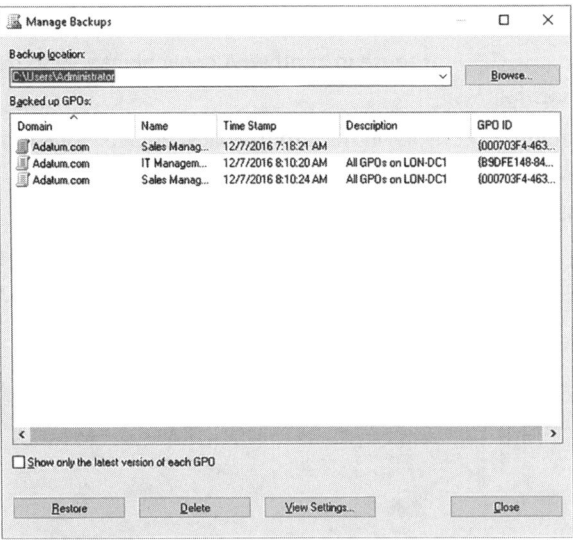

FIGURE 3-20 Managing available backups

Import a GPO

Although you can link the same GPO to multiple containers, including domains, it is not always advisable to do this. Usually, it is better to import a GPO from another domain. The import process requires that you effectively restore the settings of another GPO into a newly created, empty GPO. The process therefore starts with you creating a backup of the source GPO, as described above.

Then, to import the settings, use the following procedure:

1. In the Group Policy Management console on the target domain, create a new GPO in the Group Policy Objects node.
2. Right-click the new GPO, and then click Import Settings.
3. In the Import Settings Wizard, on the Backup GPO page, click Next. You do not need to back up your GPO because it currently contains no settings.
4. On the Backup location page, select the folder where you backed up your source GPO, and click Next.
5. On the Source GPO page, select the appropriate GPO from the Backed Up GPOs list, and then click Next.
6. Click through the wizard to complete the import process. Click Finish when prompted.

You can also use the import-gpo Windows PowerShell cmdlet. For example, to import the IT Managers GPO from the \\LON-DC1\Backup folder to a new GPO called Sales Managers, use the following command:

```
Import-GPO -BackupGpoName "IT Managers" -TargetName "Sales Managers" -Path \\LON-DC1\
Backup
```

Copy a GPO

You can duplicate the settings in one GPO for reuse in another. A convenient way to do this is to copy a GPO. The procedure is as follows:

1. In the Group Policy Management console, in the Group Policy Objects node, right-click the source GPO, and then click Copy.
2. Right-click the Group Policy Objects node, and then click Paste.
3. In the Copy GPO dialog box, shown in Figure 3-21, choose either to Use The Default Permissions For New GPOs, or choose Preserve The Existing Permissions. Click OK.

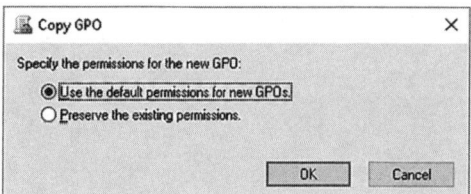

FIGURE 3-21 Configuring permissions on a copied GPO

4. When prompted, click OK.
5. In the Group Policy Objects node, rename the newly created GPO. It has the same name as the source GPO with the prefix Copy Of.

You can also use the copy-gpo Windows PowerShell cmdlet. For example, to copy the IT Manager's GPO to the Sales Manager's GPO, use the following command:

```
Copy-GPO -SourceName "IT Managers" -TargetName "Sales Managers"
```

Create and configure a migration table

Migration tables can help when you wish to use the same GPO in multiple domains. Some GPOs might contain folder redirection settings, which often contain universal naming convention (UNC) folder names, such as \\LON-SVR1\Users\Start-Menu. Others settings might contain security principals, such as computer names.

If you import a GPO from another domain, these UNC names might not be relevant in the target domain. By using migration tables, you can more easily maintain the accuracy of GPO settings when copying between domains. Using migration tables, you can reference and update the following objects types:

- Users
- Groups
- Computers
- UNC paths

To create a migration table, use the following procedure:

1. In the Group Policy Management console, right-click the Domains node, and then click Open Migration Table Editor.
2. In the Migration Table Editor – New dialog box, shown in Figure 3-22, click Tools, and click Populate From GPO.

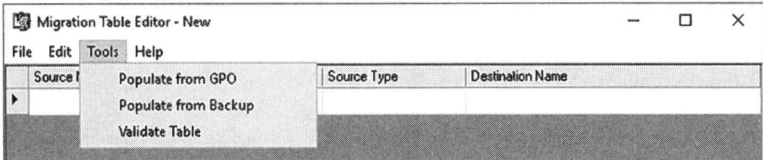

FIGURE 3-22 Populating the GPO migration table

3. In the Select GPO dialog box, shown in Figure 3-23, in the Look In This Domain list, select the source domain. In the Group Policy objects list, click the source GPO. Select the During Scan, Include Security Principals From The DACL On The GPO. Click OK.

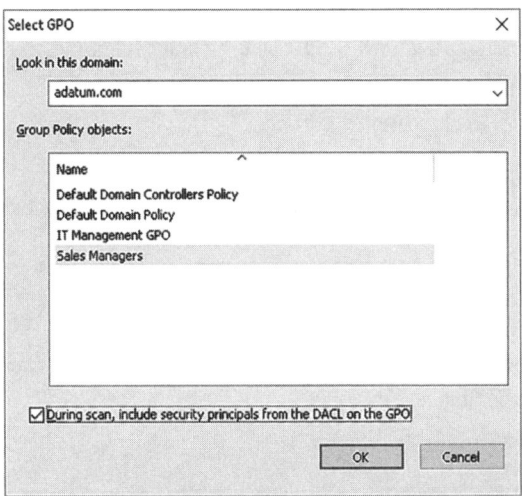

FIGURE 3-23 Selecting a GPO to use to populate the migration table

4. In the Migration Table Editor – New dialog box, shown in Figure 3-24, in the Destination Name column, enter the replacement UNC name(s) as needed.

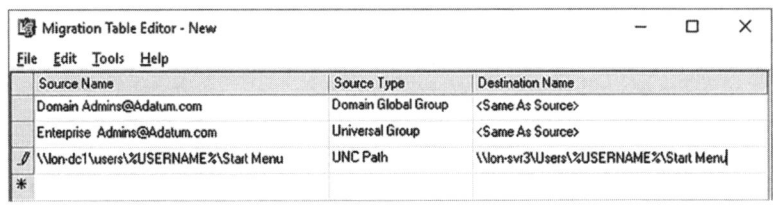

FIGURE 3-24 Editing the destination details

5. When you have made all the required changes, click File, and then click Save.
6. In the Save As dialog box, enter a valid path, enter the name of the file, and then click Save. Make sure you save the migration table to a network accessible location.
7. Close the Migration Table Editor.

EXAM TIP

Consider using the Validate Table option before saving your table. This is accessible from the Tools menu.

You can use the migration table when you import a GPO into a different domain. Use the following procedure:

1. First, back up the source GPO that you referenced in the migration table. For details on this process, see the section in this chapter titled "Back up, import, copy, and restore GPOs." Place the backup files into a network accessible folder.
2. On the target domain, open the Group Policy Management console, navigate to the Group Policy Objects node, and create a new GPO. Use a meaningful name; this does not need to be the same as the source GPO.
3. Right-click the new GPO, and then click Import Settings.
4. In the Import Settings Wizard, on the Welcome page, click Next.
5. On the Backup GPO, click Next. You do not need to back up your GPO because it contains no settings now.
6. On the Backup Location page, in the Backup folder box, type the UNC name to the shared folder that contains the backup of the source GPO, and then click Next.
7. On the Source GPO page, shown in Figure 3-25, in the Backed Up GPOs list, click the appropriate GPO, and then click Next.

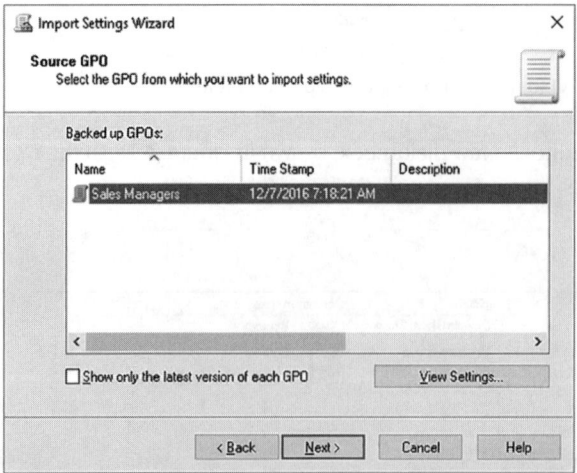

FIGURE 3-25 Specifying the GPO from which settings are migrated

8. On the Scanning Backup page, observe the message that the backup contains security principals and/or UNC paths, as shown in Figure 3-26, and then click Next.

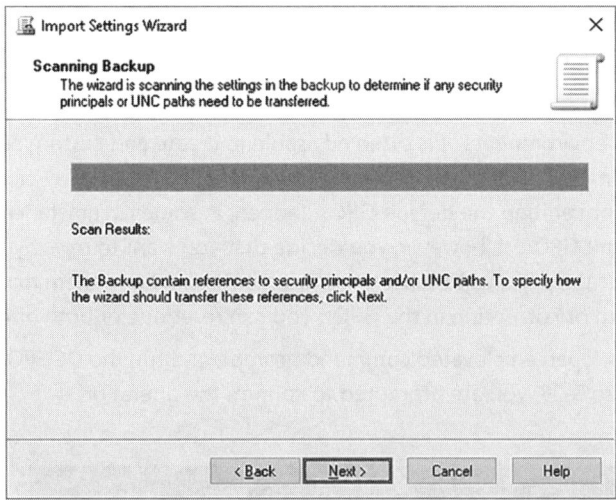

FIGURE 3-26 Viewing the scan results of a GPO import operation

9. On the Migrating References page, as shown in Figure 3-27, click Using This Migration Table To Map Them In The Destination GPO, and then browse and select the migration table from the shared folder where you saved it. Click Next.

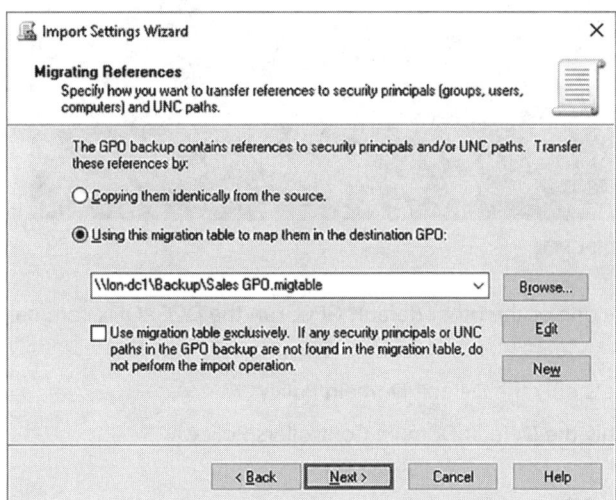

FIGURE 3-27 Specifying the migration table to use

10. On the Completing The Import Settings Wizard page, click Finish.
11. On the Import Progress page, when the Succeeded message displays, click OK.

Reset default GPOs

In an AD DS domain, there are two default GPOs. These are:

- **Default Domain Policy**   This policy is linked to the domain object.
- **Default Domain Controllers Policy**   This policy is linked to the Domain Controllers OU.

Generally, in most AD DS environments, it is often advisable to create and customize GPOs to suit your business requirements rather than editing the two default GPOs. However, there is nothing preventing you from editing the default GPOs. Indeed, in some circumstances, it makes sense to use the default GPOs. If, however, you decide that you want to revert your default GPOs to their initial state, perhaps because that's quicker than editing them manually, or because there is a problem or corruption in the GPOs, you can reset one or both of them.

To reset the default GPOs, open an elevated command prompt, and run the DCGPOFix command. As shown in Figure 3-28, you are prompted to confirm the operation.

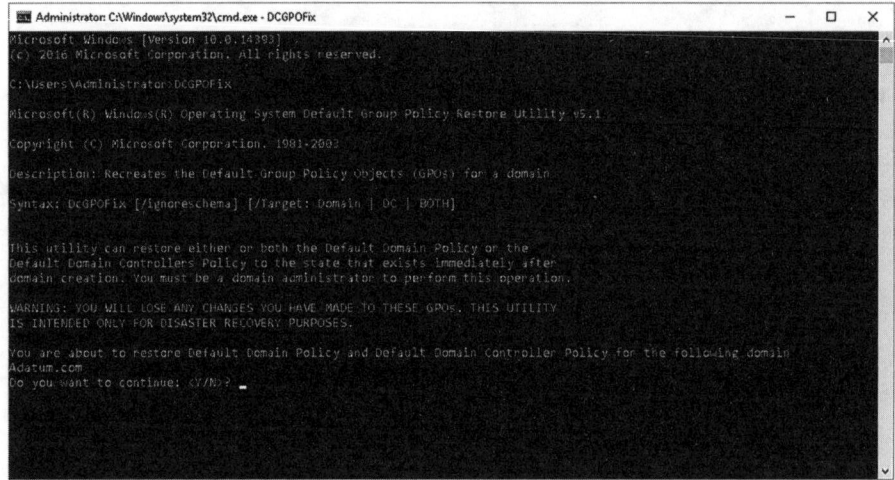

FIGURE 3-28 Resetting the default GPOs

If you wish to restore only one or the other default GPO, run the DCGPOFix command with the following parameters:

- /target:Domain   Resets only the Default Domain Policy.
- /target:DC   Resets only the Default Domain Controllers Policy.

Delegate Group Policy management

In smaller organizations, it is likely that the same person who creates GPOs is the person responsible for configuring the settings within the GPO, and for linking the GPO to the appropriate container objects in a domain. By default, in Windows Server 2016, members of the following groups have full control over all GPO management tasks:

- Enterprise Admins
- Domain Admins
- Group Policy Creator Owners
- Local System

> **EXAM TIP**
>
> Users must be able to apply GPOs for the GPO to configure their settings; this requires at least Read and Apply Group Policy permissions, which are applied by default to all newly created GPOs. These are not management permissions.

However, in larger organizations, the ability to split the administrative tasks associated with GPO management is useful. This splitting of administrative effort is known as *delegating control*. In Windows Server 2016, you can delegate control of the following GPO administrative and management tasks:

- **Creating GPOs** You can grant the required permissions to perform this task by using the Group Policy Management console.
- **Editing GPOs** To edit the settings in GPOs, users require the Read and Write permission on the GPO. Use the Group Policy Management console to assign these permissions.
- **Managing GPO links for sites, domains, or OUs** Linking allows you to enable the GPO settings on a specified container object. In Group Policy Management, use the Delegation tab on the specified container to assign these permissions. Alternatively, use the Delegation Of Control Wizard in Active Directory Users and Computers as described in Chapter 1.
- **Performing GPO modeling analyses for specified domain or OU** Modeling enables an administrator to perform 'what if' analysis for the application and processing of GPOs within the AD DS infrastructure. On a specific container, use the Delegation tab in Group Policy Management to assign these permissions. You can also use the Delegation Of Control Wizard in Active Directory Users and Computers.
- **Reading GPO results data for objects in specified domain or OU** GPO result analysis allows you to generate reports on the effect of GPO settings on target objects within your AD DS environment. As before, use the Delegation tab on a specific container to assign these permissions, or use the Delegation Of Control Wizard.
- **Creating WMI filters** Windows Management Instrumentation (WMI) filters enable you to determine whether a GPO applies to an object in an OU based on the characteristics of that object. For example, the GPO applies if the computer object is running Windows 10 and has 8GB of physical memory. In Group Policy Management, use the Delegation tab on the container to assign these permissions. You can also use the Delegation Of Control Wizard.

EXAM TIP

You can use the Windows PowerShell Get-GPPermissions cmdlet to view current GPO permissions, and the Set-GPPermissions cmdlet to modify permissions.

To use the Group Policy Management console to delegate permissions to manage GPOs, use the following procedure:

1. In the Group Policy Management console, select the container object on which you want to delegate control. For example, in the navigation pane, click the domain.

2. In the details pane, click the Delegation tab, as shown in Figure 3-29.

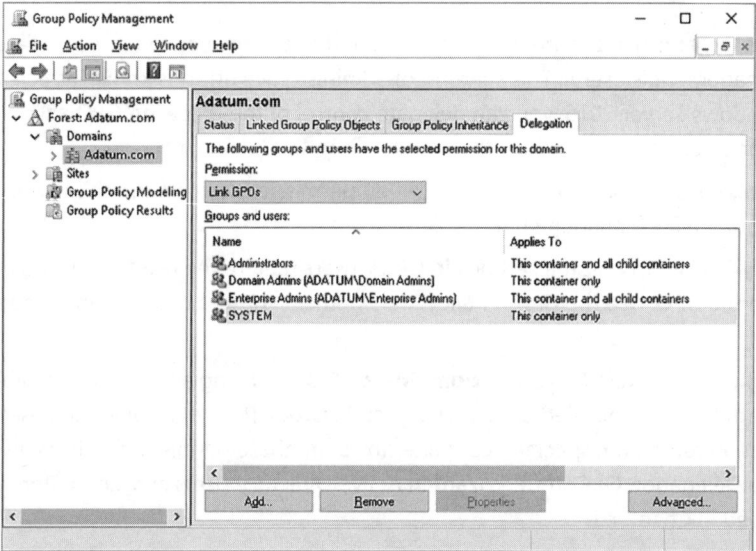

FIGURE 3-29 Delegating the Link GPOs permission using the Group Policy Management console

3. In the Permission list, click the permission that you want to delegate. Choose between: Link GPOs, Perform Group Policy Modeling Analyses, and Read Group Policy Results Data.

4. Click Add, and in the Select User, Computer, or Group dialog box, in the Enter The Object Name To Select Text box, type the group or user name to which you want to delegate the permission, and then click OK.

5. In the Add Group Or User dialog box, shown in Figure 3-30, in the Permissions list, select the required inheritance. Choose between: This Container Only and This Container And All Child Containers. Click OK.

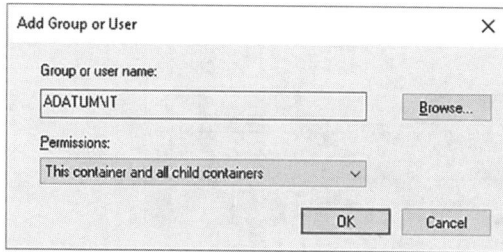

FIGURE 3-30 Selecting the group for delegation

6. Review the changes, as shown in Figure 3-31. You can use the Advanced button to fine tune the required permissions.

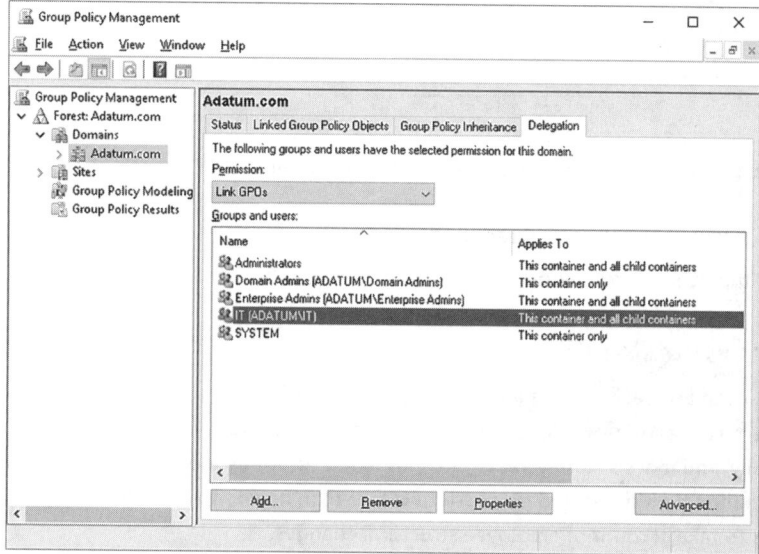

FIGURE 3-31 Verifying the newly delegated permissions

To use the Delegation Of Control Wizard to delegate permissions to manage GPO links, use the following procedure:

1. In Active Directory Users and Computers, locate and right-click your target container, and then click Delegate Control.
2. In the Delegation Of Control Wizard, on the Welcome page, click Next.
3. On the Users Or Groups page, click Add, and locate the user or group to which you want to delegate the specific task you are configuring. Click OK, and then click Next.
4. On the Tasks To Delegate page, shown in Figure 3-32, in the Delegate The Following Common Tasks list, select the check box for the Manage Group Policy links, and click Next.

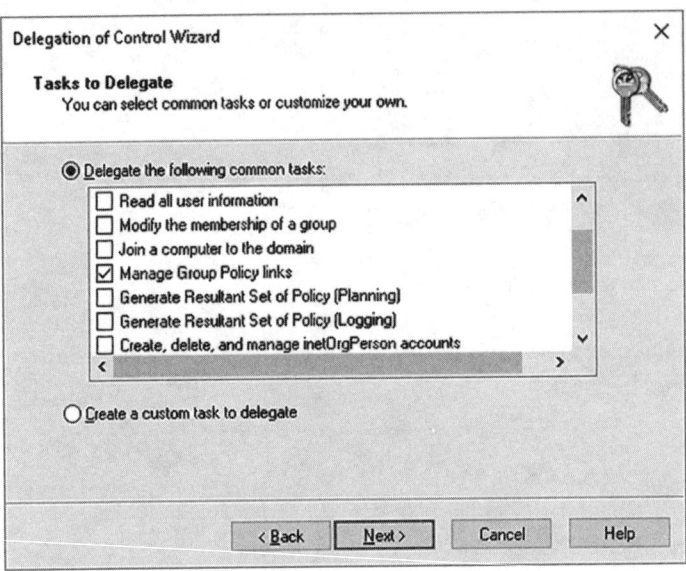

FIGURE 3-32 Using the Delegation Of Control Wizard to delegate GPO management tasks

5. AD DS permissions are configured. Click Finish.

Delegating the other permissions, such as creating WMI filters, is a broadly similar process.

> **NOTE GROUPS NOT USERS**
>
> It is important to use best practice and, unless strictly necessary to do otherwise; always delegate permissions to groups rather than to user accounts directly. This enables you to more easily, and more securely, make changes in the future by moving users between groups to change their delegated permissions rather than having to modify delegated permissions to take account of employee structural changes.

Detect health issues using the Group Policy Infrastructure Status dashboard

Windows Server 2016 AD DS provides a GPO Infrastructure Status page. This is accessible in the Group Policy Management console. To view the status, use the following procedure:

1. Select the domain object, and then click the Status tab.
2. To view the current status, click Detect Now.
3. Review the information in the details pane, as shown in Figure 3-33.

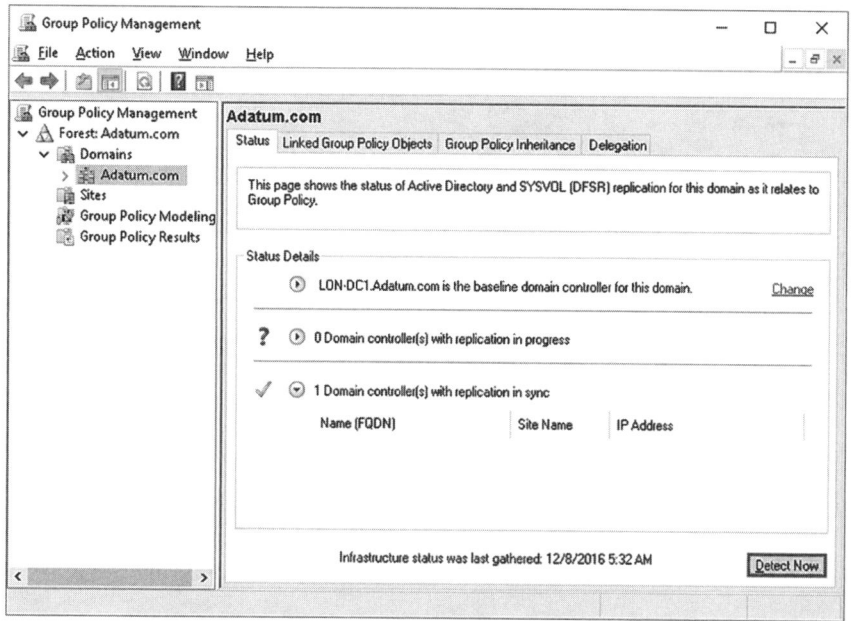

FIGURE 3-33 Checking the status of GPOs

Skill 3.2: Configure Group Policy processing

When you start thinking about using GPOs to configure user and computer settings, you must think about implementing a meaningful OU structure. This is because it is OUs (and to a lesser extent, domains and sites) to which you link GPOs. By default, this means that all objects that you place in the OU (or domain or site) are affected by the linked GPOs.

As we mentioned earlier, since each policy linked to a container might contain conflicting settings—that is, in GPO1, policy setting X is Enabled, while in GPO2, policy setting X is Disabled—we must consider factors that determine in which order GPOs are applied. Indeed, we must also consider factors such as inheritance, precedence, and both WMI and security filtering to make a proper determination.

You should group objects together into OUs because you want to delegate management permissions on those objects, or because you want to configure common settings on the objects. Figure 3-34 shows a representation of the Adatum.com forest, and shows several OUs and linked GPOs.

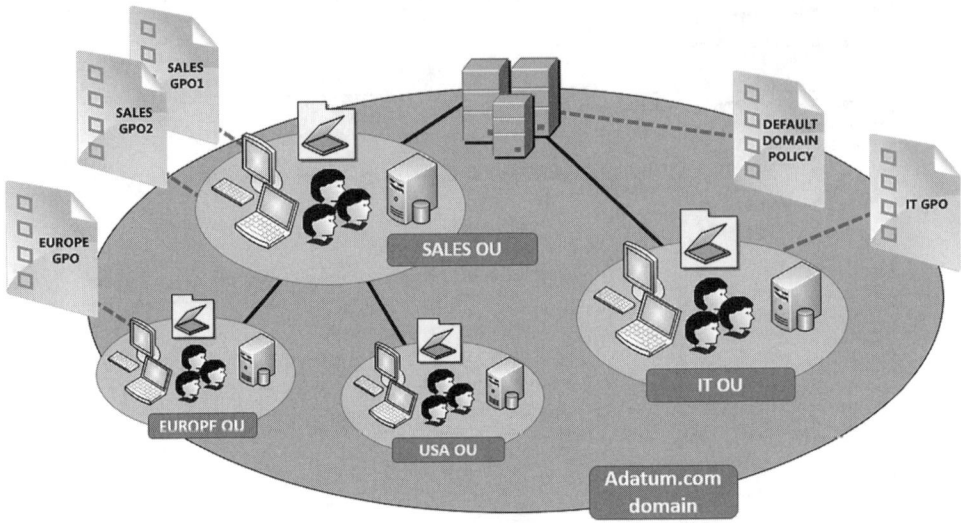

FIGURE 3-34 A representation of the Adatum.com domain and its OU and GPO infrastructure

In Figure 3-35, the Group Policy Management console shows the same structure. We discuss this infrastructure throughout this skill.

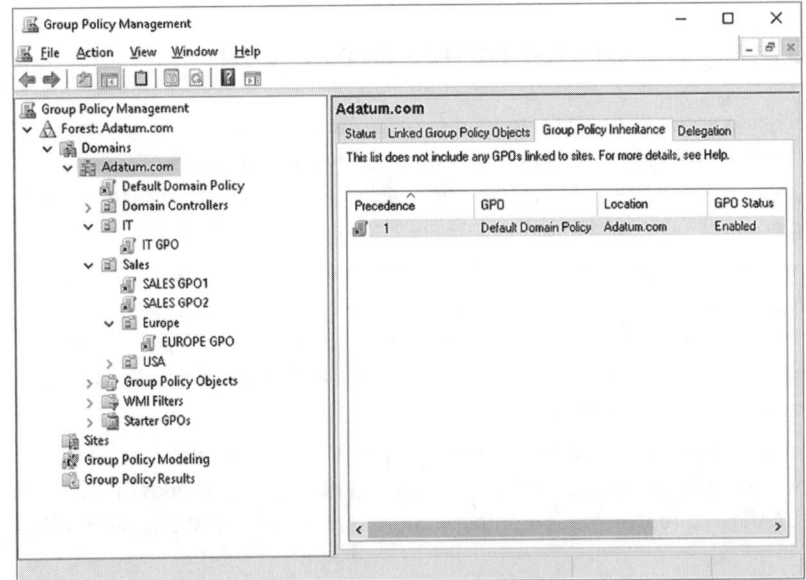

FIGURE 3-35 Group Policy Management console view on Adatum.com OUs and GPOs

This section covers how to:
- Configure processing order and precedence
- Configuring inheritance
- Configure security filtering and WMI filtering
- Configure loopback processing
- Configure and manage slow-link processing and Group Policy caching
- Configure client-side extension behavior
- Force a Group Policy update

Configure processing order and precedence

By default, if multiple GPOs apply to objects in an OU, the settings in the GPO that has the lowest link order (1 being the lowest) takes precedence. That is not to say that the whole GPO overwrites all previously applied settings. What happens depends on how the settings are configured.

For example, suppose you create a GPO that configures only the Security Settings in the Computer Configuration node. Then suppose you create another GPO linked to the same container in which you configure only the Windows Components under the Administrative Templates folder. None of these settings conflict with one another. Therefore, it doesn't matter which has the lowest link order.

However, let's suppose you configure the same two GPOs linked to the same container. This time, both GPOs configure the same settings; for example, in Windows Components in the Administrative Templates folder under the Computer Configuration node. In this instance, the setting that is applied to objects in the OU is determined by the link order.

> **EXAM TIP**
>
> If you link only a single GPO to any given container, you do not need to consider the processing order of the GPOs.

You must also consider the fact that settings are, by default, inherited from higher-level containers to which GPOs are linked. So, in our example, settings applied to the Default Domain Policy also apply to objects in the Sales OU. Likewise, objects in the Europe OU receive their settings, by default, from the Default Domain Policy as well as from both the SALES GPO1 and SALES GPO2. These settings are in addition to the settings applied to the EUROPE GPO, which is linked to the Europe OU. In the case of any conflicting settings (and only in the case of conflicting settings), the GPO applied last takes precedence, and those settings are applied. In this scenario, the last-applied GPO would be the one linked to the Europe OU.

Therefore, to configure precedence, you must link your GPOs to the correct OU. Those at the lower levels in our diagram have the higher precedence. To configure link order, open the

Group Policy Management console, as shown in Figure 3-36, and use the arrow buttons to change the link order in OUs with multiple linked GPOs.

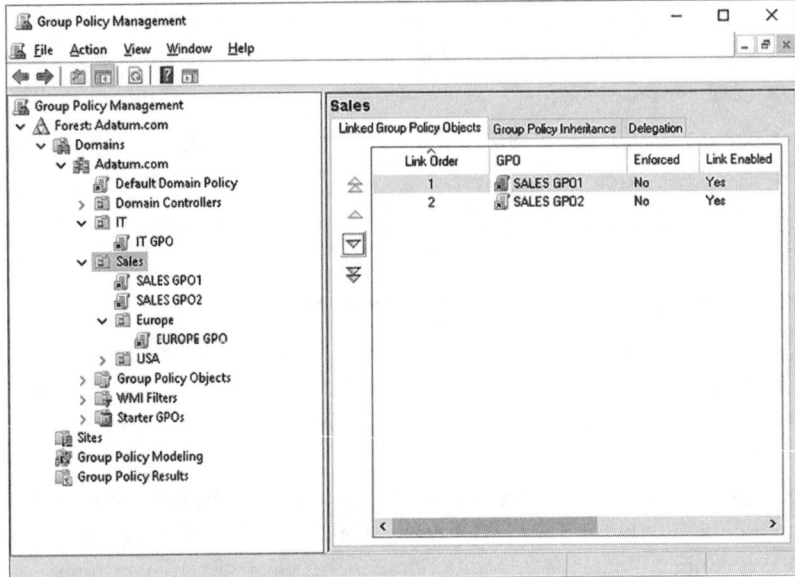

FIGURE 3-36 Configuring link order for multiple GPOs

Configuring inheritance

By default, any GPOs you create and link to high-level objects in your OU tree also apply to all objects beneath that link. For example, in our scenario in Figure 3-34, the Default Domain Policy linked to the domain is applied to all objects in all OUs beneath that point.

Again, in our example, the computers and users in the Europe OU beneath the Sales OU receive settings not only from the directly linked EUROPE GPO, but also inherit settings from the Default Domain Policy, and both SALES GPO1 and SALES GPO2.

In fact, it is beneficial that this inheritance occurs because it enables you to link GPOs high up in the OU tree with settings that you want to apply to all computers (or users), knowing that these settings apply to subordinate objects. Best practice, therefore, is to plan to take advantage of this inheritance behavior and configure the settings in high-level GPOs to apply to all objects. Then, as you move down the OU tree to sub OUs, create and link specific GPOs with settings that affect only the objects in that container.

EXAM TIP

Inherited GPOs have a lower precedence value than directly linked GPOs. This is because of the last processed principle: GPOs that apply last overwrite conflicting settings from higher-level GPOs.

Block inheritance

Occasionally, however, despite the best-planned OU structure, you might find that you want to block the inheritance of GPO settings from further up the OU tree. You can do this on a per-container basis. That is, you can block inheritance on a specific OU.

When you choose to block inheritance, you block the settings for all GPOs linked to containers above the OU you are blocking. For example, as shown in Figure 3-37, inheritance is blocked on the SALES OU. Whereas the DEFAULT DOMAIN POLICY once applied to objects in the SALES OU, as well as the EUROPE OU and the USA OU, now, the settings in the DEFAULT DOMAIN POLICY do not apply in the SALES OU and beyond.

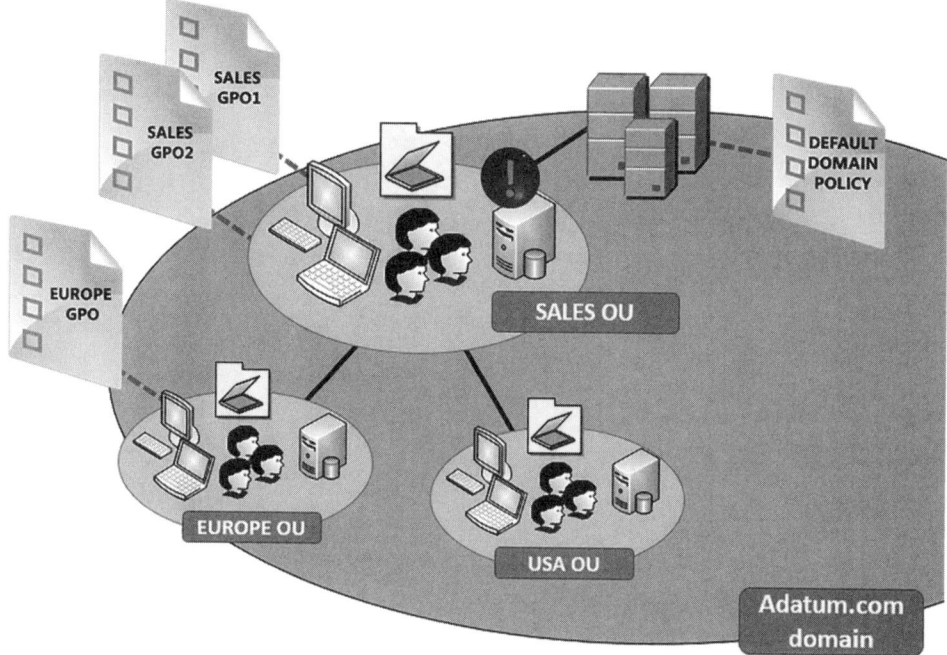

FIGURE 3-37 Blocking inheritance on the Sales OU

To configure this behavior, complete the following procedure:

1. Open the Group Policy Management console.
2. In the navigation pane, as shown in Figure 3-38, right-click the relevant OU, and then click Block Inheritance.

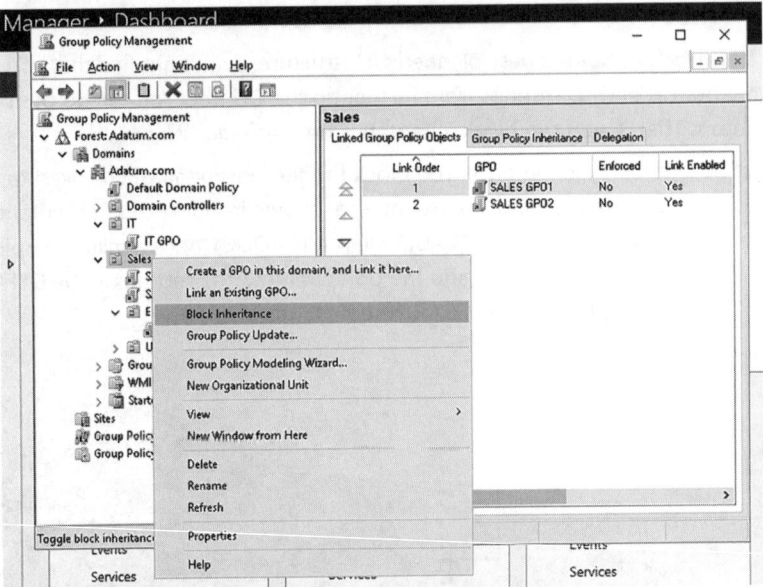

FIGURE 3-38 Enabling Block Inheritance in Group Policy Management

3. In Group Policy Management, as shown in Figure 3-39, the blue exclamation point indicates that inheritance is blocked.

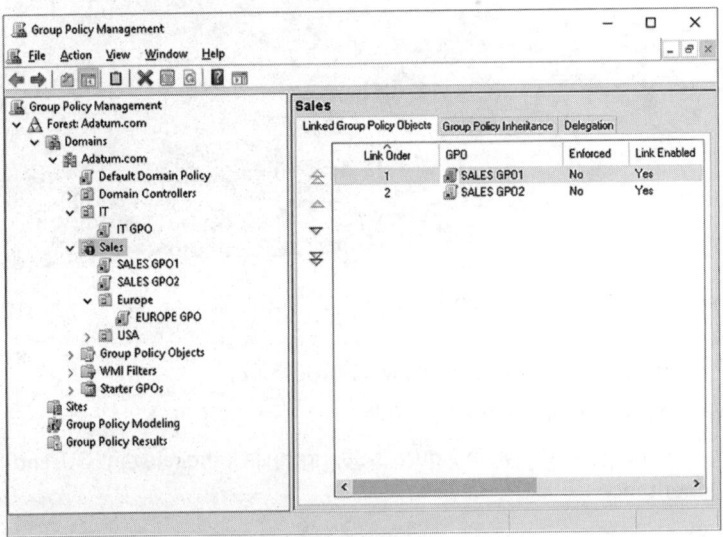

FIGURE 3-39 Inheritance blocked on the Sales OU

You can verify which GPOs settings are inherited by selecting the appropriate GPO in the Group Policy Management console, and then, in the details pane, clicking the Group Policy Inheritance tab. Only policies that are applying are displayed, as shown in Figure 3-40.

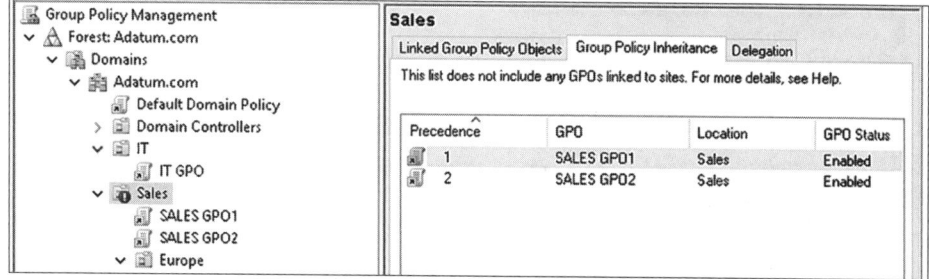

FIGURE 3-40 Viewing the inheritance status of an OU

EXAM TIP

You can use the Windows PowerShell Get-GPinheritance cmdlet to view current GPO inheritance, and the Set-GPinheritance cmdlet to modify inheritance.

Configure enforced policies

Given that an administrator of an OU can block inheritance on that OU, effectively preventing all configured settings in GPOs linked higher up the OU tree, this might not always be desirable. For example, as a domain-level administrator, you might want to ensure that your domain-linked GPO settings apply to all computers (or users) irrespective of any block settings configured by down-level admins.

This is where enforcement is useful. GPOs can be enforced, which is to say that using block inheritance cannot block them.

EXAM TIP

Whereas you configure blocking on a per-OU basis, you configure enforcement on a per-policy basis.

To configure GPO enforcement, use the following procedure:

1. Open Group Policy Management.
2. Locate the GPO you want to enforce, and right-click it, as shown in Figure 3-41.

Skill 3.2: Configure Group Policy processing **CHAPTER 3** **185**

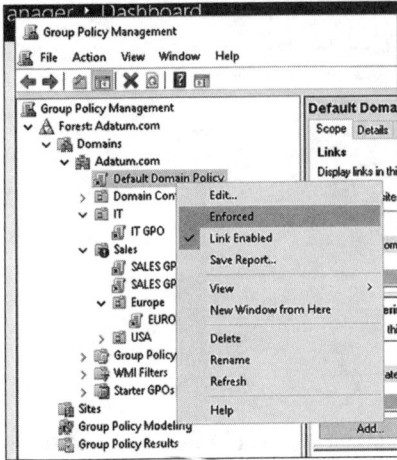

FIGURE 3-41 Enforcing a GPO

3. Click Enforced.

As shown in Figure 3-42, the padlock symbol on the GPO indicates enforcement. In the details pane, the Enforced column is set to Yes.

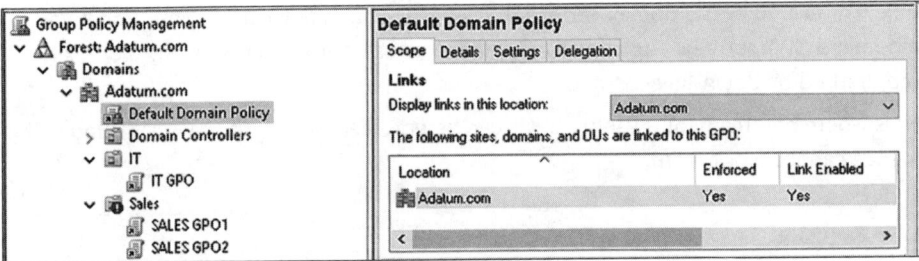

FIGURE 3-42 Verifying enforcement of a GPO

You can see the effect of the enforcement on lower level OUs. In the Sales OU, there is a block configured. But due to the enforcement of the Default Domain Policy, this policy appears, as shown in Figure 3-43, on the Group Policy Inheritance tab in the details pane for the Sales OU. This means that enforcement trumps blocking.

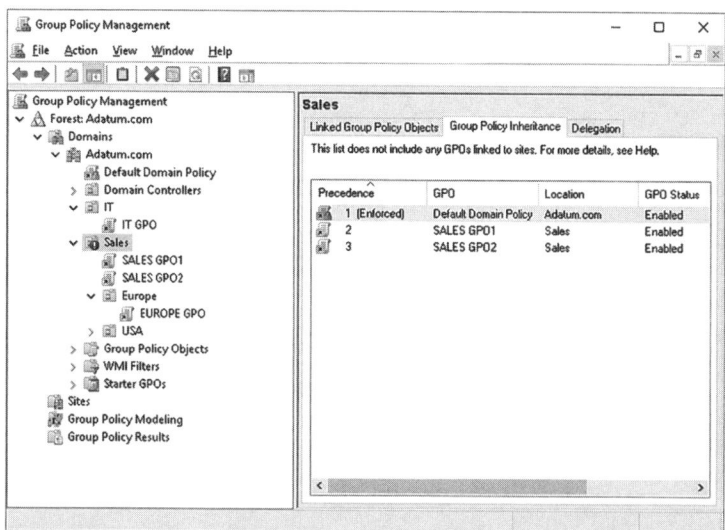

FIGURE 3-43 Verifying inheritance after enforcement

> **EXAM TIP**
>
> When you enforce a GPO, you also change its precedence. In Figure 3-43, the Default Domain Policy now has the highest precedence (but the lowest precedence value). Conflicting settings in the Default Domain Policy override those in the other linked GPOs.

Configure security filtering and WMI filtering

Until now, we have assumed that all of the configured settings in one or more GPOs should apply to all objects in an OU, either directly through a link, or indirectly, through inheritance. By using Block Inheritance and Enforced, you can control the default behavior, but this is still at the whole container level.

What if you want to apply the settings of a GPO to most, but not all the computers in a specific OU? Or maybe you want a restrictive security GPO to apply to *most* users in a department, but not all of them. Perhaps you create a GPO to distribute software updates, but don't want it to apply to computers that do not meet the minimum hardware requirements for the software. These are all examples of situations in which GPO security or WMI filtering can be useful.

Configuring security filtering

A security filter for a GPO works on the simple premise that for a policy to apply to an object, that object requires at least Read and Apply group policy permissions on the GPO. These permissions are applied by default, of course, to all GPOs. You can see the permissions assigned to the Authenticated Users group in Figure 3-44.

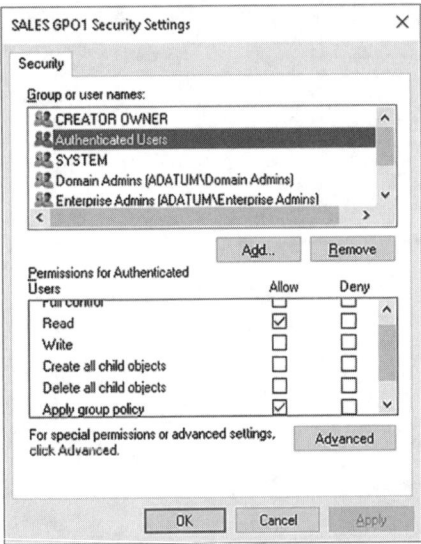

FIGURE 3-44 Viewing the security permissions on a GPO

You can use security filtering to implement one of two strategies:

- **Applies To Everyone But** In this scenario, you want your GPO settings to apply to all users (or computers) except for one (or a couple) of users or computers. To achieve this, you grant the specific user (or computer) the Deny Apply Group Policy permission. This prevents that user (or computer) from applying the policy.

- **Applies To Only** In this scenario, you want the policy to apply only to a specific user or computer. This begs the question as to whether the user or computer should be in the OU in the first place. Assuming there are sound reasons for the object's presence in the OU, you can remove the Allow Apply group policy permission from the Authenticated Users group. Next, grant the user or computer the Allow Read and Allow Apply Group Policy permissions on the GPO.

Be careful that you do not remove the Allow Read permission for the Authenticated Users group. This is because unless this group has Read permissions, the policy is not processed by the client at all.

> *NOTE* **SECURITY UPDATE 3159398, JUNE 2016**
>
> Without this update, GPOs are retrieved in the security context of the user account. With this update applied to your computers, client computers retrieve GPOs within the security context of the computer account. If you remove the Allow Read permission from the Authenticated Users group, your computers cannot retrieve the policy from the domain controller.

IMPLEMENT THE 'APPLIES TO EVERYONE BUT' STRATEGY

To implement this strategy, you must grant a user or group the deny Apply Group Policy permission. To do this, use must use the Delegation tab:

1. In the Group Policy Management console, in the Group Policy Objects container, select the appropriate GPO.
2. In the details pane, click the Delegation tab, as shown in Figure 3-45.

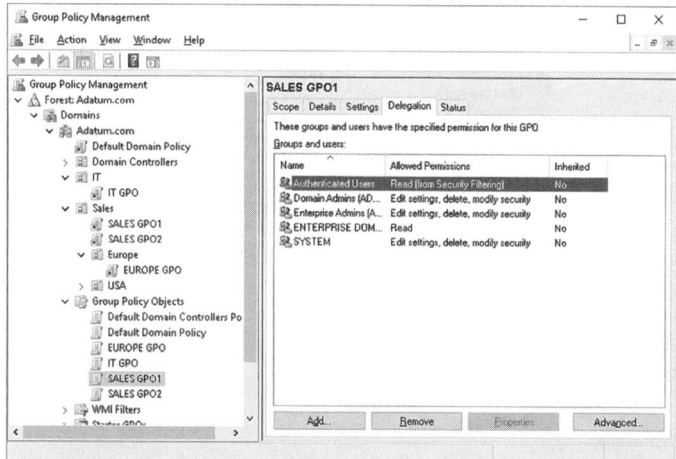

FIGURE 3-45 Viewing the current GPO security settings on the Delegation tab

3. Click Advanced, and in the GPO Security Settings dialog box, click Add.
4. In the Select Users, Computers, Service Accounts, Or Groups dialog box, type the name of the user or group you want to exclude, and then click OK.
5. The user or group that you select is granted the Allow Read permission automatically. Clear the Allow Read permission check box, and then select the Deny check box for Apply Group Policy, as shown in Figure 3-46, and then click OK.

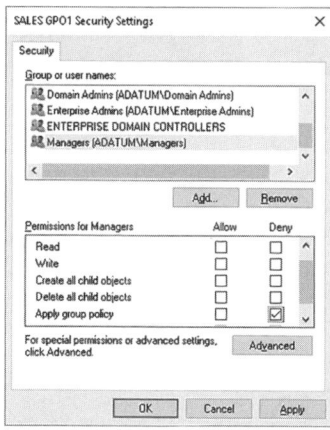

FIGURE 3-46 Configuring the Apply Group Policy permission

Skill 3.2: Configure Group Policy processing   **CHAPTER 3**   **189**

6. You receive a security warning that Deny permissions override other permissions. Click Yes to continue.

7. The user or group you specified is listed on the Delegation tab with Custom permissions, as shown in Figure 3-47.

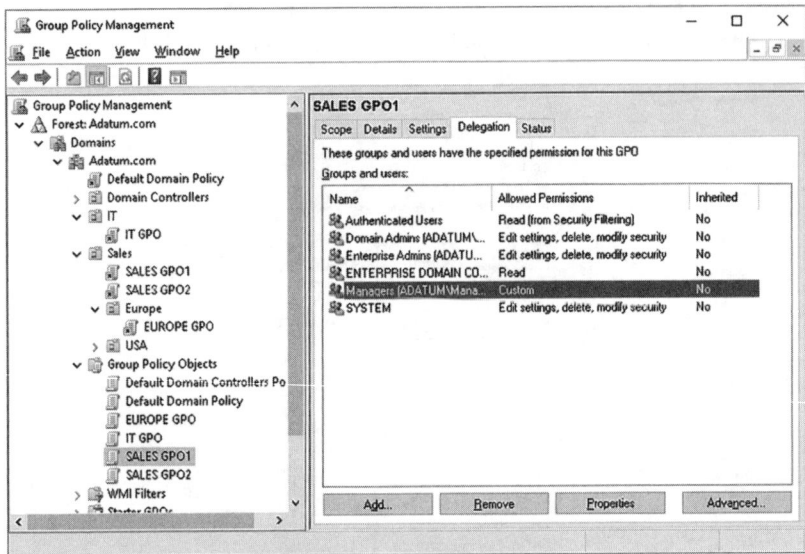

FIGURE 3-47 Reviewing the configured permissions

IMPLEMENT THE 'APPLIES TO ONLY' STRATEGY

To implement this strategy, you must remove the Authenticated Users security setting and then grant a specific security group the Allow Apply Group Policy permission. Use the following procedure:

1. In the Group Policy Management console, in the Group Policy Objects container, select the appropriate GPO.

2. On the Scope tab, in the Security Filtering section, select the Authenticated Users group, as shown in Figure 3-48, click Remove, and then click OK.

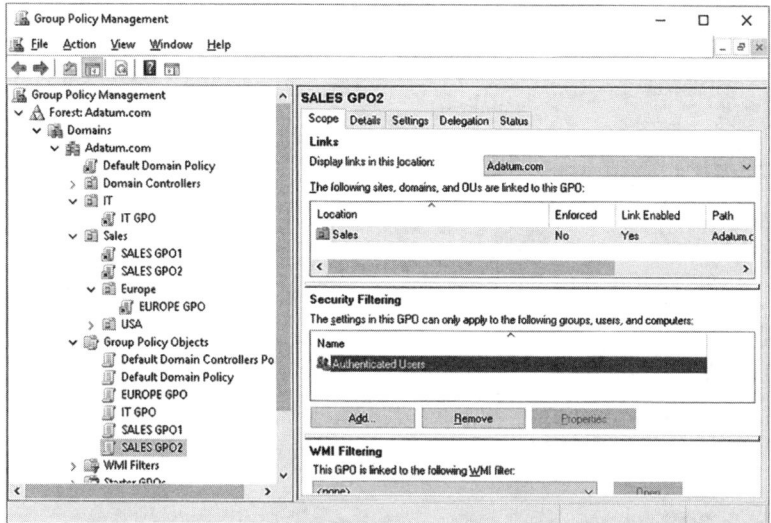

FIGURE 3-48 Using the Security Filtering option to configure GPO permissions

3. Click Add, and in the Select User, Computer, Or Group dialog box, type the name of the user or group to which you want the GPO to apply, and then click OK. The Security Filtering list contains only the object to which the GPO will apply, as shown in Figure 3-49.

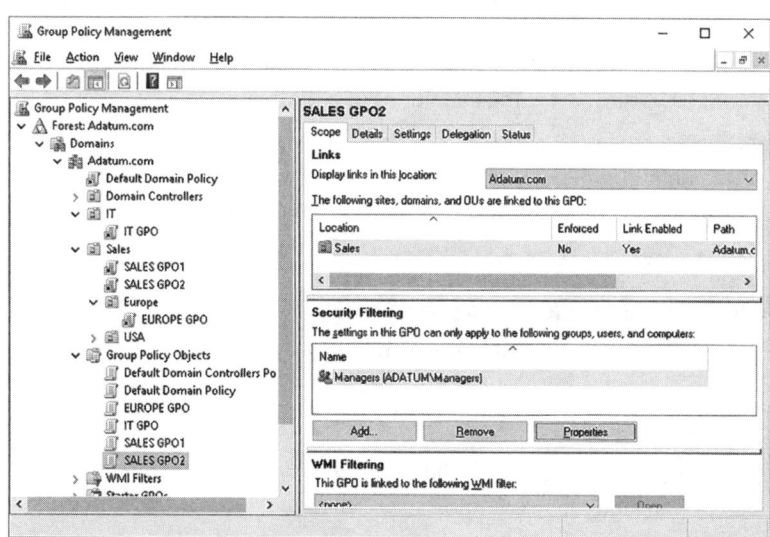

FIGURE 3-49 Verifying the Security Filtering change

You can view the configured permissions by using the Delegation tab, as shown in Figure 3-50, and selecting the appropriate security principal.

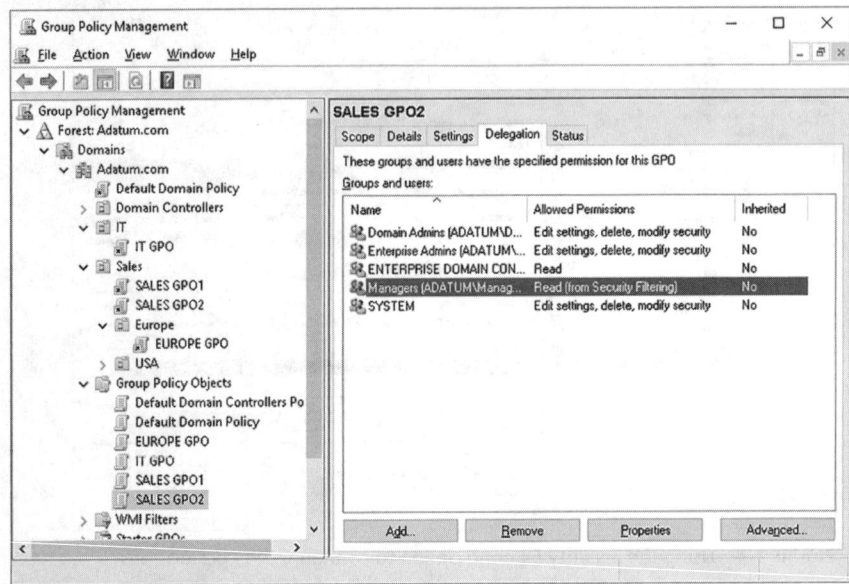

FIGURE 3-50 Viewing the applied permissions

Configuring WMI filtering

Security filtering works well when you can select a security principal that readily identifies the collection of users, groups, or computers that you want to configure. Sometimes, however, there is no such security principal. This is where using WMI filtering can be useful. For a GPO to apply to a computer, it must meet the conditions of a WMI filter.

A WMI filter is based on a WMI query that defines the properties of the objects that you are seeking. For example, you might want to select only those computers installed with Windows 10 or Windows Server 2016. The WMI filter looks something like this:

```
SELECT * FROM Win32_OperatingSystem WHERE Version LIKE "10.%"
```

To create a WMI filter, use the following procedure:

1. In the Group Policy Management console, in the navigation pane, click the WMI Filters node.
2. Right-click WMI Filters, and then click New.
3. In the New WMI Filter dialog box, in the Name box, type the name of your WMI filter, type a Description, and then click Add.
4. In the WMI Query dialog box, shown in Figure 3-51, in the Query box, type the WMI query, and then click OK.

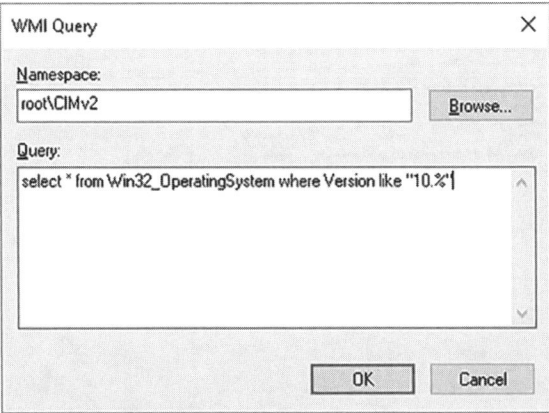

FIGURE 3-51 Configuring a WMI query

5. In the New WMI Filter dialog box, shown in Figure 3-52, click Save.

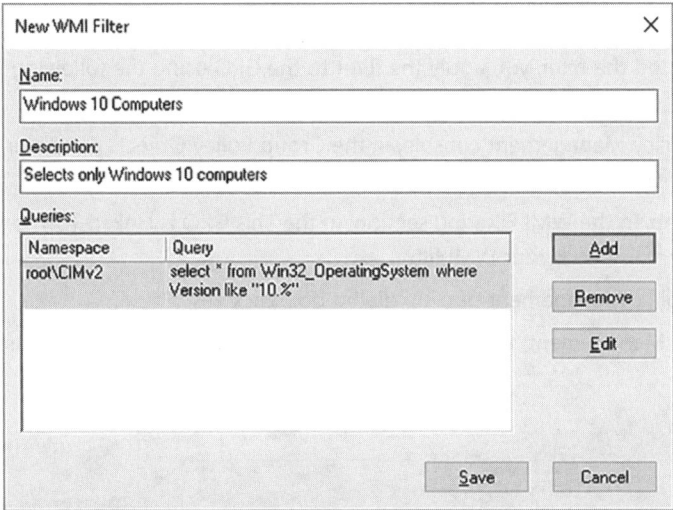

FIGURE 3-52 Configuring a WMI filter

6. Your newly defined WMI filter is listed in the Group Policy Management console in the WMI Filters node, as shown in Figure 3-53.

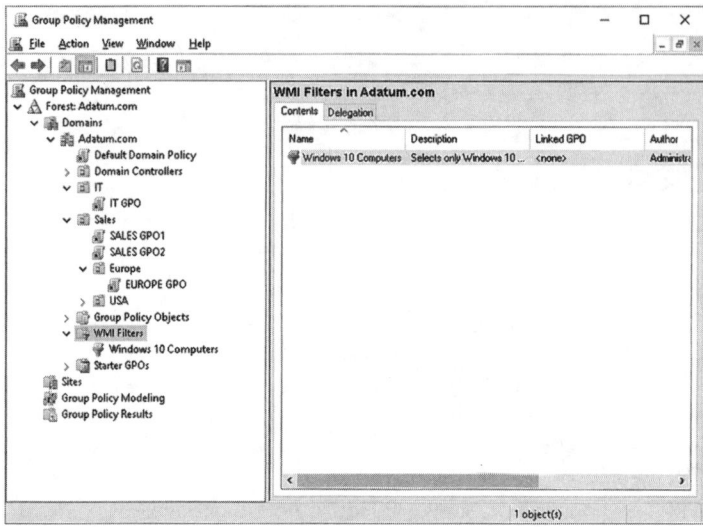

FIGURE 3-53 Viewing the available WMI filters

After you have created the filter, you apply the filter to the GPO using the following procedure:

1. In the Group Policy Management console, in the Group Policy Objects container, select the appropriate GPO.
2. On the Scope tab, in the WMI Filtering section, in the This GPO Is Linked To The Following WMI Filter list, click your WMI filter.
3. In the Group Policy Management pop-up dialog box, click Yes.
4. In Group Policy Management, the WMI Filtering is configured, as shown in Figure 3-54.

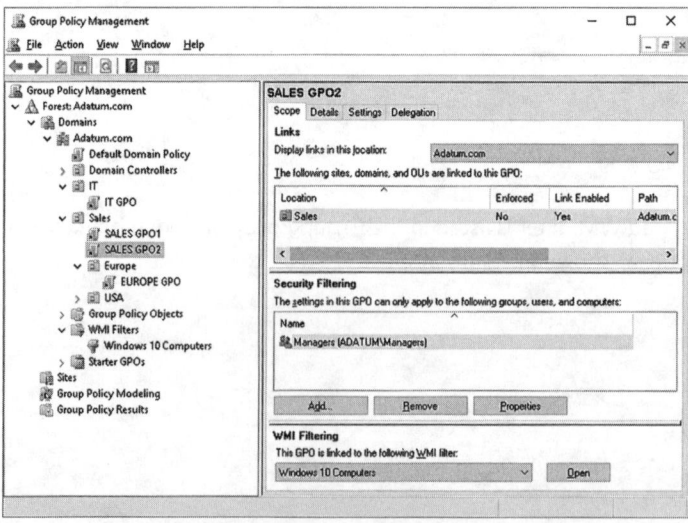

FIGURE 3-54 Verifying the application of WMI filters

In this example, we created a WMI filter with a single WMI query. However, you can easily build complex, multi-condition queries for more complex situations. In addition, once you have created your WMI filters, you can apply them to multiple GPOs; you do not need to create them separately for each GPO.

> **NEED MORE REVIEW?** **CREATE THE WMI FILTERS**
>
> To review further details about using WMI filters, refer to the Microsoft TechNet website at *https://technet.microsoft.com/library/jj899801(v=ws.11).aspx*.

Configure loopback processing

In some organizations, users sign in from more than one computer. If you are using GPOs to configure these users' desktop settings, it is important to understand how GPOs apply when a user, in one OU, signs in at a computer from another OU. When you use GPOs to configure desktop settings, by default, a user's settings are applied from the GPOs linked to the user object in AD DS. In other words, the settings that apply are determined by the OU in which the user object is stored.

However, there might be situations in which you want certain computers to present a standard desktop, irrespective of who signs in. For example, you might have kiosk computers in a public area within your organization, and it might be desirable for these computers to have an enforced, standard desktop.

Loopback processing enables you to change the default behavior so that instead of the desktop settings applying based on the user's OU, the settings that apply are determined by the location of the computer object in AD DS.

> **NOTE** **DESKTOP SETTINGS**
>
> Remember that desktop settings are stored in the User Configuration node of a GPO, and that it is therefore logical, in most situations, that the GPO that applies the User Configuration be the GPO(s) linked to the user's location in AD DS.

To enable GPO loopback processing, you edit the following location in the Administrative Templates folder of an appropriate GPO:

1. Open the appropriate GPO for editing.
2. In the Group Policy Management Editor, under the Computer Configuration node, navigate to Policies\Administrative Templates\System, and then select the Group Policy folder, as shown in Figure 3-55.

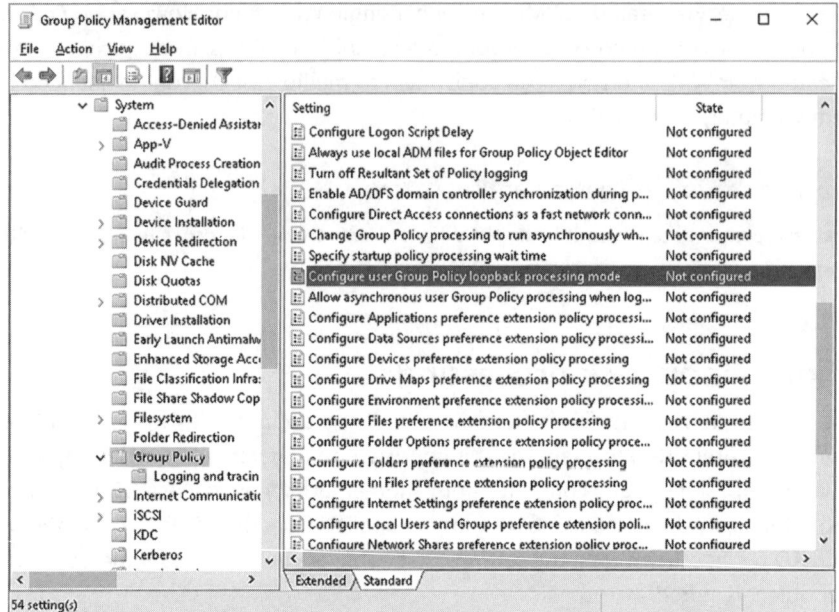

FIGURE 3-55 Configuring loopback processing

3. In the details pane, double-click the Configure User Group Policy Loopback Processing Mode policy setting.

4. In the Configure User Group Policy Loopback Processing Mode dialog box, shown in Figure 3-56, click Enabled, and then select the Mode. You can choose between:

- **Replace** Replaces the user list of GPOs entirely with the list of GPOs obtained for the computer during startup. Only the User Configuration settings of the computer's GPOs apply to the user. Use this mode to apply standard configurations, such as on a kiosk computer; for example, in a library or classroom.

- **Merge** Appends rather than overwrites the User Configuration node settings from the GPO list obtained for the computer during startup to the list of user GPOs obtained for the user during sign in. The computer settings have precedence because they apply last. Use this mode to apply additional settings to users' desktop configurations. For example, when a user signs in at a conference room computer, they receive their usual desktop settings, but the computer GPOs configure certain restrictions, or appearance settings.

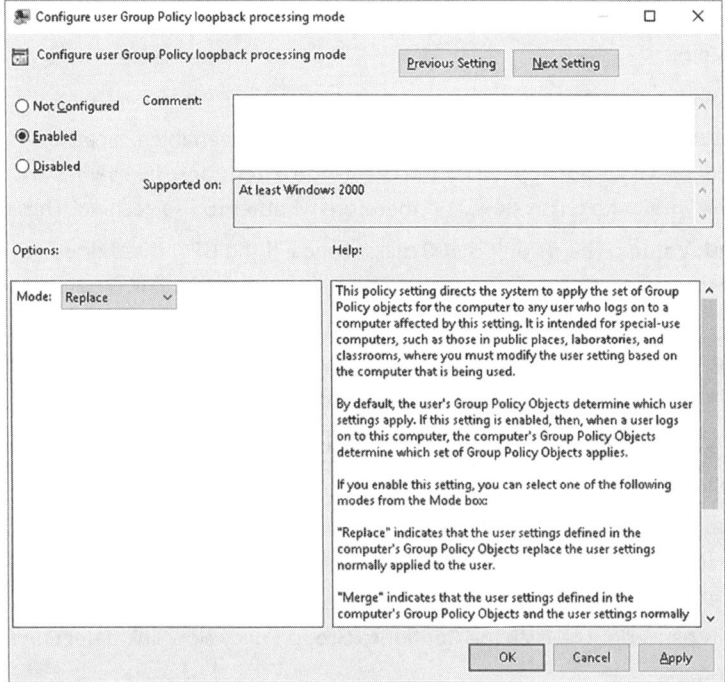

FIGURE 3-56 Enabling loopback processing replace mode

5. Click OK.

Client computers must receive this GPO update before the loopback processing mode is configured on the local computer. This might require a restart.

Configure and manage slow-link processing and Group Policy caching

If your users work from home, or branch offices connected by slow links, you might need to configure GPO processing to account for those slow links. You can configure two options:

- **Slow Link Detection** If a link between the client and the domain controller serving the GPOs is slower than 500 kilobits per second, and the Configure Group Policy slow link detection setting is enabled, the client processes GPOs differently. Specifically, some client-side extensions are disabled and do not process related policy settings. This helps optimize the available bandwidth. When a slow link is detected, the following client-side extensions are disabled:
    - Internet Explorer maintenance
    - Software Installation policy
    - Folder Redirection policy
    - Scripts policy

- Internet Protocol security (IPsec) policy
- Wireless policy
- Disk quota policy

- **Caching**   When a client detects a slow link, and caching is enabled, a cached version of the applicable GPOs are applied by the client-side extensions. Two values are used to determine whether a link is slow, and therefore whether to use caching. These are:
    - **Slow Link Value**   The default is 500 milliseconds. If the GPO client does not receive a response from a domain controller in this interval, the link is determined to be slow.
    - **Timeout Value**   The default is 5000 milliseconds. After this period, the client assumes there is no network connectivity and caching is used.

To enable and configure slow link detection, use the following procedure:

1. Open the appropriate GPO for editing.
2. In the Group Policy Management Editor, under the Computer Configuration node, navigate to Policies\Administrative Templates\System, and then select the Group Policy folder, as shown in Figure 3-55.
3. In the details pane, double-click the Configure Group Policy slow link detection setting policy setting.
4. In the Configure Group Policy slow link detection setting dialog box, shown in Figure 3-57, click Enabled, and then configure the connection speed. Remember the default is 500 kbps. Click OK.

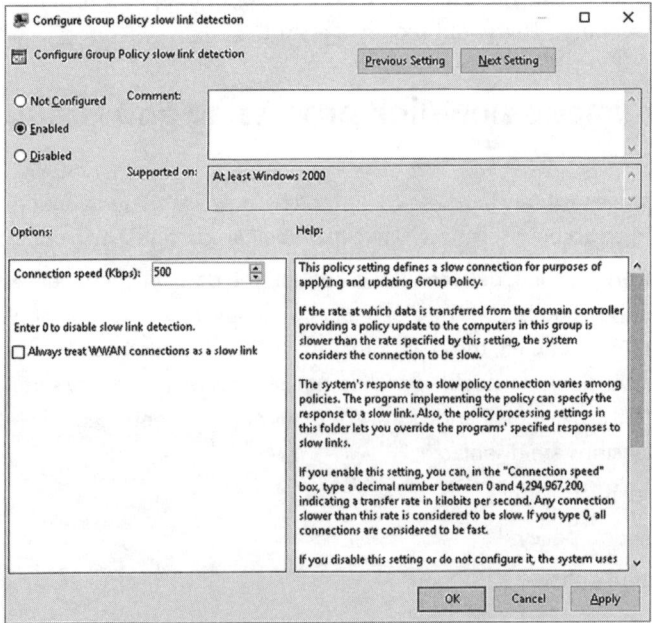

FIGURE 3-57 Configuring slow link detection

To enable and configure caching, use the following procedure:

1. In the details pane, double-click the Configure Group Policy Caching policy setting.
2. In the Configure Group Policy Caching dialog box, shown in Figure 3-58, click Enabled, and then configure the Slow Link Value and Timeout value. Click OK.

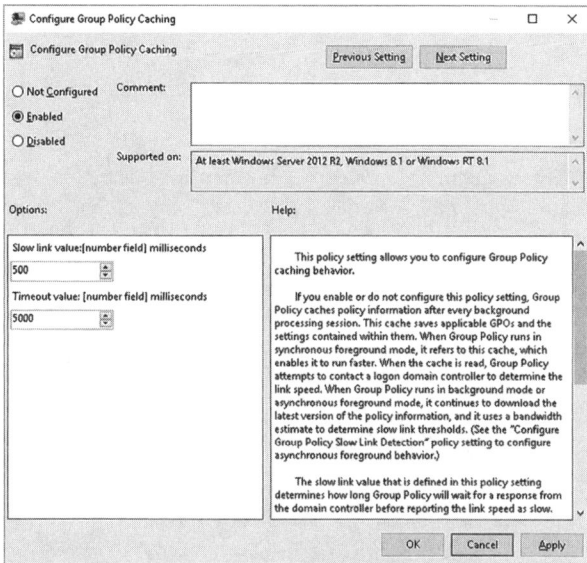

FIGURE 3-58 Enabling Group Policy caching

Client computers must receive these GPO updates before the slow link and caching settings are configured on the local computer. This might require a restart.

Configure client-side extension behavior

We have already mentioned client-side extensions, but it is worth exploring a little more about the configuration options that you have for controlling them and how they process GPO settings.

Generally, client-side extensions only apply GPO settings if those settings are changed since they were last applied. This improves performance. However, you can control this behavior with the Process Even If The Group Policy Objects Have Not Changed value in the appropriate client-side extension setting in a GPO.

For example, use the following procedure to enforce application of GPO settings for the security client-side extension:

1. Open the appropriate GPO for editing.
2. In the Group Policy Management Editor, under the Computer Configuration node, navigate to Policies\Administrative Templates\System, and then select the Group Policy folder.

3. In the details pane, double-click the Configure Security Policy Processing policy setting.

4. As shown in Figure 3-59, click Enabled, and then select the Process Even If The Group Policy Objects Have Changed check box.

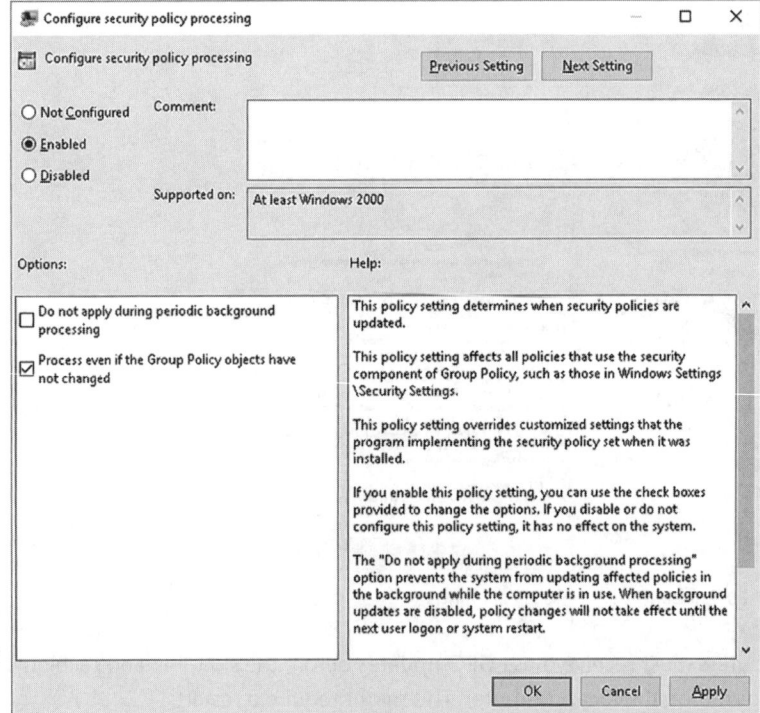

FIGURE 3-59 Configuring the security client-side extension policy processing

5. You can also determine whether the setting is updated while the computer is in use during the automatic refresh intervals for GPOs. The default behavior is that the client-side extension will process updates. If you want to change this, select the Do Not Apply During Periodic Background Processing check box. Click OK.

To configure all client-side extensions, locate the appropriate setting in the Group Policy folder, and configure the two values described above. The required settings are shown in Figure 3-60.

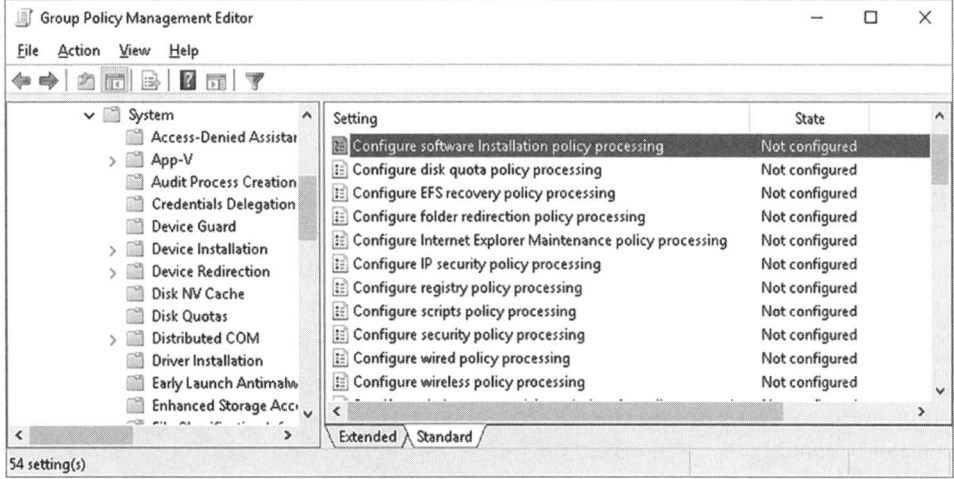

FIGURE 3-60 List of the client-side extension policy processing values

Force a Group Policy update

When you are making changes to GPOs and want to verify the application of those settings, you probably don't want to wait for the settings to automatically refresh. If you don't want to wait, you can restart a computer, or for many user settings, you can sign out and sign back in.

However, you can also use the GPUpdate.exe command-line tool from a command prompt to force the updates to apply. To refresh GPOs settings, use the following procedure:

1. Open a command prompt.
2. Run the gpupdate /force command, as shown in Figure 3-61.

> **NOTE WINDOWS POWERSHELL**
> You can also use the Windows PowerShell invoke-gpupdate cmdlet.

3. You might need to sign out or even restart your computer, depending on the setting.

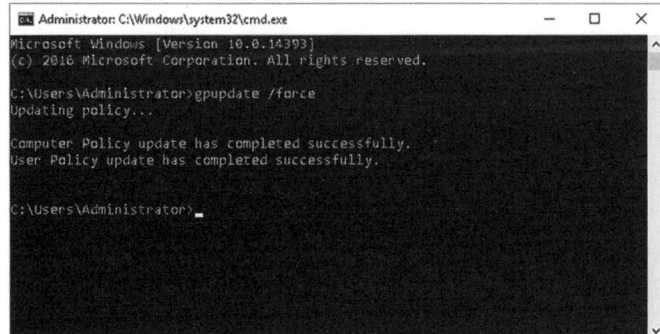

FIGURE 3-61 Force a refresh of the GPOs

> **NEED MORE REVIEW? GPUPDATE**
>
> To review further details about the gpupdate syntax and usage, refer to the Microsoft TechNet website at *https://technet.microsoft.com/library/hh852337(v=ws.11).aspx*.

Skill 3.3: Configure Group Policy settings

So far, we have looked at how to create and link GPOs to your AD DS container objects, such as sites, domains, and OUs. But to properly manage the users and devices in your organization, you must also know how to configure common settings by using GPOs.

In this skill, you learn how to use GPOs to deploy software, how to create and configure startup and login scripts, how to enforce security settings, and when to use administrative templates to control other settings.

> **This section covers how to:**
> - Configure software installation
> - Configure scripts
> - Import security templates
> - Configure folder redirection
> - Configure administrative templates

Configure software installation

One of the most common tasks for any network administrator is that of deploying and maintaining software. Windows Server 2016 provides several different ways for you to achieve this objective, including using GPOs.

With GPO-based software deployment, you can deploy software to either computers, irrespective of who is using the computer, or to users, irrespective of which computer they are using. This is possible because the Software Settings folder exists under both the Computer Configuration and User Configuration nodes in the Group Policy Management Editor, as shown in Figure 3-62.

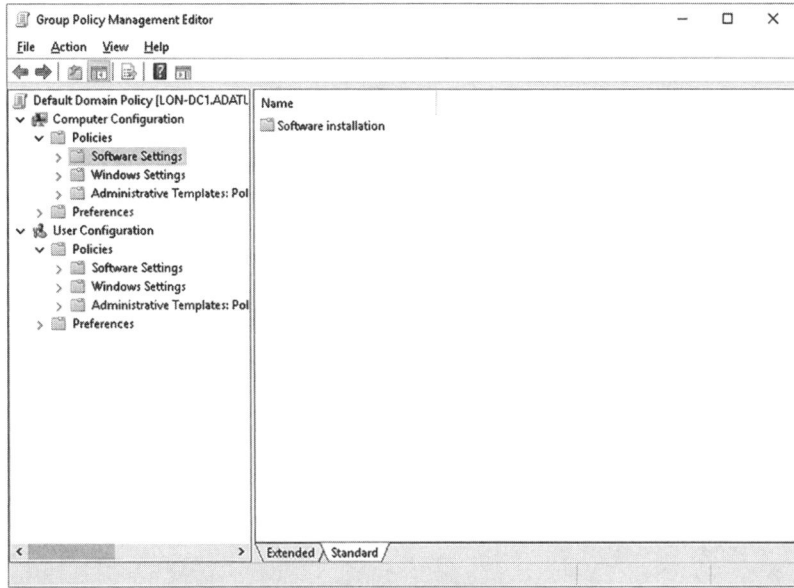

FIGURE 3-62 Preparing to deploy software using GPOs

Using GPOs to deploy software offers several benefits:

- It is relatively simple and certainly quick to set up.
- You don't need any additional infrastructure because GPOs are part of AD DS.
- You require no client-side agent software because the built-in GPO client-side extensions handle the deployment.

However, before deciding whether to use GPOs to deploy software, you should consider the following potential disadvantages:

- You can only deploy certain types of packages using GPOs; specifically, you must use .msi installer packages.
- There are no controls over when software deployment takes place.
- If you are deploying multiple packages, you have no control over which package is deployed first.
- There are no reporting features in GPO software deployment making it difficult to determine whether deployment was successful.

Given these considerations, it is likely that using GPOs to deploy and maintain application software is only suitable for organizations supporting relatively few computers within their AD DS forest.

Preparation

The first stage in using GPOs to deploy software is to store the apps that you want to deploy in an accessible location. Remember that your apps must be in the form of Windows Installer files; that is, .msi files. Place the .msi files into a shared folder on a network server. Ideally, this folder is part of a DFSR folder structure to ensure high availability of the installation files. If you are using the same shared folder for software deployment, configure the default package location. To do this, use the following procedure:

1. Open the appropriate GPO for editing, and in the Group Policy Management Editor, navigate to the Computer Configuration, Policies, Software Settings folder, and then click Software Installation.
2. Right-click Software Installation, and then click Properties.
3. In the Software Installation Properties dialog box, shown in Figure 3-63, in the Default Package Location box, type the path to the software .msi files, and then click OK.
4. If you want, repeat these steps for the User Configuration, Policies, Software Settings, and Software Installation Properties.

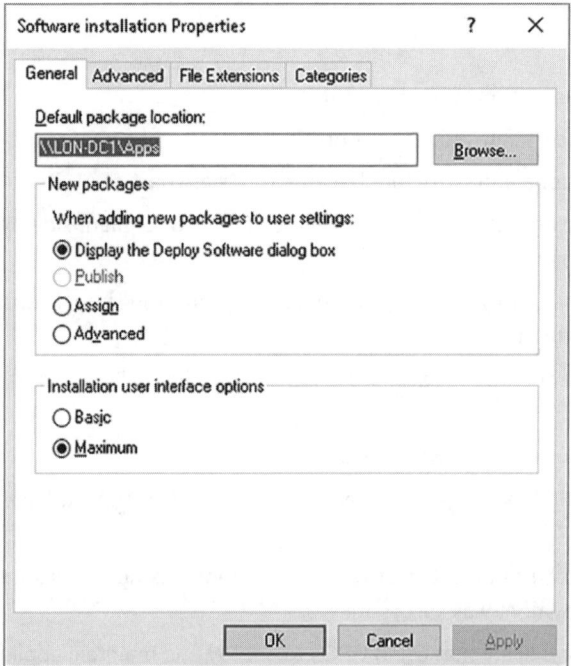

FIGURE 3-63 Defining the default package location

Deployment

Next, you must decide how you want the software to be deployed. You have two choices, which are:

- **Assigning** Assigned software is automatically installed without user intervention.
- **Publishing** Published software is available only if the user chooses to install it.

You can assign software to both users and computers. However, you can only publish software to users. To assign a software application to a computer, use the following procedure:

1. Open the appropriate GPO for editing, and in the Group Policy Management Editor, navigate to the Computer Configuration, Policies, Software Settings folder, and then click Software Installation.
2. Right-click Software Installation, point to New, and then click Package.
3. In the Open dialog box, browse and locate your software installation package, as shown in Figure 3-64.

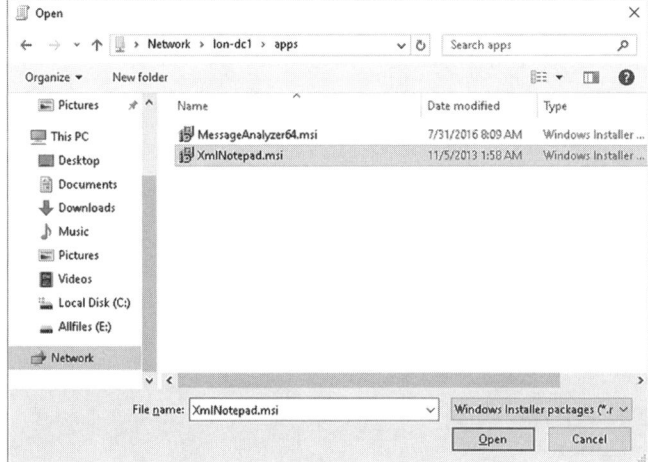

FIGURE 3-64 Locating the .msi software installation file

4. Click Open, and then in the Deploy Software dialog box, shown in Figure 3-65, click Assigned, and then click OK.

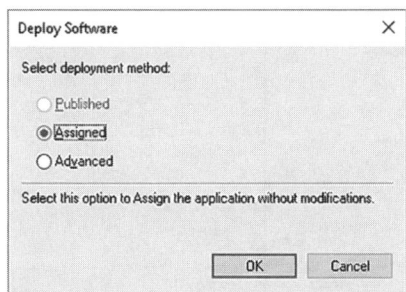

FIGURE 3-65 Selecting the deployment method

Your software package is now ready for deployment, and is listed in the Software Installation folder. As clients refresh the GPO, the new setting applies. In this instance, because you are deploying a package by assigning to a computer, the package deploys following the next computer restart after the GPOs refresh on the computer. The process for assigning to a user is broadly the same.

To deploy a package by publishing to a user, use the following procedure:

1. Open the appropriate GPO for editing, and in the Group Policy Management Editor, navigate to the User Configuration, Policies, Software Settings folder, and then click Software installation.
2. Right-click Software installation, point to New, and then click Package.
3. In the Open dialog box, browse and locate your software installation package, and then click Open.
4. In the Deploy Software dialog box, shown in Figure 3-66, click Published, and then click OK.

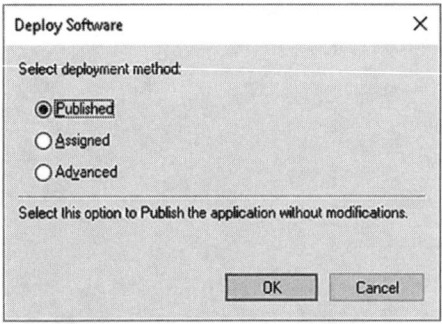

FIGURE 3-66 Publishing a package

Your software package is now ready for deployment, and is listed in the Software Installation folder. As clients refresh the GPO, the new setting applies. In this instance, because you are deploying a package by publishing to a user, the package is available for deployment by using the Control Panel once the GPOs are refreshed, as shown in Figure 3-67.

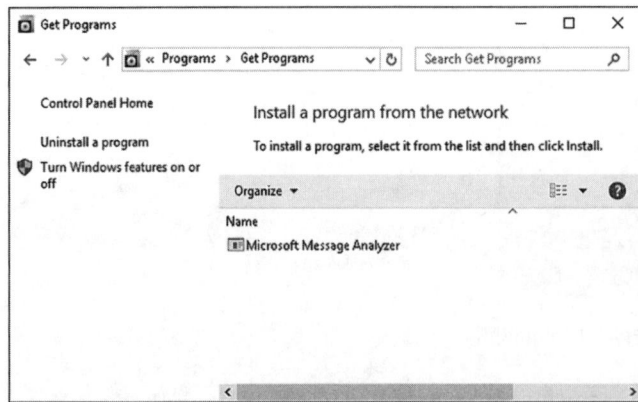

FIGURE 3-67 Accessing published packages

> **NOTE** **CATEGORIES**
>
> If you plan on deploying many software packages by using Publishing, you can create application categories and designate an appropriate category for your package during the deployment phase. To configure categories, click the Categories tab in the Software Installation Properties node shown in Figure 3-63, and add the required categories.

Aside from deploying software using assignment or publishing, you can also make software available by using file extension deployment. This works when a user attempts to open a file of a specific type; for example, they double-click on a .doc file. You can configure GPO software installation to deploy a specific application when a user invokes a specific file type. To do this, you configure the File Extensions tab of the Software Installation node.

Maintenance

After you have successfully configured and deployed the required software, you must be ready to maintain that software. This might involve upgrading or redeploying the software.

To redeploy a software package:

1. In the Group Policy Management Editor, in the Software Installation folder, right-click the appropriate software package, and then click Redeploy Application.
2. At the confirmation prompt, click Yes.

To upgrade a package, use the following procedure:

1. Right-click Software Installation, point to New, and then click Package.
2. In the Open dialog box, browse and locate your software installation package.
3. In the Deploy Software dialog box, click Advanced, and then click OK.
4. Click the Upgrades tab.
5. Click Add, and select the software package that is getting upgraded.
6. As shown in Figure 3-68, in the Add Upgrade Package dialog box, choose whether the existing package is removed before installation of the new package, or whether the new package can upgrade over the existing package. Click OK.

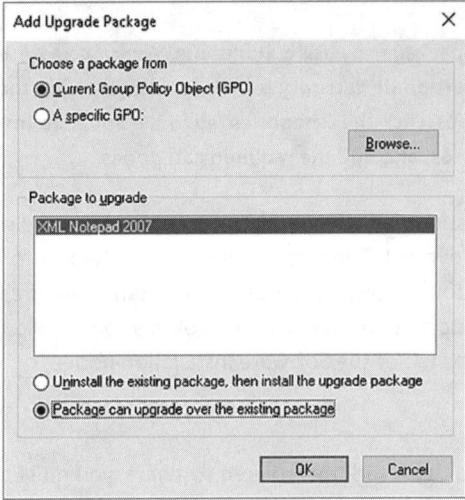

FIGURE 3-68 Upgrading a package

7. In the New Package Properties dialog box, shown in Figure 3-69, click OK.

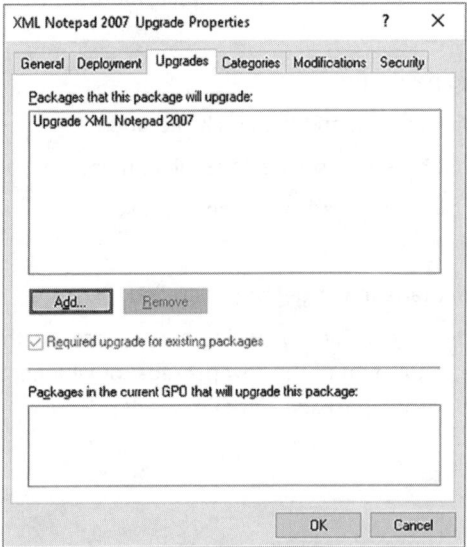

FIGURE 3-69 Completing the upgrade configuration

Removal

Once a package reaches the end of its useful life in your organization, you must remove it. You can achieve this by using GPO software installation. Use the following procedure to remove any unwanted package from your organization:

1. In the Group Policy Management Editor, in the Software Installation folder, right-click the appropriate software package, and then click Remove.
2. In the Remove Software dialog box, shown in Figure 3-70, select one of the following options, and then click OK:
   - Immediately uninstall the software from users and computers.
   - Allows users to continue to use the software, but prevent new installations.

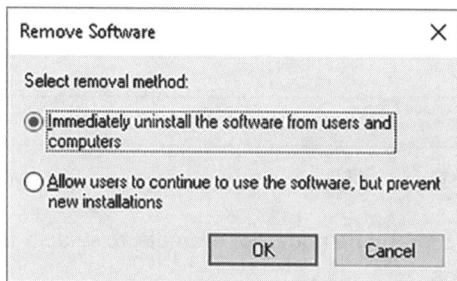

FIGURE 3-70 Removing a package

Configure scripts

It's often very useful to be able to run a script during logon, or when a computer starts up. You might want to use the script to set the user's environment, to map network drives, or to install software updates.

Windows Server 2016 enables you to use GPOs to configure scripts to run during computer startup or shutdown, and during user sign in or sign out. The procedure for configuring these various scripts is essentially the same. For example, to configure a logon script to run, use the following high-level procedure:

1. Open the Group Policy Management Editor for the appropriate GPO.
2. To configure sign in and sign out scripts, expand the User Configuration node, and navigate to Policies, Windows Settings, Scripts (Logon/Logoff), as shown in Figure 3-71.

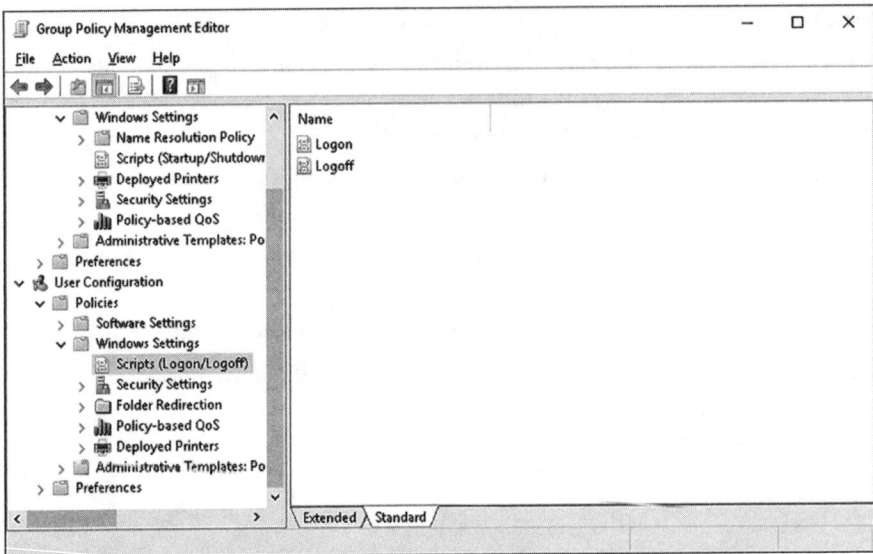

FIGURE 3-71 Configuring Logon/Logoff scripts in GPOs

3. In the details pane, double-click the appropriate node. For example, to setup a script that runs at sign in, double-click Logon.

4. In the Logon Properties dialog box, to use a Windows PowerShell script, click the PowerShell Scripts tab.

5. Click Add.

6. In the Add A Script dialog box, click Browse, locate your Windows PowerShell script, and then click OK.

> **NOTE PATHS**
>
> You must place your scripts in a shared folder to which the client computers have access and at least read permissions. Specify the path in the form of a UNC.

7. See the Logon Properties dialog box, on the PowerShell Scripts tab, shown in Figure 3-72; in the For This GPO, Run Scripts In The Following Order list, specify whether you want your Windows PowerShell script to run first or last. Otherwise, click Not Configured.

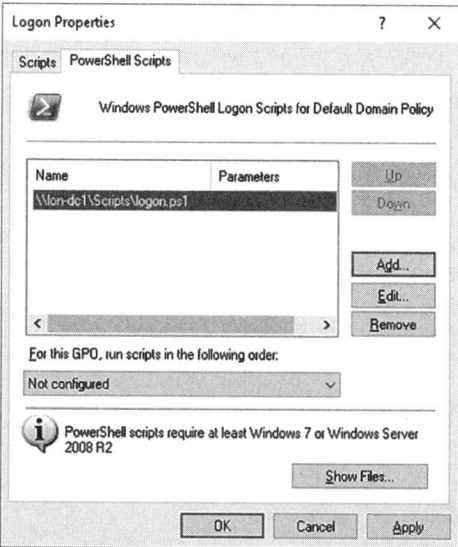

FIGURE 3-72 Defining a Windows PowerShell script as a logon script

8. If you have additional scripts to run, add them to the PowerShell Scripts list, and then click OK.

9. Refresh the GPOs on the target computers, and then sign in to test that the script runs correctly.

The process for creating and configuring scripts for logoff, and also for startup and shutdown, are almost identical. In addition to using Windows PowerShell, you can also use other scripting languages, including VBScript.

> **NEED MORE REVIEW? SCRIPT CENTER HOME**
>
> To find out more about using scripts, refer to the Microsoft TechNet website at *https://technet.microsoft.com/scriptcenter/bb410849.aspx*.

Import security templates

One of the most important responsibilities of network administrators is maintaining the security of their organization's network infrastructure. To help you make this task easier, you can use GPOs to secure your network. However, even using GPOs to secure network and related settings can be a tedious and time-consuming process, especially if you want to apply the same settings to other parts of your organization. For example, if, having secured one domain in your forest with GPO-based security settings, you had to repeat the process with the same, or very similar, settings. You can use security templates to help mitigate this issue.

With the Security Templates console, shown in Figure 3-73, you can configure the following security settings:

- **Account Policies** Includes password, account-lockout, and Kerberos policies.
- **Local Policies** Includes audit, user rights, and security options polices.
- **Event Log** Enables you to define event log settings.
- **Restricted Groups** Allows you to define and configure restricted groups.
- **System Services** Enables you to define startup behavior for system services.
- **Registry** Allows you to define registry security settings.
- **File System** Enables you to centrally define file and folder permissions.

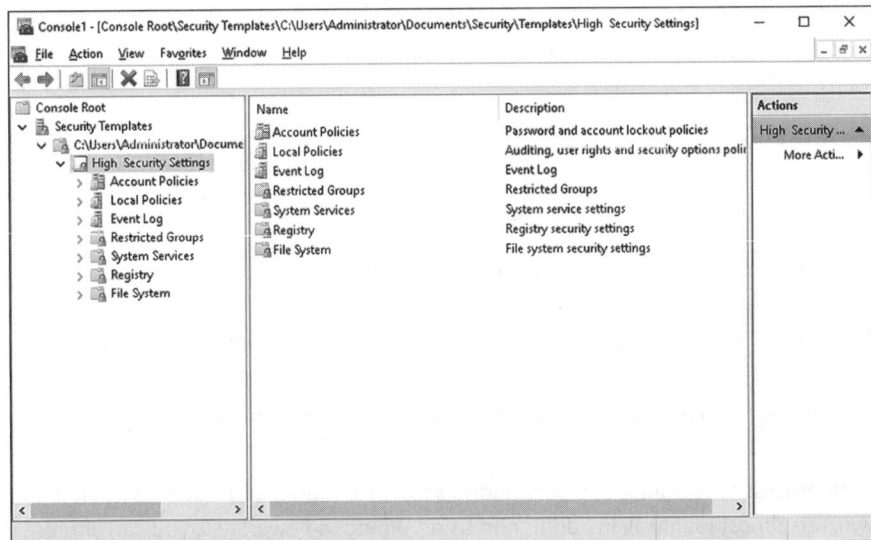

FIGURE 3-73 Creating a security template

To create and use security templates with GPOs, use the following procedure:

1. Open the management console, and add the Security Templates snap-in.
2. Expand the Security Templates node in the navigation pane, and then click the top-level folder beneath that node. Right-click the folder, and then click New Template.
3. In the unlabeled dialog box, in the Template Name text box, type the name. For example, type High Security Settings, and then click OK.
4. Click on the High Security Settings node, or whatever you named your template.
5. Configure the required security settings to help to secure your organization.

After you have created your template and configured the required security settings, save the template. To do this, right-click the template, and click Save. You can now apply the template to your GPO(s). To do this, use the following procedure:

1. Open the required GPO for editing.
2. In the Group Policy Management Editor, select the Security Settings folder in the Computer Configuration\Policies\Windows Settings node in the navigation pane.

3. Right-click the Security Settings folder, and then click Import Policy, as shown in Figure 3-74.

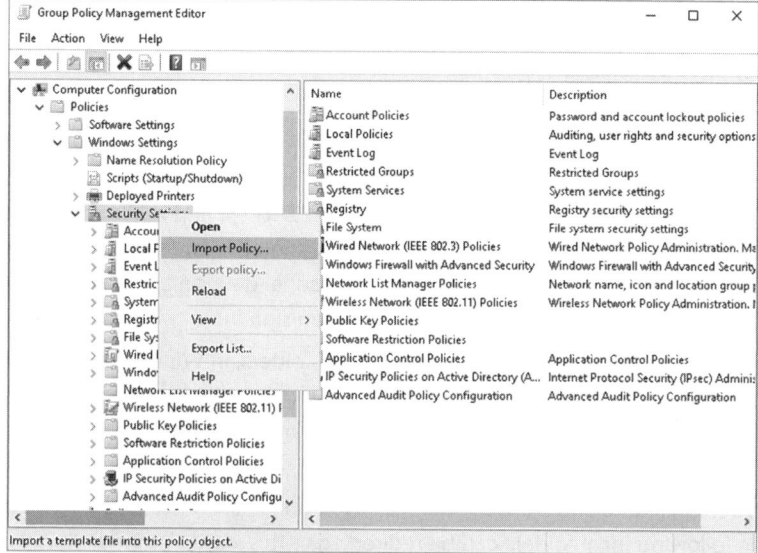

FIGURE 3-74 Importing a security template

4. In the Import Policy From dialog box, shown in Figure 3-75, double-click the policy you earlier created.

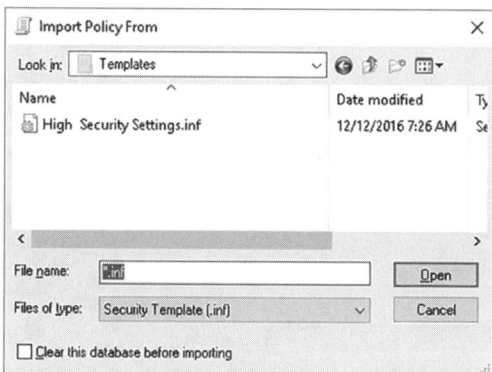

FIGURE 3-75 Selecting a template

5. Your settings are applied.

You can use the Security Compliance Manager to help you choose and configure appropriate security settings for your organization. The Security Compliance Manager is regularly updated with security baselines helping to make it easier for you to select and implement appropriate security settings in your organization.

> **NEED MORE REVIEW?** **SECURITY COMPLIANCE MANAGER**
>
> To find out more about using the Security Compliance Manager, visit the Microsoft TechNet website at *https://technet.microsoft.com/solutionaccelerators/cc835245.aspx*.

Configure folder redirection

Administrators have long sought to centralize and sometimes standardize their users' desktops. All versions of Windows Server have supported the notion of roaming desktop profiles; these enabled users to sign in at any computer in the AD DS forest and automatically apply their user-related settings. Administrators could also assign a home folder on a network server for their users; this enables users to store their personal data on a file server, making their data accessible from other computers where they can sign in.

Although you can still use roaming profiles and home folders, in Windows Server 2016, you can use Folder Redirection to help to centralize and, if desired, standardize your users' desktop and app settings. You implement Folder Redirection as a feature of GPOs.

Folder Redirection gets its name from the fact that a number of local folders, stored as part of a user's personal data and settings, can be stored on file server shared folders through redirection. The following local folders can be redirected in this way:

- AppData\Roaming
- Desktop
- Start Menu
- Documents
- Pictures
- Music
- Videos
- Favorites
- Contacts
- Downloads
- Links
- Searches
- Saved Games

Folder preparation

Before you can redirect folders, you must create the underlying shared folder structure. It is usual to redirect users' folders to a common shared folder; this folder is referred to as the root folder.

Generally, you assign permissions to security groups that contain the relevant users on the required folders. For example, if you redirect folders by department, you might assign the Sales global security group the required permissions on the root folder for sales users; likewise, the marketing security group for users in that department, and so on.

Table 3-1 shows the correct NTFS folder permissions.

TABLE 3-1 Root folder NTFS permissions

User or group	Permissions
Creator/Owner	Full Control – subfolders and files only
Administrator	None
Departmental security group of users that store data on the share	List Folder/Read Data, Create Folders/Append Data-This Folder Only
System	Full Control

Because your users will access the root folder and its subfolders through a Windows Server shared folder, you must assign shared folder permissions. Table 3-2 shows the appropriate shared folder permissions.

TABLE 3-2 Shared folder permissions

User or group	Permissions
Creator/Owner	Full Control – subfolders and files only
Departmental security group of users that store data on the share	Full Control

Thereafter, each user requires their own subfolder beneath the root folder. If you create the root folder with the correct permissions, Windows Server creates the user folders automatically during configuration of folder redirection, and applies the correct permissions. However, Table 3-3 shows the required permissions on the users' individual folders.

TABLE 3-3 User folder NTFS permissions

User or group	Permissions
Creator/Owner	Full Control – subfolders and files only
%Username%	Full Control, owner of folder
Administrators	Full Control
System	Full Control

Available redirection options

When you enable folder redirection, you can configure its behavior in a number of different ways depending on what you want to achieve. The available options are:

- **None** When you select this setting, which is the default value, folder redirection is disabled.
- **Basic** Used when you want to:

- Redirect users' folders to a common area. That is, you do not want to redirect users' folders to a different folder based on their departmental membership. In this instance, all users' folders are redirected to a single folder root. Each user has a unique folder beneath the root.
- Ensure privacy of user data. Because each user has their own folder, and because Windows Server assigned the appropriate permissions (see Table 3-3), each user can access only their own folder contents.

- **Advanced**   Used when you want to redirect groups of users to a common shared folder.
- **Follow The Documents Folder**   If you choose to redirect users' Documents folder as part of your folder redirection implementation, you can redirect the following folders to the same location without needing to individually configure them: Pictures, Music, and Videos.

Enabling and configuring basic folder redirection

You use the Group Policy Management Editor to enable and configure folder redirection. To enable and configure basic folder redirection, use the following procedure:

1. In the Group Policy Management console, locate the appropriate GPO, and open for editing.
2. In the Group Policy Management Editor, navigate to the User Configuration node, and then select the Policies folder.
3. Expand Windows Settings, and then expand Folder Redirection.
4. Select the appropriate folder from the list, as shown in Figure 3-76.

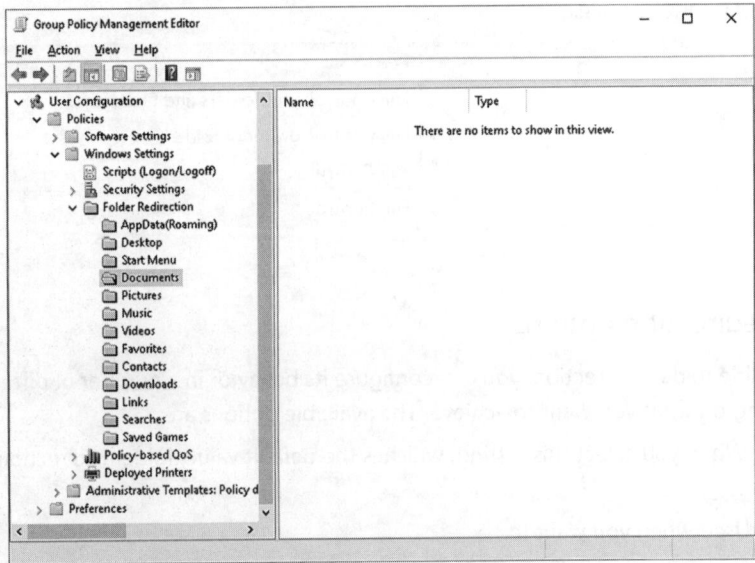

FIGURE 3-76 Enabling Folder Redirection

5. Right-click the selected folder, and then click Properties.
6. In the Folder Properties dialog box, shown in Figure 3-77, on the Target tab, in the Setting list, click Basic. You redirect your users' folders to the same location.

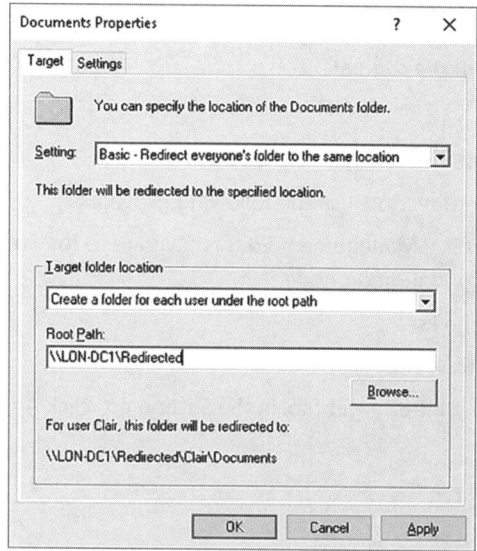

FIGURE 3-77 Enabling basic redirection

7. In the Target folder location section, select from the following options.
   - **Create A Folder For Each User Under The Root Path** If you select this option, Windows Server creates a folder in the form \\server\share\%Username%\Folder, where %Username% is the user account name, and Folder is the name of the folder being redirected. For example: \\LON-SVR1\Redirected\Claire\Documents.
   - **Redirect To The Following Location** If you select this option, Windows Server creates a single folder for multiple users, and all users use the same path for the redirected folder.
   - **Redirect To The Local Userprofile Location** If you select this option, Windows Server moves the location of the redirected folder to the user's local profile under the local Users folder.
   - **Redirect To The User's Home Directory** This option is only available for the Documents folder. Windows Server redirects the folder to the user's home folder.
8. Enter the UNC for the root folder.
9. Click OK, and in the Warning dialog box, click Yes.

When a user signs in that is affected by your GPO, their folder is redirected to the desired location, and Windows Server creates the required user folder beneath the root folder you specified, assuming you created it with the correct permissions.

> ***NOTE* WHEN TO USE BASIC FOLDER REDIRECTION**
>
> It is common to use basic redirection for folders that contain users' personal data. That means you are using folder redirection to move the contents of personal folders to a server. Typical folders to redirect using basic are: AppData/Roaming, Documents, Pictures, Favorites, Contacts, Links, and Searches. Music, Videos, Downloads, and Saved Games are less typical because of the potential size of the content.

Enabling and configuring advanced folder redirection

To enable and configure advanced folder redirection, use the following procedure:

1. In the selected GPO, in the Group Policy Management Editor, navigate to the Folder Redirection folder under the User Configuration node.
2. Select the appropriate folder from the list.
3. Right-click the selected folder, and then click Properties.
4. In the Folder Properties dialog box, on the Target tab, in the Setting list, click Advanced, as shown in Figure 3-78.

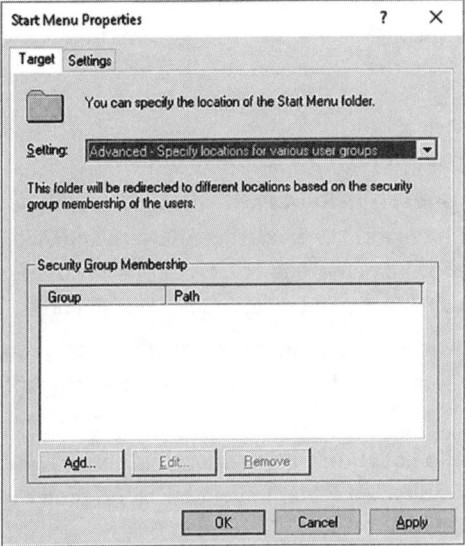

FIGURE 3-78 Enabling Advanced folder redirection

5. Under the Security Group Membership heading, click Add.
6. In the Specify Group And Location dialog box, shown in Figure 3-79, in the Security Group Membership text box, type the name of the security group.

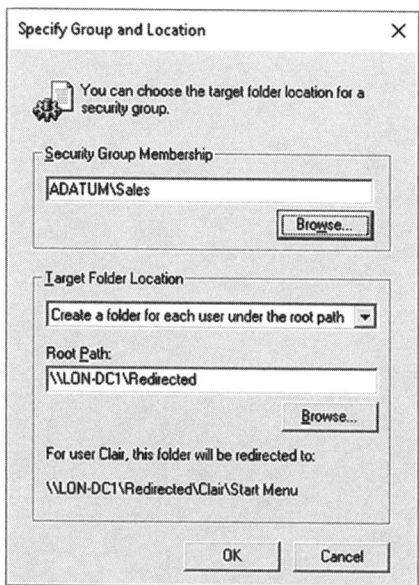

FIGURE 3-79 Configuring advanced folder redirection

7. In the Target Folder Location section, select from the following options:
   - Create A Folder For Each User Under The Root Path
   - Redirect To The Following Location
   - Redirect To The Local Userprofile Location
   - Redirect To The User's Home Directory
8. Enter the UNC for the root folder, and then click OK.
9. In the Folder Properties dialog box, repeat this procedure for other groups that you want to configure.
10. When you have configured all groups, in the Folder Properties dialog box, shown in Figure 3-80, click OK, and at the Warning, click Yes.

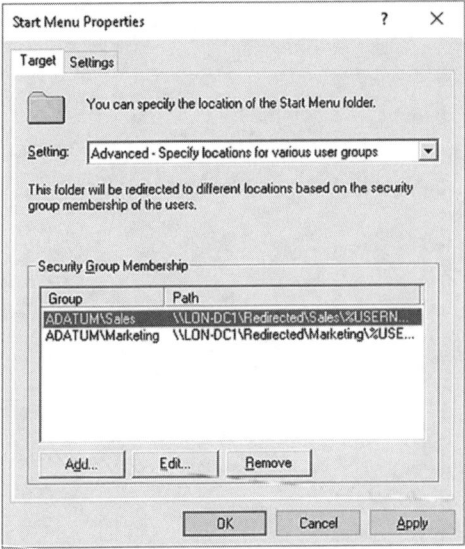

FIGURE 3-80 Completing the configuration

> **NOTE WHEN TO USE ADVANCED FOLDER REDIRECTION**
>
> It is common to use advanced redirection to create standard desktops or Start menu settings. Therefore, it is more common to implement advanced folder redirection for the Desktop and Start Menu folders. If you use advanced redirection in this way, it is common to use the Redirect to the following location option so that all users in each department use the same Desktop and Start Menu.

The Settings tab

For both basic and advanced redirection, when you select and configure the folder redirection targets, as shown, for example, in Figure 3-80, you can also configure options on the Settings tab, shown in Figure 3-81:

- **Grant The User Exclusive Rights To Folder** Ensures that each user has exclusive rights to his own folder. Enabled by default.
- **Move The Contents Of Folder To The New Location** If the local user profile contains content in the redirected folder, that content is moved to the redirected folder. Enabled by default.
- **Also Apply Redirection Policy To Windows 2000, Windows 2000 Server, Windows XP, And Windows Server 2003 Operating Systems** Enables support for older operating systems, which is not enabled by default.

- **Policy Removal** If you remove the folder redirection setting(s) from the GPO, this option determines what happens to the content in the redirected folder(s).
    - Leave the folder in the new location when policy is removed.
    - Redirect the folder back to the local userprofile location when policy is removed.

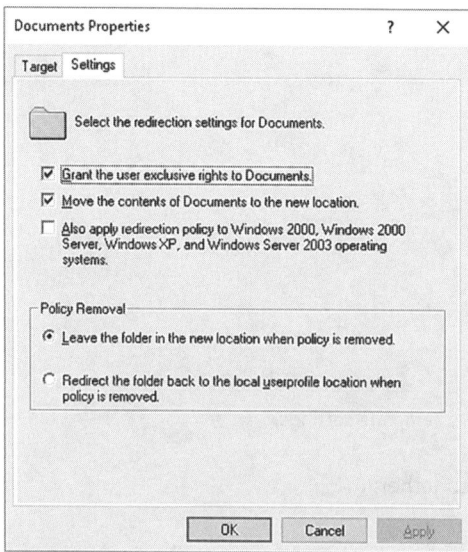

FIGURE 3-81 The settings tab

Configure administrative templates

Much of the configuration that you can achieve with GPOs is made available through the use of Administrative Templates. All the changes you make in the Administrative Templates nodes of a GPO result in changes to the affected computers' registry settings.

As with all other GPO settings, these changes are grouped into computer-related settings that modify the system elements of the registry, and user-related settings that modify the user elements of the registry. However, some settings in Administrative Templates have duplicate settings in both the Computer Configuration, and User Configuration nodes.

EXAM TIP

In the situation where you configure both these settings, the Computer Configuration takes precedence.

Because directly editing the registry can be complex, and potentially error-prone, the Administrative Templates nodes are represented in a more logical, simpler-to-navigate folder-like structure, as shown in Figure 3-82.

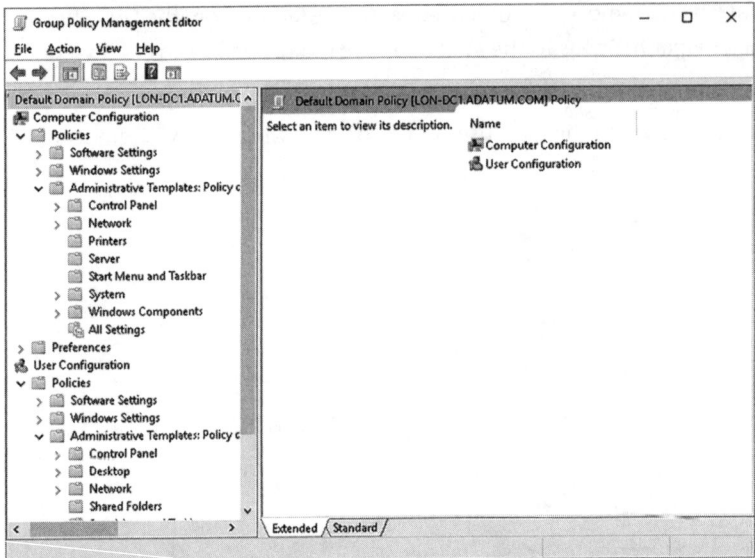

FIGURE 3-82 Viewing the available Administrative Template settings

This structure groups related elements together:

- Computer Configuration:
    - Control Panel
    - Network
    - Printers
    - Server
    - Start Menu and Taskbar
    - System
    - Windows Components
    - All Settings
- User Configuration:
    - Control Panel
    - Desktop
    - Network
    - Shared Folders
    - Start Menu and Taskbar
    - System
    - Windows Components
    - All Settings

EXAM TIP

Both of the All Settings folders represented a consolidated view of all the settings in that particular node.

Administrative template files

Although administrative templates are represented as folders in the Group Policy Management Editor, they are, in fact, stored as files on the file system of the domain controller. In earlier versions of Windows Server, these filenames had a .adm extension. In Windows Server 2016, these files have a .admx extension.

These .admx files are language neutral and in multilingual organizations, they are associated with .adml files that contain the language specific elements required to configure settings. For example, the .admx files are stored in the Windows\PolicyDefinitions folder, and the .adml files are stored in subfolders beneath the Windows\PolicyDefinitions folder, such as en-US for the US English locale.

Configure a central store

Understanding the structure of the .admx files enables you to create your own administrative templates, if needed, to configure specific settings for your users, computers, and installed apps. However, rather than creating the .admx files on a domain controller and manually copying them to all domain controllers in your forest, you can implement a central store of the Administrative Templates files. Using a central store helps to ensure that:

- All administrative templates are the same on all domain controllers.
- It is easier to update your administrative templates because you need to only update a single .admx file—in the central store—when changes are needed.

The central store is located in the SYSVOL shared folder. Specifically, for the Adatum.com domain:

1. In the \\Adatum.com\SYSVOL\Adatum.com\Policies folder, create a PolicyDefinitions subfolder.
2. Populate this new PolicyDefinitions folder with the existing contents of the Windows\PolicyDefinitions folder on a domain controller.
3. Add new or changed .admx and .adml files to the SYSVOL version of PolicyDefinitions.

EXAM TIP

When a new operating system or service pack is released, you must update the PolicyDefinitions subfolder. For example, Windows 10 and Microsoft Office 2016 have new configuration options available that can be made use of by updating your PolicyDefinitions folder.

Import a custom administrative template file

If you want to use your own .admx files, or simply add new ones that you downloaded, you must know how to make them available in the Group Policy Management Editor console. This process is known as importing a custom template.

1. Download or create your administrative template .admx file.
2. Copy them to the central store.
3. Configure the Administrative Template settings in the Group Policy Management Editor for the appropriate GPO(s).
4. Link the GPOs to the required AD DS containers, such as a relevant OU.

> **NEED MORE REVIEW?** **CREATING A CUSTOM BASE ADMX FILE**
>
> To review further details about creating custom .admx files, refer to the Microsoft TechNet website at *https://technet.microsoft.com/library/cc770905(v=ws.10).aspx*.

Configure property filters for administrative templates

The number of settings that you can configure with administrative templates is vast. By default, the Group Policy Management Editor shows all policy settings, whether the setting is managed or unmanaged, configured or not configured, and commented.

> **EXAM TIP**
>
> The Group Policy Client service controls managed policy settings but not unmanaged settings.

Wading through dozens of unmanaged settings to locate the managed setting that you want to change is time-consuming. Likewise, looking for a specific configured setting among thousands of unconfigured settings is also time-consuming. Fortunately, you can change how Group Policy Management Editor shows your Administrative Templates policy settings by using property filters. To configure a filter, select the Administrative Templates folder beneath either the Computer Configuration or User Configuration node, as required. Then complete the following procedure:

1. Right-click Administrative Templates, and then click Filter Options.
2. In the Filter Options dialog box, shown in Figure 3-83, configure the following options, and then click OK:
   - **Managed**   Yes, No, or Any.
   - **Configured**   Yes, No, or Any.
   - **Commented**   Yes, No, or Any.

- **Keyword Filter(s)** Enter the keyword to filter for. Specify whether the word appears in the policy setting title, the policy help text, and/or the comment. Then choose to search for exact match, all words, or any words.
- **Requirements Filter(s)** Configure specific requirements for the platform or application you want to filter. After selecting the appropriate filters, choose whether they must all match, or any to match.

3. The filter applies to the current view immediately.

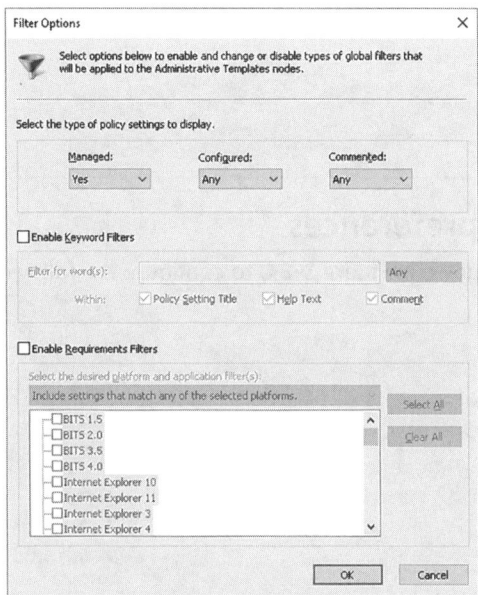

FIGURE 3-83 Configuring an Administrative Templates property filter

Skill 3.4: Configure Group Policy preferences

As we have seen, you can use logon scripts to prepare your users' desktop environment, perhaps by mapping network drives, or connecting to peripherals, such as printers. You can even deliver those scripts to your users' computer by using GPOs.

However, maintaining scripts can be a complex and time-consuming management task. It also requires knowledge of scripting languages, which you might not have available in your organization. In Windows Server 2016, you can use Group Policy preferences to deliver settings more typically made available through scripting.

There are many similarities between GPO settings and Group Policy preferences, but there are some notable and important differences. These are:

- GPO settings are strictly enforced, whereas preferences are not. It is possible, for example, for a user to reconfigure Start Menu settings configured by Group Policy preferences.
- GPOs tend to disable the area of the user interface, which has been configured by a GPO setting. Preferences do not do this.
- GPOs are automatically refreshed on a periodic basis. While this is also true for preferences, you can also configure preferences to apply only once and never refresh.

> **This section covers how to:**
> - Configuring Group Policy preferences
> - Configure item-level targeting

Configuring Group Policy preferences

You can use Group Policy preferences, shown in Figure 3-84, to configure the following settings:

- Applications
- Environment settings
- Files and folders
- Drive maps and network shares
- Registry settings
- Shortcuts
- A range of Control Panel settings, including:
    - Data sources
    - Devices
    - Folder options
    - Internet settings
    - Local Users and Groups
    - Network Options
    - Printers
    - Regional options
    - Scheduled Tasks
    - Services
    - Start Menu

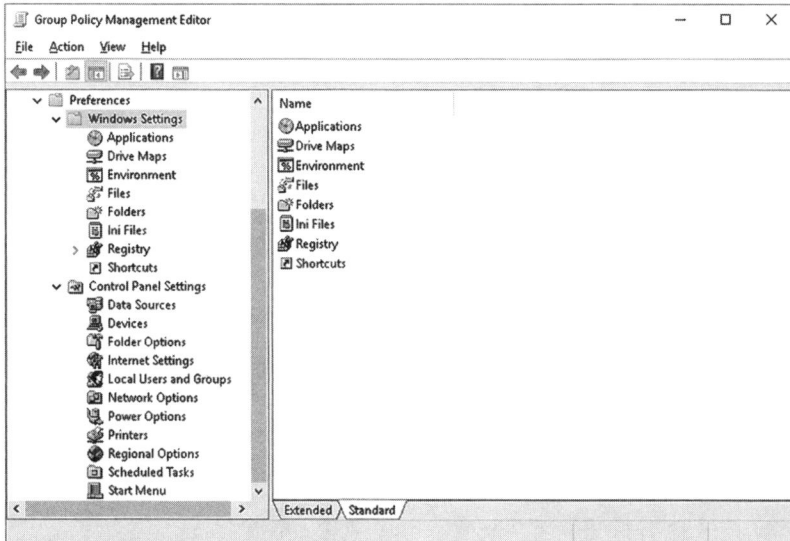

FIGURE 3-84 Group Policy Preferences node

To configure a Group Policy preference, use the following high-level procedure:

1. Open the Group Policy Management Editor for the appropriate GPO, select the User Configuration or Computer Configuration node, open the Preferences folder, and then select one of the items from the list shown earlier.
2. Perform one of the following tasks:
   - Create a new preference setting.
   - Replace an existing preference setting.
   - Update an existing preference setting.
   - Delete an existing preference setting.

EXAM TIP

The Preferences folder is not available in the Local Group Policy Editor.

Define network drive mappings

You configure Drive Maps in the User Configuration node. To add a drive mapping, complete the following procedure:

1. Select the Preferences folder, and then under Windows Settings, right-click Drive Maps, point to New, and then click Mapped Drive.
2. Then, in the New Drive Properties dialog box, on the General tab, as shown in Figure 3-85, in the Action list, click Create.
3. In the Location text box, type the UNC path to the shared folder.

4. Optionally, select the Reconnect check box to ensure that the drive mapping reconnected each time a user signs in.
5. Under Drive Letter, select the appropriate driver letter from the Use list.
6. If required, use the Connect As (Optional) section to define credentials to use to map the drive.

FIGURE 3-85 Configuring a drive mapping

7. Click the Common tab, shown in Figure 3-86.

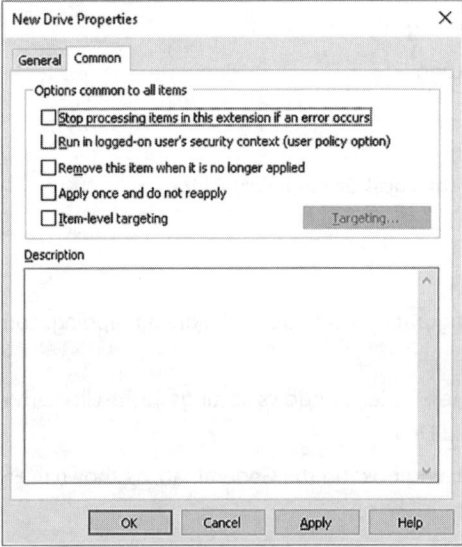

FIGURE 3-86 Configuring Common properties

8. Configure the available options, and then click OK:
   - **Stop Processing Items In This Extension If An Error Occurs**   If an error does occur, all other preferences configured in a GPO are not processed.
   - **Run In Logged-On User's Security Context**   Preferences run either in the context of the System account or the logged in user. This setting is useful when configuring drive mappings.
   - **Remove This Item When It Is No Longer Applied**   Preferences continue to apply even after the preference item is removed. This option changes that behavior.
   - **Apply Once And Do Not Reapply**   This setting overrides the default GPO refresh behavior.
   - **Item-Level Targeting**   This is discussed at the end of this skill.

If you want to modify the drive mapping, open its properties, and then on the General tab, in the Action list, click Replace, and repopulate the settings. The item is deleted from clients and replaced with the new item. Choose Update if you want to modify a setting. Finally, if the preference item is no longer needed, choose Delete.

Configure printer preferences

You can configure Printers in Group Policy preferences in both the Computer Configuration and User Configuration nodes. To setup a printer preference, complete the following procedure:

1. In the Group Policy Management Editor, navigate to the User Configuration node, and then expand the Preferences folder, expand the Control Panel Settings folder, and then click the Printers node.
2. Right-click Printers, point to New, and then click Shared Printer, TCP/IP Printer, or Local Printer depending on the way that you want to connect, as shown in Figure 3-87.

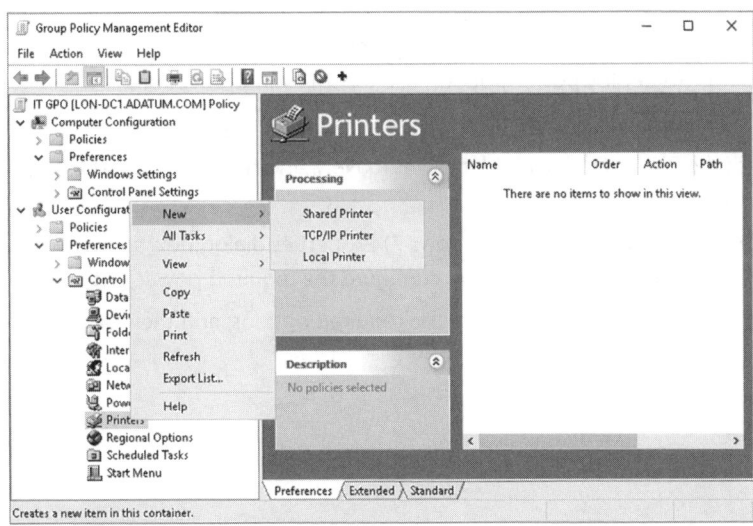

FIGURE 3-87 Adding a new printer

3. For example, click Shared Printer, and then in the New Shared Printer Properties dialog box, on the General tab, in the Action list, click Create.
4. In the Shared printer section, in the Share path, browse and locate the shared printer.
5. Optionally, select the Set This Printer As The Default Printer check box, as shown in Figure 3-88.
6. Click the Common tab, and configure the common options, and then click OK.

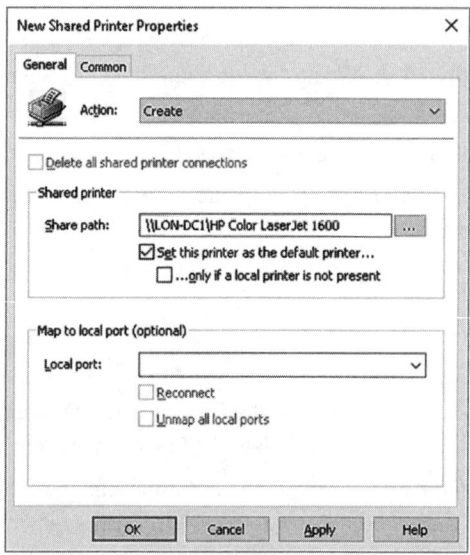

FIGURE 3-88 Configuring the printer preference

Configure power options

Configuring power options with Group Policy preferences is broadly the same as for printers and drive mappings. To deploy power options, use the following procedure:

1. Select the Power Options folder in the Control Panel Settings node.
2. Right-click the Power Options folder, point to New, and then click Power Plan (At least Windows 7).
3. In the New Power Plan (At least Windows 7) Properties dialog box, shown in Figure 3-89, select the appropriate plan, and configure the required power settings.
4. Click the Common tab, and configure the required options, and then click OK.

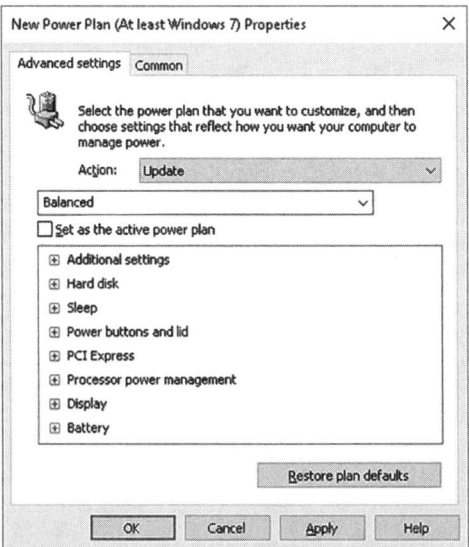

FIGURE 3-89 Configuring a new power plan

Configure shortcut deployment

It's convenient to place shortcuts to files, folders, or other objects on users' desktops. You can do this with Group Policy preferences in either the Computer Configuration or User Configuration node. To create a shortcut, use the following procedure:

1. In the Windows Settings folder in either the Computer Configuration or User Configuration node, right-click the Shortcuts folder, point to New, and then click Shortcut.
2. In the New Shortcut Properties dialog box, shown in Figure 3-90, on the General tab, select Create in the Action list.
3. In the Name box, type a name for the shortcut.
4. In the Target type list, select the type of object to which the shortcut points. Choose between File System Object, URL, or Shell Object.
5. In the Location list, select where the shortcut is to appear. For example, Desktop, Start Menu.
6. In the Target path box, enter the path to the object.
7. Configure the remaining options as needed, and then click the Common tab.
8. Configure the Common options, and then click OK.

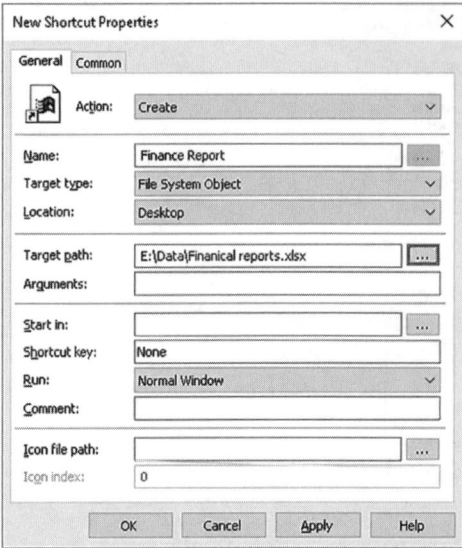

FIGURE 3-90 Creating a shortcut preference

Configure file and folder deployment

You can also configure files and folder deployment in Group Policy preferences. Again, you can also use either the Computer Configuration node or the User Configuration node.

With the Files and Folders preferences, you can use Group Policy to deploy specific files or folders to target users or computers, depending on which GPO node you select. To add a file to a user's desktop, use the following procedure:

1. In the Windows Settings folder in the User Configuration node, right-click the Files folder, point to New, and then click File.
2. In the New File Properties dialog box, shown in Figure 3-91, on the General tab, select Create in the Action list.
3. In the Source file(s) box, type the path and name of the file you want to use as a source.
4. In the Destination File box, type the path and name of the file you want to create.
5. Optionally, configure the attributes for Read-only, Hidden, and Archive.
6. Click the Common tab, and configure the common options.
7. Click OK.

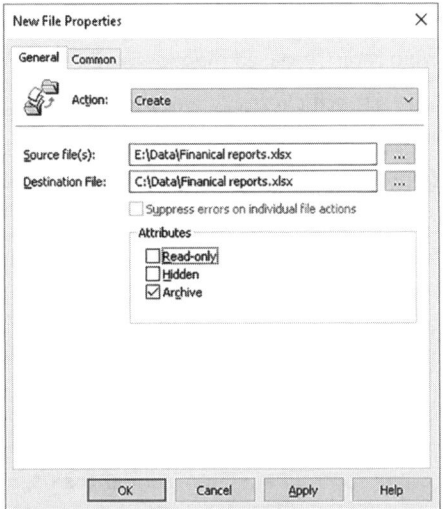

FIGURE 3-91 Adding a new file using a preference

Creating folders is broadly the same. However, when you are replacing or deleting a folder, you have some additional options over how the folder is to be managed, as shown in Figure 3-92. These are:

- Delete This Folder (If Emptied)
- Recursively Delete All Subfolders (If Emptied)
- Delete All Files In The Folder(s)
- Allow Deletion Of Read-Only Files/Folders
- Ignore Errors For Files/Folders That Cannot Be Deleted

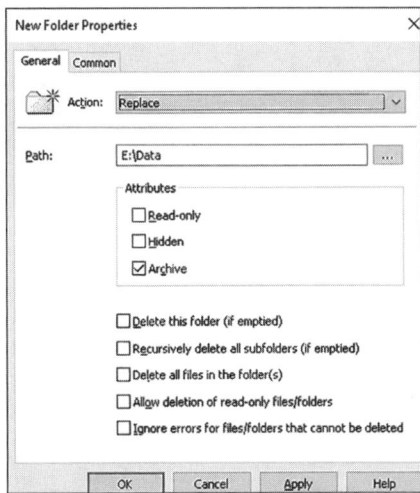

FIGURE 3-92 Configuring replace options for a folder preference

Configure custom registry settings

Using preferences, you can perform the following registry-based management tasks:

- **Add a registry item**   Enables you to add a specific registry entry to the appropriate registry hive and key.
- **Add a collection item**   Enables you to group a collection of registry items. This is useful if you want to add multiple registry entries to target users or computers.
- **Run a registry wizard**   Enables you to use a wizard on target computers to configure multiple user or computer settings in the registry on target computers.

The specific procedure for creating custom registry settings is very similar to all the other preference-based procedures.

Configure Control Panel settings

You can use preferences to configure the following Control Panel items under the User Configuration node:

- **Data Sources**   Add or configure data sources.
- **Devices**   Add or configure hardware devices.
- **Folder Options**   Configure the way files and folders are presented in File Explorer, including options such as Show Hidden Files And Folders, and Hide Extensions For Known File Types, as shown in Figure 3-93.

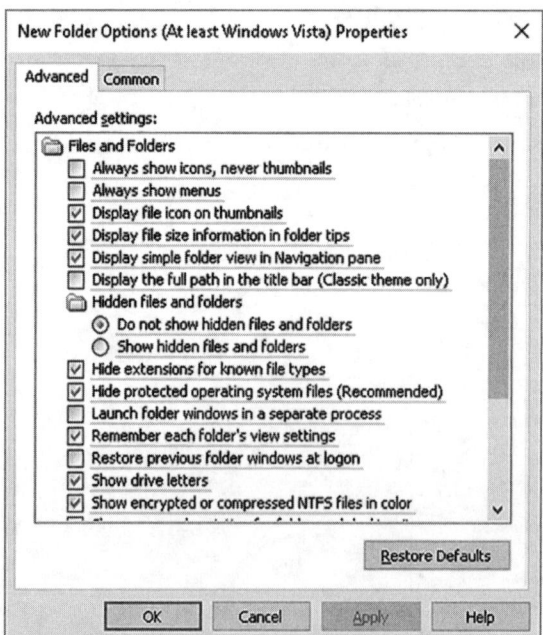

FIGURE 3-93 Configuring Folder Options with preferences

- **Internet Settings** You can configure defaults and settings for Internet Explorer, as shown in Figure 3-94.

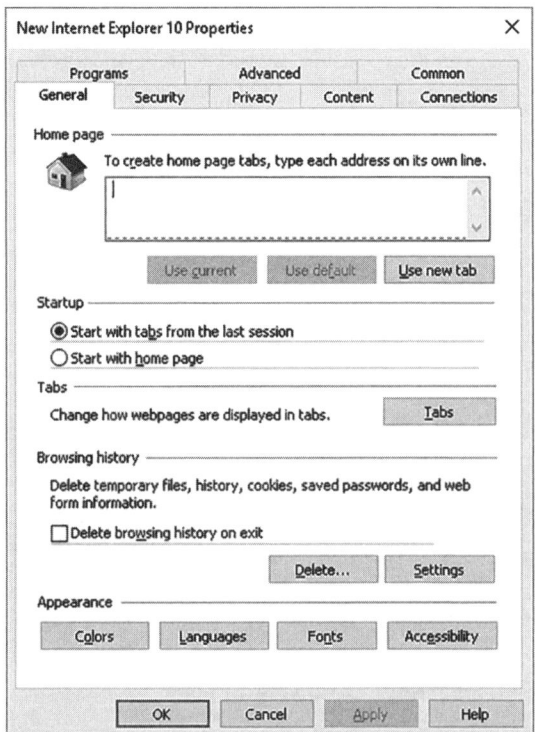

FIGURE 3-94 Configuring Internet Explorer options

> **NOTE GREEN LINES AND RED DASHES**
>
> By default, in certain Control Panel preferences, not all settings are available for configuration. If a setting is available, it is underlined with a solid green line. If a setting is not available for preference configuration, it is underlined with a red dashed line. You can change whether an item is configurable by using the function keys on your keyboard. F5 enables all settings on a tab, F6 enables the selected setting, F7 disables the selected setting, and F8 disables all settings on a tab.

- **Local Users And Groups** You can use preferences to manage local users or local groups, as shown in Figure 3-95.

FIGURE 3-95 Adding a local user

- **Network Options** Using Network Options, you can add and configure virtual private network (VPN) connections.
- **Power Options** Enables you to add and configure power plans.
- **Printers** Enables you to add and configure printer connections.
- **Regional Options** Enables you to configure regional settings.
- **Start Menu** Enables you to configure some aspects of the Start screen.

You can use preferences to configure the following additional Control Panel items under the Computer Configuration node:

- **Scheduled Tasks** Add, configure, and maintain scheduled tasks.
- **Services** Configure service startup behavior.

Configure item-level targeting

When you use GPOs, you can target specific groups or users by implementing Security filtering. You can target specific computers with WMI filters. These filters determine whether the entire GPO applies to a specific user or computer.

When you implement Group Policy preferences, you can use item-level targeting to determine whether a specific preference applies. This gives you far greater control over the application of specific settings.

Throughout this section, when looking at a particular preference, after configuring the General properties, you could optionally configure the settings on the Common tab, including the Item-level targeting option, shown in Figure 3-96.

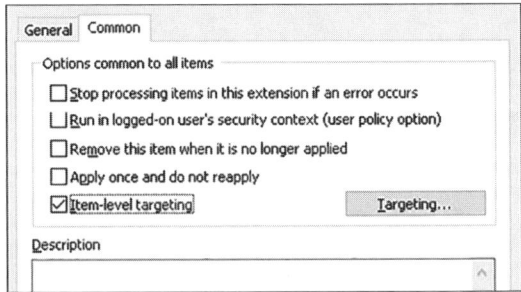

FIGURE 3-96 Enabling item-level targeting

After you have enabled this option, you can then configure targeting of the preference by using the following procedure:

1. In the Targeting Editor dialog box, click New Item, and then select from the list of objects how you want to target the preference. For example, you can select Battery Present, or Domain, or RAM, or even to use a WMI query. For example, click RAM.

2. Next, define the condition. For example, if you selected RAM, specify the amount of RAM required for the condition to bet met in order than the preference applies, as shown in Figure 3-97. Use the Item options list to define operators. For example, that total RAM **is** greater 2GB, or **is not** greater than 2GB.

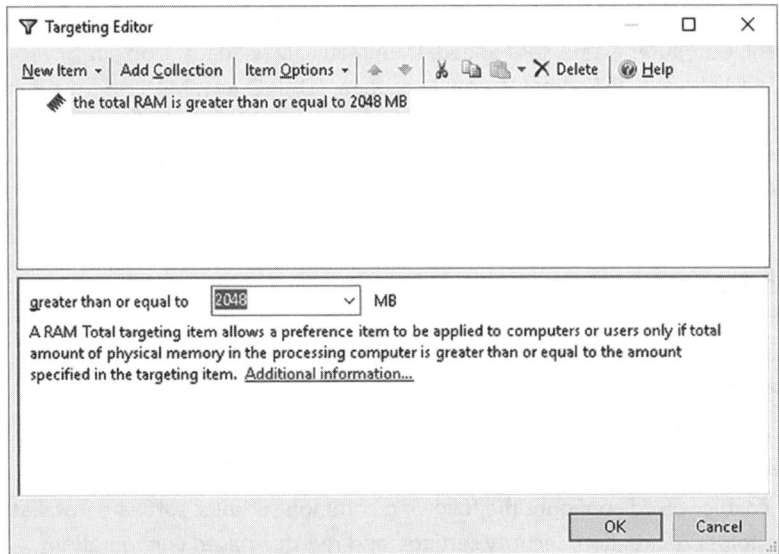

FIGURE 3-97 Adding a condition to the targeting editor

Skill 3.4: Configure Group Policy preferences **CHAPTER 3** **237**

3. Add any additional items that you require. Note that all conditions must be met for the preference to apply. Define the relationship between the conditions using the Item Options list. The default is the AND operator, as shown in Figure 3-98.

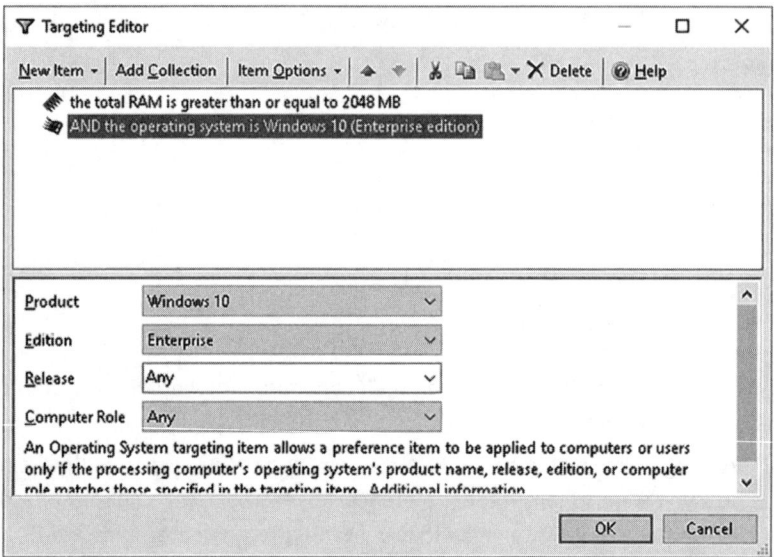

FIGURE 3-98 Adding a second condition for item-level targeting

4. When you have defined all conditions, click OK.
5. In the Preference Properties dialog box, click OK.

There are 27 available categories with which you can target your preference. These are: Battery Present, Computer Name, CPU Speed, Date Match, Disk Space, Domain, Environment Variable, File Match, IP Address Range, Language, LDAP Query, MAC Address Range, MSI Query, Network Connection, Operating System, Organizational Unit, PCMCIA Present, Portable Computer, Processing Mode, RAM, Registry Match, Security Group, Site, Terminal Session, Time Range, User, and WMI Query.

Chapter summary

- You can use GPOs to centrally configure and manage your AD DS forest's devices and user settings.
- You use the Group Policy Management console, the Group Policy Management Editor console, and Windows PowerShell to create, configure, and maintain GPOs.
- GPOs enable you to configure the following common settings: software installation, scripts, folder redirection, security settings, and registry-based configuration.
- You can link GPOs to sites, domains, and OUs.

- Settings in OUs are, by default, inherited from GPOs linked to parent OUs and the domain.
- You can use a migration table to help import GPOs into one domain from another domain where security principal names or UNC paths must be changed.
- For a GPO to apply to a user, the user must have the Read and Apply policy permissions.
- Where multiple GPOs apply to a container in AD DS, the policy that applies last has the highest precedence.
- When you block inheritance, you block at the container level and block all GPOs linked above the selected container.
- When you enforce a policy, you do so at the policy level, and enforcement overrides blocked inheritance.
- For situations where you want a specific user or computer to not receive their configuration from a policy that is linked to their container, use WMI filters or security filters.
- You can use preferences to apply drive mappings, desktop shortcuts, and Internet Explorer settings.
- Preferences assigned through GPOs are not enforced in the same way as GPO settings.

Thought experiment

In this thought experiment, demonstrate your skills and knowledge of the topics covered in this chapter. You can find answers to this thought experiment in the next section.

You work in support at A. Datum. As a consultant for A. Datum, answer the following questions about implementing and configuring Group Policies within the A. Datum organization:

1. It is necessary for all computers within the London Head Office to receive the same security settings. Computers in the other European offices receive different settings. How can you go about achieving this?
2. Users in the Paris office in France require drive mappings to be configured when they sign in. What methods could you use to address this issue?
3. You want all users throughout the single domain A. Datum organization to receive the same security settings. How is this possible?
4. The sales department in Milan has a restrictive GPO in-place. Unfortunately, this is impacting the sales manager's ability to work. It is decided that the policy should not apply to the manager. However, her user and computer account must not be moved from the Milan\Sales OU where they currently reside. How could you deal with this request?

Thought experiment answers

This section contains the solution to the thought experiment. Each answer explains why the answer choice is correct.

1. You could implement a security GPO for each of the locations in the A. Datum organization. You would configure the required security settings, perhaps using the Security Template snap-in to import similar settings between GPOs. Finally, assuming that the A. Datum forest is properly configured with AD DS sites, you could link the security GPOs to the appropriate AD DS sites.

2. There are two possible solutions. One is to implement a Logon script using GPOs and link the GPO that contains the Logon script setting to the appropriate AD DS container, perhaps a site, or appropriately configured OU. The second possibility is to implement Group Policy preferences and use the Drive Maps node to create a new drive mapping. Link the GPO containing the Group Policy preference to an appropriate AD DS container.

3. Configure the security settings that must be applied throughout the organization in a GPO that you link to the domain object. Then, enforce the GPO to ensure that the settings override any others that are configured in other GPOs.

4. One solution is to use security filtering to stop the policy from applying. Use the Applies to everyone BUT strategy. To achieve this, grant the Milan sales manager the Deny Apply group policy permission. This prevents her from applying the policy.

CHAPTER 4

Implement Active Directory Certificate Services

Many apps and services rely upon digital certificates to provide for authentication and additional security through encryption. You can install and configure Active Directory Certificate Services (AD CS) as the foundation of your public key infrastructure (PKI) to deploy and manage digital certificates within your organization.

A PKI provides the following benefits within your organization:

- **Authentication**   Enables you to identify users, computers, or services.
- **Verification**   Ensures that data in transit, such as in an email message, has not been modified. Verification also verifies that the sender is who they claim to be.
- **Privacy**   Provides a means to encrypt data, either at rest, such as on a file system, or in transit, such as an email message.

Skills covered in this chapter:

- Install and configure AD CS
- Manage certificates

Skill 4.1: Install and configure AD CS

Windows Server 2016 enables you to implement a PKI by deploying the AD CS server role. This server role consists of the following role services:

- **Certification Authority**   Certification Authorities (CAs) are responsible for managing the issuing and revocation of certificates. In small organizations, a single CA might be sufficient. However, in larger organizations, there is benefit from creating a hierarchy of CAs; this enables you to provide for high availability of certificate services, and to help distribute the workload of managing certificates across multiple CAs.
- **Certificate Enrollment Web Service**   The Certificate Enrollment Web Service (CES) enables computers running at least Windows 7 to connect to a CA through web services. CES acts as a proxy to the CA, and enables computers to download root certificates, request and install certificates, renew certificates (including automatic renewal for non-domain member computers or computers that belong to untrusted AD DS domains), and retrieve certificate revocation lists (CRLs).

EXAM TIP

Implementing the CES role service requires that your AD DS forest level is at least Windows Server 2008 R2.

- **Certificate Enrollment Policy Web Service** Enables the retrieval of certificate enrollment policy information.

EXAM TIP

When combined with CES, you can enable policy-based certificate enrollment if the retrieving computer is either not a member of an AD DS domain, or is not currently connected to the AD DS domain.

- **Certification Authority Web Enrollment** Provides a method to issue and renew certificates for users, computers, and devices that:
    - Are running non-Windows operating systems.
    - Are not AD DS domain members.
    - Are not connected directly to your network.
- **Network Device Enrollment Service** Enables devices, such as routers and switches, to obtain certificates from AD CS.
- **Online Responder** Enables you to manage Online Certificate Status Protocol (OCSP) validation and revocation checking.

You can use Add Roles and Features in Server Manager to install the required AD CS role services, as shown later in Figure 4-2. You can also use the following Windows PowerShell cmdlets to install the required AD CS role services:

- **Install-AdcsCertificationAuthority** Installs and configures the Certification Authority role service.
- **Install-AdcsEnrollmentWebService** Installs and configures the Certificate Enrollment Web role service.
- **Install-AdcsEnrollmentPolicyWebService** Installs and configures the Certificate Enrollment Policy Web role service.
- **Install-AdcsWebEnrollment** Installs and configures the Certification Authority Web Enrollment role service.
- **Install-AdcsNetworkDeviceEnrollmentService** Installs and configures the Network Device Enrollment role service.
- **Install-AdcsOnlineResponder** Installs and configures the Online Responder role service.

For example, to install an Enterprise root CA with associated management tools, use the following command:

```
Install-AdcsCertificationAuthority -CAType EnterpriseRootCa -IncludeManagementTools
```

> **NEED MORE REVIEW?** **AD CS DEPLOYMENT CMDLETS IN WINDOWS POWERSHELL**
>
> To review further details about deploying AD CS with Windows PowerShell, refer to the Microsoft TechNet website at *https://technet.microsoft.com/library/hh848387(v=wps.630).aspx*.

> This section covers how to:
> - Choosing between a standalone and an enterprise CA
> - Install standalone CAs
> - Install an AD DS integrated enterprise CA
> - Install offline root and subordinate CAs
> - Install and configure an Online Responder
> - Implement administrative role separation
> - Configure CA backup and recovery

Choosing between a standalone and an enterprise CA

Windows Server 2016 supports two CA deployment options. These are:

- **Standalone** You can deploy a standalone CA without AD DS. Standalone CAs are often deployed as offline root CAs and have the following additional characteristics:
  - Users must request certificates using web enrollment or another manual process.
  - An administrator must approve all certificate requests.
- **Enterprise** To deploy an enterprise CA, you require AD DS. Enterprise CAs cannot be deployed as offline root CAs and have the following additional characteristics:
  - CA configuration and registration information is stored in AD DS.
  - Users can request certificates using web enrollment or another manual process, but can also use autoenrollment and web services.
  - An administrator does not need to manually approve certificate requests. Instead, requests can be handled automatically based on configured settings.

Generally, the decision whether to deploy an enterprise or standalone CA is related to the decision to deploy a single or multiple tier CA architecture, based on a root CA and subordinate CAs.

> **NOTE** **SUBORDINATE CAS**
>
> Subordinate CAs are those that issue and manage certificates for users, computers, and devices. They require a subordinate certificate from their root CA before they can perform these roles.

If you intend to deploy only a single tier CA architecture in an AD DS environment, the usual deployment choice is enterprise CA. If, however, you intend to deploy a multitier CA architecture, that is, one that relies upon subordinate CAs, it is typical to choose a standalone CA for the root CA.

EXAM TIP
It is usual practice to take the standalone root CA offline after subordinate CAs have been issued their certificates.

Installing the Certification Authority role service

Before you can configure the CA, you must install the Certification Authority role service. In Server Manager, use the following procedure to complete this task:

1. Sign in as a local administrator.
2. Open Server Manager, and then on the Dashboard, click Add Roles And Features.
3. Click Next twice, select the local server on the Select Destination Server page, and then click Next.

> **NOTE RESTRICTIONS ON COMPUTER NAME AND DOMAIN MEMBERSHIP**
> You can't change the computer name, domain name, or computer domain membership after you install the Certification Authority role service on a server computer.

4. On the Select Server Roles page, shown in Figure 4-1, in the Roles list, select the Active Directory Certificate Services check box, click Next, click Add Features, and then click Next.

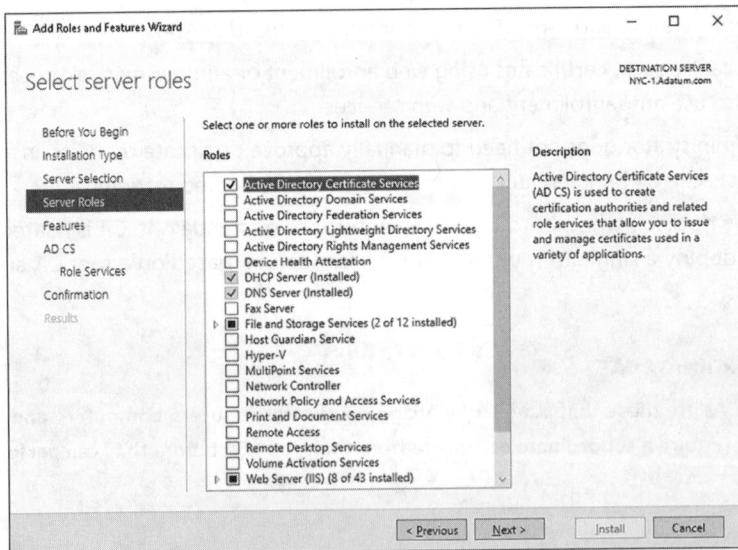

FIGURE 4-1 Installing the Active Directory Certificate Services role in Server Manager

5. On the Select Features page, click Next.
6. On the Active Directory Certificate Services page, click Next.
7. On the Select Role Services page, select the Certification Authority check box, as shown in Figure 4-2, and then click Next.

> **NOTE INSTALLING ADDITIONAL ROLE SERVICES**
> You can also install any additional role services that you require at the same time by selecting the appropriate check boxes. You can also add these role services later.

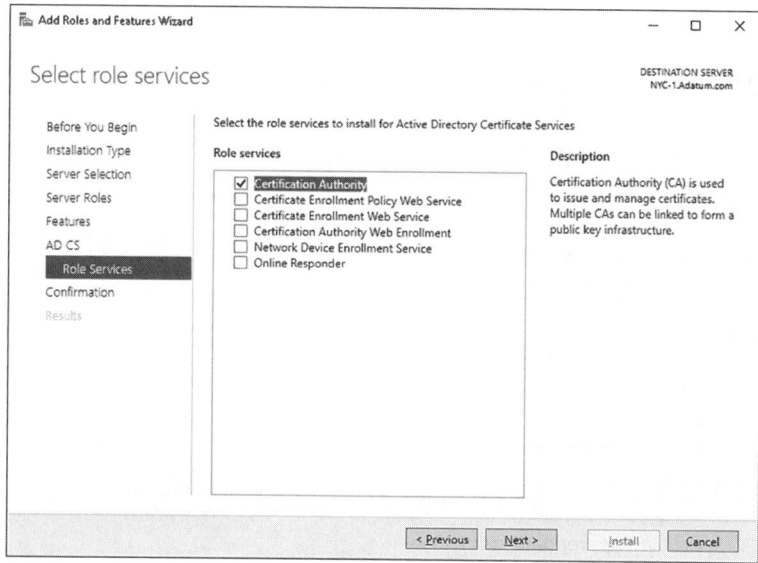

FIGURE 4-2 Installing AD CS role services with Server Manager

8. On the Confirm Installation Selections page, click Install.
9. After the role service installs, click Close.

> **EXAM TIP**
> You can install AD CS role services on Server Core deployments using Windows PowerShell, or Server Manager remotely.

After installing the Certification Authority role service, you must configure your CA as either standalone or enterprise. The following sections describe these procedures.

Install standalone CAs

After you install the Certification Authority role service, you must configure it. From Server Manager, use the following procedure to install a standalone CA:

1. In Server Manager, on the Dashboard, click the Notifications link on the toolbar.
2. Click Configure Active Directory Certificate Services on the destination server.
3. On the Credentials page, enter the credentials for a user account with at least local Administrators group membership, as shown in Figure 4-3, and then click Next.

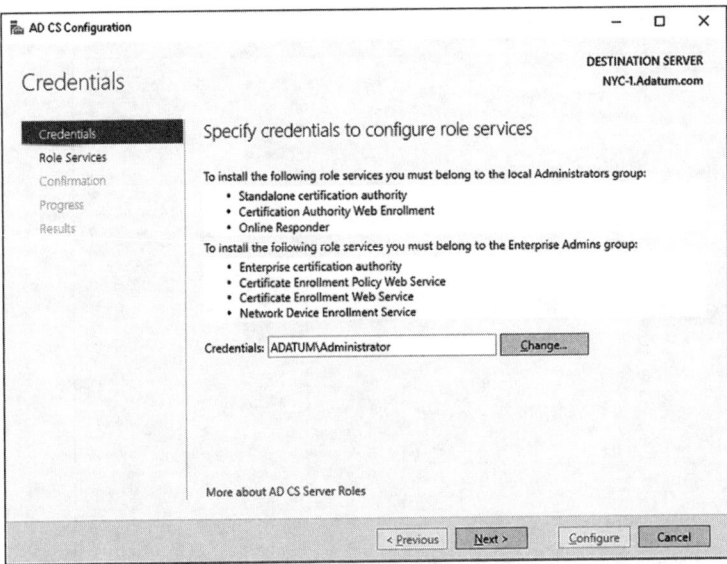

FIGURE 4-3 Specifying appropriate credentials

4. On the Role Services page, select the roles that you want to configure. In this instance, select the Certification Authority check box, as shown in Figure 4-4, and then click Configure.

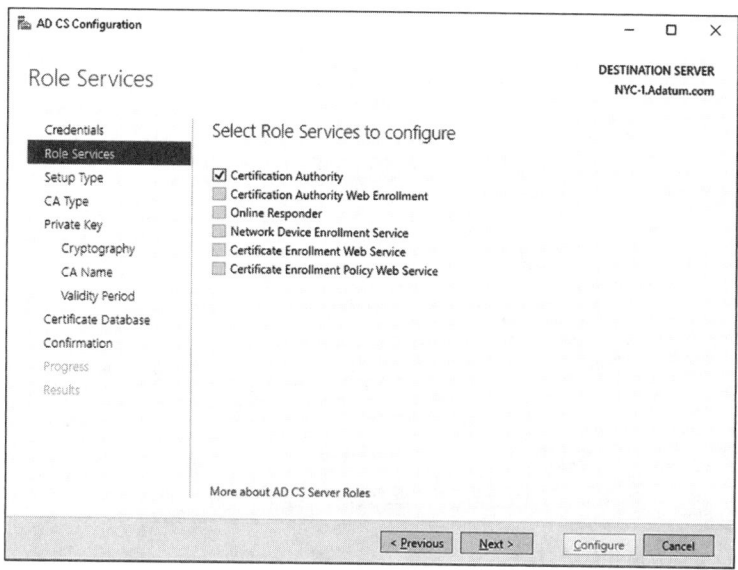

FIGURE 4-4 Selecting AD CS role services

5. On the Setup Type page, shown in Figure 4-5, select Standalone CA, and then click Next.

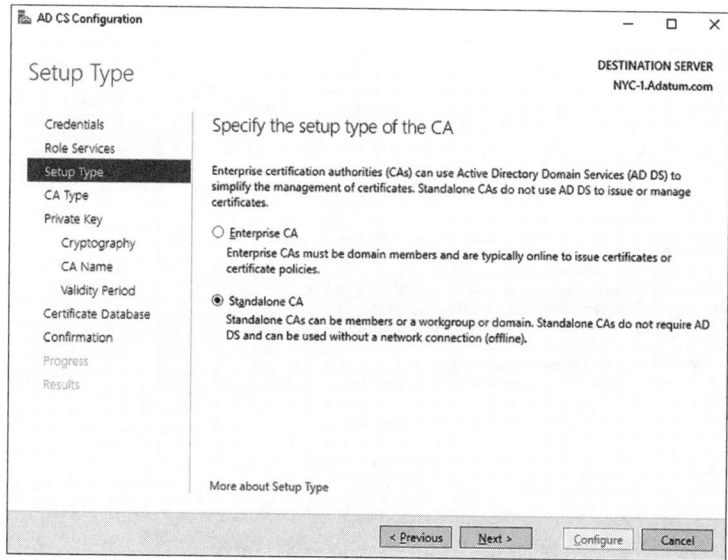

FIGURE 4-5 Choosing AD CS setup type

6. On the CA Type page, if this is the first CA, click Root CA, as shown in Figure 4-6, and then click Next.

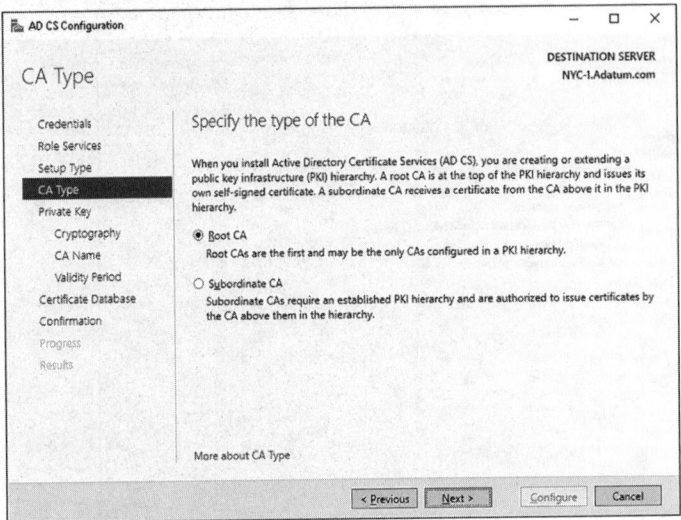

FIGURE 4-6 Specifying the CA type

7. On the Private Key page, if this is a new deployment, as shown in Figure 4-7, click Create A New Private Key, and then click Next. If you have an existing key that you want to use, click Use Existing Private Key. This might be the case if you are reinstalling a CA and want to maintain continuity with previously issued certificates.

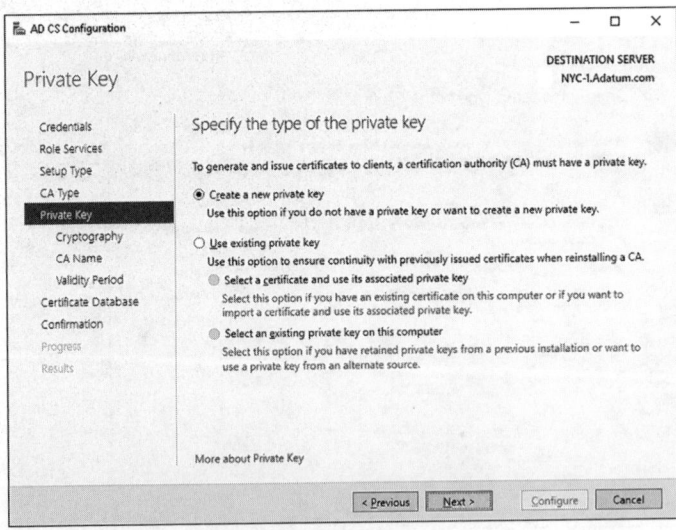

FIGURE 4-7 Defining the private key of the CA

8. On the Cryptography For CA page, select the appropriate cryptographic provider, key length, and hash algorithm, as shown in Figure 4-8, and then click Next. Note that the default values are probably suitable for many deployments.

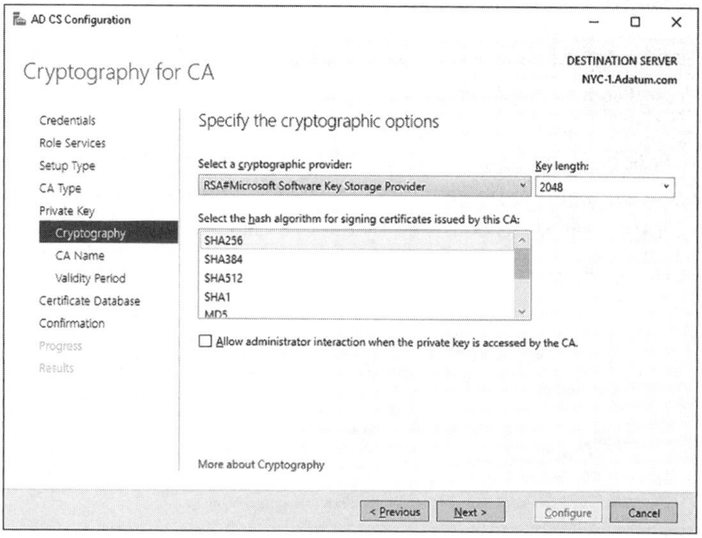

FIGURE 4-8 Specifying CA cryptographic options

> **NEED MORE REVIEW? SELECT CRYPTOGRAPHIC OPTIONS**
>
> To review further details about the configurable cryptography options, refer to the Microsoft TechNet website at *https://technet.microsoft.com/library/hh831574#crypto*.

9. On the CA Name page, enter a common name and distinguished name for the CA, as shown in Figure 4-9, and then click Next.

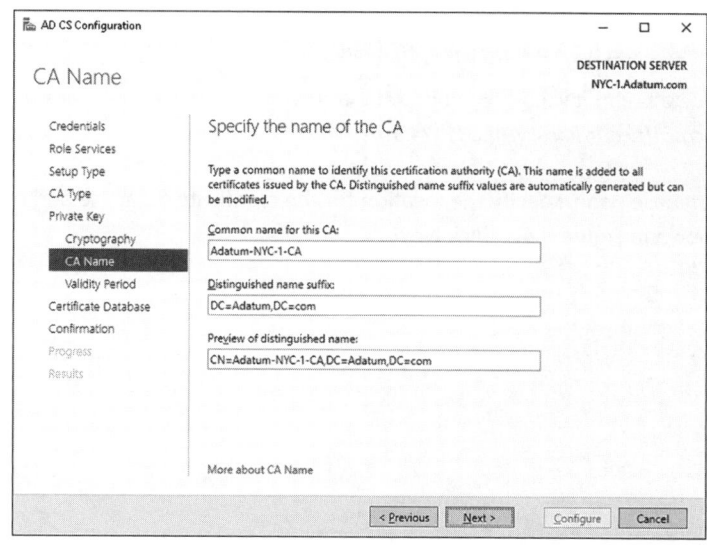

FIGURE 4-9 Specifying the CA name

> **NEED MORE REVIEW?** **ESTABLISH A CA NAME**
>
> To review further details about CA naming, refer to the Microsoft TechNet website at *https://technet.microsoft.com/library/hh831574.aspx#CAName*.

10. On the Validity Period page, shown in Figure 4-10, select the appropriate validity period for the certificate that is to be generated for the CA. This must exceed the validity period for certificates that are to be issued by the CA. Click Next.

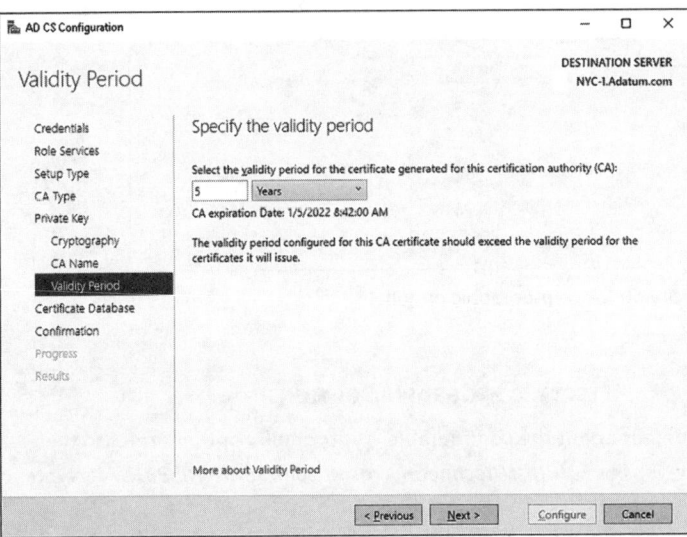

FIGURE 4-10 Setting the CA validity period

> **NEED MORE REVIEW?** **VERIFY THE VALIDITY PERIOD**
>
> To review further details about validity periods, refer to the Microsoft TechNet website at *https://technet.microsoft.com/library/hh831574.aspx#Validity*.

11. On the CA Database page, specify the location for the certificate database and related log files, as shown in Figure 4-11. Click Next.

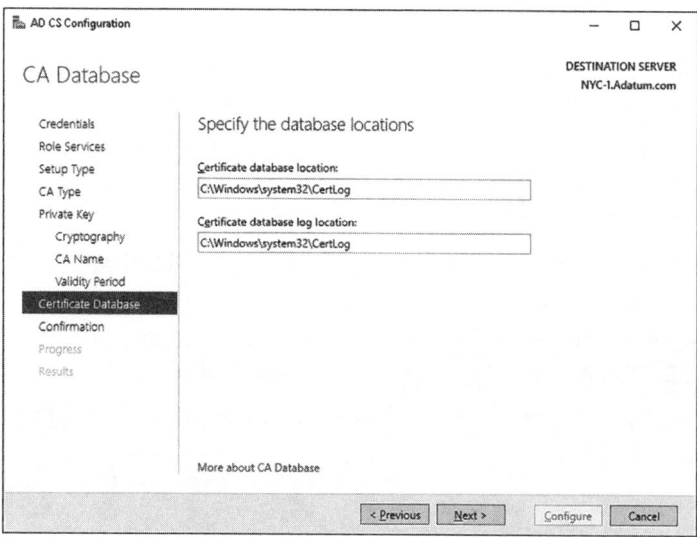

FIGURE 4-11 Defining the location of the CA database

12. On the Confirmation page, shown in Figure 4-12, verify your configuration choices, and then click Configure.

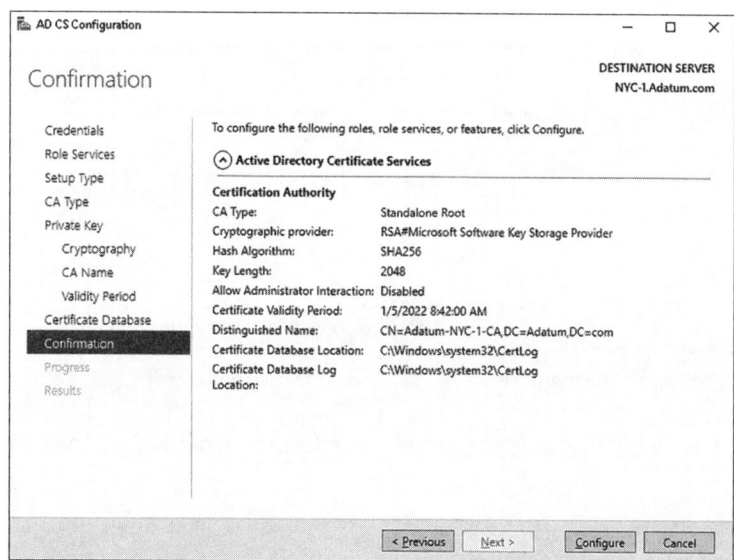

FIGURE 4-12 Confirming installation choices

13. After configuration is complete, when prompted, click Close.

Install an AD DS integrated enterprise CA

The procedure for deploying and configuring an enterprise CA is almost identical to the process for installing a standalone CA. Use the following procedure to complete the process:

1. Install the Certification Authority role service, and then, in Server Manager, on the Dashboard, click the Notifications link on the toolbar, and then click Configure Active Directory Certificate Services on the destination server.
2. On the Credentials page, enter the credentials for a user account with Enterprise Admins group membership, and click Next.
3. On the Role Services page, select the roles that you want to configure. In this instance, select the Certification Authority check box, and then click Next.
4. On the Setup Type page, select Enterprise CA, as shown in Figure 4-13, and then click Next.

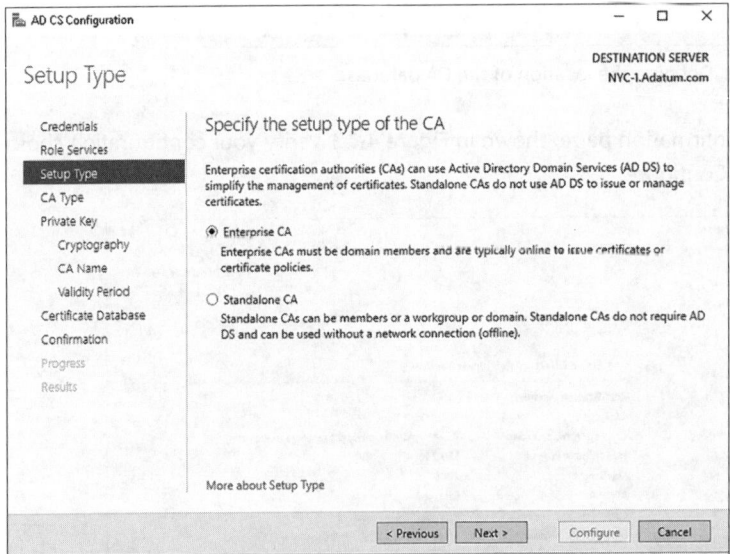

FIGURE 4-13 Deploying an Enterprise CA

The rest of the configuration is the same as the procedure for deploying a standalone CA.

> **NOTE CAPOLICY.INF**
>
> You can use a CAPolicy.inf file to help automate the configuration of your AD CS server. This simple text file contains settings that you can use to customize your deployments. For further information, visit the Microsoft TechNet website at *https://technet.microsoft.com/library/hh831574(v=ws.11).aspx#Anchor_2*.

Install offline root and subordinate CAs

If your root CA is compromised, all certificates issued by the CA, including certificates issued to subordinate CAs, are also compromised. Essentially, this means that everything in your organization that relies on digital certificates for security is now at risk. However, as previously mentioned, if you deploy a standalone CA, you have the option to take it offline. Taking a root CA offline helps to secure your PKI by reducing the opportunity for it to be compromised.

Considerations for an offline root CA

Before you take your root CA offline, there are several things to consider and several tasks to perform. These are:

- **Define a certificate revocation list (CRL) distribution point (CDP)**   By default, the CDP resides on the standalone root CA. If this CA is offline, the CDP is inaccessible. Define an alternative location and manually copy the CRL information to the new CDP location.
- **Define CRL validity period**   When a CRL expires, you must publish a new CRL and distribute this to your configured CDPs. If the validity period is short, you must bring your offline root CA online to create and publish an updated CRL. If you configure a longer CRL validity period, for example, a year, you need to only bring the offline root CA online once a year to update and publish your organization's CRLs.
- **Define an authority information access (AIA) point**   By default, the AIA also resides on the root CA. Again, if the CA is offline, the AIA is inaccessible. Define an alternative location and manually copy the AIA information to the new location.
- **Export the root CA certificate**   Subordinate CAs require this certificate. You must export the root CA certificate and subsequently install the root CA certificate on all subordinate CAs.
- **Publish the root CA certificate**   Use Group Policy to publish the root CA certificate to all client and server computers. An enterprise root CA performs this task automatically, but a standalone root CA does not.
- **Subordinate CAs**   You must deploy subordinate CAs; these are responsible for issuing, revoking, and managing certificates in your organization. Subordinate CAs require an appropriate certificate from the root CA (in addition to the root CA certificate). It makes sense to deploy the subordinate CAs while the root CA is accessible so that they can obtain the appropriate certificate from the root CA.

> **NEED MORE REVIEW?**   **OFFLINE ROOT CA**
>
> To review further details about deploying and configuring an offline root CA, refer to the Microsoft TechNet website at *http://social.technet.microsoft.com/wiki/contents/articles/2900.offline-root-certification-authority-ca.aspx.*

Configure CRL distribution and AIA points

Before you deploy your subordinate CAs, you must configure both the CDP and AIA locations. These locations are important for the following reasons:

- **A revoked certificate should not be used to provide security and identity services** CDPs enable apps and services that rely on certificates to establish the revocation status of a certificate by enabling the app or service to find the CRL that is maintained by your organization's CAs.
- **Apps and services must trust issuing CAs** If an app or service does not explicitly trust a CA which issues a certificate, the app or service uses AIA addresses to determine the validity of the certificate issuing CA. AIA addresses are URLs that define the location of the issuing CA's certificate.

> **NOTE WHAT'S IN A CERTIFICATE?**
>
> Every certificate issued by your CAs contains the CDP and AIA locations. This ensures that all certificate verifiers in app and services within your organization know where to go to locate CDP and AIA information.

You can configure CDP and AIA locations by using the following procedure on your root CA:

1. Sign in as a local administrator (or domain administrator if the server is a domain member) on your root CA, open Server Manager, click Tools, and then click Certification Authority.
2. In the certsrv – [Certification Authority (Local)] console, shown in Figure 4-14, right-click your root CA, and then click Properties.

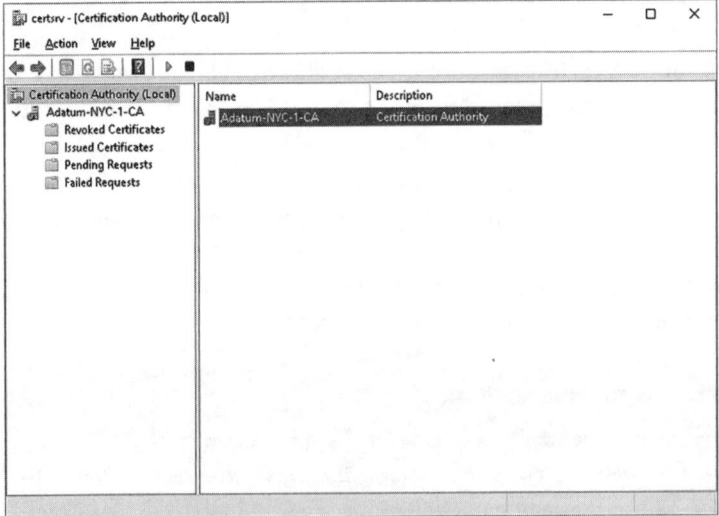

FIGURE 4-14 Selecting the Root CA server

3. In the Root CA Properties dialog box, on the Extensions tab, in the Select Extension list, click CRL Distribution Point (CDP), as shown in Figure 4-15, and then click Add.

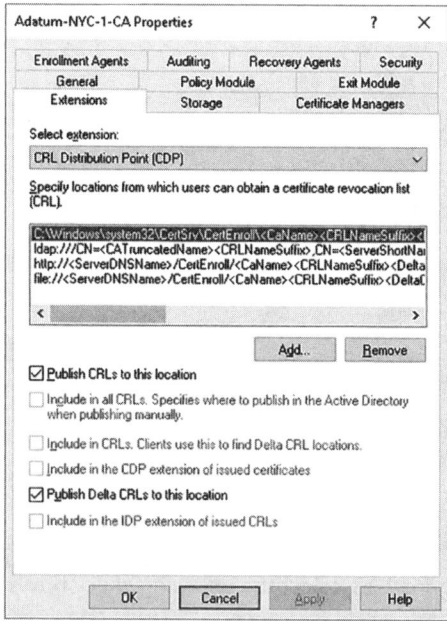

FIGURE 4-15 Configuring the CDP

4. In the Add Location dialog box, in the Location text box, type the URL for the website that hosts the CRL. For example, type **http://lon-svr2.adatum.com/Cert/**.

5. In the Variable list, click <CaName>, as shown in Figure 4-16, and then click Insert. The variable is appended to the URL in the Location text box.

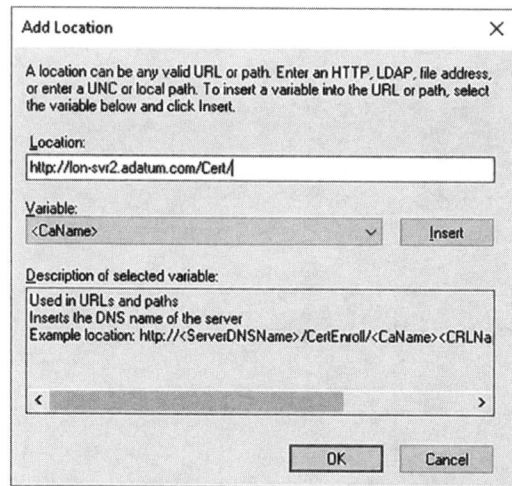

FIGURE 4-16 Defining the URL for the CDP

6. In the Variable list, click <CRLNameSuffix>, and then click Insert.
7. In the Variable list, click <DeltaCRLAllowed>, and then click Insert.
8. In the Location box, at the end of URL, type **.crl**, as shown in Figure 4-17, and then click OK.

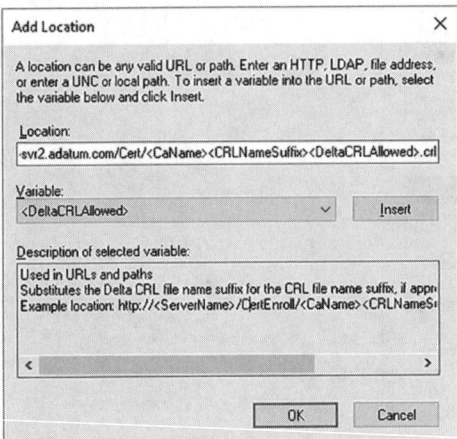

FIGURE 4-17 Completing the CDP URL name

9. On the Extensions tab, as shown in Figure 4-18, select the following check boxes and then click Apply:
   - Include in CRLs. Clients use this to find Delta CRL locations.
   - Include in the CDP extension of issued certificates.

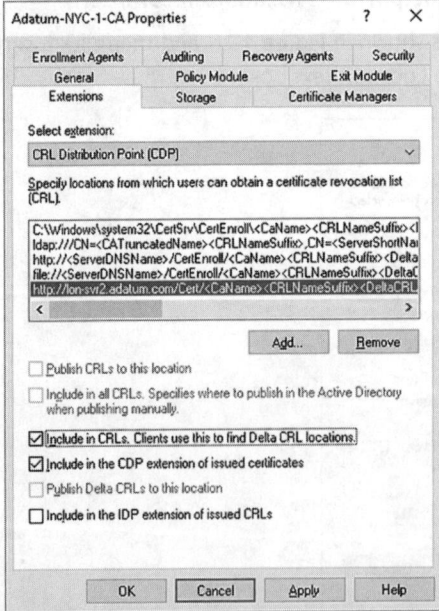

FIGURE 4-18 Completing the CDP configuration

10. Do not restart AD CS when prompted. On the Extensions tab, in the Select Extension list, click Authority Information Access (AIA), and then click Add.
11. In the Location box, type the URL for the website that hosts the AIA. For example, type http://lon-svr2.adatum.com/Cert/.
12. In the Variable list, click <ServerDNSName>, and then click Insert. This variable is added to the end of the typed URL in the Location text box.
13. In the Location box, type an underscore (_) at the end of the URL, then, in the Variable list, click <CaName>, and then click Insert.
14. In the Location box, click the end of URL, and then in the Variable list, click <CertificateName>, and then click Insert.
15. In the Location box, at the end of URL, type **.crt**, as shown in Figure 4-19, and then click OK.

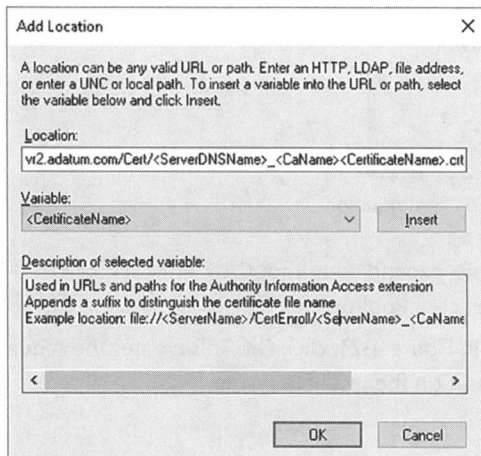

FIGURE 4-19 Defining the AIA location

16. As shown in Figure 4-20, select the Include In The AIA Extension Of Issued Certificates check box, and then click OK. Restart the Certification Authority service when prompted.

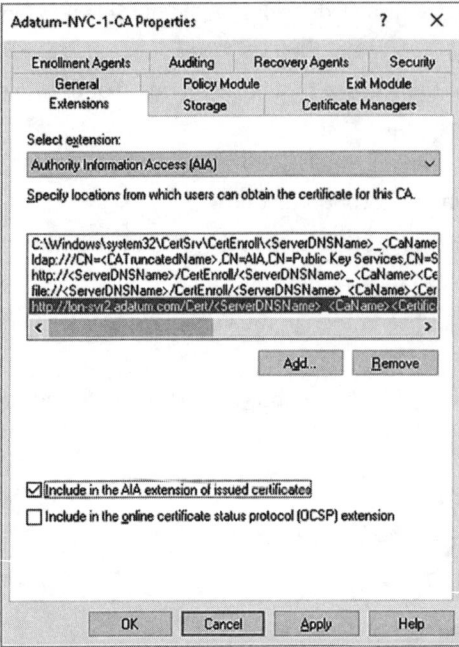

FIGURE 4-20 Completing the AIA location configuration

17. In the Certification Authority console, expand your Root CA, right-click Revoked Certificates, point to All Tasks, and then click Publish.

18. In the Publish CRL window, shown in Figure 4-21, click OK. This creates the required CRL and AIA information and stores it on the local file system.

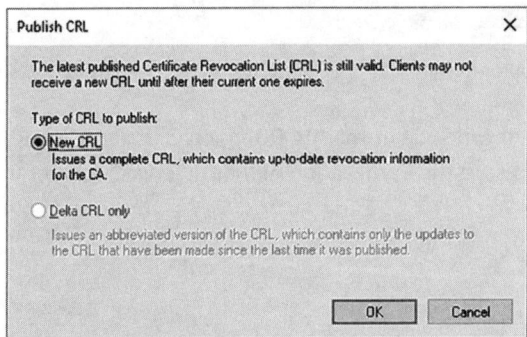

FIGURE 4-21 Publishing the CRL

19. Ensure that the website that hosts the CDP and AIA is online. Copy the contents, shown in Figure 4-22, from the C:\Windows\System32\CertSrv\CertEnroll folder on your Root CA to the website that hosts the CDP and AIA data. For example, copy to http://lon-svr2.adatum.com/Cert/.

NOTE **WEB SERVER**

The CDP and AIA information must be available on a web server. Therefore, when you copy the contents of the C:\Windows\System32\CertSrv\CertEnroll folder, you must place the files onto a web server in a folder identified by the URL that you configured. In our example, place them into a folder called Cert on *http://lon-svr2.adatum.com*.

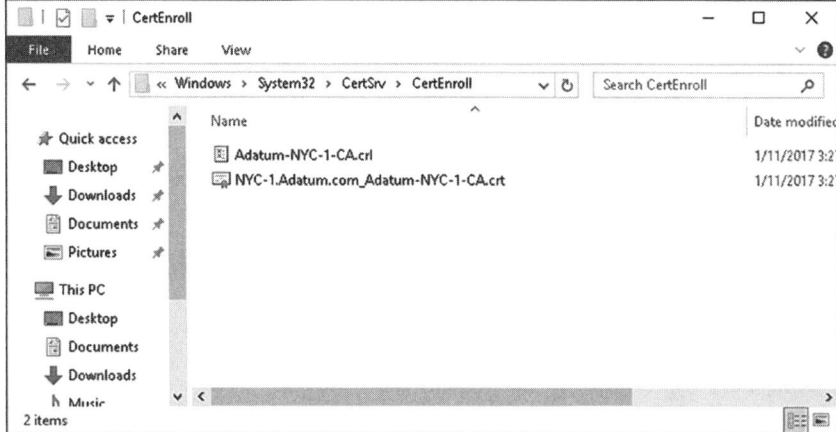

FIGURE 4-22 Viewing the CRL information in File Explorer

EXAM TIP

If you are using an Enterprise root CA, the CDP and AIA information is automatically configured and maintained in AD DS and replicated throughout your AD DS forest.

Export the root CA certificate

It is common to deploy a standalone root CA as part of a workgroup; this means that subordinates do not trust the certificate used when you deploy the Certification Authority role service. Consequently, you must export this certificate on the root CA and then, later, install the certificate on all subordinate CAs. To do this, complete the following procedure:

1. On the root CA in the Certification Authority console, right-click the Root CA in the navigation pane, and then click Properties.
2. In the Root CA Properties dialog box, click View Certificate.
3. In the Certificate dialog box, on the Details tab, click Copy To File.
4. In the Certificate Export Wizard, on the Export File Format page, shown in Figure 4-23, click DER Encoded Binary X.509 (.CER), and then click Next.

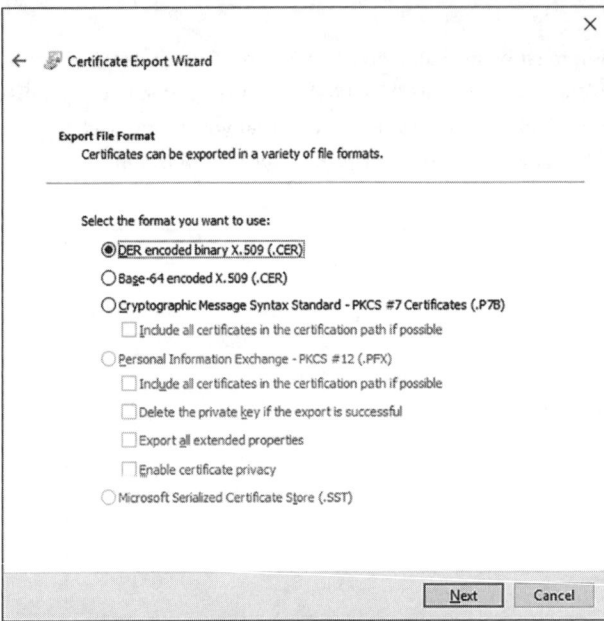

FIGURE 4-23 Exporting the Root CA certificate to a file

5. On the File To Export page, click Browse.
6. In the File name box, type a location that is to be accessible to the subordinate CAs. This could be a shared folder, or even a USB memory stick.
7. In the File name box, type a meaningful name for the exported certificate, for example, type RootCA, click Save, and then click Next.
8. Click Finish, and then click OK three times.

Install the root CA certificate

On the servers that you intend to use as subordinate CAs, install the root CA certificate in the Trusted Root Certification Authorities store. To do this, complete the following procedure:

1. On the target subordinate CA, sign in as a local administrator, and then navigate to the location where you placed the root CA certificate.
2. Right-click the certificate, which has a .cer file extension, and then click Install Certificate.
3. In the Certificate Import Wizard, click Local Machine, and then click Next.
4. On the Certificate Store page, click Place All Certificates In The Following Store, and then click Browse.
5. Select Trusted Root Certification Authorities, click OK, and then, as shown in Figure 4-24, click Next, and then click Finish.

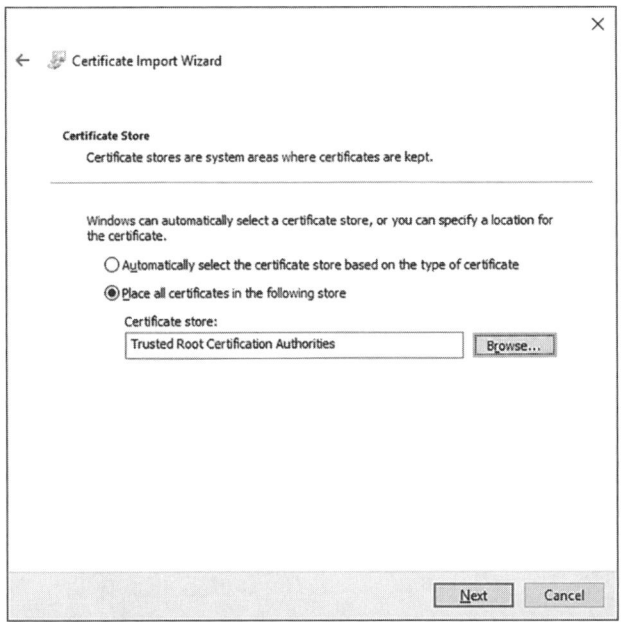

FIGURE 4-24 Installing the root CA certificate on a subordinate CA

6. When the Certificate Import Wizard window appears, click OK.

Deploy subordinate CAs

After you have deployed and configured your root CA, you can deploy subordinate CAs. There are a number of scenarios for deploying subordinate CAs, as shown in Figure 4-25. These are:

- **By certificate purpose**   You can use certificates for many purposes, including file encryption, to help secure email, to help secure remote access client, such as those using virtual private network (VPN) connections. Because you might want to implement differing issuing policies for certificates for each of these purposes, you can deploy subordinate CAs, each with distinct certificate purposes. You could then configure administrative separation based on certificate purpose.

- **By location**   If your organization spans multiple geographic locations, you could choose to deploy subordinate CAs based on those locations. Each subordinate would service client and server computers' certificate needs within that region. This approach would enable you to separate administration based on region.

- **By business group**   Your certificate policies might vary according to business group. In this instance, deploy your subordinate CAs according to the operating divisions or departments within your organization. This scenario allows you to separate administration based on department.

- **For load balancing or high availability** Deploying multiple subordinate CAs enables you to help to ensure availability of certificate services. It also enables you to distribute the workload to help ensure timely responses by the CA servers in your infrastructure.

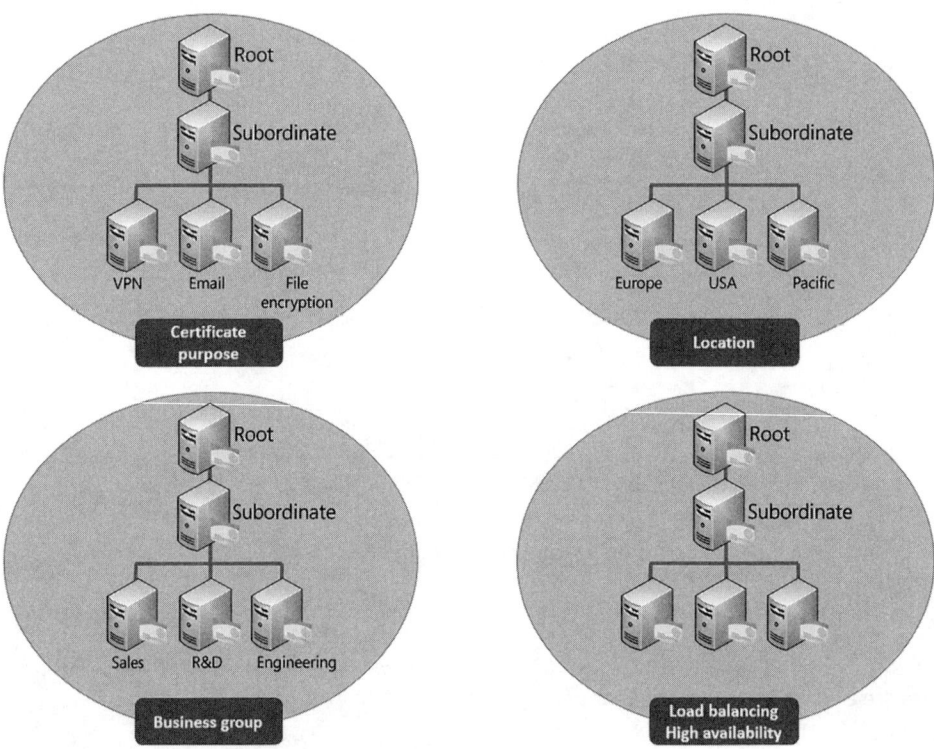

FIGURE 4-25 Choosing a deployment scenario

After you have deployed your root CA and have chosen the appropriate scenario, to deploy a subordinate CA, use the following procedure:

EXAM TIP

It is common to deploy an enterprise CA as a subordinate in AD DS environments, as described in the following procedure.

1. Install the Certification Authority role service.
2. Configure Active Directory Certificate Services on the destination server as previously described, and on the Setup Type page, click Enterprise CA, and then click Next.
3. On the CA Type page, click Subordinate CA, and then click Next.
4. Complete the configuration using the guidance previously provided, but on the Certificate Request page, click Save A Certificate Request To File On The Target Machine, and

then click Next, as shown in Figure 4-26. You must make this file available to the root CA later in this procedure. Either place it in a shared folder accessible from the Root CA, or copy it to a memory stick.

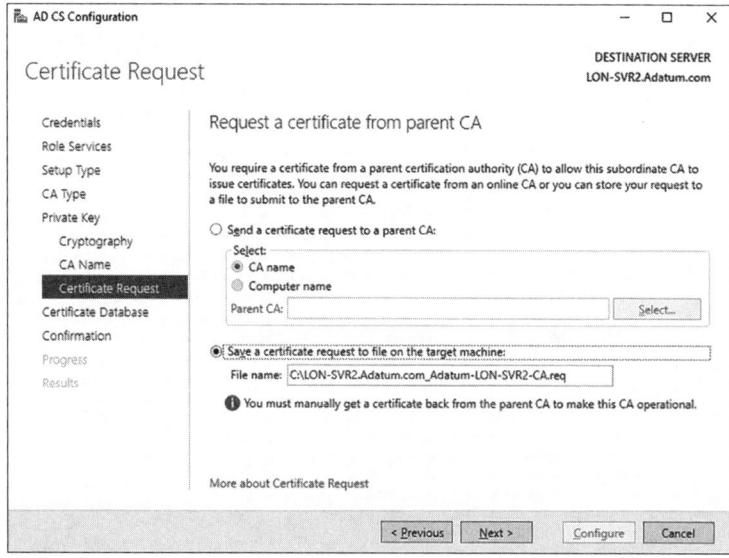

FIGURE 4-26 Saving a certificate request file on a subordinate CA

5. On the CA Database page, click Next.
6. On the Confirmation page, click Configure.
7. On the Results page, read the warning messages, shown in Figure 4-27, and click Close.

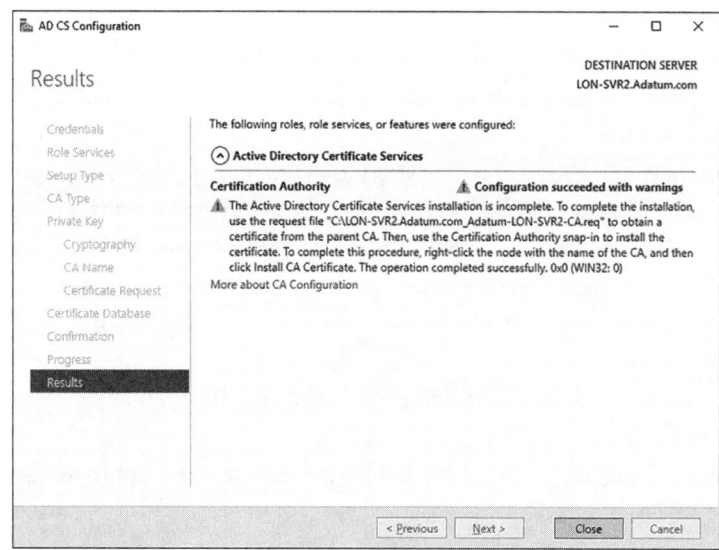

FIGURE 4-27 Viewing configuration results for a subordinate CA

8. On the server installed as your root CA, in the Certificate Authority console, right-click the root CA server, point to All Tasks, and then click Submit New Request.

9. In the Open Request File dialog box, navigate to the .req file you created in step 4, and then click Open. You might have placed this file on a shared folder, as shown in Figure 4-28, or it might be accessible on a memory stick, or other removable media.

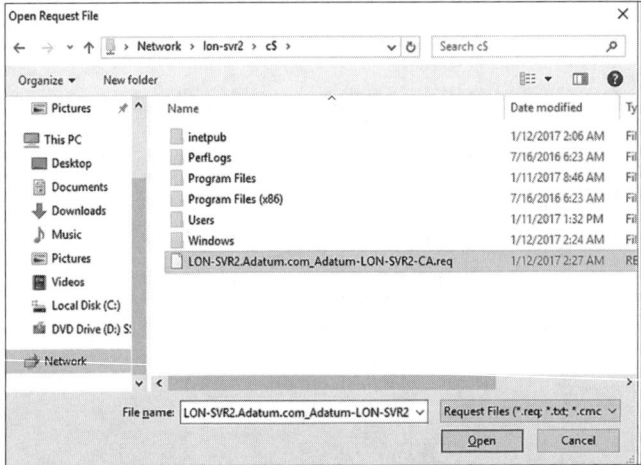

FIGURE 4-28 Opening a request file

10. In the Certification Authority console, click the Pending Requests container, right-click Pending Requests, and then click Refresh. You should see a request that is a result of the open request action you just performed. In the details pane, right-click the request (which has an ID of 2), point to All Tasks, and then click Issue.

11. You must now export the issued request and import it on your subordinate CA. In the Certification Authority console, click the Issued Certificates container.

12. In the details pane, double-click the certificate, click the Details tab, and then click Copy To File.

13. In the Certificate Export Wizard, on the Export File Format page, click Cryptographic Message Syntax Standard – PKCS #7 Certificates (.P7B), select the Include All Certificates In The Certification Path If Possible check box, and then click Next.

14. On the File To Export page, enter a location that is accessible from the subordinate CA, and then type a meaningful name for the file, and then click Next, and complete the export process.

15. Switch to the subordinate CA, and in Server Manager, click Tools, and then click Certification Authority.

16. In the Certification Authority console, right-click the local server, point to All Tasks, and then click Install CA Certificate.

17. In the Select File To Complete CA Installation dialog box, navigate to the location of the certificate you just exported in step 13. Double-click the PKCS #7 Certificates file, as shown in Figure 4-29. You can now start the CA on the subordinate CA server.

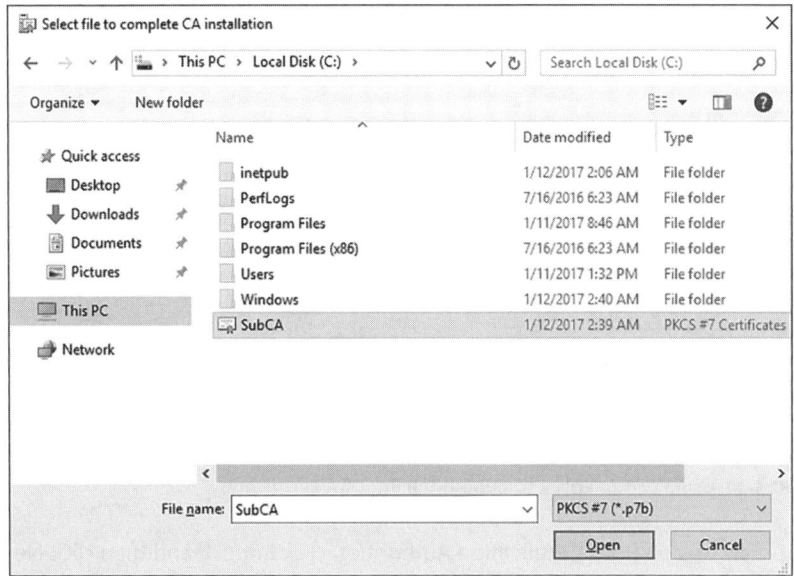

FIGURE 4-29 Installing the subordinate CA certificate

After you have completed the deployment of your subordinate CAs, you can shut down the root CA.

Publish the root CA in AD DS

If you configured your subordinates in an AD DS environment, you should publish the root CA certificate to all client and server computers in your domain by using Group Policy. Use the following procedure to complete this final task:

1. On a domain controller, open Group Policy Management.
2. In the Group Policy Management Console, open the Default Domain Policy for editing.
3. In the Computer Configuration node, navigate to Policies, Windows Settings, Security Settings, Public Key Policies, Trusted Root Certification Authorities, as shown in Figure 4-30.

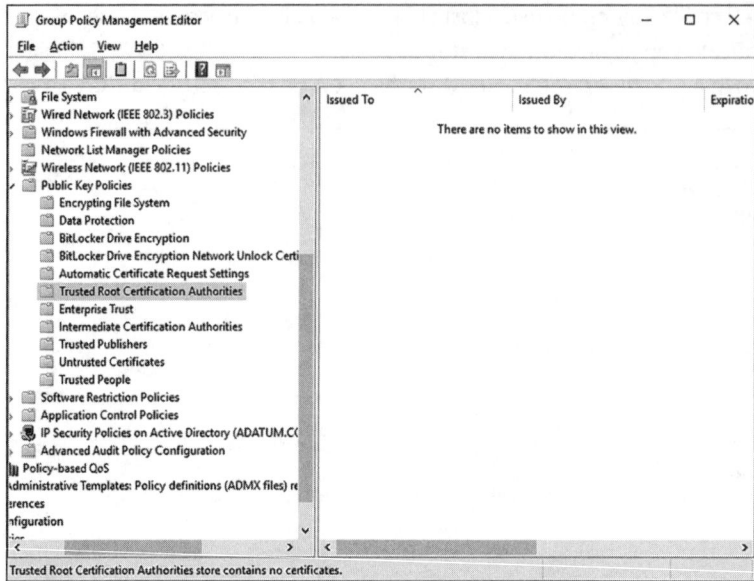

FIGURE 4-30 Using Group Policy to publish the Root CA certificate

4. Right-click Trusted Root Certification Authorities, click Import, and then click Next.
5. Navigate to the place where you stored the exported root CA, and double-click the certificate file. This has a .cer file extension.
6. Click Next two times, and then click Finish.
7. In the Certificate Import Wizard dialog box, click OK.
8. You can close the Group Policy Management Editor, and the Group Policy Management Console.

Install and configure an Online Responder

Online responders can provide certificate revocation information and offer an alternative to using CRLs. Because online responders provide revocation status about a specific certificate rather than all certificates, they offer several advantages over CRLs, as follows:

- **Provide better support for remote clients** Computers that connect remotely, for example, over a VPN, might lack the bandwidth to download the entire CRL to check a single certificate.
- **Avoid excessive network activity** During certain times of the day, for example, when users sign in, your network handles peaks in certificate revocation checking.
- **Improve revocation checking throughput** Rather than provide an entire CRL to check a single certificate, placing unnecessary load on your PKI, using an online responder enables you to provide only the required revocation checking data.

> **NEED MORE REVIEW?** **HOW ONLINE RESPONDERS WORK**
>
> To review further details about OCSP, refer to the Microsoft TechNet website at https://technet.microsoft.com/library/cc731001(v=ws.11).aspx.

Install the Online Responder role service

You can install the Online Responder role service to provide online responder function in Windows Server 2016. To add the Online Responder role service, use the following procedure:

1. Sign in as a local administrator on your CA server and open Server Manager.
2. Click Manage, and then click Add Roles And Features.
3. Click through the wizard, and on the Server Roles page, expand Active Directory Certificate Services, and then select the Online Responder check box.
4. Because OCSP uses HTTP to handle revocation requests, you must install several Web Server components. In the Add Roles And Features Wizard dialog box, in the Add Features That Are Required For Online Responder list, click Add Features, and then click Next.
5. Complete the wizard to install the Online Responder role service.

> **EXAM TIP**
>
> Do not combine the Online Responder role service on the same server computer that hosts the Certification Authority role service.

Configure the Online Responder role service

After the role service is installed, use the following procedure to configure the Online Responder role service:

1. In Server Manager, in Notifications, click Configure Active Directory Certificate Services on the destination server.
2. In the AD CS Configuration Wizard, on the Credentials page, enter the required credentials to perform the configuration. These should be set to at least Local Administrator. Click Next.
3. On the Role Services page, select the Online Responder check box, and click Next.
4. Click Configure, and when prompted, click Close.

You must also issue the OCSP Response Signing certificate template. To do this, complete the following steps:

1. In the Certification Authority console, right-click the Certificate Templates node.
2. Point to New, and then click New Certificate Template To Issue.
3. In the Enable Certificate Templates dialog box, locate the OCSP Response Signing Certificate, and then click OK.

Finally, you must create a revocation configuration for the online responder:

1. In Server Manager, click Tools, and then click Online Responder Management.
2. In the navigation pane, right-click the Revocation Configuration node, and then click Add Revocation Configuration.
3. In the Add Revocation Configuration Wizard, click Next.
4. On the Name The Revocation Configuration page, type a name of the configuration, and click Next.
5. On the Select CA Certificate Location page, click the option for the location of your CA certificate, and then click Next. Choose from:
   - Select A Certificate For An Existing Enterprise CA (default)
   - Select A Certificate From The Local Certificate Store
   - Import Certificate From A File
6. On the Choose CA Certificate page, select the certificate that you want to use, and click Next.
7. On the Select Signing Certificate page, shown in Figure 4-31, choose from the following options, and then click Next:
   - Automatically Select A Signing Certificate (default)
   - Manually Select A Signing Certificate
   - Use The CA Certificate For The Revocation Configuration

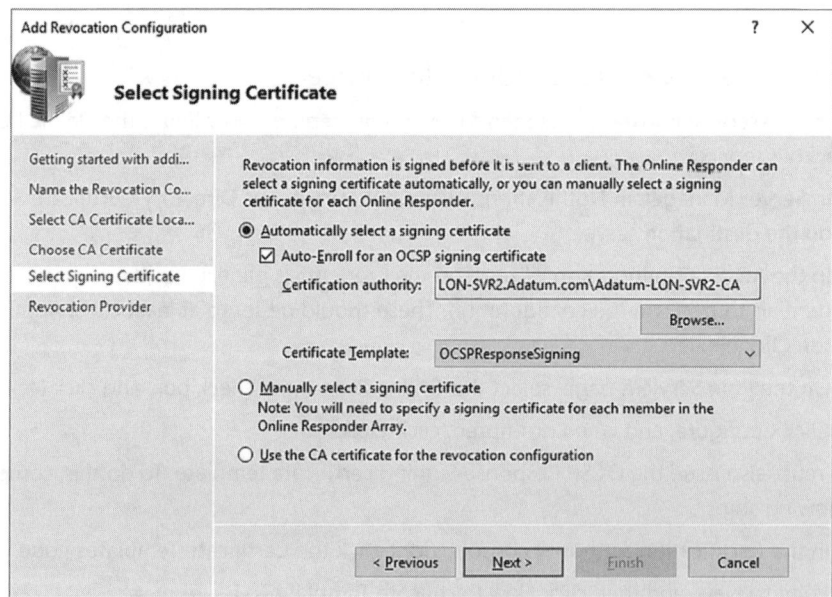

FIGURE 4-31 Adding a revocation configuration

8. On the Revocation Provider page, click Provider, and in the Revocation Provider Properties dialog box, enter the location of the CRLs. For example, click Add, type http://lon-svr2.adatum.com/cert/Adatum-NYC-1-CA.crl and then click OK twice.
9. Click Finish.

> **NEED MORE REVIEW? CREATING A REVOCATION CONFIGURATION**
>
> To review further details about configuring an online responder, refer to the Microsoft TechNet website at *https://technet.microsoft.com/library/cc731099(v=ws.11).aspx*.

Implement administrative role separation

While it is common in small organizations for a single group of administrators to perform all administrative tasks in a network, as an organization grows, this approach becomes less suitable. For this reason, you should consider separating the administration of your AD CS architecture into distinct roles, each with responsibility for different aspects of AD CS management. For example: CA administration, certificate management, backup management, and auditing.

Windows Server 2016 does not provide built-in roles for AD CS administration; you must create these yourself. It is recommended that you create appropriately named security groups in AD DS and assign the required administrative roles to the respective groups by using AD CS permissions. Use the information in Table 4-1 to help plan the required groups.

TABLE 4-1 Administrative role separation

Role or Group Name	Ad CS Permissions	Explanation
CA Admin	Manage CA	■ This is a CA role and includes the ability to: 　■ Assign all other CA roles. 　■ Renew the CA certificate. 　■ Configure and maintain the CA. ■ Assign these permissions using the Certification Authority console.
Certificate Manager	Issue and Manage Certificates	■ This is a CA role and enables members to issue and manager certificates, including approving certificate enrollment and revocation requests. ■ Assign these permissions using the Certification Authority console.
Backup Operator	■ Back up file and directories. ■ Restore file and directories.	■ Perform system backup and restore operations. ■ Built-in to the operating system.
Auditor	Manage auditing and security log	■ Enables members to configure and maintain audit logs. ■ Built-in to the operating system.

EXAM TIP

By default, the local Administrators group has Manage CA, and Issue and Manage Certificates permissions. In enterprise CAs, the Domain Admins Global Security Group and the Enterprise Admins Universal Security Group has Manage CA, and Issue And Manage Certificates permissions.

To configure the required permissions for any groups that you create, use the Certification Authority console, as described in the following procedure:

1. In the Certification Authority console, right-click your CA, and then click Properties.
2. In the CA Properties dialog box, click the Security tab.
3. Add the required groups and then, in the Permissions list below, configure the desired permissions for each group.

The exact groups that you establish and the roles that you assign to those groups vary depending on your AD CS deployment and what you want to achieve in terms of administrative separation. For example, consider the following scenario.

You have deployed a standalone root CA that is a member of an AD DS domain and two enterprise subordinate CAs, one of which issues user certificates, while the other issues computer certificates. You want a single group to have both CA admin and Certificate manager permissions on all CAs in your organization, and another group that has CA admin and Certificate manager permissions only on the two subordinate CAs.

To set up role-based administration to support this scenario, perform the following steps:

1. Using Active Directory Users And Computers, create the following security groups in AD DS:
   - Enterprise CA Admins
   - Subordinate CA Admins
   - User Cert Managers
   - Computer Cert Managers
2. On all CAs, assign the Enterprise CA Admins group both the Manage CA and Issue And Manage Certificates permissions as described above.
3. On both subordinate CAs, assign the Subordinate CA Admins group the Manage CA and Issue And Manage Certificates permissions.
4. On the subordinate CA for user certificates, assign the User Cert Managers group the Issue And Manage Certificates permission, as shown in Figure 4-32.

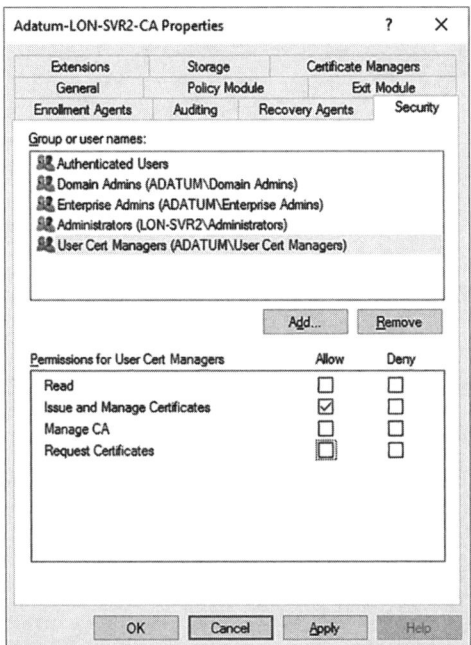

FIGURE 4-32 Configuring AD CS administrative role separation with permissions

5. Then, on the Certificate Managers tab of the CA properties, shown in Figure 4-33, restrict the User Certificate Managers group to only the User certificate template:

   A. Click Restrict Certificate Managers. The configured security groups display in the Certificate Managers: (configured on the Security tab) list.

   B. Click Add, and in the Enabled Certificate Templates dialog box, select the User certificate, and click OK.

   C. In the Certificate Templates list, click All, and then click Remove.

   D. Click OK.

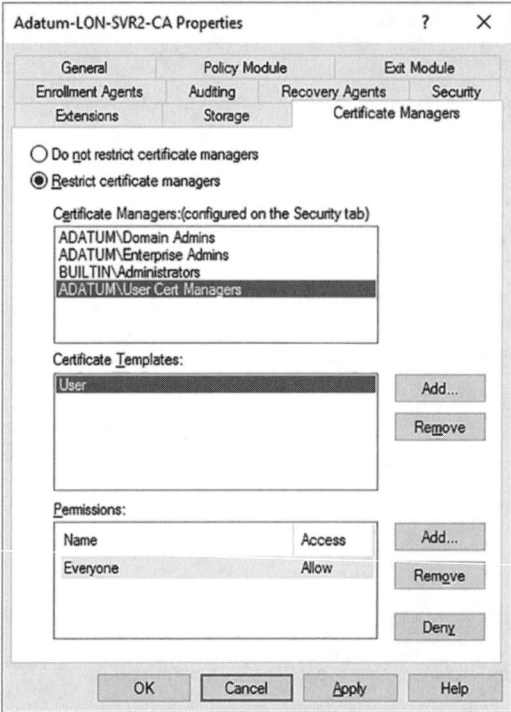

FIGURE 4-33 Restricting certificate managers

6. On the subordinate CA for computer certificates, assign the Computer Cert Managers group the Issue And Manage Certificates permission. Then restrict the Computer Cert Managers group to only the Computer certificate template.

> **NEED MORE REVIEW?** **IMPLEMENT ROLE-BASED ADMINISTRATION**
>
> To review further details about implementing AD CS administrative role separation, refer to the Microsoft TechNet website at *https://technet.microsoft.com/library/cc732590(v=ws.11).aspx*.

Configure CA backup and recovery

Given the importance of certificates in helping to secure your organization's app and services, it is vital that you know how to back up and restore your CAs. You can use the Certification Authority console, Windows PowerShell, and the Certutil.exe command-line tool to perform both backup and restore operations.

Backing up the CA

To back up your CA using the Certification Authority console, use the following procedure:

1. In the navigation pane, right-click the CA, point to All Tasks, and then click Back Up CA, as shown in Figure 4-34.

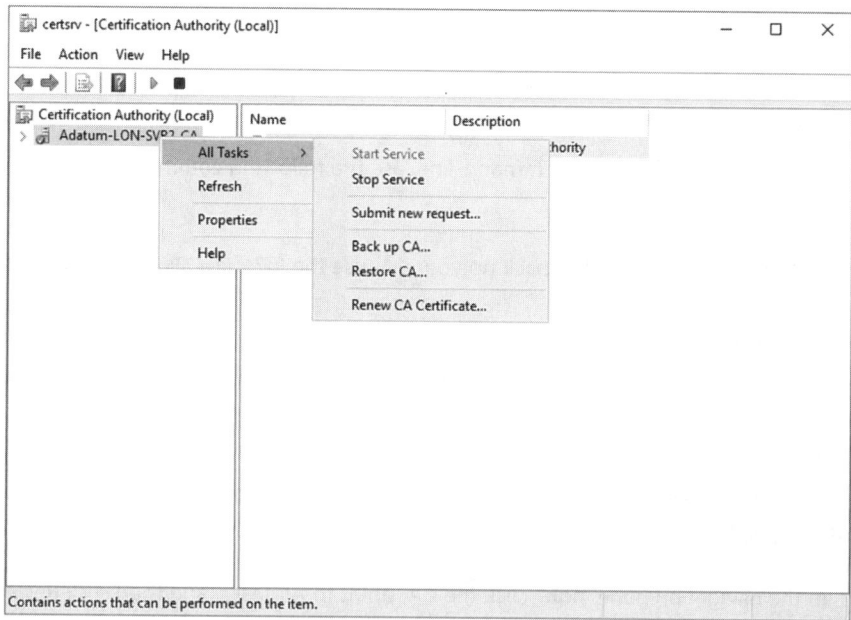

FIGURE 4-34 Backing up your CA

2. In the Certification Authority Backup Wizard, click Next, and then on the Items To Back Up page, shown in Figure 4-35, select the Private Key And CA Certificate and Certificate Database And Certificate Database Log check boxes.

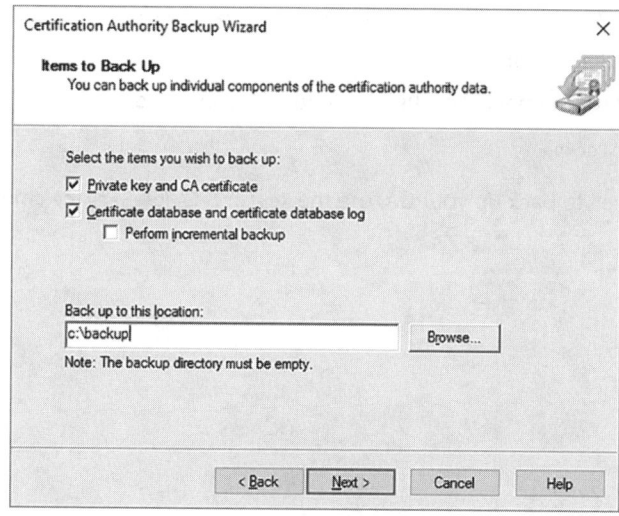

FIGURE 4-35 Specifying CA backup options

Skill 4.1: Install and configure AD CS   **CHAPTER 4**   273

3. If you have performed backups previously, you can choose the Perform Incremental Backup option.
4. Define a location for your backup to be stored, and then click Next.
5. On the Select A Password page, enter a password to protect the security of your backup files, and then click Next.
6. Click Finish.

To back up your CA from the command-line, use the following command:

```
Certutil -Backup c:\Backup
```

To use Windows PowerShell to back up your CA, use the `Backup-CARoleService` cmdlet.

Restoring your CA

To restore your CA using the Certification Authority console, use the following procedure.

EXAM TIP

Note that the Active Directory Certificate Services service cannot be running during a restore operation.

1. In the navigation pane, right-click the CA, point to All Tasks, and then click Restore CA.
2. When prompted, click OK to stop the AD CS services running on your server.
3. In the Certification Authority Restore Wizard, click Next, and then on the Items To Restore page, select the Private Key And CA Certificate and Certificate Database And Certificate Database Log check boxes.
4. Specify the location of your backup files, and then click Next.
5. Enter the password that was used to protect the backup files, and click Next.
6. Click Finish to complete the procedure.

To restore your CA from the command-line, use the following command:

```
Certutil -Restore c:\Backup
```

To use Windows PowerShell to back up your CA, use the `Restore-CARoleService` cmdlet.

Skill 4.2: Manage certificates

Deploying and configuring CAs as part of your PKI is only part of the story. It is also necessary for you to configure and manage certificate templates, certificates, autoenrollment, and key archival and recovery.

> **This section covers how to:**
> - Manage certificate templates
> - Implement and manage certificate deployment, validation, and revocation
> - Configure and manage key archival and recovery

Manage certificate templates

You can use digital certificates for many different purposes. Certificate templates enable you to define these purposes, and also how users or computers can request specific certificates. You can quickly and easily create new certificates templates using both graphical and command-line tools.

Template versions

Windows Server 2016 supports four different template versions. These template versions have different features and characteristics, as described below:

- **Version 1** Created by default when you install the Certification Authority Role Service. You can make only limited changes to version 1 templates; specifically, the certificate permissions.

> **EXAM TIP**
>
> Autoenrollment is not available for version 1 templates.

- **Version 2** Several version 2 templates are created automatically when you install the Certification Authority Role. You can modify these templates, or create your own version 2 templates as your needs dictate.
- **Version 3** Support more advanced features, including Cryptography Next Generation (CNG).
- **Version 4** Available since Windows Server 2012, provides for newer features, including support for cryptographic service providers (CSPs) and for key storage providers.

Managing template security

You can use template security to determine which users have what level of access to templates. Access is defined using the Security tab on the Template Properties dialog box, and includes the following permissions:

- **Read** Enables a user or computer to read the properties of a template when enrolling a certificate.

EXAM TIP

Ensure that the default Read permission for the Authenticated Users group is not removed from a template.

- **Write** Enables a user or computer to modify the template properties.
- **Full control** Enables users to modify all properties of the template, including the security settings for the template.
- **Enroll** Assuming that the user, or computer, has the Read permission, the Enroll permission enables a user or computer to enroll a certificate based on a template.
- **Autoenroll** If the user, or computer, has the Read and Enroll permissions, the Autoenroll permission enables a user or computer to enroll a certificate using autoenrollment.

EXAM TIP

Always assign permissions on templates to global or universal security groups because the certificate templates are stored in AD DS.

Managing other template properties

Aside from the security settings that determine whether a user or computer can read, modify, and enroll a certificate based on a template, you can also configure the intended certificate purpose by modifying a template. By default, when you deploy the CA server role, Windows Server 2016 installs several templates, most with multiple purposes, as shown in Figure 4-36.

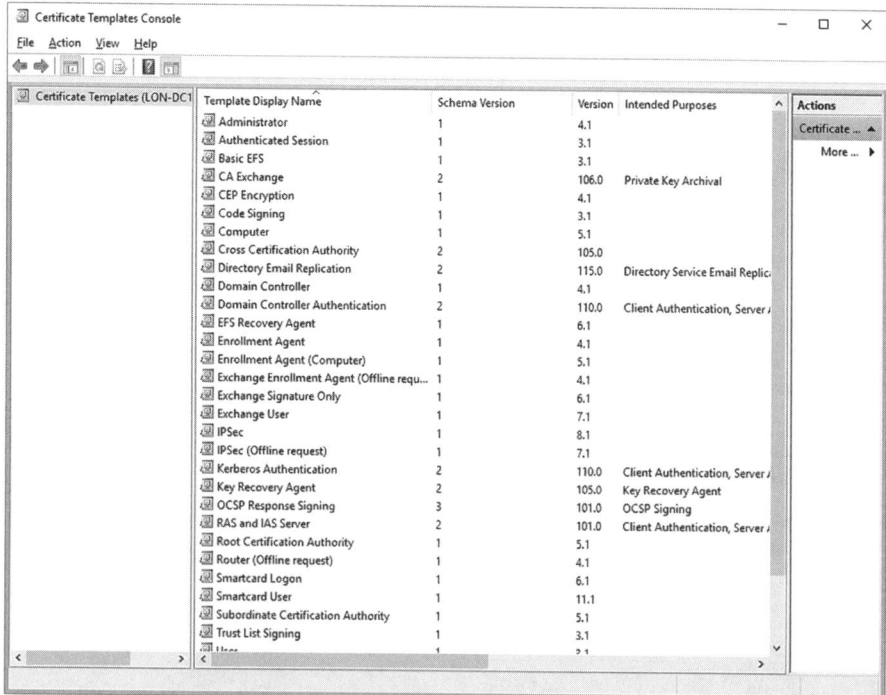

FIGURE 4-36 Viewing default templates

When planning to create or modify templates, you must consider several factors, including the following:

- What the certificate is for
- What methods are required for users or computers to submit a valid certificate request
- The key length and validity period for certificates
- The enrollment process and requirements

EXAM TIP

Certificates can be single purpose or multipurpose. Multipurpose certificates are used to simplify administration; for example, when all users require a certificate to achieve three things, such as email signing, EFS, and smart card sign in, it can make sense to combine these purposes in a single certificate.

Creating and managing a template

To create and manage certificate templates, from the Certification Authority console, right-click the Certificate Templates node, and then click Manage. For example, to create a new template based on the existing User template, use the following procedure:

1. In the Certificate Templates Console, shown in Figure 4-36, right-click the User template, and then click Duplicate Template.
2. In the Properties Of New Template dialog box, on the General tab, shown in Figure 4-37, in the Template Display Name box, type a meaningful name for your new template. For example, type Standard A Datum User Template.

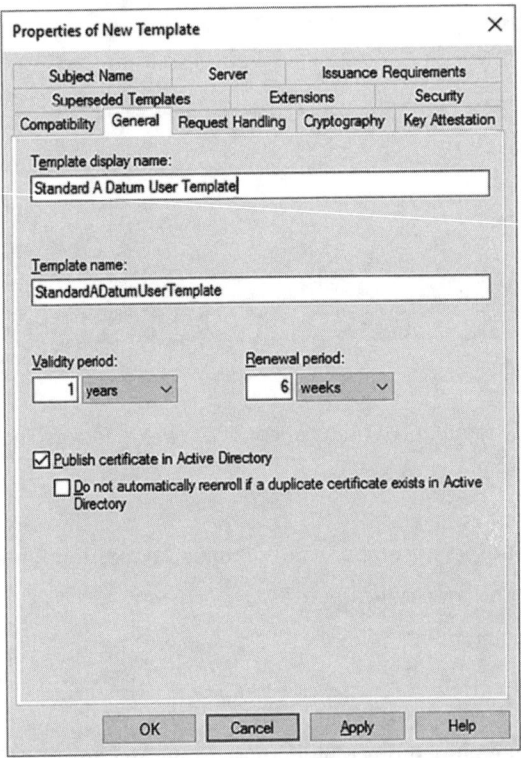

FIGURE 4-37 Configuring a template's General properties

3. Configure the Validity and Renewal periods.
4. On the Request Handling tab, shown in Figure 4-38, configure the intended purpose in the Purpose list, and then configure the enrollment settings. Choose between:
   - Enroll Subject Without Requiring Any User Input (default)
   - Prompt The User During Enrollment
   - Prompt The User During Enrollment And Require User Input When The Private Key Is Used

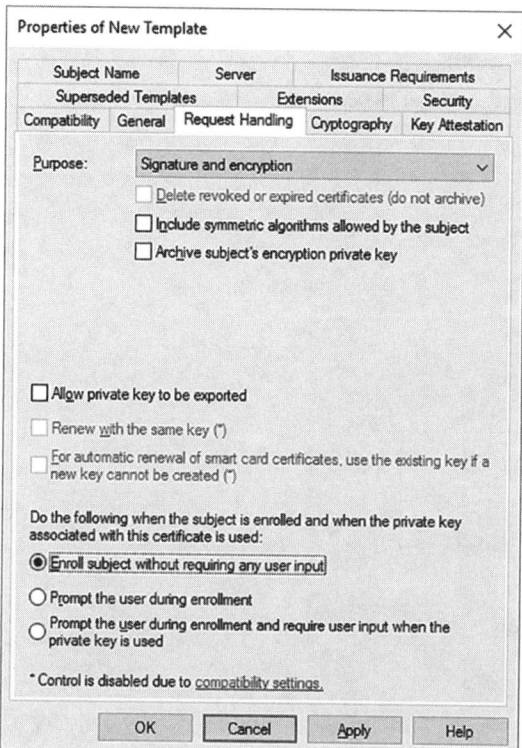

FIGURE 4-38 Configuring request handling options

5. Click the Security tab. Add any additional groups that require permissions on the template, and then configure the required permissions. For example, to enable all users to enroll and autoenroll certificates for this template, click Authenticated Users, and then in the Permissions For Authenticated Users section, enable the Enroll and Autoenroll Allow check boxes, as shown in Figure 4-39.

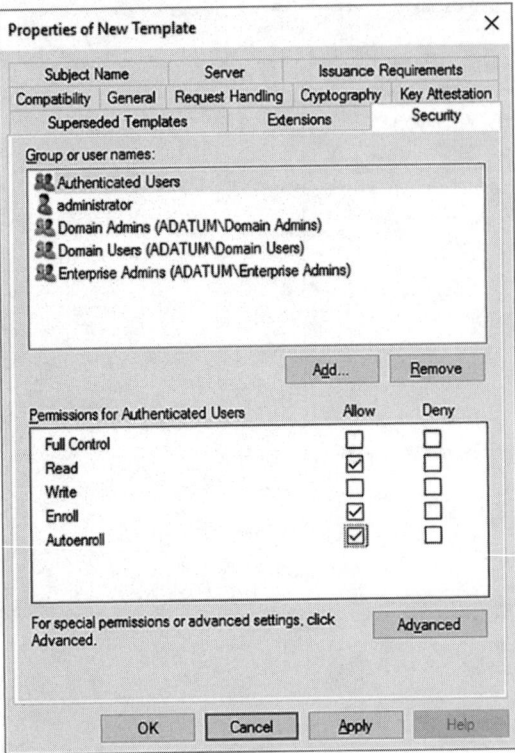

FIGURE 4-39 Configuring template security

6. On the Issuance Requirements tab, shown in Figure 4-40, configure any requirements. For example, if you require CA Manager Approval, select the CA Certificate Manager Approval check box.

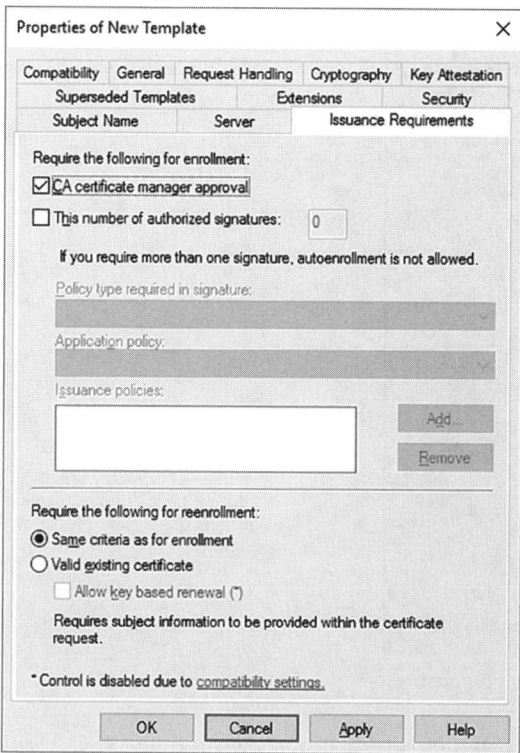

FIGURE 4-40 Configuring template issuance requirements

7. On the Extensions tab, shown in Figure 4-41, if you want to modify the template's intended purpose(s), click Application Policies in the Extensions Included In This Template list, and then click Edit.

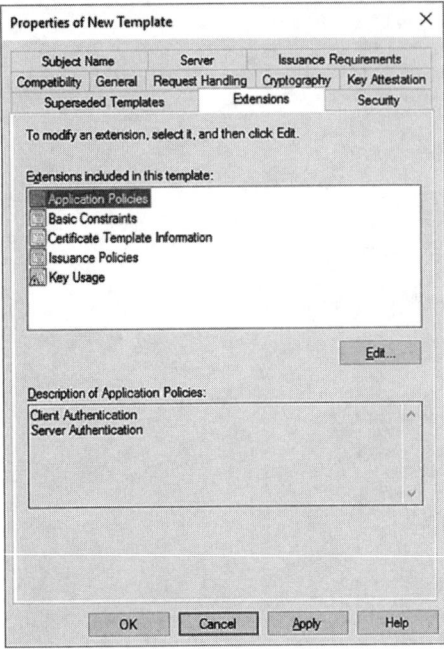

FIGURE 4-41 Modifying a template's purpose

8. In the Edit Application Policies Extension dialog box, shown in Figure 4-42, click Add.

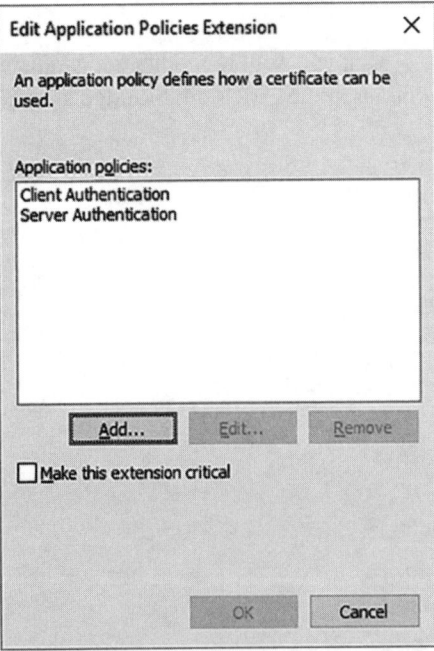

FIGURE 4-42 Modifying a template's purpose

9. Select any additional purposes from the Application Policies list. Click OK twice.
10. In the Properties Of New Template dialog box, click OK.

To make the template available, switch to the Certification Authority console, and then use the following procedure:

1. Right-click the Certificate Templates node.
2. Point to New, and then click New Certificate Template To Issue.
3. In the Enable Certificate Templates dialog box, locate the template you created, and then click OK.

Modify or supersede?

To modify a template, duplicate an existing template that closely matches your requirements, and then modify the intended purpose(s), or other properties of your duplicate, as described above. Ensure that you give the duplicate a meaningful name that best describes its purpose(s).

When you update a certificate template, you can choose to modify the original template or you can choose to supersede existing templates.

- **Modify**   Modification is used when you want to change the original certificate template, perhaps because you want to add a new purpose to it, or change its security settings. After you make the modification, all new certificates issued based on the template reflect the changes you made.

- **Supersede**   You might choose to supersede certificate templates in the situation where you have multiple templates that have similar (or identical) purposes. In this scenario, after you have superseded the various old templates, your new template replaces them. Any users that have older certificates are issued new certificates.

Implement and manage certificate deployment, validation, and revocation

After you have planned and created your certificate templates, you can begin the process of deploying and managing certificates to support your organization's security needs. As part of this process, you must consider how best to make certificates available to your users (and their computers).

When a user or computer obtains a certificate, this is referred to as enrollment. There are several certificate enrollment methods available:

- **Manual**   As the name suggests, when a user requires a certificate, they perform a manual procedure to obtain it. Typically, the user generates the request locally on their computer, and then transfers the request file to the CA for processing. Assuming the request is valid, the CA issues the appropriate certificate, which must then be transferred back to the requesting user for installation. Users can use the Certificates console or the Certreq.exe command-line tool to perform manual enrollment.

EXAM TIP

Manual enrollment is used when the user cannot communicate directly with the CA.

- **Autoenrollment** This is perhaps the most convenient form of enrollment because it requires no user intervention. After you have configured autoenrollment through Group Policy for the certificate, AD DS domain member computers can use this method for requesting, retrieving, and renewing their certificates. Where possible, this is the preferred method for enrollment.
- **Web enrollment** Users can request and retrieve their certificates by using a web site on the CA. The user signs in to the website and selects the appropriate template. Assuming all enrollment conditions are met, the CA issues the certificate. To enable this enrollment method, you must install the Certification Authority Web Enrollment role service on your CAs. If you are unable to use autoenrollment, web enrollment is a good alternative.
- **On behalf** Not all users are skilled at using the tools required to request and install certificates. For this reason, you can use the enrollment on behalf method. This might be appropriate when a manager is installing certificates for users to enable smart card authentication. To use enrollment on behalf, you must create an enrollment agent; this is a user account that is used to request certificates on behalf of other users.

EXAM TIP

To enable the enrollment agent, the designated user account must hold a certificate based on the Enrollment Agent template. Microsoft recommends that you only publish this template on your CAs when you need to create an enrollment agent.

The method(s) you choose depend upon your organizational requirements and the PKI components that you have in place.

Manage certificate enrollment and renewal for computers and users using Group Policies

Autoenrollment offers many benefits for the CA administrator, chief among these being the relative simplicity of establishing the certificate infrastructure. Autoenrollment enables your users (and computers) to obtain and renew certificates without user intervention.

EXAM TIP

Autoenrollment is not available with standalone CAs. You must implement an enterprise CA to configure autoenrollment. However, as previously discussed, you can implement an offline standalone root CA with enterprise subordinate CAs.

Consider implementing Group Policy-based enrollment in situations where all users and computers require the same certificate(s), for example, to provide for user or computer authentication.

To enable autoenrollment, you must sign in to your enterprise CA as a member of either the Domain Admins global security group, or the Enterprise Admins universal security group. Any certificates that you want to autoenroll must be based on a certificate template on which you have assigned the Autoenroll permission. Finally, you must configure the required Group Policy Object (GPO) settings to enable autoenrollment.

To perform this last step, use the following procedure:

1. On a domain controller, sign in as a member of Domain Admins.
2. In Server Manager, click Tools, and then click Group Policy Management.
3. Locate the Default Domain Policy and open it for editing.
4. In the Group Policy Management Editor dialog box, navigate to Computer Configuration, Policies, Windows Settings, Security Settings, Public Key Policies, as shown in Figure 4-43.

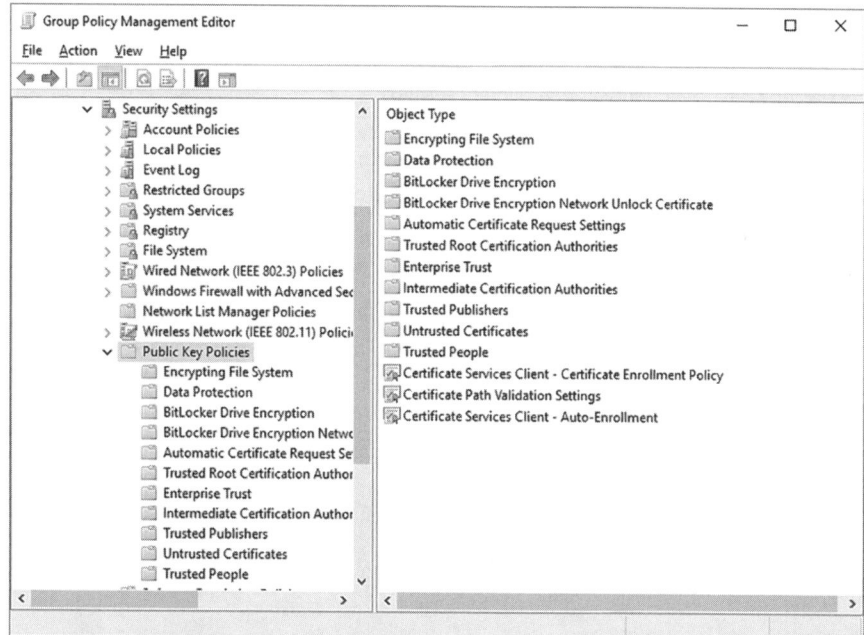

FIGURE 4-43 Enabling autoenrollment in GPO

5. In the details pane, double-click Certificate Services Client - Auto-Enrollment. The Properties dialog box opens, as shown in Figure 4-44.
6. Configure the following items, and then click OK:
    - In the Configuration Model list, click Enabled.

- Select both the Renew Expired Certificates, Update Pending Certificates, And Remove Revoked Certificates and Update Certificates That Use Certificate Templates check boxes.

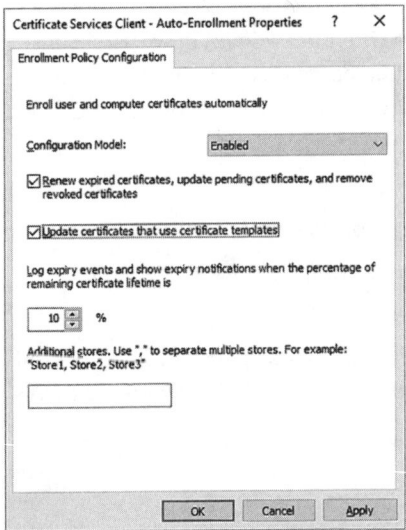

FIGURE 4-44 Configuring autoenrollment settings

You can also configure the certificate enrollment policy in the same GPO node. To complete this task, in the Group Policy Management Editor:

1. In the details pane, double-click the Certificate Services Client – Certificate Enrollment Policy value.
2. In the Certificate Services Client – Certificate Enrollment Policy dialog box, in the Configuration Model list, click Enabled, as shown in Figure 4-45.

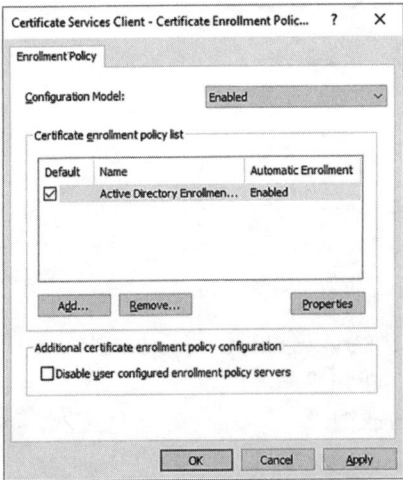

FIGURE 4-45 Configuring enrollment policy settings

3. The Active Directory Enrollment Policy is automatically Enabled.
4. If you want to configure additional enrollment policy servers, click Add, and in the Certificate Enrollment Policy Server dialog box, shown in Figure 4-46, enter the enrollment policy server's URI, and then click Validate Server. Click Add.

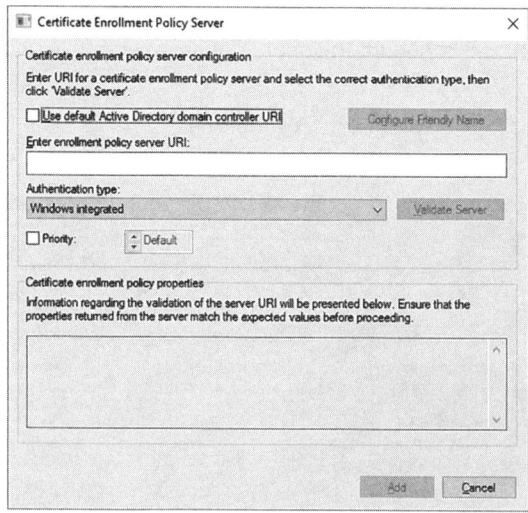

FIGURE 4-46 Configuring enrollment policy settings

5. Click OK, and then close the Group Policy Management Editor.

> **NEED MORE REVIEW? MANAGE CERTIFICATE ENROLLMENT POLICY BY USING GROUP POLICY**
>
> To review further details about managing certificate enrollment with GPOs, refer to the Microsoft TechNet website at *https://technet.microsoft.com/library/dd851772(v=ws.11).aspx*.

Certificate revocation

Certificate revocation allows you to indicate that a certificate is no longer valid. When you revoke a certificate, information about the revocation is stored in the CRL. Client and server computers can access the published CRL either directly, or via an online responder, as discussed earlier in this chapter.

Typical reasons to revoke a certificate include:

- The certificate's key has been compromised.
- The issuing CA has been compromised.
- The certificate is no longer valid for its intended purpose.
- The certificate has been superseded.
- The user or computer no longer qualifies to use the certificate.

To revoke a certificate, in the Certification Authority console:

1. In the Issued Certificates folder, in the Details pane, right-click the certificate that you want to revoke.
2. Point to All Tasks, and then click Revoke Certificate.

It is important that certificate revocation information is maintained accurately. Changes must be published to the CRL, and you can configure the publishing interval from within the Certification Authority console:

1. Right-click Revoked Certificates folder, and then click Properties.
2. In the Revoked Certificates Properties dialog box, shown in Figure 4-47, on the CRL Publishing Parameters tab, configure the appropriate CRL Publication Interval and Publish Delta CRLs Interval.
3. Click OK.

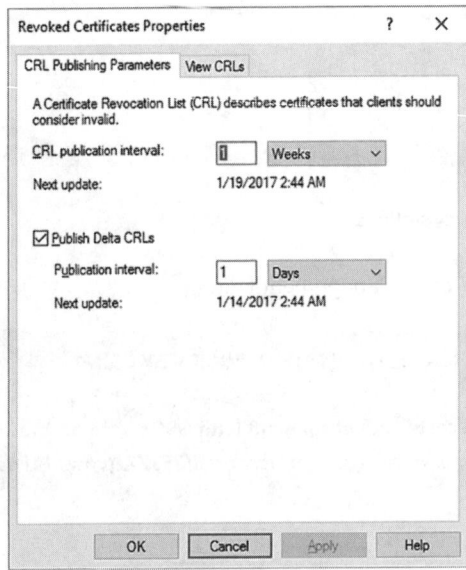

FIGURE 4-47 Configuring CRL publishing intervals

Configure and manage key archival and recovery

It is vitally important that digital certificates and their corresponding keys are kept secure. If you lose the keys that were used to encrypt data files, you might no longer be able to access those data files.

Keys can be compromised in the following situations:

- You reinstalled the operating system.

- A hard disk is corrupted.
- A user's computer is stolen or lost.
- A user desktop profile is corrupted or deleted.

To help protect against data loss arising from the loss of keys, you can configure key archival and key recovery agents. Key archival must be enabled both on the CA and on the specific certificate templates. To enable key archival, you must also enable a key recovery agent; this requires that you install a key recovery agent certificate in the context of the user account that you want to enable as a key recovery agent.

Enabling and configuring a key recovery agent

Use the following procedure to enable and configure a key recovery agent. Start by enabling the Key Recovery Agent certificate template:

1. Open the Certificate Template console, and locate the Key Recovery Agent template.
2. Right-click this template, and then click Properties.
3. On the Issuance Requirements tab, shown in Figure 4-48, clear the CA Certificate Manager Approval check box, and then click OK.

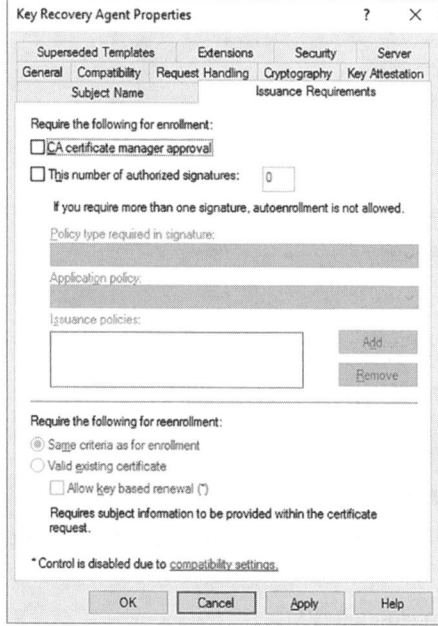

FIGURE 4-48 Configuring the key recovery agent template

4. Switch to the Certification Authority console.
5. Right-click Certificate Templates, point to New, and then click Certificate Template To Issue.

6. In the Enable Certificate Templates dialog box, select the Key Recovery Agent template, and then click OK.

Next, enroll a certificate using the Key Recovery Agent Template. Open the Certificates console and enroll a Key Recovery Agent certificate:

1. Run mmc.exe and add the Certificates console and set the focus to Current User.
2. Right-click the Personal folder, and point to All Tasks.
3. Click Request New Certificate.
4. In the Certificate Enrollment Wizard, on the Select Certificate Enrollment Policy page, click Active Directory Enrollment Policy, and then click Next.
5. On the Request Certificates page, shown in Figure 4-49, select the Key Recovery Agent check box, and click Enroll.

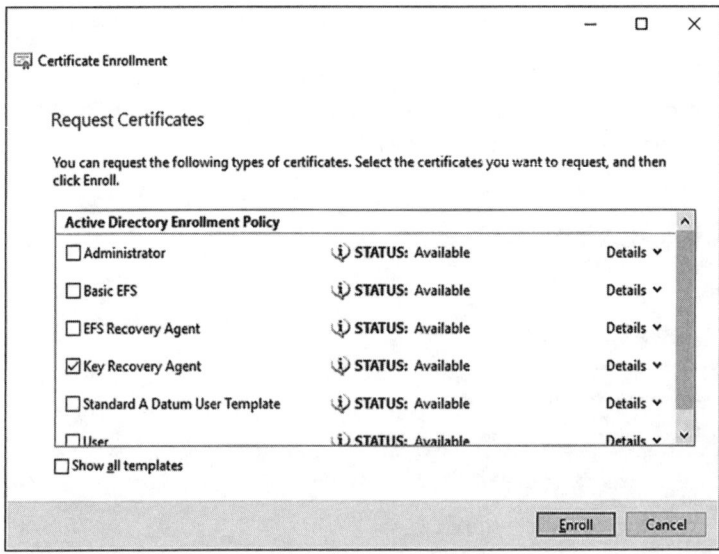

FIGURE 4-49 Installing the key recovery agent certificate

6. Close the console.

Finally, you must configure the CA to allow for key recovery:

1. In the Certification Authority console, right-click your CA in the navigation pane, and then click Properties.
2. Click the Recovery Agents tab, shown in Figure 4-50.
3. Select the Archive The Key check box, and then click Add.
4. In the Windows Security pop-up dialog box, click OK to select the Key Recovery Agent certificate.

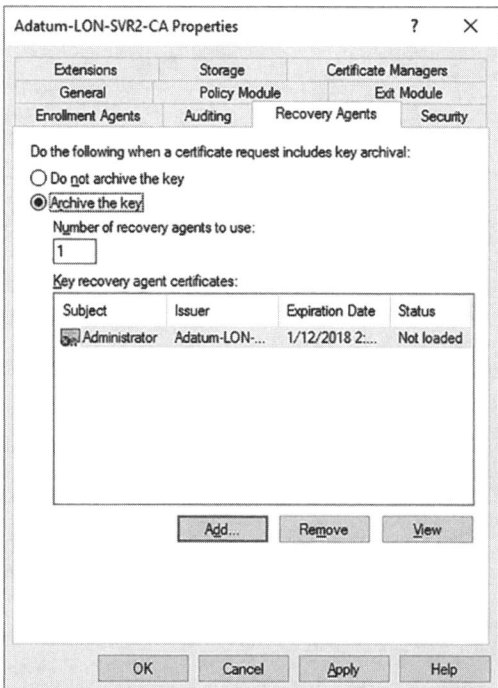

FIGURE 4-50 Enabling key recovery agents on the CA

5. Click OK, and then restart the CA when prompted.

Enabling and configuring key archival

After you have enabled the key recovery agent, you must modify the templates for any certificates for which you wish to enable key archival. Use the following procedure to complete this process:

1. In the Certificate Templates console, right-click any certificate template that you want to enable for key archival, and then click Duplicate Template.
2. Configure any general settings for the template including, on the General tab, the name for the template.
3. On the Superseded Templates tab, click Add to select the templates that this template replaces.
4. On the Request Handling tab, shown in Figure 4-51, select the Archive Subject's Encryption Private Key check box.

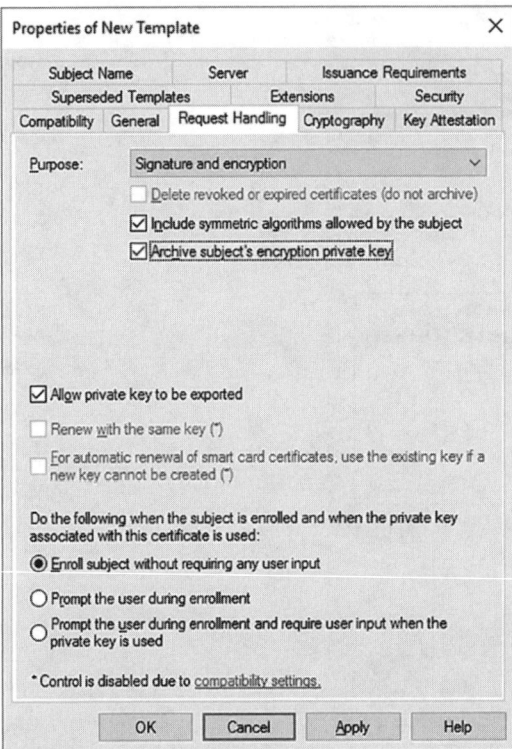

FIGURE 4-51 Enabling key archival

5. Click OK.
6. Switch to the Certification Authority console.
7. Right-click Certificate Templates, point to New, and then click Certificate Template To Issue.
8. In the Enable Certificate Templates dialog box, select the template you just duplicated and configured, and then click OK.

Chapter summary

- AD CS can provide the required components to support your PKI and your organization's digital certificate needs.
- You can deploy CAs as standalone or integrated with AD DS.
- You can take your standalone root CA offline to enhance security of your PKI.
- Deploying subordinate CAs as enterprise CAs enables you to take advantage of AD DS features such as autoenrollment and configuring AD CS features by using Group Policy.
- It is important to configure the CDP and AIA information before you take your root CA offline.
- The Online Responder role service enables you to respond to client requests for specific revocation requests.
- You can use GPOs to publish the root CA certificate and to enable autoenrollment for AD DS users and computers.
- Role-based administration enables you to separate administrative tasks in AD CS.
- Certificate templates can make managing certificates easier.
- Configuring a key recovery agent enables you to help protect against data loss in the event of user keys being lost or corrupted.

Thought experiment

In this thought experiment, demonstrate your skills and knowledge of the topics covered in this chapter. You can find answers to this thought experiment in the next section.

You work in support at A. Datum. As a consultant for A. Datum, answer the following questions about deploying and managing CAs within the A. Datum organization:

1. A Datum has many thousands of users distributed across many locations. You must deploy CAs throughout the organization to enable the deployment of digital certificates. What strategies might you consider?
2. Before taking your root CA offline, what must you consider?
3. Why is it necessary to publish the standalone root CA certificate?
4. In addition to the Autoenroll permission, what permissions on a certificate template does a user require to be able to use autoenrollment?
5. How do you modify a certificate's purpose?

Thought experiment answers

This section contains the solution to the thought experiment. Each answer explains why the answer choice is correct.

1. It is likely that more than one CA is required. Using multiple CAs helps to provide for high availability and load balancing. In addition, for an organization as large as A Datum, a multitier CA infrastructure is appropriate. Deploy the root CA as a standalone CA. Then deploy enterprise CAs as subordinates. Configure these based on location, department, or other appropriate factors. After you have configured the subordinates, take the root CA offline.

2. Before you take the root CA offline, it is important to deploy the subordinate CAs. This involves installing the root CA certificate on each subordinate. It is also important to configure the CDP and AIA location information.

3. Users and computers do not trust the root CA certificate, which means that they do not trust the subordinate CAs. By publishing the root CA certificate in AD DS, you can ensure that all users and computers trust the root CA, and therefore its subordinates and all certificates issued by them.

4. Users require the Read and Enroll permissions, together with the Autoenroll permission to be able to autoenroll a certificate.

5. Typically, you modify the purpose on a duplicate template of the template that you wish to modify. Use the Extensions tab and modify the Application Policies for additional purposes. Then, use the Superseded Templates tab to define which template the duplicate template supersedes. Finally, issue the new template so that it is available in your organization. If the template is enabled for autoenroll, users and computers automatically receive the updated template.

CHAPTER 5

Implement identity federation and access solutions

Windows Server 2016 provides several features and services that enable you to make your organization's content securely available to users in other organizations, to users on the Internet, and to users that have a Microsoft Azure Active Directory (Azure AD) account. These features include Active Directory Federation Services (AD FS), Active Directory Rights Management Services (AD RMS), and Web Application Proxy. It is important that you know how to deploy and configure these services in order to allow users from outside of your organization to access your resources in a secure way.

Skills covered in this chapter:
- Install and configure AD FS
- Implement Web Application Proxy
- Install and configure AD RMS

Skill 5.1: Install and configure AD FS

Deploying AD FS allows your users to use single sign-on (SSO) to authenticate with app and services located in Azure, your on-premises network infrastructure, or the network of a partner organization, depending upon configuration.

AD FS is based on trust relationships that you establish between organizations to enable the sharing of resources; these trusts are known as *federation trusts*. You can establish federation trusts across Active Directory Domain Services (AD DS) forest boundaries and between organizations based on business requirements.

As with AD DS trusts, in each organization, the administrator defines what resources are accessible through the trust and who has access to those resources.

> **EXAM TIP**
>
> Federation trusts are not related to AD DS forest trusts and it is not a requirement that each organization's AD FS servers communicate with one another directly.

For example, theater staff might want to view ticket sales for an upcoming performance where the ticket sales are handled by an external organization. The theater network administrator must put all user accounts that require access to this information into a group. The ticket sales organization's administrator must grant the required access to the ticketing sales database to that group through the trust. However, the ticket sales organization's administrator must ensure that only the remote organization's ticketing staff can access the ticketing data for their theater, and only that data.

It is important when establishing a federation trust that each party in the trust understands how user identities are to be used; specifically, what type of user credentials are required, and how this information is stored and used. It is also necessary for each organization to define a policy that can help to ensure the privacy of data that is not to be made available through the trust.

> **NEED MORE REVIEW? ACTIVE DIRECTORY FEDERATION SERVICES OVERVIEW**
>
> To review further details about AD FS, refer to the Microsoft TechNet website at
> *https://technet.microsoft.com/library/hh831502(v=ws.11).aspx.*

> **This section covers how to:**
> - Examine AD FS requirements
> - Install the AD FS server role
> - Configure the AD FS server role
> - Implement claims-based authentication, including relying party trusts
> - Configure authentication policies
> - Implement and configure device registration
> - Configure for use with Microsoft Azure and Microsoft Office 365
> - Configure AD FS to enable authentication of users stored in LDAP directories
> - Upgrade and migrate previous AD FS workloads to Windows Server 2016

Examine AD FS requirements

Windows Server 2016 provides the Active Directory Federation Service server role to facilitate federation. This server role provides the following components:

- **Federation Server** Each party requires at least one federation server. This component is the engine of the implementation, and is responsible for issuing and validating identity claims.

- **Web Application Proxy** This is an optional component. You usually deploy the Web Application Proxy to your perimeter network where it functions as a web proxy and reverse web proxy for your AD FS deployment. In this role, it is referred to as an AD FS proxy.

> **EXAM TIP**
>
> You install the Web Application Proxy as a separate role service, which is part of the Remote Access server role.

- **Claims** A trusted party in the federation trust makes a statement about a security principal, such as a user that is used to provide authentication through the trust. The claim might include one or more attributes of the object, perhaps including the user name or department.
- **Claim Rules** The trusting party uses claim rules to determine how to process claims. For example, a claim rule might state that a user's user principal name (UPN) is a valid claim.
- **Claims Providers** The trusted party hosts the claims provider component. This component is responsible for managing user authentication and issuing claims that users present.
- **Claims Provider Trust** Provides the rules that define when a client can request claims from a claims provider, which the client then submits to a relying party.
- **Attribute Store** An attribute store, such as AD DS, contains claim values. Simply put, a directory service that contains user objects with appropriate properties, such as UPNs or email addresses. AD DS is a common choice with AD FS deployments because any AD FS server must be domain-joined, and therefore AD DS is easily accessible as an attribute store.

> **EXAM TIP**
>
> AD DS is automatically available as an attribute store on your AD FS servers without requiring any administrative configuration.

- **Relying Parties** The relying party resides at the resource holding, or trusting, end of the federation trust. Provided by a web service that has the Windows Identity Foundation (WIF) installed. Relying parties can use the AD FS 1.0 claims-aware agent as an alternative to WIF.

> **NEED MORE REVIEW?** **WHAT IS WINDOWS IDENTITY FOUNDATION?**
>
> To find out more about WIF, refer to the Microsoft MSDN website at *https://msdn.microsoft.com/library/ee748475.aspx*.

- **Relying Party Trust** Consists of rules and identifiers and used to provide claims to a relying party.

- **Certificates** Used extensively throughout the AD FS architecture to provide for security. The AD FS server can use:
    - Self-signed certificates
    - Certificates from either an internal Certificate Authority (CA)
    - Certificate from an external CA

    It is important that whatever type of certificate you use, all communicating parties trust the certificates. Consequently, when implementing a federation trust between two separate organizations, it is highly likely that you must implement a public key infrastructure (PKI) for your AD FS architecture based on public certificates.

> *NOTE* **USING AN INTERNAL CA**
> If you are using AD FS solely within your organization to facilitate SSO to multiple web apps, you can use an internal enterprise CA to deploy and manage the required certificates. In this instance, you can use Group Policy Objects (GPOs) to deploy the required certificates.

To help understand what each component does, consider the following scenario. Two organizations, A Datum and Contoso, want to share resources. Specifically, Contoso hosts a web-based app that users in A Datum require access to. The IT department deploy AD FS and related components to facilitate this requirement. In this scenario, Contoso is the resource holding entity, and A Datum the account holding entity. In federation terms, A Datum is the Claims Provider, while Contoso is the Relying Party. As shown in Figure 5-1, when a user from A Datum attempts to connect to the web-based app in Contoso, the following high-level process takes place:

1. The user at A Datum uses Internet Explorer to open a connection to the web server at Contoso. The web-based app determines that the user is not authenticated, and redirects the client to the Contoso federation server.
2. The client computer sends a request to the Contoso federation server. The federation server determines that A Datum is the home realm for the user. The web server now redirects the client to the A Datum federation server.
3. The client sends a request to the A Datum federation server.
4. The AD DS domain controller at A Datum authenticates the user and communicates this success with the A Datum federation server.
5. The federation server at A Datum creates a claim for the user based on rules defined for the federation partner (Contoso). The federation server sends the claims to the client computer.
6. The client sends the claim to the Contoso federation server.
7. The Contoso federation server validates the trust in the token and creates and signs a new token, which it sends to the client computer.
8. The client computer sends the new token to the original web server.

9. The app on the web server validates the token and provides access to the app based on the claims in the token.

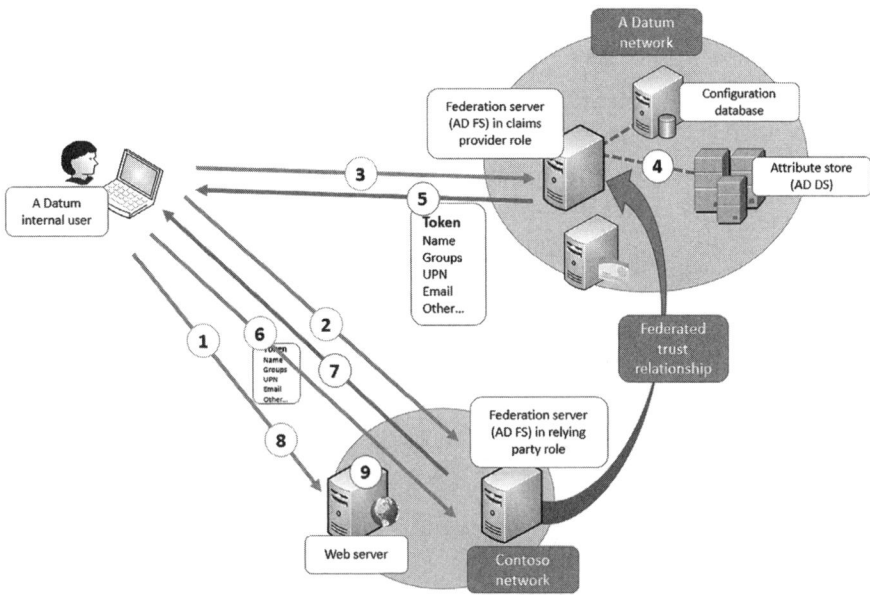

FIGURE 5-1 Overview of AD FS components

AD FS requirements

Before you can deploy AD FS as part of your federation solution, you network infrastructure must meet several requirements. These are:

- **AD DS** All federation servers in a Windows Server 2016 AD FS deployment must be domain-joined.
- **Attribute Store** Contains the attributes for security principals.
- **Name Resolution** Name resolution is provided by Domain Name System (DNS). Internal client computers must be able to resolve the DNS name for the federation server (or farm). External client computers must be able to resolve the name of the federation proxy in your perimeter network.
- **Network** Client computers must be able to establish network connections with the federation server or federation proxy. Federation servers must be able to establish network connections with domain controllers. The federation proxy must also be able to establish connections with the federation server.

EXAM TIP

AD FS communications is based on Hypertext Transfer Protocol over Secure Sockets Layer (HTTPS).

Install the AD FS server role

All AD FS deployments rely on the initial deployment of the Active Directory Federation Services server role. To deploy this role, use the following procedure:

1. On a domain-joined server computer, sign in as a member of the Domain Admins global security group.
2. Open Server Manager, click Manage, and then click Add Roles And Features.
3. On the Select Server Roles page, in the Roles list, select the Active Directory Federation Services check box, as shown in Figure 5-2, and then click Next.

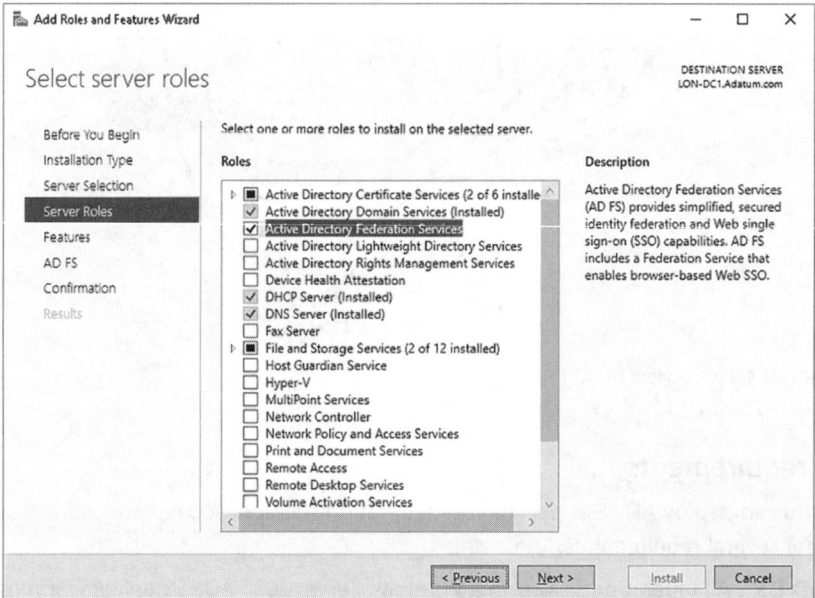

FIGURE 5-2 Installing the Active Directory Federation Services server role

4. Click through the rest of the wizard, and then click Install.
5. When prompted, click Close.

You can also use the Windows PowerShell Install-WindowsFeatures cmdlet to install the Active Directory Federation Services server role. Use the following command to install the role and all management tools:

```
Install-WindowsFeature -Name adfs-federation -IncludeManagementTools
```

Configure the AD FS server role

After you have deployed the server role, you must configure it. This requires that you define the service account, configuration database, certificate configuration, and the directory service. Use the following procedure to complete this task:

1. In Server Manager, click the notifications icon, and then click Configure The Federation Service On This Server.
2. On the Welcome page, click either of the following options, and then click Next:
   - Create The First Federation Server In A Federation Server Farm
   - Add A Federation Server To A Federation Server Farm
3. On the Connect To Active Directory Domain Services page, enter the credentials required to perform the configuration. Typically, this is a member of the Domain Admins group. Click Next.
4. On the Specify Service Properties page, shown in Figure 5-3, select the appropriate SSL Certificate, verify the Federation Service Name, and then type the Federation Service Display Name. Click Next.

> *NOTE* **SELECTING THE CERTIFICATE**
> The Federation Service Name matches the subject name of the certificate you select and should also be the same as the FQDN of the federation server in DNS. You must obtain and install the required certificate, with the appropriate subject name, before you launch the Active Directory Federation Services Configuration Wizard.

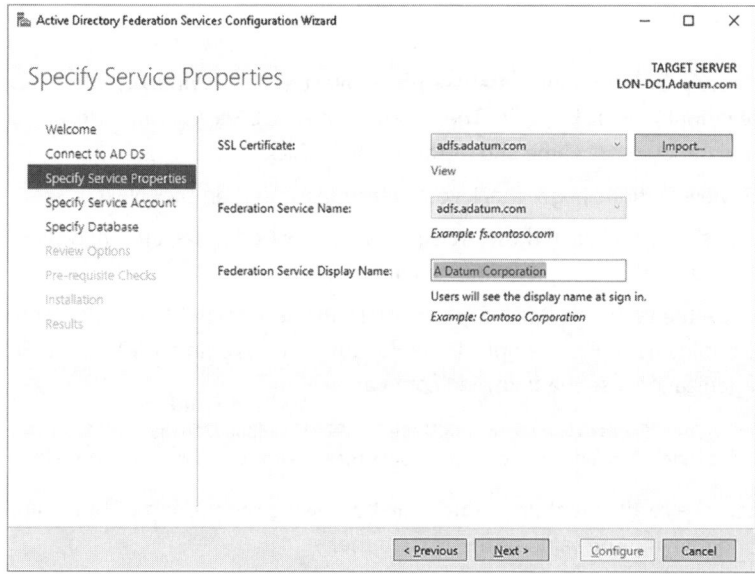

FIGURE 5-3 Selecting the AD FS server certificate and federation service display name

5. On the Specify Service Account page, shown in Figure 5-4, select a suitable service account. Ideally, create a group managed service account (group MSA). Click Next.

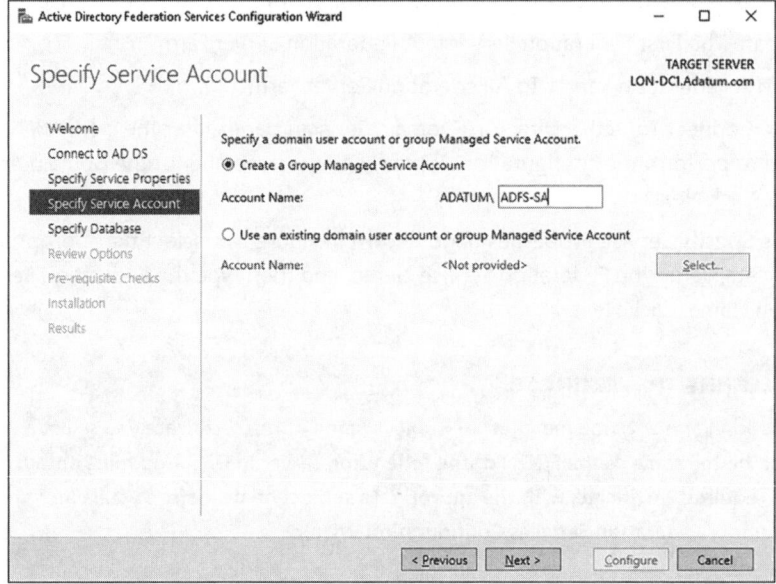

FIGURE 5-4 Specifying the service account for AD FS

6. On the Specify Configuration Database page, select either a Windows Internal Database (the default), or click Specify The Location Of A SQL Server Database, and then enter the database host name and instance name. Click Next.
7. On the Review Options page, check your selections, and then click Next.
8. Prerequisites are checked. If these are successful, click Configure, and then click through the wizard to complete the configuration.

You can also use the Windows PowerShell `Install-ADFSFarm` cmdlet to configure and manage your AD FS deployment. For example, to deploy the first server in an AD FS farm in the Adatum.com organization, use the following command:

```
Install-AdfsFarm -CertificateThumbprint ⊠8d4ece8e4397923563868d3f61b944103573a248
-FederationServiceName adfs.adatum.com -GroupServiceAccountIdentifier ADATUM\ADFS-SA
```

You can obtain the certificate thumbprint value by viewing the properties of the appropriate certificate and copying the value to the paste buffer.

> **NEED MORE REVIEW?** **AD FS CMDLETS IN WINDOWS POWERSHELL**
>
> To find out more about configuring AD FS with Windows PowerShell, refer to the Microsoft TechNet website at *https://technet.microsoft.com/library/dn479343.aspx*.

After you have deployed your AD FS server, you can configure it to perform one or both of the following functions:

- Claims provider
- Relying party

In business-to-business scenarios, where one organization holds users accounts and the other holds resources, you configure AD FS to perform the claims provider function in the account holding organization, and the relying party function in the resource holding organization. But you can also implement AD FS within a single organization. In this scenario, both the users and the resources are in the same organization, and consequently, a single AD FS server can act as the claims provider and relying party. In the next section, we look at how to configure the claims provider and relying party components in AD FS.

Implement claims-based authentication, including relying party trusts

To implement claims-based authentication, you must complete the following tasks:

- Configure a claims provider trust
- Configure a relying party trust

Configuring a claims provider trust

To configure a claims provider trust, complete the following procedure on the AD FS server that is providing the claims provider function:

1. From Server Manager, click Tools, and then click AD FS Management.
2. In the AD FS Management console, click Claims Provider Trusts. You can see the default Active Directory object in the details pane.
3. In the Actions pane, under Active Directory, click Edit Claim Rules.
4. In the Edit Claim Rules For Active Directory dialog box, shown in Figure 5-5, on the Acceptance Transform Rules tab, click Add Rule.

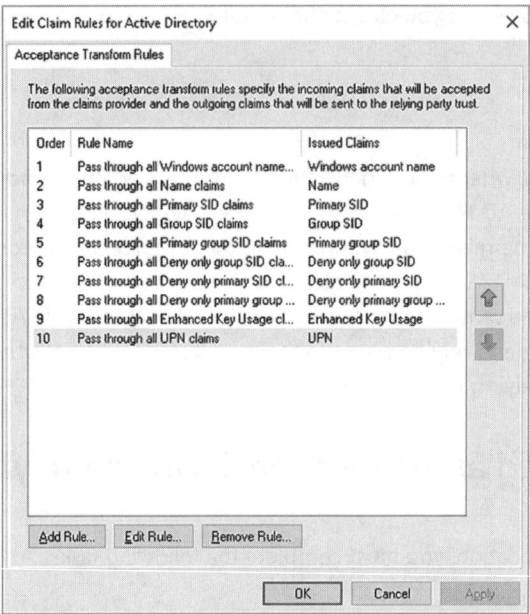

FIGURE 5-5 Viewing acceptance transform rules

5. In the Add Transform Claim Rule Wizard, on the Select Rule Template page, shown in Figure 5-6, in the Claim Rule Template list, select from the following options:

   - **Send LDAP Attributes As Claims** Use this template to select one or more Lightweight Directory Access Protocol (LDAP) attributes from an LDAP store, for example AD DS or Active Directory Lightweight Directory Service (AD LDS). The rule extracts one or more specified values from the designated store and sends the values as one or more outgoing claims.

   - **Send Group Membership As A Claim** Use this template to send as a claim the membership of an AD DS security group.

   - **Transform An Incoming Claim** Use this template to create a rule that transforms incoming claims by changing the rules' types, and optionally, values.

   - **Pass through Or Filter An Incoming Claim** Use this template to filter incoming claims and pass through those that meet your specified criteria. For example, you might create a rule that only passes UPN-based claims that end with the @Adatum suffix.

   - **Send Claims Using A Custom Rule** Use this template if none of the preceding templates address your specific needs.

6. For example, click Send LDAP Attributes as Claims, and then click Next.

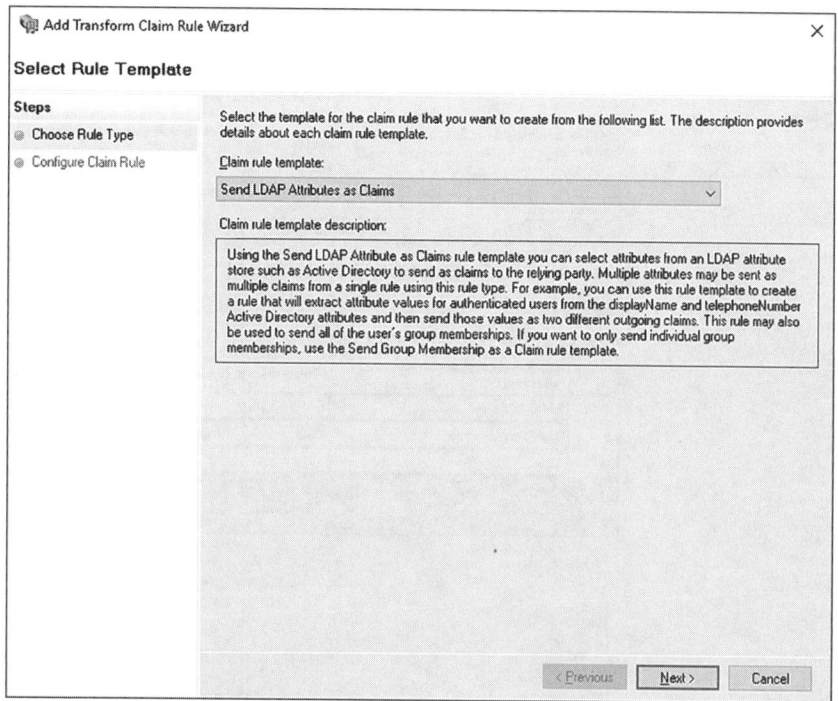

FIGURE 5-6 Selecting a rule template

7. On the Configure Rule page, shown in Figure 5-6, enter a claim name in the Claim Rule Name box. For example, type Outbound LDAP Rule.
8. In the Attribute store list, click Active Directory.
9. Under the Mapping Of LDAP Attributes To Outgoing Claim Types Heading, select the appropriate values for the LDAP Attribute and the Outgoing Claim Type. For example, select the following, as shown in Figure 5-7.
    - E-Mail-Addresses Maps To E-Mail Address
    - User-Principal-Name Maps To UPN
10. Click Finish, and then click OK.

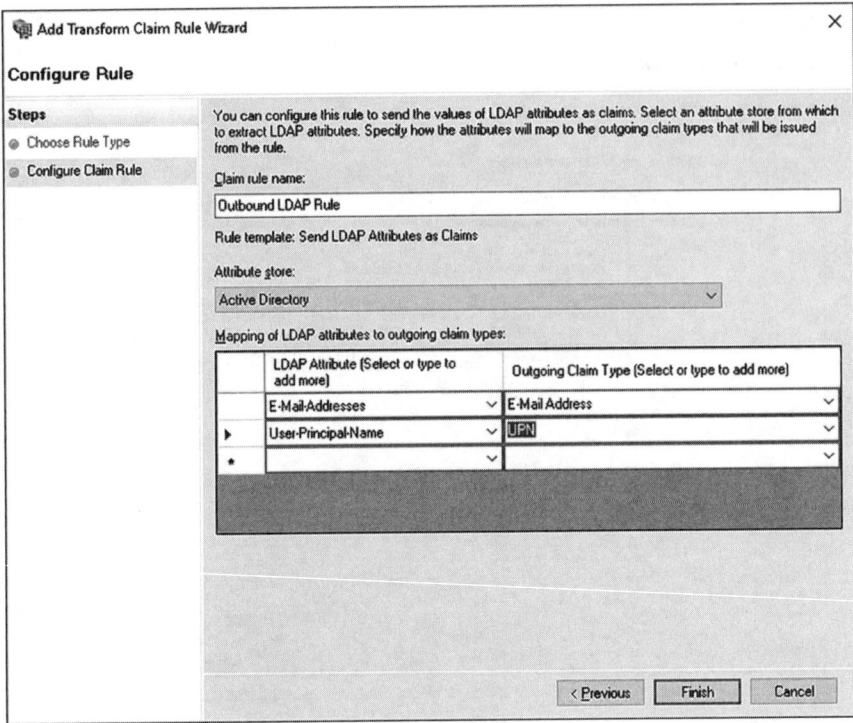

FIGURE 5-7 Configuring an outbound LDAP claim rule

> **NEED MORE REVIEW? CREATE A CLAIMS PROVIDER TRUST**
>
> To review further details about creating a claims provider trust, refer to the Microsoft TechNet website at *https://technet.microsoft.com/library/dn486771(v=ws.11).aspx*.

Configuring a relying party trust

After you have configured the claims party trusts, on the AD FS server that you want to use as a relying party, you must create and configure a relying party trust. This might be the same AD FS server in a single organization scenario, or it might be on a different server in a different organization for a business-to-business federation trust. Use the following procedure to create and configure the relying party trust:

1. On the AD FS server, open AD FS Management, and then click Relying Party Trusts.
2. Right-click Relying Party Trusts, and then click Add Relying Party Trust.
3. In the Add Relying Party Trust Wizard, on the Welcome page, click Claims Aware, and then click Start.

4. On the Select Data Source page, shown in Figure 5-8, you must enter the information to enable the configuration wizard to locate information about the relying party. Choose from:
    - Import Data About The Relying Party Published Online Or On A Local Network
    - Import Data About The Relying Party From A File
    - Enter Data About The Relying Party Manually

5. For example, click Import Data About The Relying Party Published Online Or On A Local Network, and in the Federation Metadata Address (Host Name Or URL) text box, type the path to the app that holds the relying party metadata, and then click Next.

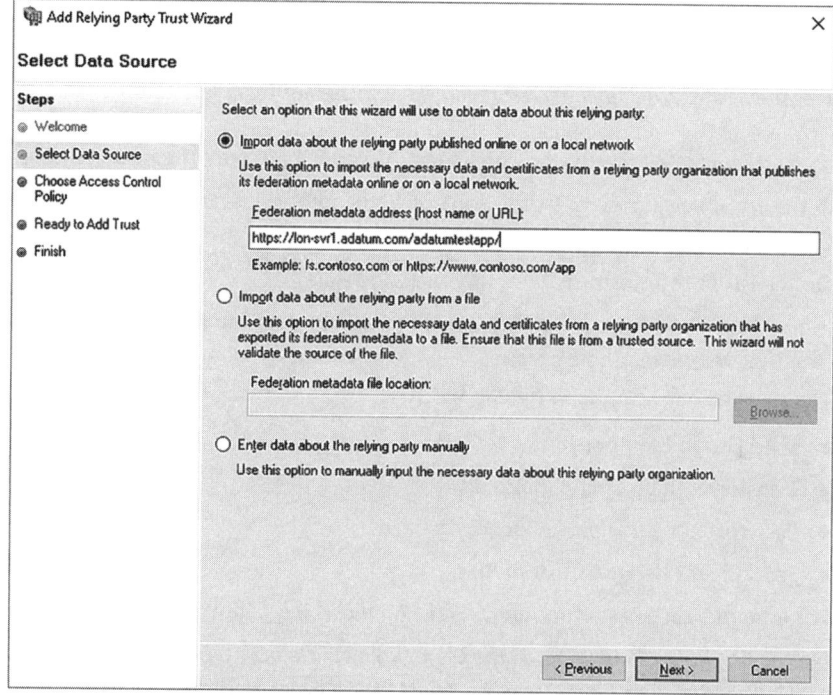

FIGURE 5-8 Specifying a data source for a relying party trust

6. On the Specify Display Name page, in the Display Name box, type a name for your trust, and then click Next.

7. On the Choose Access Control Policy page, choose the appropriate access control policy. Select from:
    - Permit Everyone
    - Permit Everyone And Require MFA
    - Permit Everyone And Require MFA For Specific Group

- Permit Everyone And Require MFA From Extranet Access
- Permit Everyone And Require MFA From Unauthenticated Devices
- Permit Everyone And Require MFA, Allow Automatic Device Registration
- Permit Everyone For Intranet Access
- Permit Specific Group

8. For example, click Permit Everyone, and then click Next.
9. To complete the configuration, on the Ready To Add Trust page, click Next, and when prompted, click Close.

> **NEED MORE REVIEW? CREATE A RELYING PARTY TRUST**
>
> To review further details about creating a relying party trust, refer to the Microsoft TechNet website at *https://technet.microsoft.com/library/dn486828(v=ws.11).aspx*.

After you have created the relying party trust, you must configure the issuance policy rules:

1. In the list of Relying Party Trusts, right-click the appropriate trust, and then select Edit Claim Issuance Policy.
2. On the Issuance Transform Rules tab, click Add Rule.
3. In the Claim Rule Template dialog box, in the Claim Rule Template list, select the appropriate template. Choose from:
   - Send LDAP Attributes As Claims
   - Send Group Membership As A Claim
   - Transform An Incoming Claim
   - Pass Through Or Filter An Incoming Claim
   - Send Claims Using A Custom Rule
4. For example, click Pass Through Or Filter An Incoming Claim, and then click Next.
5. On the Configure Rule page, in the Claim Rule Name box, type the name for your rule, and in the Incoming Claim Type list, select the relevant attribute. For example, click Windows Account Name, as shown in Figure 5-9.

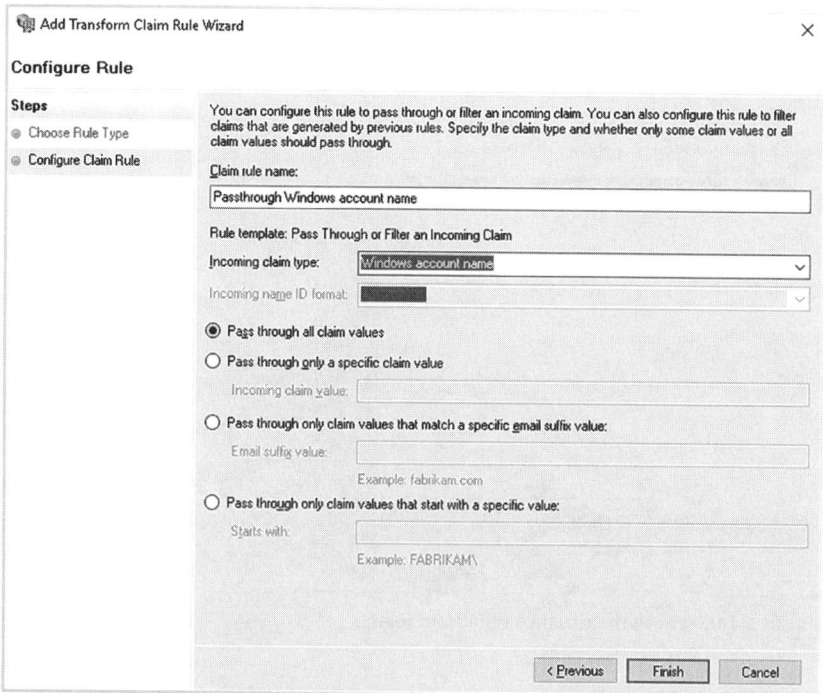

FIGURE 5-9 Defining a transform claim rule for an issuance policy

6. Then choose whether to:
   - Pass Through All Claim Values
   - Pass Through Only A Specific Claim Value
   - Pass Through Only Claim Values That Match A Specific Email Suffix Value
   - Pass Through Only Claim Values That Start With A Specific Value
7. Click Finish.
8. Now define any additional transform rules by repeating this process. For example, add a rule for passing through claims with an E-Mail address or UPN. Then, as shown in Figure 5-10, click OK to complete the configuration of the trust's issuance policy.

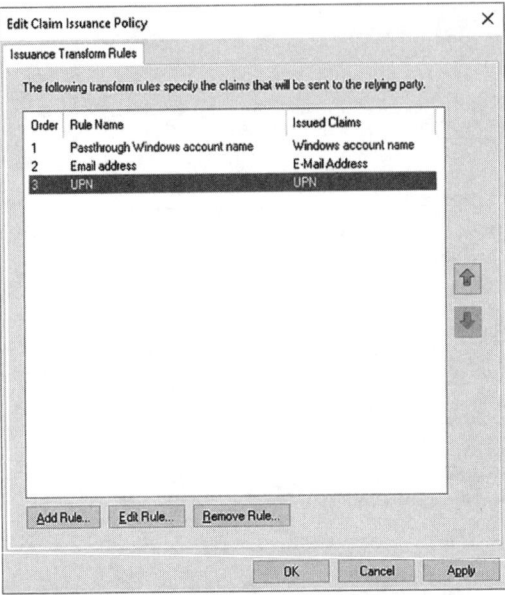

FIGURE 5-10 Viewing the issuance transform rules

> **NEED MORE REVIEW?** **CONFIGURING CLAIM RULES**
>
> To review further details about claim rules in AD FS, refer to the Microsoft TechNet website at *https://technet.microsoft.com/library/dn486796(v=ws.11).aspx*.

Configure authentication policies

Authentication policies enable you to define acceptable authentication mechanisms to help secure access to your resources through a federation trust. You can specify an authentication policy at two levels:

- **Globally** You can create a globally scoped authentication policy that applies to all services and app that AD FS secures. Your global authentication policy is used when no authentication policy exists for a specific relying party trust.
- **Specifically** You can create an authentication policy for a specific service or app that AD FS secures by creating a per relying party trust policy. If you create a specific per relying party trust authentication policy, it does not override any global authentication policy that you create.

EXAM TIP

If an authentication policy requires multi-factor authentication (MFA), when the user attempts to authenticate, MFA is triggered.

To configure a global authentication policy, use the following procedure:

1. In the AD FS console, expand the Service node in the navigation pane.
2. Click Authentication Methods.
3. As shown in Figure 5-11, under the Primary Authentication Methods heading, click Edit.

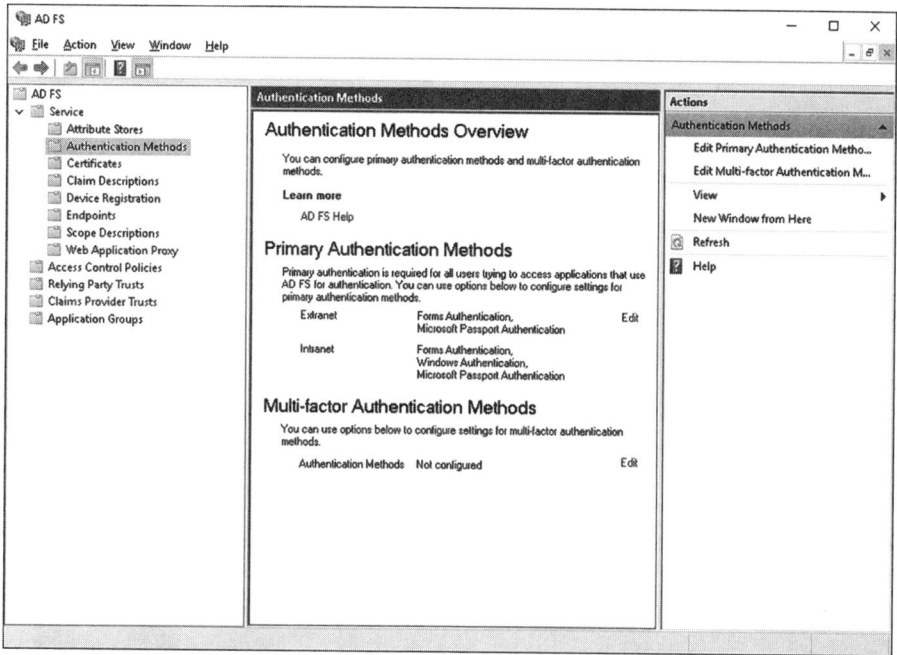

FIGURE 5-11 Configuring authentication methods

4. In the Edit Authentication Methods dialog box, shown in Figure 5-12, on the Primary tab, configure the appropriate methods for your organization. You can configure settings that apply for both Intranet and Extranet-based users. Available methods are:
   - Forms Authentication
   - Windows Authentication (Available For Intranet Only)
   - Certificate Authentication
   - Device Authentication
   - Microsoft Passport Authentication

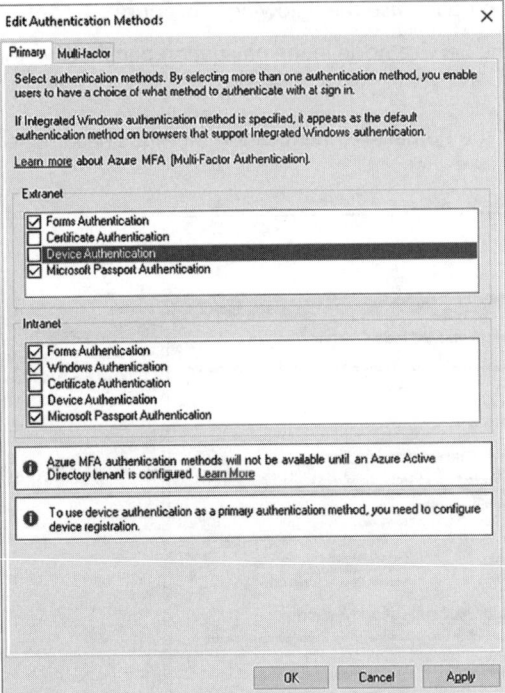

FIGURE 5-12 Configuring primary authentication methods

Configure MFA

Traditional computer authentication is based on user name and password exchange with an authentication authority. Although password-based authentication is acceptable in many circumstances, AD FS in Windows Server 2016 provides for a number of additional, more secure methods for users to authenticate with their devices, including MFA.

MFA is based on the principle that users who want to authenticate must have two (or more) things with which to identify themselves. Specifically, they must have knowledge of something, they must be in possession of something, and they must be something. For example, a user might know a password, possess a security token (in the form of a digital certificate), and be able to prove who they are with biometrics, such as fingerprints.

In AD FS in Windows Server 2016, to enable MFA, you must select at least one additional authentication method. By default, Certificate Authentication and Azure MFA are available. To enable and configure MFA in AD FS, use the following procedure:

1. In the AD FS console, expand the Service node in the navigation pane.
2. Click Authentication Methods.

3. In the Edit Authentication Methods dialog box, on the Multi-factor tab, shown in Figure 5-13, configure the appropriate authentication methods and click OK. Select from:
   - Certificate Authentication
   - Azure AD

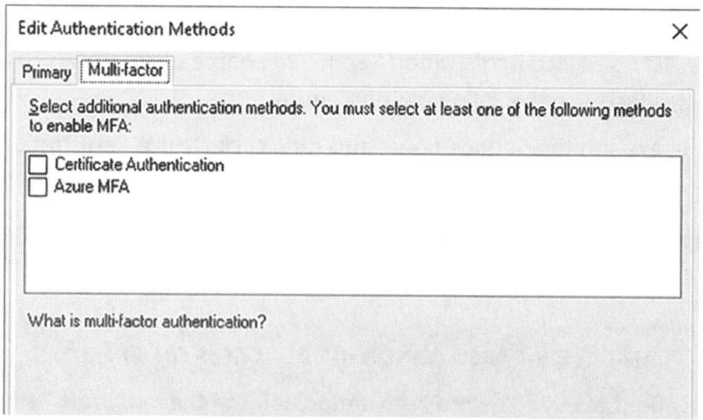

FIGURE 5-13 Configuring multi-factor authentication methods

> **NEED MORE REVIEW? AZURE MULTI-FACTOR AUTHENTICATION**
>
> To review further details about Azure MFA, refer to the Microsoft website at *https://docs.microsoft.com/azure/multi-factor-authentication/multi-factor-authentication-get-started-adfs-w2k12*.

Implement and configure device registration

These days, many users want to be able to access corporate resources from their own devices. However, enabling users to connect their own devices to your organization's network poses potential security risks, and certainly involves additional administrative effort.

By using Device Registration with AD FS, you can extend some of the features available to domain-joined devices to those devices that are not domain-joined. You can provide this facility while maintaining your organization's security.

> **NOTE FOREST FUNCTIONAL LEVEL**
>
> Your AD DS forest functional-level must be Windows Server 2016 to support device registration and integration with Microsoft Passport.

For example, when you implement Device Registration, users with their own devices can use SSO to access company resources and app.

> **NOTE CERTIFICATES**
>
> Users' devices must trust the CA that issues certificates for SSL on your AD FS servers. If you use an internal private CA for certificates, users' devices must obtain the root CA certificate. Because these devices are not domain-joined, you cannot use GPOs to achieve this and must distribute the certificate by other means.

You must configure the AD FS Device Registration Service to enable on-premises device registration. To complete this task, use the following procedure:

1. In the AD FS console, expand the Service node, and then click Device Registration.
2. In the details pane, click Configure Device Registration, and then click OK.

You can also complete this task by using the Windows PowerShell `Initialize-ADDeviceRegistration` cmdlet.

> **NEED MORE REVIEW? PLAN DEVICE-BASED CONDITIONAL ACCESS ON-PREMISES**
>
> To review further details about planning device registration, refer to the Microsoft TechNet website at *https://technet.microsoft.com/windows-server-docs/identity/ad-fs/operations/plan-device-based-conditional-access-on-premises*.

Integrate AD FS with Microsoft Passport

To avoid using password authentication, Microsoft provides an authentication system called Microsoft Passport; this enables secure authentication without sending a password to an authenticating authority, such as an AD DS domain controller. Microsoft Passport uses two-factor authentication based on Windows Hello–based biometric authentication (or a PIN) together with the ownership of a specific device.

> **EXAM TIP**
>
> Windows Hello is a biometric authentication mechanism built into Windows 10 to address the requirement that users must be able to prove who they are by something they uniquely have. When you implement Windows Hello, users can unlock their devices by using facial recognition or fingerprint scanning. Note that when Windows 10 first shipped, Windows Hello and Microsoft Passport were two separate but related security features. Microsoft has now combined the two features under the Windows Hello name.

Using Microsoft Passport provides two benefits for your organization.

- **User convenience** After your users set up Windows Hello, they can access enterprise resources without needing to remember user names or passwords.
- **Security** Because no passwords are used, Microsoft Passport helps protect user identities and user credentials.

> **NEED MORE REVIEW?** **WINDOWS HELLO FOR BUSINESS**
>
> To review further details about Microsoft Passport and Windows Hello, refer to the Microsoft TechNet website at *https://technet.microsoft.com/itpro/windows/keep-secure/microsoft-passport-guide*.

To integrate AD FS with Microsoft Passport, complete the process outlined above to enable on-premises device registration, and then use the following procedure to complete the integration with Microsoft Passport:

1. Open the Group Policy Management console.
2. Create a new GPO, and open the GPO for editing.
3. In the Group Policy Management Editor, navigate to Computer Configuration, Policies, Administrative Templates, Windows Components, Device Registration.
4. In the details pane, double-click the Register Domain Joined Computers As Devices.
5. In the Register Domain Joined Computers As Devices dialog box, shown in Figure 5-14, click Enabled, and then click OK.

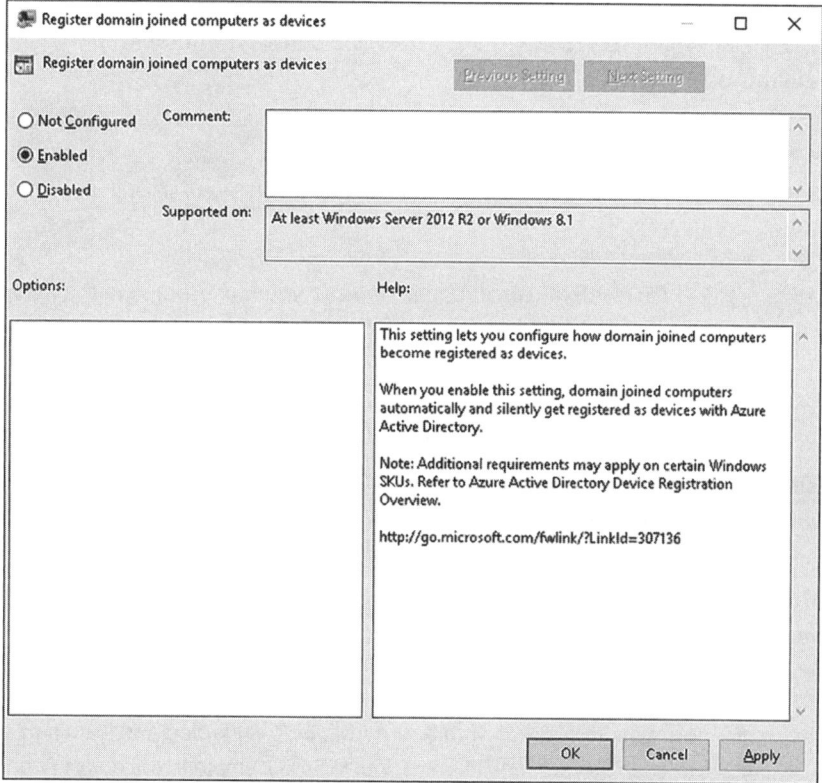

FIGURE 5-14 Enabling the Register Domain Joined Computers As Devices GPO setting

6. In the navigation pane, locate Computer Configuration, Policies, Administrative Templates, Windows Components, Windows Hello For Business.
7. In the details pane, double-click Use Windows Hello For Business.
8. In the Use Windows Hello For Business dialog box, click Enabled, and then click OK.
9. Finally, link the GPO to the appropriate container. For example, to enable the following settings for all devices, link the GPO to the domain object.

> **NEED MORE REVIEW?** **CONFIGURE AD FS TO USE MICROSOFT PASSPORT ON-PREMISES**
>
> To review further details about configuring AD FS with Microsoft Passport, refer to the Microsoft TechNet website at *https://technet.microsoft.com/library/mt732271.aspx*.

Configure for use with Microsoft Azure and Microsoft Office 365

Many organizations are moving some or all their app and services to online platforms, such as Microsoft Azure or Microsoft Office 365. You can integrate AD FS with these Microsoft online platforms, enabling your users to use SSO to access app and services both within your on-premises infrastructure, and online.

> **EXAM TIP**
>
> In addition to Microsoft online services, you can integrate AD FS with several other cloud providers.

To configure AD FS SSO with Microsoft online services, you must complete the following high-level steps:

1. Configure AD FS extranet access. This requires that you deploy the Web Application Proxy role to a server in your perimeter network. Web Application Proxy is discussed in Skill 5.2: Implement Web Application Proxy.
2. Establish a trust between AD FS and Azure AD by using the `New-MsolFederatedDomain` cmdlet in Windows PowerShell.

> **EXAM TIP**
>
> You must install the Microsoft Azure Active Directory Module before you can use this cmdlet.

3. Set up directory synchronization with Azure AD by downloading and installing Azure AD Connect to enable synchronization of your AD DS domain in Microsoft Azure.

> **NEED MORE REVIEW?** **CONNECT ACTIVE DIRECTORY WITH AZURE ACTIVE DIRECTORY**
>
> To review further details about connecting to Azure AD, refer to the Microsoft website at *https://docs.microsoft.com/azure/active-directory/connect/active-directory-aadconnect*.

4. Finally, verify that you have configured SSO correctly:
   - On a domain-joined computer, sign in to the appropriate Microsoft cloud service. Use your domain credentials. When you click inside the password box, if single sign-on is set up, the password box is shaded, and you see the following message:

     "You are now required to sign in at <your company>."

   - Click the Sign in at <your company> link. If sign in is successful, you have established SSO correctly.

Configure AD FS to enable authentication of users stored in LDAP directories

AD FS can use support authentication of objects stored in LDAP directories, such as AD LDS. To configure an LDAP-compliant directory as an attribute store in AD FS, use the following procedure:

1. Open the AD FS console.
2. Under the Service node, click Attribute Stores. The Active Directory store is visible in the details pane.
3. Right-click Attribute Stores, and then click Add Attribute Store.
4. In the Add An Attribute Store dialog box, shown in Figure 5-15, in the Display Name box, type a name, and then in the Attribute store type list, click LDAP.

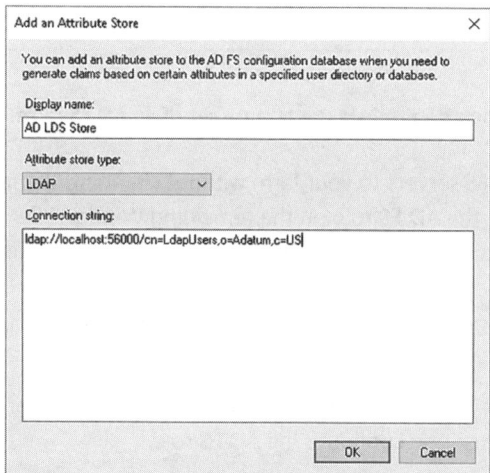

FIGURE 5-15 Configuring an LDAP attribute store

5. In the Connection String box, type the connection string, and then click OK. The string looks something like this: `ldap://localhost:56000/cn=LdapUsers,o=Adatum,c=US`. The specifics vary based on where the LDAP directory is hosted. In this example, the local host is running the AD LDS server role, and it is available on port 56000.

> **NEED MORE REVIEW? CONFIGURE AD FS TO AUTHENTICATE USERS STORED IN LDAP DIRECTORIES**
>
> To review further details about configuring AD FS for an LDAP attribute store, refer to the Microsoft TechNet website at *https://technet.microsoft.com/library/dn823754(v=ws.11).aspx*.

After creating the attribute store, you create a new claims provider trust. When you define the claim rules for the trust, you select the newly created attribute store.

Upgrade and migrate previous AD FS workloads to Windows Server 2016

Windows Server 2016 introduces some new and improved features in AD FS. These include:

- Support for LDAP v3 compliant directories.
- Support for Azure MFA.
- The introduction of application policies and delegated service management.
- Device registration improvements.

Consequently, if you are implementing AD FS on Windows Server 2012 R2 or earlier, you might consider upgrading or migrating your current AD FS workloads to AD FS on Windows Server 2016. If you add a new Windows Server 2016 AD FS server to an existing Windows Server 2012 R2 AD FS farm, the farm continues providing the same features; in other words, it operates at the same farm behavior level (FBL); in this case, Windows Server 2012 R2.

> **EXAM TIP**
>
> FBL is a Windows Server 2016 feature that determines the feature set of an AD FS farm.

This allows you to add additional AD FS servers to your farm without changing the features of the farm. You can then decommission the AD FS role on the remaining Windows Server 2012 R2 servers, and then raise the FBL to Windows Server 2016 to take advantage of the new and improved AD FS features.

To upgrade or migrate to AD FS with Windows Server 2016, use the following high-level procedure:

1. Deploy AD FS on Windows Server 2016 and choose the Add A Federation Server To A Federation Server Farm option when you configure the AD FS role.
2. Set the Windows Server 2016 AD FS server as the primary federation server. Use the Windows PowerShell `Set-AdfsSyncProperties -Role PrimaryComputer` cmdlet.

3. On any Windows Server 2012 R2 computers, run the `Set-AdfsSyncProperties -Role SecondaryComputer -PrimaryComputerName {FQDN}` cmdlet.

4. On the Windows Server 2016 AD FS server computer, open an elevated command prompt and run the `adprep /forestprep` and `adprep /domainprep` commands from the Windows Server 2016 product DVD support\adprep folder. This prepares the AD DS forest and domain for the presence of Windows Server 2016 AD FS.

5. In Windows PowerShell, run the `Invoke-AdfsFarmBehaviorLevelRaise` cmdlet to raise the FBL to Windows Server 2016.

6. When you are ready, you can decommission the Windows Server 2012 R2 AD FS servers.

> **NEED MORE REVIEW? UPGRADING TO AD FS IN WINDOWS SERVER 2016**
>
> To review further details about upgrading workload to AD FS in Windows Server 2016, refer to the Microsoft TechNet website at *https://technet.microsoft.com/windows-server-docs/identity/ad-fs/deployment/upgrading-to-ad-fs-in-windows-server-2016*.

Skill 5.2: Implement Web Application Proxy

Most organizations want to provide app and services to users outside of their intranet. This usually means enabling connections to remote users over the Internet. If you want to extend any services and app to remote users, you can configure a server with the Web Application Proxy role service and deploy the server to your perimeter network. The Web Application Proxy enables you to publish app and services from your internal network to users on external networks.

This section covers how to:
- Install and configure Web Application Proxy
- Integrate Web Application Proxy with AD FS
- Implement Web Application Proxy in pass-through mode
- Publish Remote Desktop Gateway applications

Install and configure Web Application Proxy

Installing and configuring the Web Application Proxy is fairly straightforward. You can use either Server Manager or Windows PowerShell to deploy the Web Application Proxy role service. To deploy the role service, use the following procedure:

1. In Server Manager on the target server, click Manage, and then click Add Roles And Features.

2. In the Add Roles And Features Wizard, on the Server Roles page, in the Roles list, select the Remote Access check box, and click Next.

3. On the Select Role Services page, as shown in Figure 5-16, select the Web Application Proxy check box, click Add Features, and then click Next.

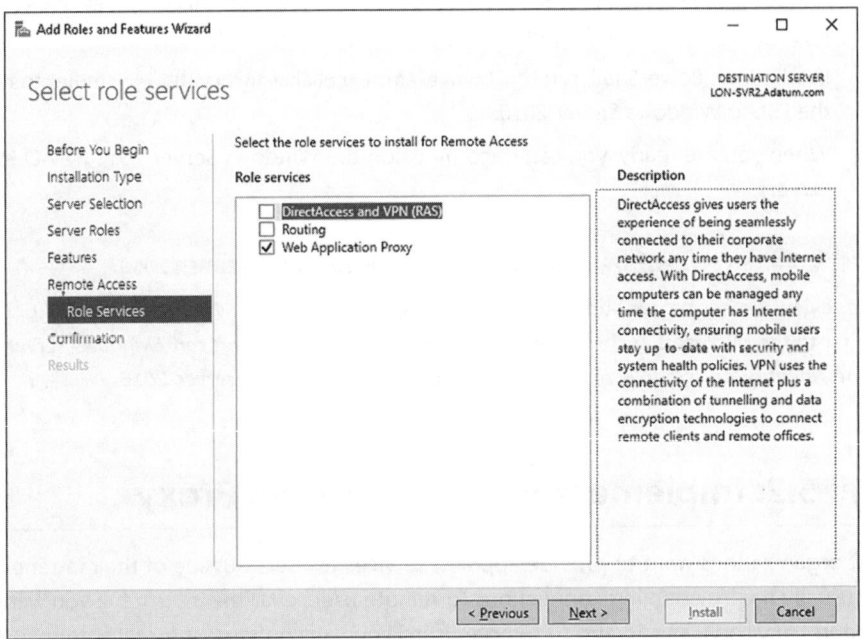

FIGURE 5-16 Installing the Web Application Proxy role service

4. Click Install, and when prompted, click Close.

You can also use the Install-WindowsFeature Web-Application-Proxy -IncludeManagement-Tools command to deploy the Web Application Proxy role service.

After you have installed the Web Application Proxy role service, in Server Manager, click the Open The Web Application Proxy Wizard link in the notifications area. Then use the following procedure to configure the server:

1. In the Web Application Proxy Configuration Wizard, on the Welcome page, click Next.

2. On the Federation Server page, in the Federation Service Name box, type the FQDN of the federation service name. You defined this name when you configured AD FS. For example, as shown in Figure 5-17, type adfs.Adatum.com.

3. Enter a user name and password to connect to the federation servers, and then click Next.

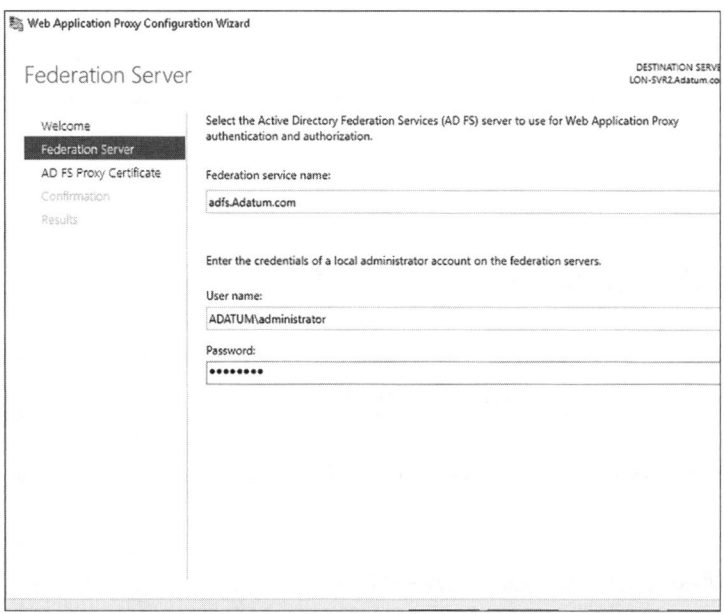

FIGURE 5-17 Defining the federation server name on the Web Application Proxy server

4. On the AD FS Proxy Certificate page, shown in Figure 5-18, in the Select A Certificate To Be Used By The AD FS Proxy list, click the appropriate certificate, and then click Next.

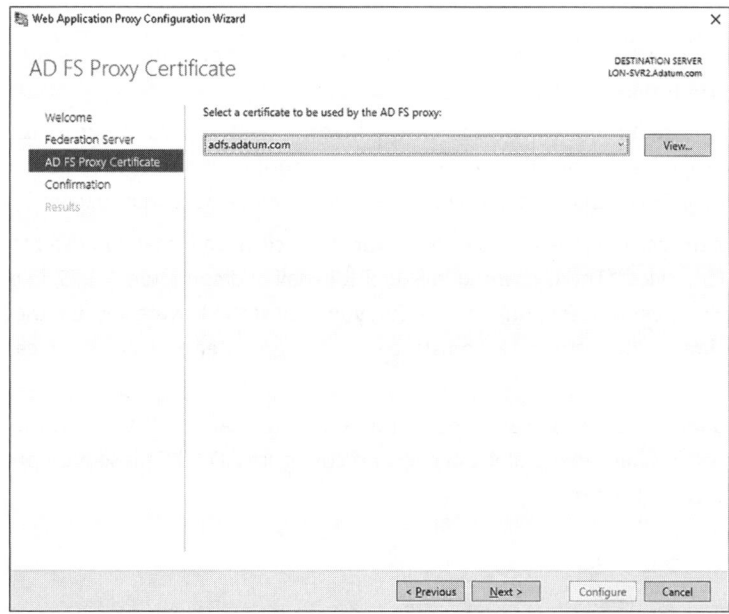

FIGURE 5-18 Configuring the Web Application Proxy certificate for AD FS

> **NOTE CERTIFICATES FOR AD FS INTEGRATION**
>
> You must install an appropriate certificate on the Web Application Proxy server before you configure the role service. This is discussed in the Integrate Web Application Proxy with AD FS section at the end of this Skill.

5. On the Confirmation page, click Configure, and when prompted, click Close.

Integrate Web Application Proxy with AD FS

You can integrate AD FS with the Web Application Proxy role, thereby enabling SSO for published app and services. This enables your remote users to access your internal resources without being repeatedly prompted for their credentials.

When you use AD FS with the Web Application Proxy, you can choose to enable pass-through authentication for web apps, or you can use AD FS preauthentication for your claims-aware app.

> **NOTE ADDITIONAL SKILLS COVERED IN THIS SECTION**
>
> The following exam skills are also covered in this section: Publish web apps via Web Application Proxy, Configure HTTP to HTTPS redirects, and Configure internal and external FQDNs.

Configure AD FS requirements

When a user attempts to connect to AD FS from outside the corporate network, DNS is used to resolve the name of the computer running the AD FS role in the internal network. However, the computer to which remote users actually connect is the Web Application Proxy rather than the AD FS server itself.

Therefore, an important requirement is to ensure that the Web Application Proxy is installed with an appropriate certificate. The certificate must contain the correct subject name, which must match the DNS name of the AD FS server, for example, adfs.adatum.com.

To ensure this is the case, on the AD FS server, export the certificate that you used to configure the AD FS service. (This is covered in Skill 5.1: Install and configure AD FS, in the Configure the AD FS server role section). Ensure that you export the private key. On the Web Application Proxy, import the certificate, and store it in the computer personal certificate store.

For further guidance on exporting and importing certificates, refer to the Export the root CA certificate section in Chapter 4: Skill 4.1: Install and configure AD CS. This section provides non-specific guidance on the process.

Implement Web Application Proxy as AD FS proxy

When your remote users want to access published claims-aware app, it is not desirable to enable direct connectivity to the AD FS server from Internet-based users. For this reason, you can implement Web Application Proxy as an AD FS proxy. In this scenario, users connect to the Web Application Proxy in your perimeter network.

To implement the Web Application Proxy as an AD FS proxy, complete the deployment and configuration process outlined above. Then, to publish claims-aware applications, use the following procedure on the Web Application Proxy:

1. From Server Manager, click Tools, and then click Remote Access Management.
2. In the Remote Access Management Console, under the Configuration node, click Web Application Proxy, and then in the Tasks pane, click Publish.
3. In the Publish New Application Wizard, on the Welcome page, click Next.
4. On the Preauthentication page, shown in Figure 5-19, click Active Directory Federation Services (AD FS), and then click Next.

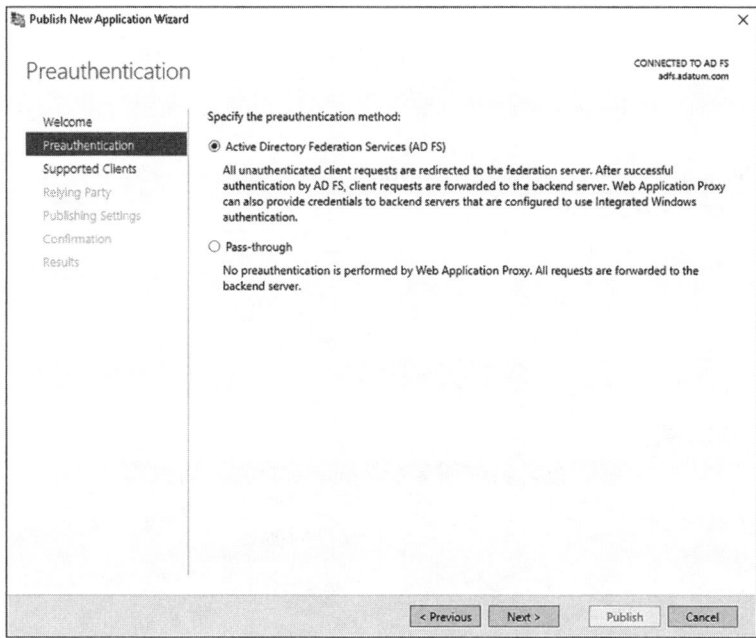

FIGURE 5-19 Enabling preauthentication on the Web Application Proxy

5. On the Supported Clients page, choose the preauthentication method, as shown in Figure 5-20, and then click Next. Choose between:
   - **Web And MSOFBA**   Used by Microsoft Office app
   - **HTTP Basic**   Used by Exchange ActiveSync clients
   - **OAuth2**   Supported by Windows Store app

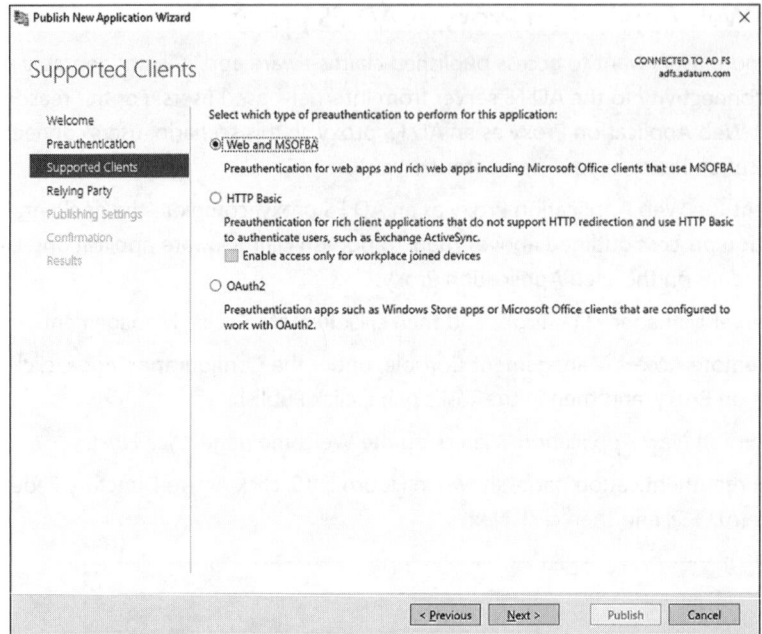

FIGURE 5-20 Selecting the appropriate client type

6. On the Relying Party page, select the appropriate relying party trust, as shown in Figure 5-21, and then click Next.

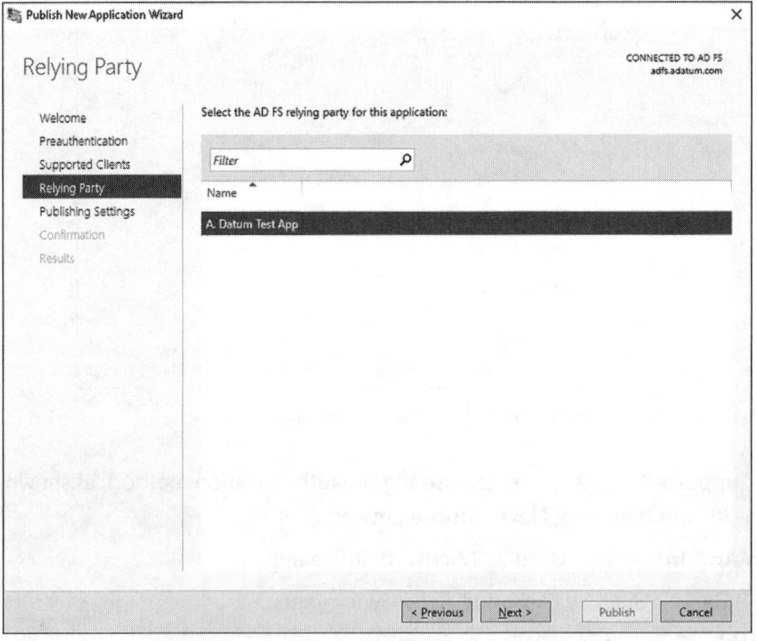

FIGURE 5-21 Selecting the relying party trust

7. On the Publishing Settings page, shown in Figure 5-22, in the Name box, type the name of the app that you want to publish.
8. In the External URL box, type the external URL, and then in the External Certificate list, select the certificate that has a subject name that matches the URL you specified. The backend server URL should match the external URL.

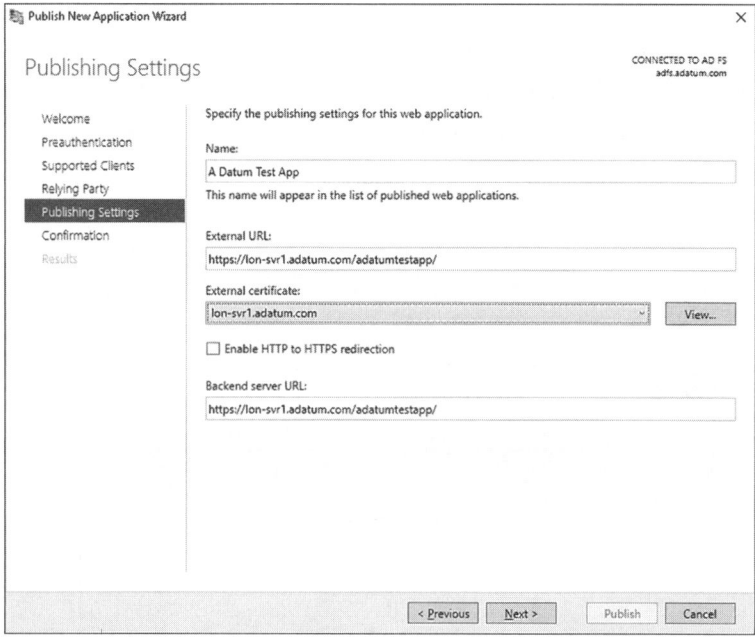

FIGURE 5-22 Configuring the internal and external URLs and the certificate

> *NOTE* **EXTERNAL AND INTERNAL URLS**
>
> For each app that you publish, you must configure both an external URL and an internal URL. The Web Application Proxy uses the internal URL to access the app on behalf of external users. External users use the external URL to access the published app. When you define the external URL, you must also choose a certificate that contains the host name in the external URL, and you must install that certificate on the local server.

9. Optionally, select the Enable HTTP To HTTPS Redirection check box, and then click Next.

> *NOTE* **HTTP TO HTTPS REDIRECTION**
>
> The Enable HTTP to HTTPS redirection feature is new to Windows Server 2016. This option helps ensure users can access your published app even if they omit to type https as the prefix of the published app URL.

10. On the Confirmation page, click Publish, and when prompted, click Close.

Implement Web Application Proxy in pass-through mode

When you publish a web application, you can choose whether to use AD FS preauthentication, as described in the last section. Alternatively, you can use pass-through mode. When you select pass-through mode, the Web Application Proxy does not use AD FS to perform preauthentication; instead, it passes the authentication request to the backend server that hosts the published application.

To publish an app using pass-through mode, use the following procedure:

1. In the Remote Access Management Console, in the Tasks list, click Publish.
2. In the Publish New Application Wizard, on the Welcome page, click Next.
3. On the Preauthentication page, shown in Figure 5-23, click Pass-through, and then click Next.

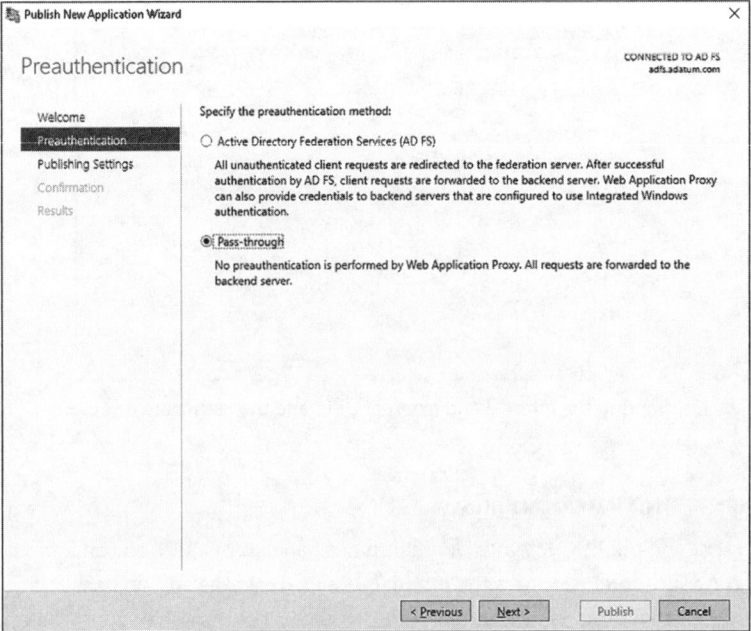

FIGURE 5-23 Configuring pass-through mode

4. On the Publishing Settings page, configure the Name, External URL, External Certificate, and Backend Server URL.
5. Optionally select the Enable HTTP To HTTPS Redirection check box, click Next, and then click Publish.

Publish Remote Desktop Gateway applications

Many organizations that provide Remote Desktop Gateway applications for their users want to make these app available to their users remotely. However, when you use the Web Application Proxy role service to publish Remote Desktop Gateway app, you help to make your infrastructure more secure by reducing the exposure of the Remote Desktop Gateway server.

> *NOTE* **ASSUMPTIONS**
>
> The following documentation assumes that you have already deployed and configured the Remote Desktop Gateway and related components and have created and configured the Remote Desktop Gateway app you want to make available to your users.

To publish Remote Desktop Gateway app without using preauthentication, use the same procedure described in the preceding section: Implement Web Application Proxy in pass-through mode. On the Publish Settings page, enter the root FQDN of the RD Web Access server as the External URL.

> *EXAM TIP*
>
> If your RD Web Access and RD Gateway are on different RDG servers, you must publish two virtual directories separately.

To publish Remote Desktop Gateway app using preauthentication, use the following procedure:

1. On the AD FS server, in the AD FS console, create a Relying Party Trust:

   A. Use the Add Relying Party Trust Wizard, and choose the option Enter Data About The Relying Party Manually, as shown in Figure 5-24.

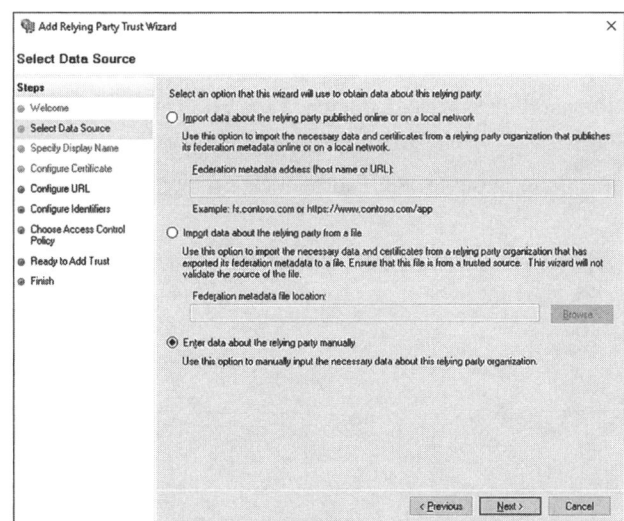

FIGURE 5-24 Specifying the data source for a relying party trust

B. Click through the wizard accepting default values.

   C. On the Configure Identifiers page, in the Relying Party Trust Identifier box, type the external FQDN you want to use for Remote Desktop Gateway access, as shown in Figure 5-25. Click Add, and then click through the rest of the wizard.

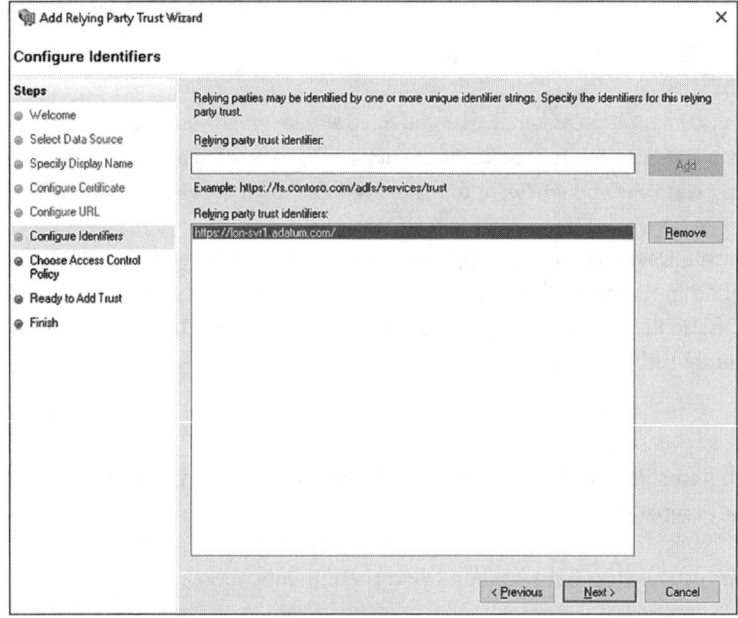

FIGURE 5-25 Defining the relying party trust identifier

2. Switch to the Web Application Proxy, and in the Remote Access Management Console, under Configuration, click Web Application Proxy.

3. In the Tasks list, click Publish.

4. In the Publish New Application Wizard, on the Welcome page, click Next.

5. On the Preauthentication page, click Active Directory Federation Services (AD FS), and then click Next.

6. On the Supported Clients page, choose the preauthentication method, and then click Next.

7. On the Relying Party page, select the relying party trust you just created, as shown in Figure 5-26, and then click Next.

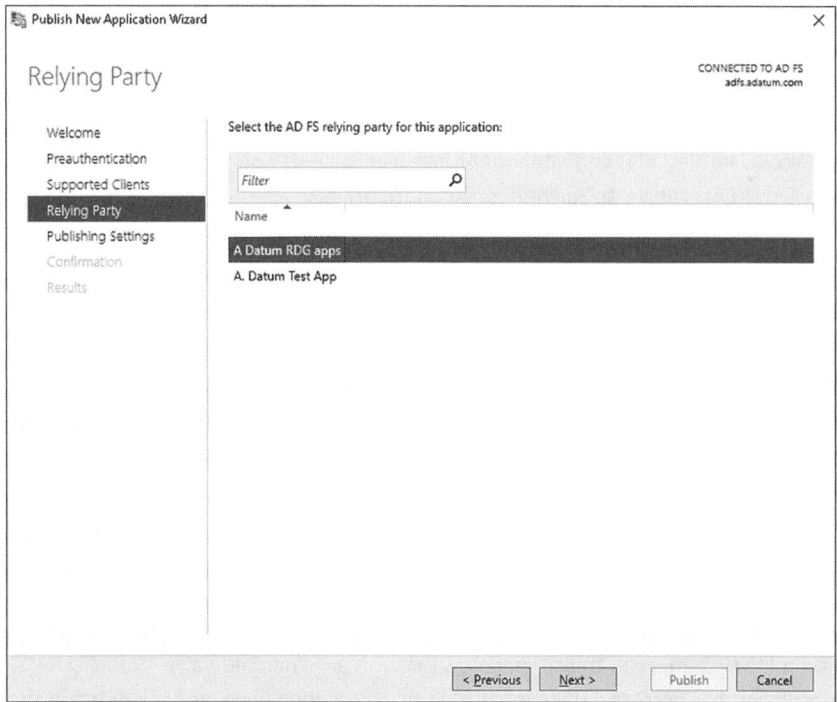

FIGURE 5-26 Selecting the relying party trust

8. On the Publishing Settings page, type the name of the app that you want to publish. In the External URL box, type the external URL, and then in the External certificate list, select the certificate that has a subject name that matches the URL you specified. The backend server URL should match the external URL. Optionally, select the Enable HTTP To HTTPS Redirection check box, and then click Next.
9. On the Confirmation page, click Publish, and when prompted, click Close.

> **NEED MORE REVIEW?** **PUBLISHING APPLICATIONS WITH SHAREPOINT, EXCHANGE AND RDG**
>
> To review further details about publishing remote desktop gateway app with Web Application Proxy, refer to the Microsoft TechNet website at *https://technet.microsoft.com/library/dn765486.aspx*.

Skill 5.3: Install and configure AD RMS

One of the ongoing problems for network administrators is to find ways to protect their organization's data from inappropriate access. You can use NTFS file permissions to determine who has access to files. You can implement features, such as Encrypting File System (EFS) and BitLocker Drive Encryption, to further control data privacy.

> **This section covers how to:**
> - An AD RMS overview
> - Deploying an AD RMS server
> - Manage rights policy templates
> - Configure exclusion policies
> - Backup and restore AD RMS

An AD RMS overview

AD RMS enables you to add to these capabilities, and enables you to protect data files, both at rest on a file system, or in transit, perhaps through an email message. With AD RMS, you can control who has access to data, what type of access they have, and even define the specific access duration.

Typical scenarios for using AD RMS to secure data include the following:

- **Prevent propagation**   You do not want sensitive information to be sent by email.
- **Restrict actions**   You want to restrict users to being able to view a document, but not to edit it, nor to print it.
- **Protect data**   You want to protect data on removable storage devices. If a storage device containing sensitive data is lost, you want to know that the data cannot be accessed by unauthorized persons.

Components

Before you can implement AD RMS to help protect your organization's data, you must know how to deploy and configure the AD RMS architecture, including understanding how it works. AD RMS consists of the following components:

- **AD RMS Server**   A server computer that is domain-joined and installed with the Active Directory Rights Management Services role. Servers publish their AD RMS capability by using a service connection point (SCP) in AD DS, enabling clients to locate them.

- **AD RMS Client** Windows 7 and later support AD RMS, and this capability is built-in to the client operating system. If a device is not AD RMS-aware, the device cannot access AD RMS-protected content.
- **AD RMS Apps** Applications, such as Microsoft Office Outlook are AD RMS-aware and can interact with AD RMS-protected content.
- **Database** AD RMS stores its configuration in a database, either a Microsoft SQL Server database for large deployments, or else the Windows Internal Database for smaller deployments.
- **PKI** AD RMS is dependent on digital certificates. Consequently, you require a properly configured PKI. AD RMS uses the following certificates and licenses:
    - **Server Licensor** Generated when you deploy an AD RMS cluster (group of AD RMS servers). Allows the AD RMS server to issue:
        - Additional server licensor certificates to other AD RMS servers
    - Rights account certificates to clients
    - Client licensor certificates
    - Publishing licenses
    - Use licenses
    - Rights policy templates
        - **Client Licensor** Enables a user to publish protected content.
        - **Machine Certificate** Used to identify a computer or device.
        - **Rights Account Certificate** Identifies a specific user.
        - **Publishing Licenses** Determines applied rights on protected content.
        - **End-user License** Enables a user to access protected content.

> **NEED MORE REVIEW?** **ACTIVE DIRECTORY RIGHTS MANAGEMENT SERVICES OVERVIEW**
>
> To review further details about AD RMS, refer to the Microsoft TechNet website at *https://technet.microsoft.com/library/hh831364(v=ws.11).aspx*.

Deploying an AD RMS server

The following exam skills are also covered in this section: Installing a licensor certificate and manage an AD RMS SCP.

You can deploy and configure the Active Directory Rights Management Services role by using Server Manager. To do so, use the following procedure:

1. In Server Manager, click Manage, and then click Add Roles And Features.
2. Click through, and on the Server Roles page, select the Active Directory Rights Management Services check box, click Add Features, and then click Next.

3. On the Active Directory Rights Management Services page, click Next, and on the Role Services page, select the Active Directory Rights Management Server check box, as shown in Figure 5-27, and then click Next. The Identify Federation Support check box is used to enable integration with AD FS.

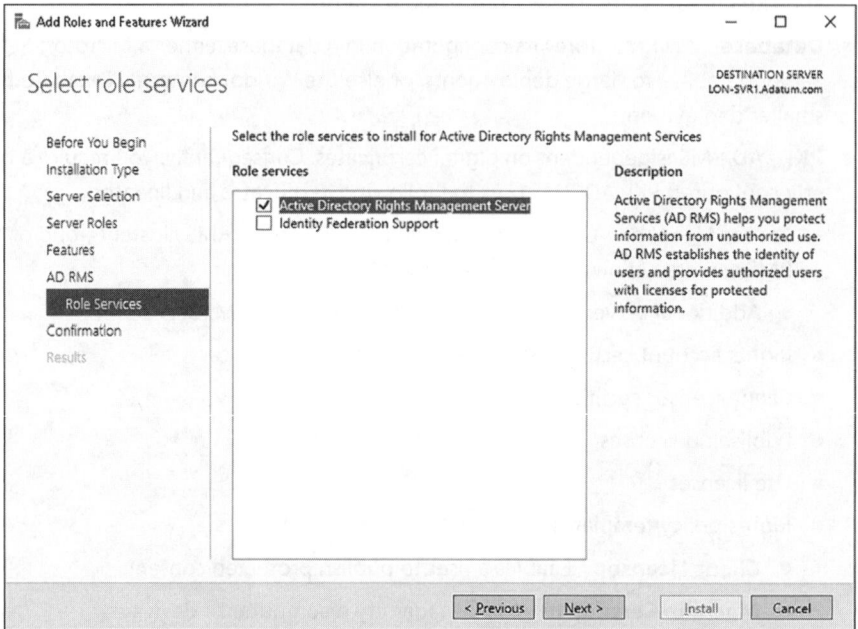

FIGURE 5-27 Deploying the Active Directory Rights Management Services role

4. Click Install, and when prompted, click Close.

You can also use the Windows PowerShell `Install-WindowsFeature ADRMS -IncludeManagementTools` command to install the Active Directory Right Management Services server role.

> **NEED MORE REVIEW?** **AD RMS CMDLETS IN WINDOWS POWERSHELL**
>
> To review further details about managing AD RMS with Windows PowerShell, refer to the Microsoft TechNet website at *https://technet.microsoft.com/library/ee617271.aspx*.

After deploying the role, you must configure it. Use the following procedure:

1. In Server Manager, in the notifications area, click Perform Additional Configuration. The AD RMS Configuration Wizard launches.
2. In the AD RMS Configuration Wizard, on the AD RMS page, click Next.
3. On the AD RMS Cluster page, shown in Figure 5-28, click Create A New AD RMS Root Cluster, and then click Next.

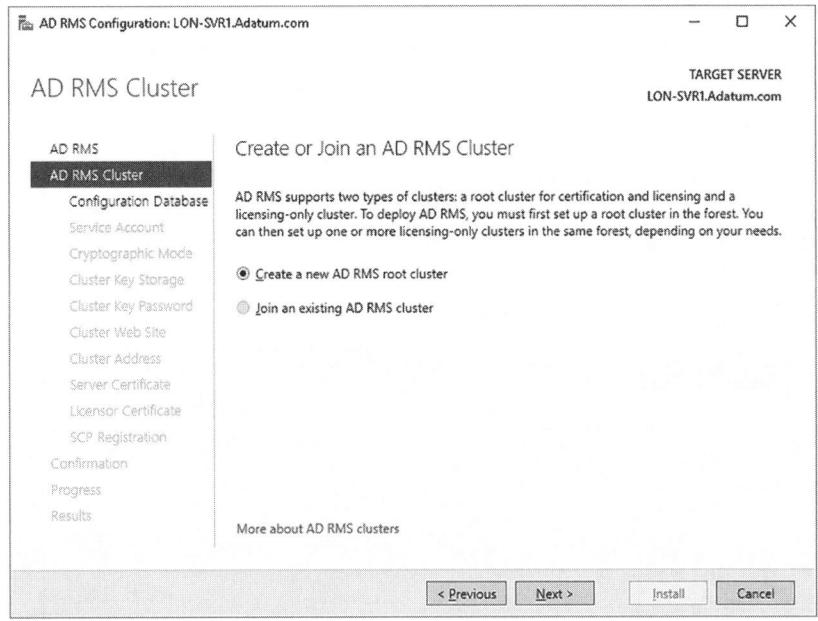

FIGURE 5-28 Creating an AD RMS cluster

4. On the Configuration Database page, specify to use a Windows Internal Database on the local server, as shown in Figure 5-29, or else enter the details to connect to a SQL Server database instance. Click Next.

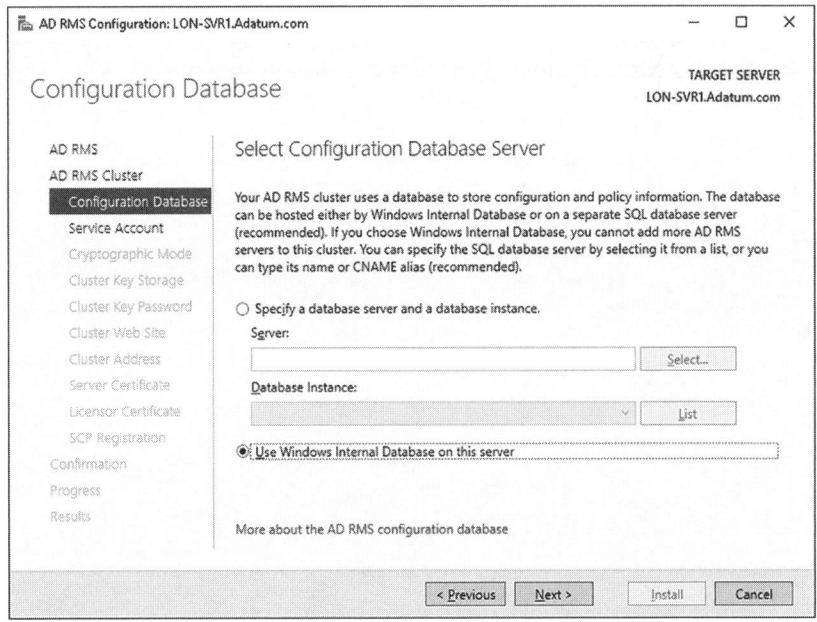

FIGURE 5-29 Defining the AD RMS database

5. On the Service Account page, enter the details for a domain user account that is to be used as a service account, as shown in Figure 5-30. Click Next. Ensure that this password is configured with both the User Cannot Change Password and Password Never Expires options.

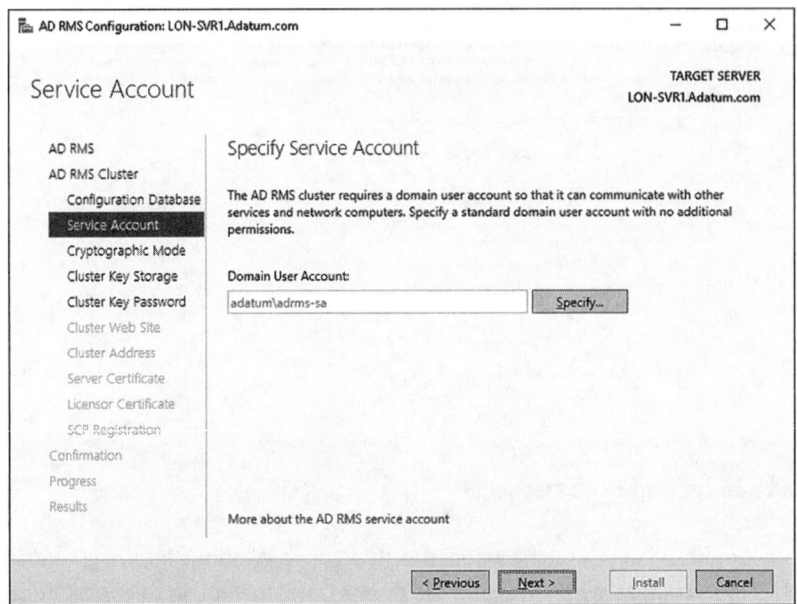

FIGURE 5-30 Defining the service account

6. On the Cryptographic Mode page, as shown in Figure 5-31, select the cryptographic mode, and click Next. Cryptographic Mode 2 is recommended.

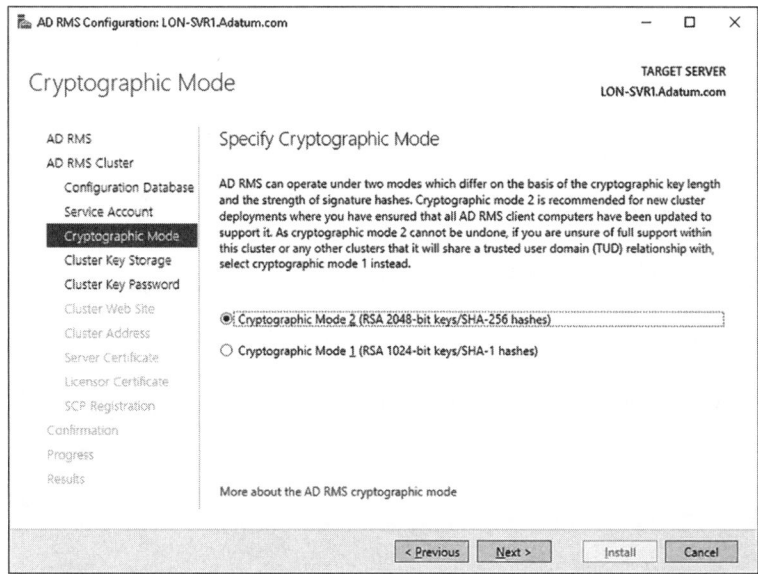

FIGURE 5-31 Selecting a cryptographic mode

7. On the Cluster Key Storage page, shown in Figure 5-32, specify the AD RMS cluster key storage mode. This key is used in disaster recovery, or when you add servers to the AD RMS cluster. Choose between:
   - AD RMS Centrally Managed Key Storage
   - Cryptographic Service Provider (CSP) Key Storage

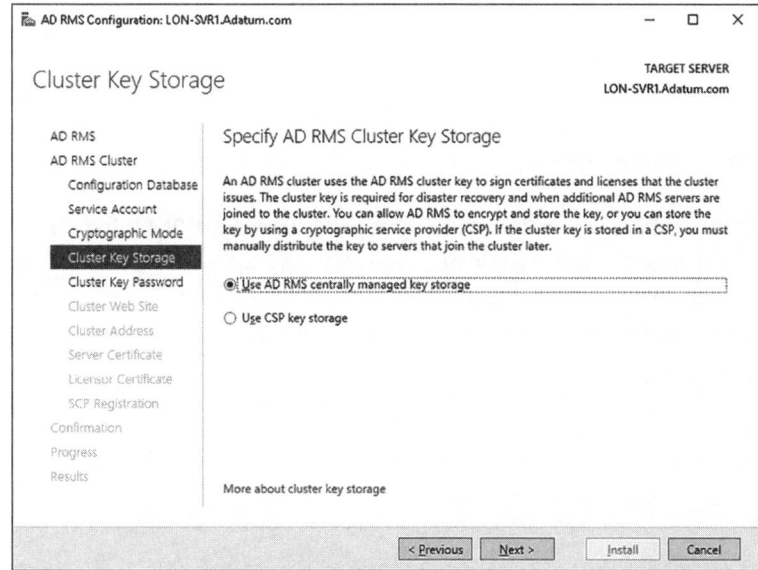

FIGURE 5-32 Defining the cluster key storage method

> **NEED MORE REVIEW?** **UNDERSTANDING AD RMS KEY PROTECTION AND STORAGE**
>
> To review further details about AD RMS key storage, refer to the Microsoft TechNet website at *https://technet.microsoft.com/library/cc754905.aspx*.

8. On the Cluster Key Password page, enter a password, and confirm the password. Click Next. This password is used to encrypt the cluster key. To add servers to the cluster, you must specify this password.

9. On the Cluster Web Site page, select the appropriate website on the local server to host AD RMS components. The Default Web Site is used by default, as shown in Figure 5-33. Click Next.

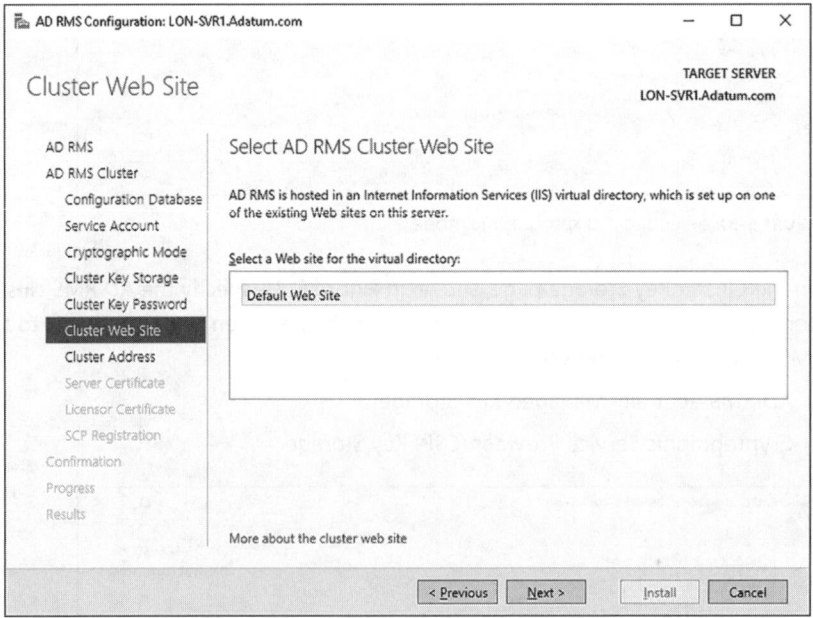

FIGURE 5-33 Selecting the website

10. On the Cluster Address page, shown in Figure 5-34, enter the URL for the cluster server. You cannot change this information after you configure the AD RMS server. Click Next. The FQDN you enter must be resolvable in DNS. Also, if you use SSL, which is recommended, you need a certificate with the appropriate subject name.

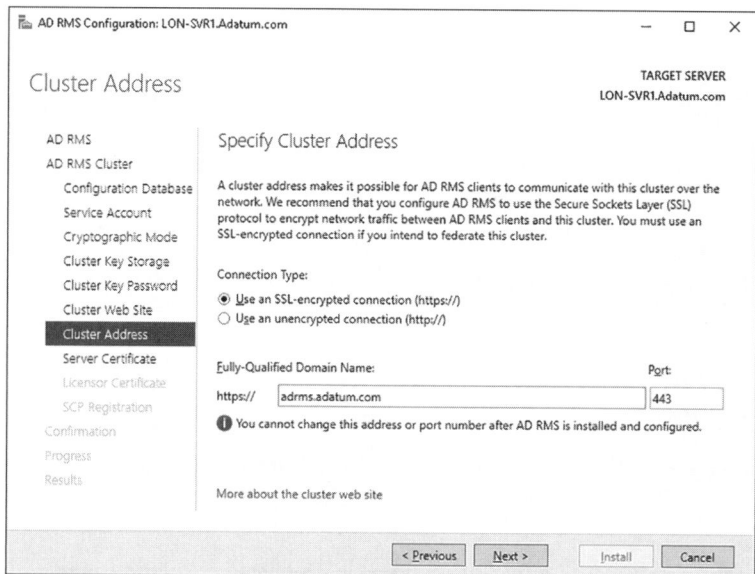

FIGURE 5-34 Specifying the cluster address

11. On the Server Certificate page, shown in Figure 5-35, specify the certificate that you want to use for SSL. Note that you should avoid using a self-signed certificate in production environments. Click Next.

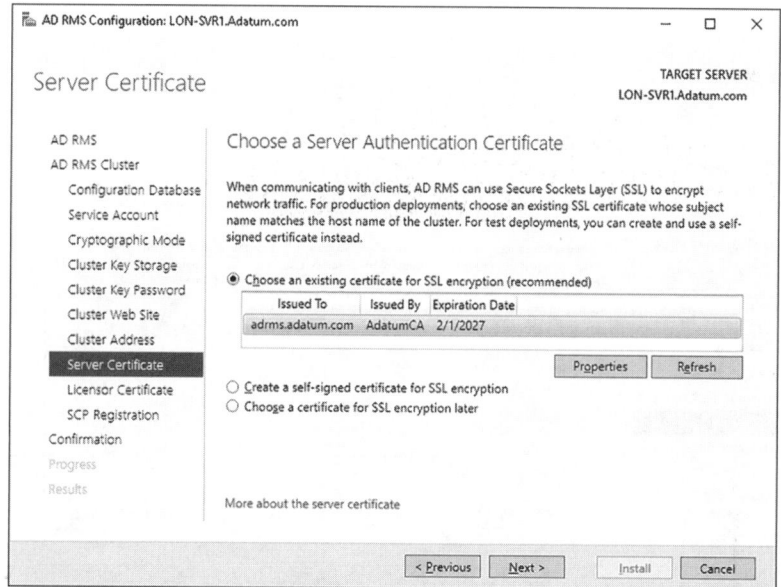

FIGURE 5-35 Selecting an authentication certificate

12. On the Licensor Certificate page, shown in Figure 5-36, click Next.

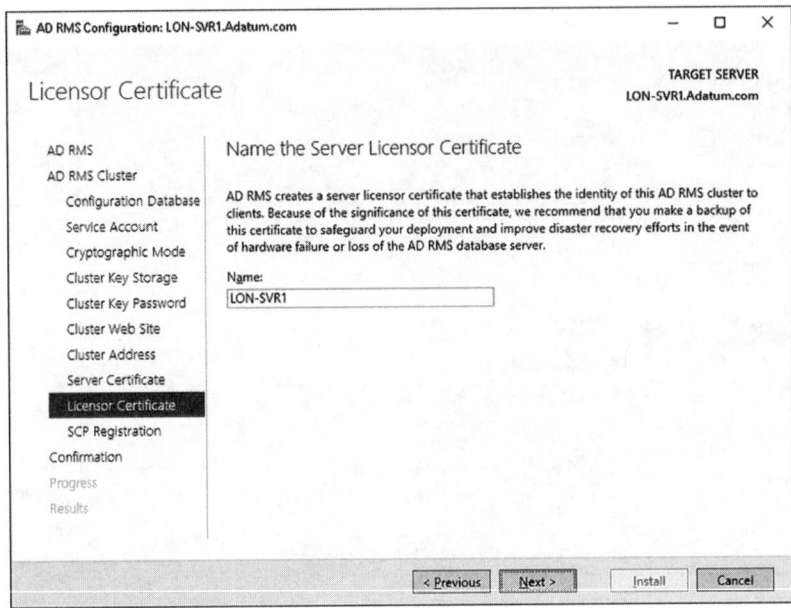

FIGURE 5-36 Configuring the licensor certificate

13. On the SCP Registration page, shown in Figure 5-37, click Register The SCP Now, and click Next.

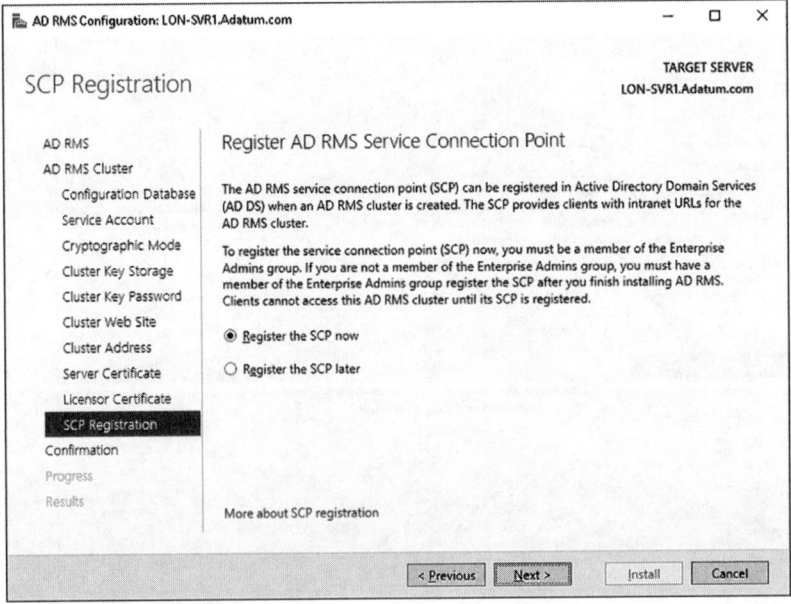

FIGURE 5-37 Registering the SCP

14. On the Confirmation page, click Install, and when prompted, click Close.

Manage rights policy templates

You can use AD RMS rights policy templates to simplify the administration of rights throughout your organization. For example, you can configure templates that enable viewing-only rights on Word documents. After you create your rights policy templates, users can apply them to content using AD RMS-aware app, such as Microsoft Office Word, by using the Protect Document option.

The rights policy templates are stored in the AD RMS database, and you can configure them by using either the AD RMS console, or Windows PowerShell cmdlets. To create rights policies, in Server Manager, click Tools, and then click Active Directory Rights Management Services. Then, use the following procedure:

1. In the Active Directory Rights Management Services console, in the navigation pane, click the Rights Policy Templates node.
2. In the action pane, click Create Distributed Rights Policy Template.
3. In the Create Distributed Rights Policy Template Wizard, on the Add Template Identification Information page, click Add to specify any languages for this template. You must specify at least one, as shown in Figure 5-38. Click Next.

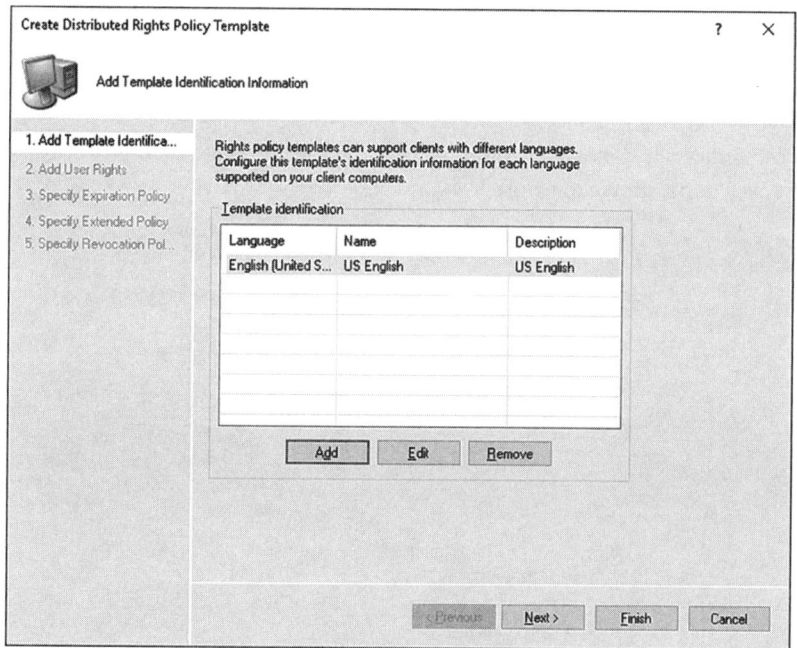

FIGURE 5-38 Defining available languages for a rights policy template

4. On the Add User Rights page, shown in Figure 5-39, click Add to select the appropriate users or groups. You can use the wildcard Anyone. Otherwise, you must specify users or groups by email address. Then, in the Rights list, select the appropriate rights, and click Next.

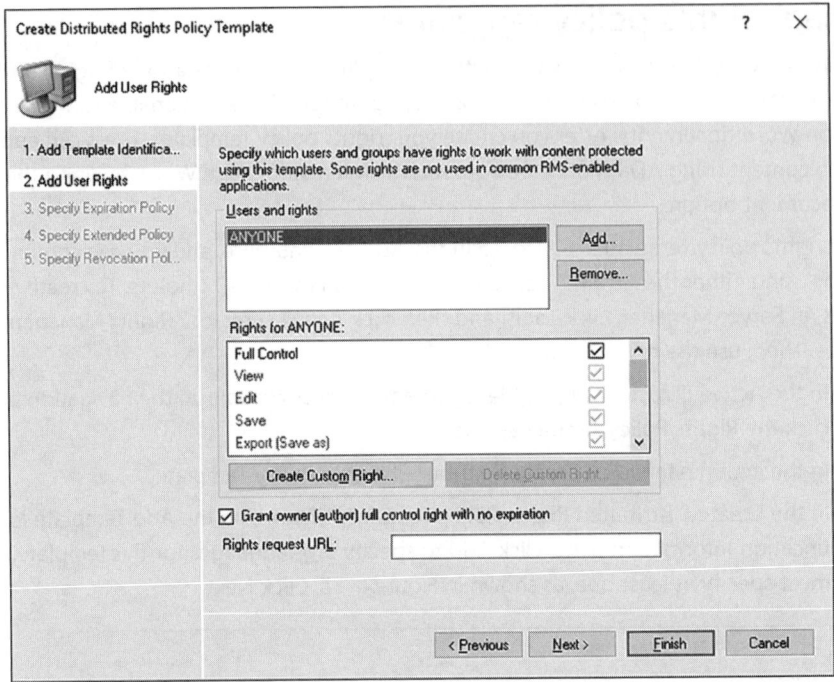

FIGURE 5-39 Adding specific rights to a template

5. You can optionally define an expiration for the rights template on the Specify Expiration Policy page, shown in Figure 5-40.

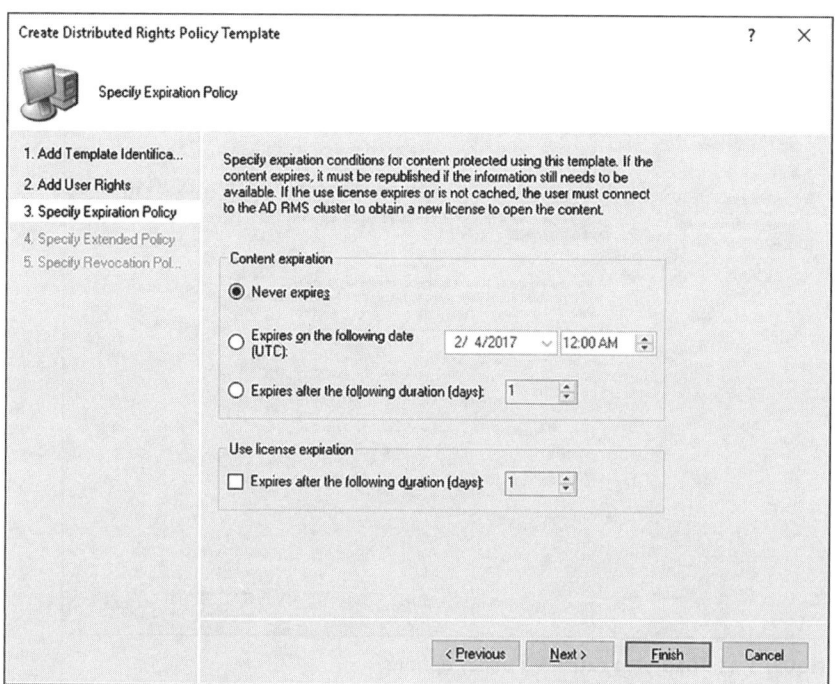

FIGURE 5-40 Setting expiration

6. On the Specify Extended Policy page, you can define the following extensions, as shown in Figure 5-41:

- Enable Users To View Protected Content Using A Browser Add-On
- Require A New Use License Every Time Content Is Consumed

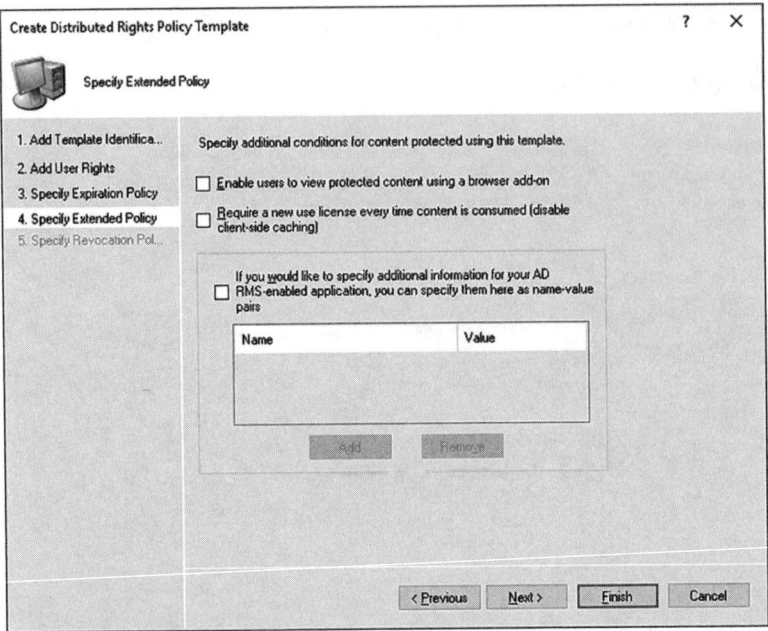

FIGURE 5-41 Specifying extended policy options

7. On the Specify Revocation Policy page, you can configure revocation options for the policy, as shown in Figure 5-42. Click Finish to create the template.

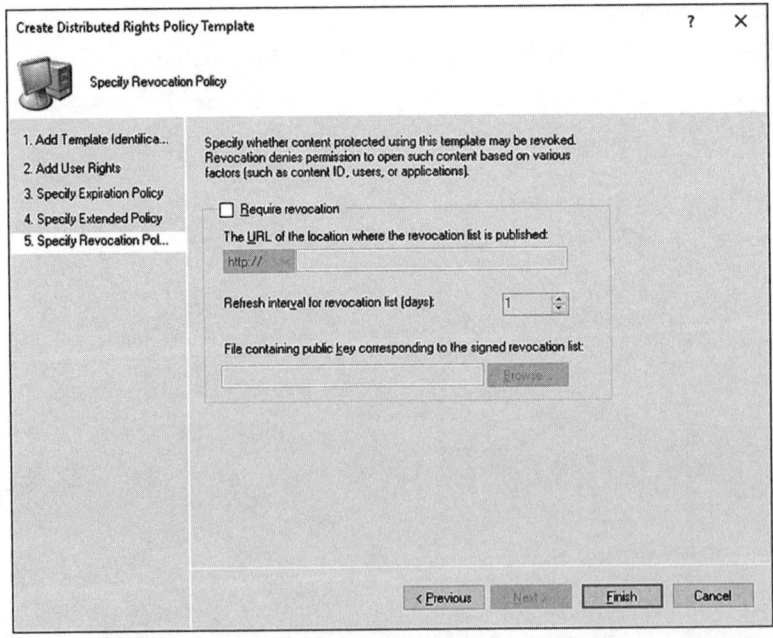

FIGURE 5-42 Revocation policy settings

EXAM TIP

If you subsequently change the details of a template, documents protected with that template are updated to reflect those changes.

Configure exclusion policies

You can create and use exclusion policies to prevent specific users or app from using AD RMS. You can configure three types of exclusion policies:

- **Application** Enables you to block specific app, such as Microsoft Office Word.
- **User** Enables you to name specific excluded users.
- **Lockbox Version** Enables you to block specific client versions, for example, Windows XP.

To create and manage exclusion policies, use the Active Directory Rights Management Services console. For example, to block Microsoft Word, use the following procedure:

1. In the navigation pane, click the Exclusion Policies node, shown in Figure 5-43.

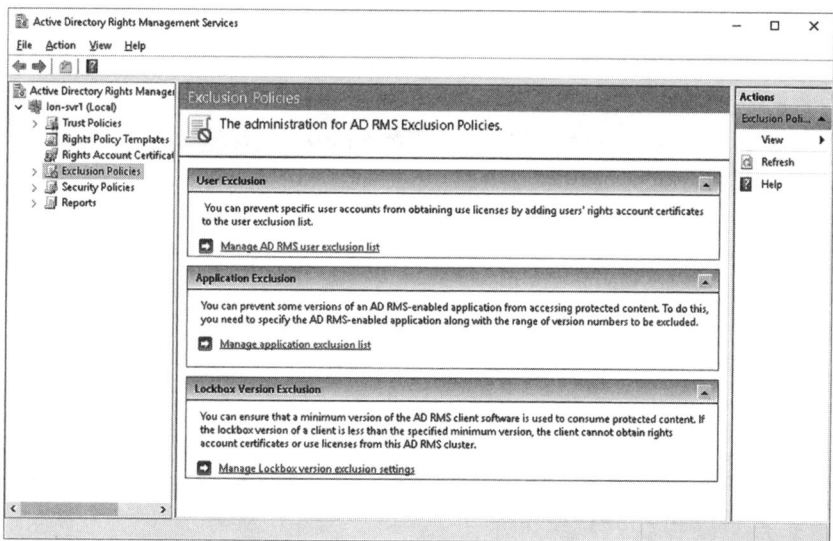

FIGURE 5-43 Exclusion policy node

2. In the details pane, click Manage Application Exclusion List.
3. In the Actions pane, click Enable Application Exclusion.
4. In the Actions pane, click Exclude Application.
5. In the Exclude Application dialog box, enter the following information, and then click Finish:
   - Application File Name: Word.exe
   - Minimum Version: 14.0.0.0
   - Maximum Version: 16.0.0.0

Backup and restore AD RMS

It is important that you know how to protect your AD RMS deployment from data loss. If AD RMS is not available, protected content cannot be accessed.

The more important AD RMS components are:

- **Private Key And Certificates**   The simplest way of protecting your AD RMS private key and related certificates is to export the certificates, with the private key, to an offline location.
- **The AD RMS Database**   The method you use depends on whether AD RMS is configured to use Windows Internal Database or a SQL Server database instance. A full system backup includes the Windows Internal Database. This won't necessarily be the case if you use SQL Server because the database might be located elsewhere. Use appropriate methods to back up the SQL database.
- **Configured Templates**   To back up the templates, export the templates to a shared folder, and then back them up as files.

> **NEED MORE REVIEW?   DISASTER RECOVERY GUIDE FOR ACTIVE DIRECTORY RIGHTS MANAGEMENT SERVICES**
>
> To review further details about recovery for AD RMS, refer to the Microsoft TechNet website at *https://social.technet.microsoft.com/wiki/contents/articles/9111.disaster-recovery-guide-for-active-directory-rights-management-services.aspx*.

Chapter summary

- AD FS federation trusts are not related to AD DS forest trusts.
- The Active Directory Federation Service role issues, manages, and validates identity claims.
- The claims provider hosts the attribute store and manages user authentication.
- The relying party hosts resources.
- You can implement Web Application Proxy to publish both claims-aware and non-claims-aware app.
- Integrating AD FS with the Web Application Proxy enables you to implement preauthentication for published app and websites.
- AD RMS enables you to protect content consumption and define rights on content for users.

Thought experiment

In this thought experiment, demonstrate your skills and knowledge of the topics covered in this chapter. You can find answers to this thought experiment in the next section.

You work in support at A. Datum. As a consultant for A. Datum, answer the following questions about implementing identity federation and access solutions within the A. Datum organization:

1. You are setting up the first AD FS server in the A. Datum organization. The server is called LON-SVR1. What name should you assign to the AD FS service host name?
2. In AD FS, what are claims rules used for?
3. You have been told that you must obtain a certificate for SSL on your AD RMS server. What is the purpose of this certificate?
4. Your manager doesn't want users to protect content in Microsoft Word. How could you achieve this?
5. Your remote users use their own computers when working from home. They attempt to connect to a claims-aware app through the web application proxy that you deployed in your perimeter network. They receive a certificate error. Why might this be?

Thought experiment answers

This section contains the solution to the thought experiment. Each answer explains why the answer choice is correct.

1. You should avoid using the actual server name. This is because if you add additional servers to the farm, they share the initial name. By using a physical server name, you make this impossible.
2. Claims rules are used by AD FS to define which incoming claims are acceptable, to determine which outbound claims are routed to relying parties, and to apply configured authorization rules.
3. The SSL certificate enables you to secure network traffic between the AD RMS clients and the AD RMS server.
4. In the AD RMS console, create an Application Exclusion policy for Microsoft Word.
5. It is likely that the certificate you used for the app is not from a trusted CA. If you are likely to extend your app to computers that are not part of your organization, consider using a public CA to issue the certificates for any published app.

Index

A

account lockout settings 87–88
Account Operators group 46
account policies
   configuration of 83–89
Active Directory Administrative Center 45
   creating PSOs with 92–94
Active Directory Certificate Services (AD CS) 241–294
   administrative role separation 269–272
   certificate management 275–292
   installation and configuration 241–274
      Certificate Authority role service 244–245
      standalone CAs 246–252
   online responders 266–269
   role services 241–242
Active Directory Domain Services (AD DS) 1–76
   backup and recovery 102–109
   bulk operations 60–61
   computer accounts 44, 53–57
   configuration
      domain and forest functional levels 122–124
      multi-domain and multi-forest 120–122
      name suffix routing 135–136
      sites and subnets 136–144
      trusts 126–136
      user principal names 123–125
   containers 2
   defragmentation 97–99
   domain controllers
      adding or removing 9–18
      cloning 28–34
      configuration 6–8
      installation 18–24
      operations master roles 36–41
      upgrading 33–35
   domains 2
   enterprise CA installation 252–253

   forests 2–3
      installation 4–8
   fundamentals 2–5
   groups 62–69
      built-in 62
      configuration of 66–67
      configuring group nesting 63–65
      converting 65
      creating 65–66
      management of 67–69
   in complex enterprise environment 120–144
   installation
      domain controllers 18–24
      on Server Core installation 17
   logical components 2–5
   maintaining 96–119
   metadata cleanup 99–103
   object permissions 73–75
   offline domain joins 57–58
   offline management of 96–103
   organizational units 2, 69–75
   partitions 4
   physical components 2
   publishing root CA in 265–266
   replication 4, 21, 113–119
   restartable 96
   restore 109–110
   schema 2
   service authentication and account policies 77–95
   sites 2–3
   SRV records 41–43
   subnet 3
   trees 2
   trust relationships 4
   user accounts 44–53
      adding 44–50
      configuration of 47–50
      managing 51–53
      templates 51
   user rights 58–60

Active Directory Federation Services (AD FS)

Active Directory Federation Services
    (AD FS) 295, 295–318
  authentication of users stored in LPAD
        directories 317–318
  authentication policies configuration 310–313
  claims-based authentication 303–309
  components 296–299
  device registration 313–316
  federation trusts 295–296
  implementing Web Application Proxy 319–329
  Microsoft Passport integration 314–316
  migrating to Windows Server 2016 318–319
  proxy 323–325
  requirements 299, 322
  server role
      configuration 300–303
      installation 300
  upgrading 318–319
  with Microsoft Azure 316–317
  with Microsoft Office 365 316–317
Active Directory Recycle Bin 102–103, 109
Active Directory Rights Management Services
    (AD RMS) 295
  authentication certificate 337
  backup and restore 344
  cluster key storage 335–336
  clusters 333
  components 330–331
  database 333
  exclusion policies 343
  install and configure 330–343
  licensor certificate 337–338
  overview 330
  rights policy templates 339–342
  server deployment 331–338
  service connection point 338–339
Active Directory snapshots 104–105
  mounting 104
Active Directory Users and Computers 45
Add-ADComputerServiceAccount cmdlet 79
Add-DnsServerResourceRecord cmdlet 144
Add-FineGrainedPasswordPolicySubject cmdlet 91
administrative roles 269–272
administrative templates
  central store 223–224
  configuration of 221–225
  files 223
  importing custom 224
  property filters for 224–225

AD RMS apps 330
AD RMS client 330
AD RMS server 330
AIA. *See* authority information access (AIA) point
Allow Apply Group Policy permissions 190
Allowed RODC Password Replication Group 24
Allow Read permissions 188
application partitions 113
"Applies to Everyone But" strategy 189–190
"Applies to Only" strategy 190–192
Apply Group Policy permissions 189
attribute store 297, 299, 317–318
authentication
  biometric 314
  claims-based 303–309
  Microsoft Passport 314–316
  multi-factor 310, 312–313
  of users stored in LDAP directories 317–318
  policies, configuring 310–313
authentication delegation 82
authentication scope 134–135
authoritative restores 109–110
authority information access (AIA) point 253, 254–260
autoenrollment
  of certificates 284, 284–286
Azure multi-factor authentication 312–313

B

backups
  Active Directory 102–109
  AD RMS 344
  Certificate Authority 272–273
  GPOs 166–167
      managing 168–169
  SYSVOL 105–108
bare metal recovery 106
biometric authentication 314
block inheritance 183–185
bridgeheads 21
built-in containers 3
bulk operations 60–61

C

Certificate Authorities (CAs) 241
  backing up 272–274
  CRL distribution and AIA points 254–260

cryptographic options 248–249
database location 251
enterprise 243
    installation 252–253
naming 249
offline root 253–254
private key of 248–249
restoring 274
root 253
    exporting 259–260
    publishing in AD DS 265–266
standalone 243
    installation 246–252
subordinate 253
    deployment 261–265
validity period 250
Certificate Authority role service
    installation 244–245
Certificate Enrollment Policy Web Service 242
Certificate Enrollment Web Service (CES) 241
certificate revocation list (CRL) 253
certificate revocation list (CRL) distribution point
    (CDP) 253, 254–260
certificates
    AD FS 297
    authentication 337
    enrollment 283–287
    key archival and recovery 288–292
    licensor 337–338
    management of 275–292
        using Group Policy 284–287
    multipurpose 277
    revocation of 287–288
certificate services. *See* Active Directory Certificate
    Services (AD CS)
certificate templates
    creating 278–282
    managing 275–281
    modifying or superseding 283
    properties 276–277
    security 276–277, 280
    versions 275
Certification Authority Web Enrollment 242
child domains 13, 14, 121
claim rules 297
claims
    in federation trusts 297–298, 304

claims-based authentication
    claims provider trust configuration 303–306
    implementing 303–309
    relying party trust configuration 306–309
claims providers 297, 303
claims provider trust 297
    configuration 303–306
client-side extensions (CSEs)
    configuration of 199–200
    for GPOs 161–162
Cloneable Domain Controllers security group 28
cloning
    domain controllers 28–34
cluster key storage 335–336
comma separated value (CSV) files 60–61
computer accounts 44, 53–57
    adding 54–55
    managing 55–57
    permissions for 53
    resetting secure channel 56–57
Computers container 53
configuration
    account lockout policy 87–88
    account policies 83–89
    Active Directory Rights Management Services
        330–343
    Active Directory snapshots 104–105
    AD DS sites and subnets 136–144
    AD FS server role 300–303
    administrative templates 221–225
    authentication policies 310–313
    CA backup and recovery 272–274
    claims provider trust 303–306
    client-side extensions 199–200
    cloning 28–34
    Control Panel settings 234–236
    CRL distribution and AIA points 254–260
    device registration 313–316
    domain and forest functional levels 122–124
    domain controllers 6–8
    drive mapping 227–229
    enforced policies 185–187
    exclusion policies 343
    file and folder deployment 232–233
    Folder Redirection 214–221
    global catalog server 24–27

configuration partitions

    GPO links 164–166
    Group Policy Objects 158–160
    Group Policy preferences 225–238
    Group Policy processing 178–201
    Group Policy settings 202–224
    inheritance 182–187
    item-level targeting 236–238
    Kerberos constrained delegation 82
    Kerberos policy settings 88–89
    key archival and recovery 288–292
    local Group Policies 150–155
    loopback processing 195–197
    MSAs and gMSAs 78–80
    multi-factor authentication 312–313
    name suffix routing 135–136
    online responders 267–269
    Password Settings Objects 89–94
    power options 230–231
    printer preferences 229–230
    read only domain controllers 20–23
    registry settings 234
    relying party trust 306–309
    replication to RODCs 118
    scripts 209–210
    security filtering 187–192
    security settings 211
    shortcut deployment 231–232
    site links 139–141
    slow-link processing 197–200
    software installation 202–208
    trusts 126–136
    user principal names 123–125
    virtual accounts 82–83
    Web Application Proxy 319–322
    WMI filtering 192–195
configuration partitions 113–114
constrained delegation 82
containers
    built-in 3
    defined 3
Control Panel
    settings 234–236
Cryptographic Service Provider (CSP) 335

D

DCCloneConfig.xml file 30, 33
DcDiag.exe 116, 117
DCGPOFix command 174
Default-First-Site-Name 3, 137
defragmentation 97–99
delegation 69
Delegation Of Control Wizard 71–73
Deleted Objects folder 109
Denied RODC Password Replication Group 23
device registration
    implement and configure 313–316
DFS Replication (DFSR) 118–119
dfsrmig.exe 119
digital certificates. *See* certificates
directory services restore mode (DSRM) 96
Directory Services Restore Mode (DSRM)
    password 7, 11
Disable-ADAccount cmdlet 53
Distributed File System (DFS) replication 99
Distributed File System Replication agent (DFSR) 156
DNS stub zones 127
Domain Admins global security group 10
domain-based GPOs 156–162
domain controllers
    adding or removing 9–18
    built-in groups 62
    configuration 6–8
        cloning 28–34
        global catalog server 24–27
    deploying 121
    forcibly removing 99
    installation
        RODCs 20–23
        using Install from Media 18–21
    moving between sites 142–143
    operations master roles 36–41
    read only 7, 11, 96
        deployment 21–23
        install and configure 20–23
        management of 110–113
    site coverage management 145
    SRV record registration issues 41–43
    upgrading 33–35
domain functional level 33, 35

domain-linked GPOs 165
Domain Name System (DNS) 299
    zone delegation 14
Domain Name System (DNS) server 7
domain naming master 36, 39
domain partitions 113–114
domain password policies 85–86
domains 120
    adding 121
    adding computers to 54–55
    child 121
    defined 2
    functional levels 122–124
    offline domain join 57–58
    tree 121
    upgrading existing 122
drive mapping 227–229
dsadd.exe command-line tool 44
Dsmod.exe command-line tool 56, 57
DSRM. *See* directory services restore mode

E

EffectiveImmediately parameter 79
Enable-ADAccount cmdlet 53
Enable-ADOptionalFeature cmdlet 102
enrollment agents 284
Enterprise Admin universal security group 12
enterprise CAs 243
    installation 252–253
exclusion policies 343
external trusts 132–133
external URLs 325

F

federation servers 296
federation services. *See* Active Directory Federation Services (AD FS)
federation trusts 295–296
    certificates 298
    claims in 297–298, 304
file deployment 232–233
File Replication Service (FRS) 118, 156
flexible single master operations (FSMO) roles 36

folder deployment 232–233
folder permissions 215
folder redirection
    advanced 218–220
    available options 215
    basic 216–218
    configuration 214–221
    preparation for 214
    Settings tab 220–221
forest functional level 6, 33
forests 120
    adding 121
    defined 2–3
    functional levels 122–124
    installation 4–8
    upgrading existing 122
forest trusts 127–131
forest-wide authentication 130
FRS. *See* File Replication Service

G

Get-ADDCCloneingExcludedApplicationList cmdlet 29
Get-AdDomain cmdlet 37
get-ADForest cmdlet 36
Get-ADReplicationConnection cmdlet 118
Get-ADReplicationFailure cmdlet 118
Get-ADReplicationPartnerMetadata cmdlet 118
Get-ADReplicationSite cmdlet 118
Get-ADReplicationSiteLinkBridge cmdlet 118
Get-ADReplicationSiteLink cmdlet 118
Get-ADReplicationSubnet cmdlet 118
get-ADUser cmdlet 125
Get-GPPermissions cmdlet 176
global catalog (GC) servers 7
    adding attributes to 26–27
    configuration 24–27
globally unique identity (GUID) 156
gMSAs. *See* Group Managed Service Accounts
GPO Infrastructure Status dashboard 178–179
GPUpdate.exe 201
Group Managed Service Accounts (gMSAs) 77–80
Group Policy caching 197–200
Group Policy container 156
Group Policy Management console 156–157, 180

Group Policy Management Editor

Group Policy Management Editor 83, 84
Group Policy Management Editor console 157, 216
group policy objects (GPOs) 3
   for managing group membership 68–69
   for user rights 58–59
Group Policy Objects (GPOs) 136, 149–179
   backups 166–167
      managing 168–169
   certificate management using 284–287
   checking status of 178–179
   client-side extensions 161–162
   configuration of 158–160
   copying 170
   domain-based 156–162
   domain-linked 165
   forced update 201–202
   importing 169
   link configuration 164–166
   linking 161
   local 150–155
   management delegation 174–177
   management tools 156–158
   migration tables 170–173
   preferences configuration 225–238
      Control Panel settings 234–236
      file and folder deployment 232–233
      item-level targeting 236
      network drive mappings 227–229
      power options 230–231
      printer preferences 229–230
      registry settings 234
      shortcut deployment 231–232
   processing configuration 178–201
      client-side extensions 199–200
      enforced policies 185–187
      inheritance 182–187
      loopback processing 195–197
      order and precedence 181–182
      security filtering 187–192
      slow-link processing 197–200
      WMI filtering 192–195
   publishing root CA using 265–266
   resetting default 174
   restoring 167–168
   security templates 211–214
   settings configuration 202–224
      administrative templates 221–225
      Folder Redirection 214–221
      scripts 209–210
      security 211
      software installation 202–208
   site-linked 165
   Starter 162–164
   structure of 156
   use of 149–150
Group Policy template 156
groups 62–69
   built-in 62
   configuration of 66–67
   configuring group nesting 63–65
   converting 65
   creating 65–66
   group membership 68–69
   management of 67–69
   scope 63–64, 65
   special identities 63
   types 64, 65

H

high availability 262
Hypertext Transfer Protocol over Secure Sockets Layer (HTTPS) 299

I

IGDLA 64
IGUDLA 64
Import-csv cmdlet 60
import-gpo cmdlet 169
infrastructure master 37
inheritance
   block 183–185
   GPO, configuration of 182–187
in-place upgrades 33
Install-AdcsCertificationAuthority cmdlet 242
Install-AdcsEnrollmentPolicyWebService cmdlet 242
Install-AdcsEnrollmentWebService cmdlet 242
Install-AdcsNetworkDeviceEnrollmentService cmdlet 242
Install-AdcsOnlineResponder cmdlet 242
Install-AdcsWebEnrollment cmdlet 242
Install-ADDSDomainController cmdlet 6, 17
Install-ADDSDomainController -ReadOnlyReplica command 24
Install-ADFSFarm cmdlet 302
Install-ADServiceAccount cmdlet 79
installation
   AD DS on Server Core installation 17
   AD FS server role 300

Certificate Authority role service 244–245
domain controllers
    read only 20–23
    using Install from Media 18–21
enterprise CA 252–253
forests 4–8
offline root and subordinate CAs 253–267
online responders 266–267
root CAs 260–261
standalone CAs 246–252
Web Application Proxy 319–322
Install from Media (IFM)
   install domain controller using 18–21
Install-WindowsFeature AD-Domain-Services cmdlet 5, 17
Install-WindowsFeature ADRMS -IncludeManagement-Tools cmdlet 332
internal URLs 325
intersite replication 114, 136, 145
intrasite replication 114, 115, 136
Invoke-AdfsFarmBehaviorLevelRaise cmdlet 319
IP site links 139
IP subnets
  creating 138–139
issuance policy rules 308
item-level targeting 236–238

K

KCD. *See* Kerberos constrained delegation
Kerberos 80, 143
   policy settings 88–89
Kerberos constrained delegation (KCD) 82
Kerberos V5 authentication protocol (KPASSWD) 143
key archival and recovery 288–292
key recovery agents 289–291
knowledge consistency checker (KCC) 115, 118, 143

L

LDAP. *See* Lightweight Directory Access Protocol (LDAP)
LDAP-compliant directories 317–318
Lightweight Directory Access Protocol (LDAP) 143
Lightweight Directory Access Protocol (LDAP) attributes 304
load balancing 262

local Group Policies 150–155
local password policies 86–87
local service (NT AUTHORITY\LOCAL SERVICE) account 78
local system (NT AUTHORITY\SYSTEM) account 78
loopback processing 195–197

M

Managed Service Accounts (MSAs) 77–80
manual enrollment
   of certificates 283
metadata cleanup 99–103
MFA. *See* multi-factor authentication (MFA)
Microsoft Azure
   integration of AD FS with 316–317
Microsoft Office 365
   integration of AD FS with 316–317
Microsoft Passport 314–316
migration tables 170–173
Move-ADDirectoryServer cmdlet 142
Move-ADDirectoryServerOperationMasterRole cmdlet 40
Move-ADDirectoryServerOperationMasterRole -force cmdlet 40
Move-ADObject cmdlet 52
MSAs. *See* Managed Service Accounts
msDS-DeletedObjectLifetime 104
msDS-PasswordSettingsPrecedence PSO attribute 90
multi-factor authentication (MFA) 310, 312–313

N

name resolution 299
name suffix routing 135–136
Nano Server 17
NetBIOS domain name 8
Netdom.exe 56
NETLOGON service 43
network connections 299
Network Device Enrollment Service 242
network service (NT AUTHORITY\NETWORK SERVICE) account 78
New-ADDCCloneConfigFile cmdlet 29, 30
New-ADFineGrainedPasswordPolicy cmdlet 91
New-ADReplicationSiteLink cmdlet 140
New-ADReplicationSubnet cmdlet 139

new-ADServiceAccount cmdlet 79
New-ADUser cmdlet 53
New-GPLink cmdlet 164, 166
New-MsolFederatedDomain cmdlet 316
Nltest.exe 56
nonauthoritative restores 109–110
nslookup.exe 43
NtdsUtil.exe 97, 101–102, 104–105
Ntdsutil.exe command line tool 41
NTFS folder permissions 215

O

object permissions 72–75
objects
  recovering deleted 104
offline domain joins 57–58
Online Certificate Status Protocol (OCSP) 242
online responders
  advantages of 266
  configuration of 267–269
  installation 266–267
operations master roles 21, 36–41
  defined 36–38
  determining current 37, 38
  seizing 40–41
  transferring 38–40
organizational units (OUs) 3, 62, 69–75, 165
  account policies 89
  creating 70
  delegating management of 71–75
  management of 70–75
  strategies for 69–70

P

Partial Attribute Set 26
partitions 4
pass-through mode 326
passwords
  DSRM 7, 11
  management 78
    delegation of 95–96
  policy settings 85–86
  replication policy 23–24, 110–113
  resetting 51–52
  user accounts 47, 51

Password Settings Container 90
Password Settings Objects (PSOs) 89–94
PDC. *See* primary domain controller
PDC Emulator 37, 38
permissions
  certificates 270–272
  folder 215
  GPO 187–192
PKI. *See* public key infrastructure (PKI)
power options 230–231
primary domain controller (PDC) 89
primary domain controller (PDC) emulator operations master 28
PrincipalsAllowedToRetrieveManagedPassword parameter 79
printer preferences 229–230
private keys 248–249
PSOs. *See* Password Settings Objects
public key infrastructure (PKI) 298, 331

R

read only domain controllers (RODCs) 7, 11, 96
  considerations for using 20–21
  delegated adminisrator 23
  deployment 21–23
  install and configure 20–23
  management of 110–113
  password replication policy 23–24
  password replication policy for 110–113
Read permissions 188
realm trusts 133
recovery
  bare metal 106
  key 288–292
  of deleted objects 104
Recycle Bin 102–103, 109
Register Domain Joined Computers As Devices setting 315
registry settings
  custom 234
relying party 297, 303
relying party trust 297, 324, 328, 327–329
  configuration 306–309
Remote Desktop Gateway applications 327–329
Remove-ADUser cmdlet 53
Rename-ADObject cmdlet 52

Repadmin.exe 116, 118
replication 4, 21
    AD DS 113–119
    intersite 114, 136, 145
    intrasite 114, 115, 136
    password, for RODC 110–113
    rebuilding topology 143
    upgrading SYSVOL to DFSR 118–119
replication boundaries 9
request files 264
restartable AD DS 97
restores
    Active Directory 109–110
    AD RMS 344
    CA 274
    GPOs 167–168
Restricted Groups 68–69
revocation configuration 268–269
revocation policy settings 342
RID master 37
rights management. *See* Active Directory Rights
        Management Services (AD RMS)
rights policy templates 339–342
role-based administration 269–272
root CAs 253
    exporting 259–260
    publishing in AD DS 265–266

S

schema 3
schema master 36, 38–39
schema partitions 113–114
scoping 161
scripts
    configuration of 209–210
secure channel
    resetting computer's 56–57
security
    certificate templates 276–277, 280
Security Compliance Manager 213
security filtering
    for GPOs 187–192
security templates
    creating 212
    importing 211–214

selective authentication 130, 135
Server Core installation
    install AD DS on 17
servers
    DNS 7
    global catalog 7
service accounts 77
    account lockout settings 87–88
    account policies 77, 83–89
    Group Managed Service Accounts 77–80
    Managed Service Accounts 77–80
    virtual 82–83
service connection point (SCP) 330, 338–339
service location (SRV) records
    elements of 143
    registration issues 41–43
    registration of 143–144
service location (SRV) resource record 136
Service Principal Names (SPNs) 78, 80–81
Set-ADAccountExpiration cmdlet 53
Set-ADAccountPassword cmdlet 51, 53
Set-ADComputer cmdlet 61
Set-ADGroup cmdlet 61
Set-ADOrganizationalUnit cmdlet 61
Set-ADUser cmdlet 53, 61, 125
Set-DnsServerResourceRecord cmdlet 144
Set-GPPermissions cmdlet 176
Setspn.exe 81
Settings tab 220–221
shortcuts
    deployment of 231–232
shortcut trusts 134
SID filtering 134
single sign-on (SSO) 295, 322
site-linked GPOs 165
site links
    bridges 141
    creating and configuring 139–141
    IP 139
    SMTP 139
sites 3–4
    coverage management 145
    creating AD DS 136–137
    default 137
    moving domain controllers between 142–143

slow-link processing 197–200
SMTP site links 139
snapshots
  Active Directory 104–105
  mounting 104
software
  deployment 204–207
  installation configuration 202–208
  maintenance 207–208
  redeployment 207
  removal 209
  upgrading 207–208
special identities 63
SSO. *See* single sign-on (SSO)
standalone CAs 243
  installation 246–252
Starter GPOs 162–164
subnets 3
  creating AD DS 138–139
subordinate CAs 253
  deployment 261–265
system state 106
SYSVOL 156
  backing up 105–108
  replication 118–119

T

templates
  user accounts 51
transform rules 304, 309
transitive trusts 126
Transmission Control Protocol (TCP) 143
tree domain 13
tree domains 121
trees 121
  defined 2
trust relationships 4
trusts
  authentication scope 134–135
  configuration 126–136
  defined 126
  external 126, 132–133
  forest 126, 127–131
  name suffix routing 135–136

parent/child 126
realm 126, 133
shortcut 126, 134
SID filtering 134
transitive 126
tree-root 126
two-factor authentication 314

U

universal naming convention (UNC) 170
Unlock-ADAccount cmdlet 52, 53
upgrades
  domain controllers 33–35
  in-place 33
UPNs. *See* universal principal names
user accounts 44–53
  account lockout settings 87–88
  adding 44–50
  configuration of 47–50
  inactive/disabled 53
  managing 51–53
  moving 52
  naming standards for 44
  passwords 47, 51–52
  renaming 52
  standard 78
  templates 51
  unlocking 52
User Datagram Protocol (UDP) 143
user permissions 58
user principal names (UPNs) 123–125
user profile properties 48–50
user rights
  configuration of 58–60

V

virtual accounts
  configuration of 82–83
virtual domain controllers
  cloning 28–34
virtual machines (VMs)
  generation identifiers 28

W

WBadmin.exe 109
Web Application Proxy 295, 296
  implementing 319–329
  implementing as AD FS proxy 323–325
  install and configure 319–322
  integrating with AD FS 322–325
  pass-through mode 326
  preauthentication 323
  publishing Remote Desktop Gateway
      applications 327–329
web enrollment
  of certificates 284
WIF. *See* Windows Identity Foundation (WIF)
Windows Hello 314–315
Windows Identity Foundation (WIF) 297
Windows Management Instrumentation (WMI)
      filters 175
Windows PowerShell
  creating PSOs with 91–92
  for GPO management 157–158
  group management in 67
  modifying AD DS objects using 61
  OU management in 70
Windows Server 2016
  migrating AD FS workloads to 318–319
  upgrading domain controllers to 33–35
Windows Server Backup feature 105–108
WMI filtering 192–195

About the author

ANDREW WARREN runs his own training and consultancy business in the UK. He has served as subject matter expert for Windows Server 2016 courses, technical lead for Windows 10 courses, and co-developer of TechNet sessions covering Microsoft Exchange Server. He has over thirty years of IT experience. He lives in rural Somerset in the UK.

From technical overviews to drilldowns on special topics, get *free* ebooks from Microsoft Press at:

www.microsoftvirtualacademy.com/ebooks

Download your free ebooks in PDF, EPUB, and/or Mobi for Kindle formats.

Look for other great resources at Microsoft Virtual Academy, where you can learn new skills and help advance your career with free Microsoft training delivered by experts.

Microsoft Press

Hear about it first.

Get the latest news from Microsoft Press sent to your inbox.

- New and upcoming books
- Special offers
- Free eBooks
- How-to articles

Sign up today at MicrosoftPressStore.com/Newsletters

Visit us today at

microsoftpressstore.com

- **Hundreds of titles available** – Books, eBooks, and online resources from industry experts

- **Free U.S. shipping**

- **eBooks in multiple formats** – Read on your computer, tablet, mobile device, or e-reader

- **Print & eBook Best Value Packs**

- **eBook Deal of the Week** – Save up to 60% on featured titles

- **Newsletter and special offers** – Be the first to hear about new releases, specials, and more

- **Register your book** – Get additional benefits

Tell us what you think!

Was it useful?
Did it teach you what you wanted to learn?
Was there room for improvement?

Let us know at https://aka.ms/tellpress

Your feedback goes directly to the staff at Microsoft Press, and we read every one of your responses. Thanks in advance!